Lecture Notes in Computer Science 3530

Commenced Publication in 1973
Founding and Former Series Editors:
Gerhard Goos, Juris Hartmanis, and Jan van Leeuwen

Andreas Prinz   Rick Reed
Jeanne Reed (Eds.)

SDL 2005:
Model Driven

12th International SDL Forum
Grimstad, Norway, June 20-23, 2005
Proceedings

 Springer

Volume Editors

Andreas Prinz
Agder University College, Faculty of Engineering and Science
Grooseveien 36, 4876 Grimstad, Norway
E-mail: andreas.prinz@hia.no

Rick Reed
Jeanne Reed
Telecommunications Software Engineering Limited
The Laurels, Victoria Road, Windermere, Cumbria LA23 2DL, United Kingdom
E-mail: {rickreed, jeanne}@tseng.co.uk

Library of Congress Control Number: 2005927490

CR Subject Classification (1998): C.2, D.2, D.3, F.3, C.3, H.4

ISSN   0302-9743
ISBN-10   3-540-26612-7 Springer Berlin Heidelberg New York
ISBN-13   978-3-540-26612-9 Springer Berlin Heidelberg New York

Springer is a part of Springer Science+Business Media

springeronline.com

© Springer-Verlag Berlin Heidelberg 2005
Printed in Germany

Typesetting: Camera-ready by author, data conversion by Scientific Publishing Services, Chennai, India
Printed on acid-free paper   SPIN: 11506843   06/3142   5 4 3 2 1 0

Preface

This volume contains the papers presented at the 12th SDL Forum, Grimstad, Norway.

The SDL Forum was first held in 1982, and then every two years from 1985. Initially the Forum was concerned only with the Specification and Description Language that was first standardized in the 1976 Orange Book of the International Telecommunication Union (ITU). Since then, many developments took place and the language has undergone several changes.

However, the main underlying paradigm has survived, and it is the reason for the success of the Specification and Description Language in many projects. This paradigm is based on the following important principles of distributed applications:

Communication: large systems tend to be described using smaller parts that communicate with each other;

State: the systems are described on the basis of an explicit notion of state;

State change: the behavior of the system is described in terms of (local) changes of the state.

The original language is not the only representative for this kind of paradigm, so the scope of the SDL Forum was extended quite soon after the first few events to also include other ITU standardized languages of the same family, such as MSC, ASN.1 and TTCN. This led to the current scope of System Design Languages covering all stages of the development process including in particular SDL, MSC, UML, ASN.1, eODL, TTCN, and URN. The focus is clearly on the advantages to users, and how to get from these languages the same advantage given by the ITU Specification and Description Language: code generation from high-level specifications.

Not only have the languages and the scope of the SDL Forum evolved, but for the first time the Programme Committee for SDL2005 decided to have short papers as well as the normal full papers with a strong scientific background for full presentation and publication. The rationale is that the SDL Forum is targeted at a mixture of participants from research to industrial engineering backgrounds, and the inclusion of the short papers allows more issues to be presented and discussed while still maintaining normal conference standards for full papers. The short papers are of essentially three kinds:

Application reports. The SDL Forum has a tradition of publishing application papers, and users need such reports to benefit from the experience of other users, in particular where the reports contain quantitative results on cost effectiveness. Typically such reports do not contain advances in techniques or technology that justify presentation as full papers.

Tool reports. Similarly, reports on new tools or new releases of tools are of interest, without requiring the paper to describe a major advance – though it may be an advance in use or technology for the particular tool.

Position papers. These are papers that raise legitimate issues that need discussion, and the paper is a contribution to the discussion but from its content it could not be considered on the same basis as a fully investigated research paper.

No doubt the concept of short papers will be further developed for future events.

One important facet of the SDL Forum is the concentration on real-world examples mentioned above, which is also present in the SDL design contest: following a 'tradition' started in 2002, the 12th SDL Forum hosted an SDL design competition sponsored by SAFIRE SDL with cash prizes for the winning designs.[1]

As editors of this volume, we have read through all the papers and are pleased with the interesting and varied selection taken by the Programme Committee. You will find all aspects of System Design Languages covered in this volume, ranging from state-of-the-art research results to modern application examples.

April 2005   Andreas Prinz and Rick Reed

SDL Forum Society

The SDL Forum Society is a not-for-profit organization that in addition to running the SDL Forum:

- runs the SAM (SDL and MSC) workshop every 2 years between SDL Forum years;
- is a body recognized by ITU-T as co-developing the Z.100 to Z.109 and Z.120 to Z.129 standards;
- promotes the ITU-T System Design Languages.

For more information on the SDL Forum Society, see `www.sdl-forum.org`.

---

[1] The descriptions of the winning entries are to be found at the SOLINET web pages.

Organization

Each SDL Forum is organized by the SDL Forum Society with the help of local organizers. The Organizing Committee consists of the Board of the SDL Forum Society plus the local organizers and others as needed depending on the actual event. For SDL 2005 the local organizers from Agder University College need to be thanked for their effort to ensure that everything was in place for the presentation of the papers in this volume.

Organizing Committee

Chairman, SDL Forum Society: Rick Reed (TSE Ltd.)
Treasurer, SDL Forum Society: Uwe Glässer (Simon Fraser University)
Secretary, SDL Forum Society: Andreas Prinz (Agder University College)
ITU-T: Georges Sebek (Counsellor to Study Group 17)
Local Organizers Prof. Andreas Prinz
   Agder University College: Maren Assev, Lisanne Prinz, Ingunn Espedal

Programme Committee

Daniel Amyot, University of Ottawa, Canada
Laurent Doldi, TransMeth Sud-Ouest, France
Fabrice Dubois, France Télécom, France
Anders Ek, Telelogic, Sweden
Joachim Fischer, Humboldt-Universität zu Berlin, Germany
Emmanuel Gaudin, PragmaDev, France
Uwe Glässer, Simon Fraser University, Canada
Reinhard Gotzhein, University of Kaiserslautern, Germany
Jens Grabowski, Georg-August University Göttingen, Germany
Susanne Graf, Verimag, France
Øystein Haugen, University of Oslo, Norway
Dieter Hogrefe, Georg-August University Göttingen, Germany
Eckhardt Holz, Hasso-Plattner-Institut Potsdam, Germany
Sune Jakobsson, Telenor, Norway
Ferhat Khendek, Concordia University, Canada
Martin von Löwis, Hasso-Plattner-Institute Potsdam, Germany
Birger Møller-Pedersen, University of Oslo, Norway
Ian Oliver, Nokia, Finland
Anders Olsen, Cinderella, Denmark
Andreas Prinz, Agder University College, Norway

Steve Randall, PQM Consultants, UK
Rick Reed, TSE Ltd., UK
Richard Sanders, SINTEF, Norway
Amardeo Sarma, NEC, Germany
Ina Schieferdecker, Fraunhofer FOKUS, Germany
Edel Sherratt, University of Wales Aberystwyth, UK
William Skelton, SOLINET, Germany
Bent Vale, Ericsson, Norway
Thomas Weigert, Motorola, USA
Milan Zoric, ETSI, France

Thanks

A volume such as this could not, of course, exist without the contributions of
the authors who are thanked for their work.

Moreover the organization was greatly assisted through the various sponsors
that provided valuable support. SDL 2005 was sponsored by:

- Grimstad Kommune
- Cinderella ApS
- Xactium Ltd.
- PragmaDev
- Telelogic

Table of Contents

Applications and Tools (Short Papers)

Model Driven Architecture (Short Papers)

Test and Validation

Code Generation

ULF-Ware – An Open Framework for Integrated Tools for ITU-T Languages

Joachim Fischer, Andreas Kunert, Michael Piefel,
and Markus Scheidgen

Humboldt-Universität zu Berlin, Institut für Informatik,
Unter den Linden 6, 10099 Berlin, Germany
{fischer, kunert, piefel, scheidge}@informatik.hu-berlin.de

Abstract. Model driven engineering is a popular attempt to deal with the complexity of modern software systems. For the telecommunication sector a model driven approach means that you have to handle several ITU-T modelling languages in a single process to cover all aspects of telecommunication system development. Unfortunately, this is a difficult task, because the ITU-T languages are hard to use together. That is why the ITU-T started the Unified Language Family (ULF) initiative with the goal to unify the ITU-T language definitions and allow an easier alignment and integrated use of these languages.

We present a tooling framework for those ULF languages: ULF-ware. Our framework uses metamodelling and a shared use of common language concepts for a tight language integration. Around these language models it incorporates a set of tools to cover the various responsibilities of development environments such as program parsing, model checking, model transformation and code generation.

This paper shows work in progress. We demonstrate our ideas on a tool chain for a subset of SDL. But the overall goal is an open framework that is extendable with other languages, even beyond ULF, and with tools for other software engineering tasks such as model simulation or software deployment.

1   Introduction

Over the past decades the ITU-T developed a series of modelling languages; each to cover a special aspect of telecommunication system specification. These languages are called: *eODL* – used for high-level component description; *SDL* [1] and *MSC* – to define different approaches to behaviour description and modelling; *ASN.1* – to define data; and *TTCN* – to write test cases. So there is virtually a modelling technique for every need, but in reality this is meaningless if these languages cannot be used together.

Different methodologies used in language development and definition make it hard to align and relate these languages with each other, so that integration is not trivial – it is barely possible. Of course, this is not news, and various calls for integration have been made. The ITU-T proposed the idea of a *Unified Language*

A. Prinz, R. Reed, and J. Reed (Eds.): SDL 2005, LNCS 3530, pp. 1–15, 2005.

Family (ULF): a consistent, uniform foundation for all ITU-T languages, but what is the method of choice to produce this foundation?

Two rivals have emerged: the field-tested and well-founded context free grammars, versus the new (incarnation of an old idea) metamodelling that has proven itself by building the base for ULF's "antagonist" UML [2]. Omitting all political arguments, metamodelling seems the more promising, and therefore scientifically more interesting approach. This paper proposes an approach to language tool development that uses metamodelling that is named after its overall goal: ULF-Ware.

ULF-Ware concerns utilizing metamodelling's potential for: faster tool and language development cycles, reuse of language concepts, and language integration. The metamodelling method gives us two advantages: first, you can define the abstract syntax of many languages as a combined model; second, it allows the various tools that are needed to use a language properly to be developed separately.

The first point is founded on the independence from concrete notation and metamodelling's ability to form reusable object-oriented structures. It is the independence from concrete syntax that allows modelling of language concepts abstractly, independent from syntax details. It is object-orientation that allows reuse and specialization of the common, abstract concepts in concrete languages. In these ways the separate ULF languages can become the ULFamily.

The second point is based on metamodels that are data models specifying (and can even standardizing) all the interfaces needed between different language tools. The use of abstract, coherent concepts in the metamodel further loosens the coupling between concept implementations and enables reuse.

With ULF-Ware we propose a metamodel-based, extendable framework for the implementation of ULF in the spirit of the OMG's MDA [3]. Section 2 explains the overall idea and philosophy of ULF-Ware, and we introduce a first piece of ULF-Ware that we are implementing right now – an SDL/UML compiler tool chain. In section 3 we present our current work in progress; this section gives interesting insights into the various aspects of metamodel-based compiler construction. The concluding section discusses the future of ULF.

2   ULF-Ware

The label ULF-Ware denotes all our tools around the Unified Language Family. We constituted all ULF-Ware components around a conceptual model based architecture: the ULF-Ware philosophy. We have begun to implement combined SDL and UML compiler tools. These first ULF-Ware pieces have to prove the applicability of the ULF-Ware philosophy.

2.1   Philosophy Behind ULF-Ware

ULF-Ware uses a centralized architecture; it has orbits placed around a core. Figure 1 gives an overview on ULF-Ware.

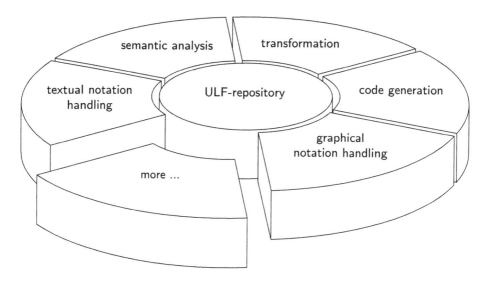

Fig. 1. An Overview of the ULF-Ware

The core's responsibility is to handle all models: these are M1-models such as specifications and programs as well as M2-metamodels, the metamodels. It is a model-centered architecture. It is responsible for model storage and representation; the core also facilitates functionality for model exchange, and therefore connects the various language tools. It offers all the functionality needed to integrate the orbiting tools. It can be understood as a provider for all common functionality and shared data that the language tools need. We realize the core by using a MOF-compliant repository, where MOF (*Model Object Facility*) is the standardized metamodelling architecture of the OMG [4].

The orbits around the core use, import and modify the models in the core; they use the core's operational interface. The distinct orbits act independently of each other, except that their behaviour is based on the shared data provided by the core repository. Because all orbits are independent of each other, the architecture is not fixed to the initial given orbits and is easily extensible.

If we step back from this structural viewpoint and look at core and orbits in terms of languages, we see the core handles abstract syntax and the orbits handle semantics, where the concrete notations are considered a part of semantics.

The core handles the metamodels and provides a repository for actual language instances (specifications or programs). The language instances are realized by the *extent* concept. An extent is a conceptual space, where the lifecycle of model elements takes place. An extent is automatically generated from the metamodel for which it provides an instance.

The orbits add meaning to the abstract syntax stored in the core. Examples for those semantics are: static semantics – the check of models for static

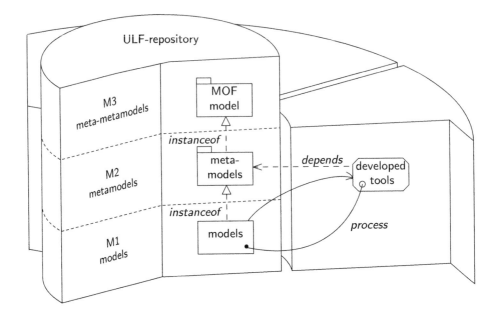

Fig. 2. The philosophy of the distinct ULF-Ware orbits

correctness; model transformation – as a possible representation of dynamic semantics; code generation – the question of how a model can be represented by implementation code; textual and graphical representations – which relate graphical or textual tokens to abstract model entities. There are many other possible semantics, such as simulation or deployment.

Figure 2 provides a closer view of the ULF-Ware philosophy. The core is a realization of a 4-layered metamodelling architecture: The models of every layer are described by a more abstract (*more 'meta'*) model in the layer above. An example: the M1-layer represents SDL specifications; the M2-layer contains the language description, the SDL metamodel; and the third layer defines the language used to write metamodels: for a MOF-repository this is the MOF-model.[1]

The semantics are realized by tools. In the first development state these might be hand-written tools that depend on the languages that they are written for. This dependency shows itself in the fact that the tools rely on the metamodel, they rely on the syntax. Tools can express semantics by modifying, creating and using models in the repository – they process models.

An SDL model checker, for example, is a tool that implements rules such as: *every agent of process kind must only contain other processes.* Such a rule depends on the SDL metamodel, because uses the metamodel elements *agent,*

---

[1] Please refer to [5] for an introduction into metamodelling architectures.

agent-kind, process, containment. The model checker applies this rule to SDL metamodel instances: that is, to SDL specifications.

Another example is model transformation. A transformer simply implements rules for metamodel entities such as: *every agent can be realized with a Java class.* It depends on the metamodels for SDL and Java; it uses the elements *agent (SDL) and class (Java).* The transformer uses SDL instances; it reads SDL specifications. Based on this model data, it fills a Java extent; it successively creates all Java elements required according to the transformation rules.

Both semantic orbits depend on the same language model (SDL), and they both access the same language instance (the SDL specification). They share the functionality of modifying SDL extents and they exchange SDL models. The orbits are connected through the core. In the context of a compiler tool chain, the model checker proves a model's correctness, the checked model is passed on and is used by the transformer as the model transformation source.

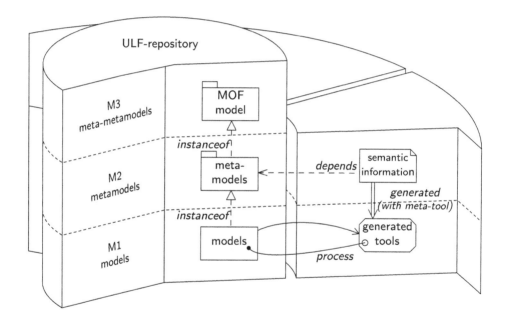

Fig. 3. Realization of an ULF-Ware orbit with a Meta-tool

Beside the hand-written-tools approach a more sophisticated realization of semantic orbits exists. We call those tools meta-tools (figure 3). Using meta-tools, we detach the language-dependent part of a semantics implementation. As an example, compare two model checkers for two different languages: they basically do the same thing; they apply static semantic rules to models. The only difference and the only language dependency lays in the rules.

Thus meta-tools take semantic descriptions as input, and they realize the described semantics by creating a generated tool. For example, such a meta-

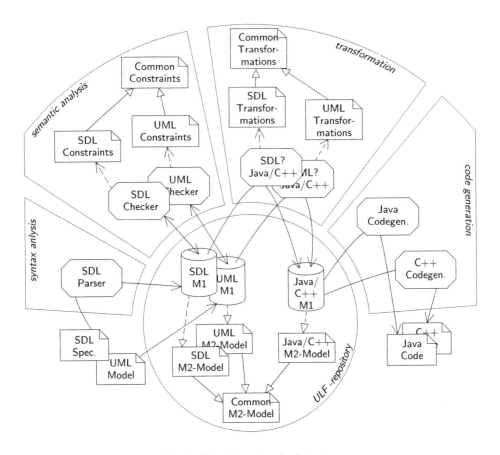

Fig. 4. The Compiler Architecture

tool might take a set of static semantic rules from a file of specified format and generate a checker from these rules. This checker can then instantly be applied. An actually existing example are OCL implementations: programs that allow you to write rules for arbitrary metamodels and allow application of these rules to instances of these metamodels.

2.2   Utilizing the ULF-Ware Philosophy – An SDL/UML Compiler

Around the previously described, more philosophical, conceptual ideas we implement actual language tools. Our first goal is a compiler tool chain for an integrated SDL/UML language. These tools will translate the models into Java or C++ code and finally allow the execution of the generated code in different run-time environments.

Figure 4 shows the compiler's architecture: The core entities (extents for the various languages – the syntax) and the different semantic descriptions that are used to build these tools, as well as the model flow between them. According to the ULF-Ware philosophy, the four boxes represent the semantic orbits *syntax analysis, semantic analysis, transformation* and *code generation.*

2.3   What We Gain

The overall ULF idea is to unify the definition of languages. We use MOF meta-modelling to describe the syntax of SDL and UML with the same method. We use this unified definition to relate and align those languages with each other. This unified definition, a common metamodel of descriptions for common modelling concepts, is an evolving product. We hope that it will be further filled with concepts contributed from the other ULF languages.

In addition to the reuse of shared abstract syntax (common metamodel), we hope that we can utilize further reuse in the tools and descriptions that describe semantics. The idea is that when a common concept is shared, then the semantics depending on this concept are shared as well.

3   Realization

We begin by implementing a compiler for a very simple language, and we plan to successively extend this language. This course of action allows us to focus on the development of methods and techniques without the hassle of very complex languages. The language SDL- is a small subset of SDL-2000; it is a small feature set that allows the specification of executable systems. The language is barely usable in real applications, and its only purpose is to give us a research playground. The language is described using an simplified version of the SDL-2000 abstract syntax grammar.

We used the technique described in [6] to develop a metamodel for SDL-based on its grammar. It is part of the technique used to derive and use a set of common concepts. With this metamodel and the corresponding repository, the SDL- compiler core is established. It is planned to successively extend the definition of SDL- (and the used metamodel) with other concepts of the SDL-2000 standard. Later on UML will be integrated, sharing the same concepts and implementations that were written for SDL. This concrete ULF-Ware is planned as an evolving product.

3.1   Common Concepts in the Metamodel Space

Common concepts are modelled with abstract MOF classes, which are reused and specialized in different concrete language definitions. Thus the definitions of the various languages are simple specializations of a common metamodel. Due to the shared core, all languages use the same common concepts. If you want to learn more about the idea of common concepts, refer to [7]; the publications [8, 9] are standard material for the object-oriented method and terminology.

There are several ways to obtain those common concepts: There are well-known concepts from different domains such as the object-oriented paradigm or state automata; there are the results of decomposing the concepts of existing languages into smaller, more abstract and potentially common concepts; and it possible to directly integrate languages and compare related concepts.

Common concepts blur the boundaries between the modelled languages; this is clearly a positive point. There are two important properties that we would like to emphasize: a common concept is polymorphic, and represents concrete concepts in (different) languages, and a common concept relates concrete concepts in (different) languages. Where the second simply helps to align languages to each other and helps to integrate languages, the first enables reuse of implementations for languages. A transformation or a static condition can be built at a more abstract level, for a polymorphic concept class. Then it can be reused for concrete concepts that act in place of the polymorphic concept.

We understand meta-models as a collection of packages with well-defined relations. They describe language concepts on different abstraction levels, with different levels of detail, and with a maximum of reuse between the distinct packages. This is the same method that is used to define the UML, where the different diagram sorts (each of them is a language of its own) are described by one large model that consists of a diversity of packages and is commonly known as the UML meta-model.

In our example, SDL, UML and even Java as well as C++ use the same basis. Even though the languages are melded together at an abstract level, it does not mean that the individual languages get lost. When you imagine the model as a tree-like abstraction hierarchy of language concepts, then the leaves of that hierarchy represent the concrete concepts, and these concrete features of one language can be clearly distinct from those of another language.

3.2   Tools for Static Language Aspects

Figure 5 shows the model flow from SDL specification until the model is passed for transformation.

The first tool in the chain is the parser. On the input side there is nothing special; it takes a textual SDL specification as input and analyzes it with context free grammar based techniques. We used *JavaCC*, a tool that allows lexical analysis and syntactical analysis with LL-1 grammars.

The result of the syntax analysis is a filled repository. Therefore the parser creates an extent of a special variant of the SDL metamodel, the SDL M2 WCSE. The actions triggered by the various grammar rules then simply create proper elements in that extent.

The SDL metamodel with the affix WCSE (*with concrete syntax extensions*) is basically an extension to the SDL metamodel. The reason for this extra package is that the SDL model is rather abstract; it omits syntactical details that cannot be resolved by the parser on its own. The idea is to use a model transformation from a model that still contains syntax details, to a model in which these details are resolved.

Most of these syntax details are string references (names, identifier) in the specification text. Take a variable definition as example. A variable definition assigns a type to a variable. In the textual syntax the type is specified, using an

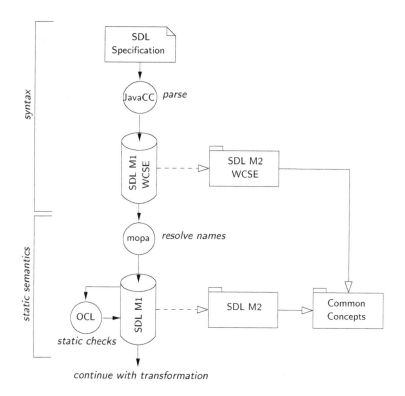

Fig. 5. Model flow from Specification to Model Transformation

identifier. Later in the SDL model this identifier is replaced with a link between the variable element and the type element.

Figure 6 shows a few of these concrete syntax extensions and how they relate to the given example. The syntax extensions contain two kinds of elements: first, elements (such as *ConcreteSyntaxExtension, StringReference, PathItem, Qualifier, Identifier*) that describe concepts exclusive to the concrete syntax; second, the placeholder elements elements that are specializations of concepts in the normal SDL metamodel. The instances of a placeholder are temporary representatives of the elements that are yet to be resolved.

The variable example again: the parser reads a variable definition; it creates a variable element (a specialization of `TypedElement`) in the repository; it does not know which `type` it shall assign to the created variable, because the parser does not know how to resolve the identifier that is used in the variable definition. Thus the only thing the parser can do is create a `PlaceHolder for NamedElement` and to save the identifier into that place holder.

The syntax extensions are partially hand-written; the place holder elements could be generated automatically.

The analysis of static semantics is done in two steps. The first step is to resolve all concrete elements from the *wcse* model and to create a real instance

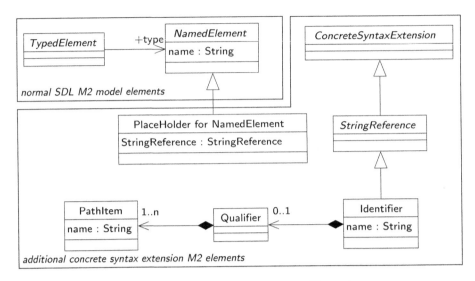

Fig. 6. Concrete Syntax Extension Example

of the SDL metamodel. To do that, the wcse model is traversed for place holder elements. If a place holder is recognized, the reference in it is resolved, and the place holder is replaced by the referenced element.

After all concrete syntax elements are resolved, the SDL specification is a true instance of the SDL metamodel (all WCSEs have been removed), and semantic rules can be applied to check the model's static correctness.

We use the *Object Constraint Language* [10] to implement semantic rules. These OCL constraints are basically predicate logic expressions that use elements from the M2 level and are evaluated against M1 models. The example OCL constraint in figure 7 expresses *An SDL agent of system kind must not be contained in another agent.* The OCL constraints themselves are part of the metamodel. They are attached to the model classes that they constrain. Evaluation of static semantic rules means that for every class all attached constraints are evaluated against every instance of this class.

3.3   Transformations and Code Generation

The repository is now filled with an SDL specification. For the tools further down the chain, it is immaterial *how* the repository was filled. It could also have been the working repository of a metamodel based, graphical SDL tool. While tools like this do not exist for SDL, they may exist for other languages, such as UML, where metamodel based tools are not rare.

In short, there are two easy steps. Step one is to perform a *model transformation* from the SDL M1 model that we use as input to the combined Java/C++ M1 model. Step two is to generate Java or C++, which should not be more than simple pretty-printing. These steps are shown in Fig. 8.

```
context SDLAgent inv: this.kind = SYSTEM implies
this.container->isEmpty()
```

Fig. 7. Example OCL constraint

The challenging part is, of course, the model transformation. To understand the elements of the transformation, it is necessary to look deeper into the target model. Therefore, we first discuss the target of the transformation before we turn to the transformation itself.

The Combined Java/C++ Model. One of the key strengths of ULF-Ware is the relative ease with which source or target language can be replaced by something else. As long as the metamodel of the new language is similar to that of the old one, only a few transformation rules will have to be adapted. This is partly due to the inheritance of transformation rules as explained in Sect. 3.

In our ULF-Ware prototype SDL- compiler we use yet another approach for the target model: a combined M2 model for both Java and C++. Many languages share common concepts, as has been shown and made use of in [11], such as the quite abstract concept of namespace. For programming languages, the similarities go even further.

Many differences in those languages are purely syntactical or for simple static semantics, such as the declaration of variables before use. The most important differences are support for crash-avoidance (which is irrelevant in a theoretical context) and the extent of the available libraries, neither of which affect the metamodel.

Java and C++ in particular are very similar to each other. Still, a complete metamodel would exhibit a number of fine differences such as visibility and the (non-)existence of multiple inheritance. However, we want to use Java and C++ as output languages only.[2] This allows us to build a metamodel that can represent only the intersection of features from Java and C++.

Since Java and C++ have so much in common, the combined metamodel is still expressive enough to allow arbitrarily complex models. It also inherits from the package `Common Concepts`, which will make the transformation simpler.

To generate source code from the model in the repository is a straightforward unparsing process. In Fig. 8 and 9 these unparsers are called cgc and cgj. The results of the pretty-printing are sometimes almost identical, as in the figure.[3]

Run-Time Libraries. When generating target source-code, it is usually convenient not to overburden the code generator with too much intelligence, but to put as much functionality as possible into a common run-time library. As an

---

[2] Although the idea of complete "roundtrippability" is very tempting, it seems almost impossible to build up an SDL specification for an arbitrary Java or C++ program in general. Note that the existing tools that generate UML from Java only cover the structural aspects.

[3] Note that in the figure the left-hand side is in UML syntax for easier recognition.

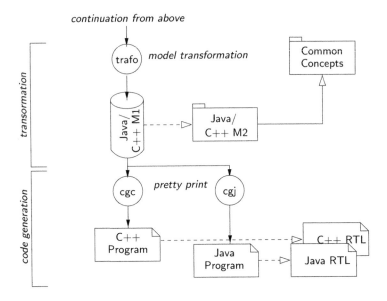

Fig. 8. Transforming the models (continuation of Fig. 5)

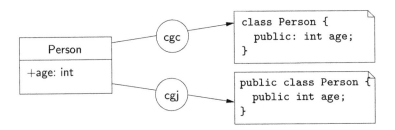

Fig. 9. Pretty printing for C++ and Java

example, when generating code for an SDL `output`, you *could* generate the code that looks for the correct route, puts the signal in the corresponding queue etc. in place, thereby letting the code generator do all the work. Alternatively, the code generator only produces a function call; the function will be defined in the run-time library.

We have used this technique in our SITE tool chain [12]; an explanation of the library can be found in [13]. The main benefit there was that it is possible to exchange the library to make the generated code behave differently; for example to generate statistics for a simulation run versus fast execution or exchange of signals to the environment via a selectable method.

In the context of ULF-Ware this separation has another advantage: It allows us to flatten the differences in the target languages by abstraction, such as the different data types used for the signal queues. This makes it easier to write the code generators, at the expense of having to write the run-time libraries.

Model Transformations. In SITE, we have gathered experience with the transformation of abstract syntax trees. We have used Kimwitu++ [14] for the definition of the abstract grammar and the pattern matching. The transformation of models in repositories is similar to this; the main difference is that the number and order of children is usually not fixed, but expressed through relations between objects. To this end we will use a newly-written pattern matcher for models, called MOPA, already used in earlier stages of the ULF-Ware process.

Just as the source metamodels share common concepts, expressed as a package inherited by both the SDL and the UML metamodels, the transformations for these languages share common transformations as well. The concrete transformations will inherit the common transformations and complete them with the rules specific for the source metamodel.

Some of the transformations will be trivial: The target metamodel also inherits from the Common Concepts package. Consequently, some transformations will comprise of merely a copy of the source model element into the target model.

3.4   Meta-tools

The tools discussed so far are sufficient to implement the described metamodel-based SDL- compiler. However, it is very hard to extend our compiler to support additional input languages (in compiler construction terms: to add additional frontends) due to two reasons:

– The first one is that usual (textual) programming languages do not have a metamodel. Most programming languages are defined by a grammar that describes the syntactical structure and English text explaining the semantic behaviour. As shown in [11] it is not possible to automatically generate a good metamodel from a given grammar. The metamodels automatically generated are as a matter of principle rather representations of the grammar than of the programming language. However, you can use such metamodels as a base and create good metamodels by refinement, but this requires a lot of writing by hand.
– The second problem is that even if you have a grammar and a corresponding metamodel you still do not have a parser for the language nor you have a model-generator. In the SDL- compiler this part has to be hand-coded as well.

The solution to both problems mentioned are meta-tools. One of our planned meta-tools is a program which reads grammars from the desired (input-)language specification and generates a corresponding metamodel. To avoid the mentioned handwritten metamodel refinement we plan to make annotations to the grammar description. These annotations shall be used by the meta-tool to directly generate a good metamodel.

Another meta-tool (or an addition to the first one) is planned that deals with the automatic generation of frontends. These frontends should be able to parse languages according to a given grammar and generate a corresponding model according to a given metamodel in the repository.

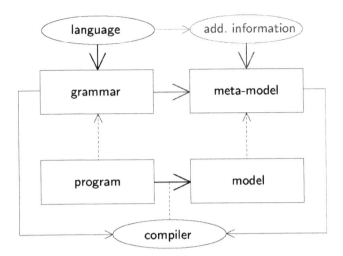

Fig. 10. Connections between grammar-based languages and the metamodelling tools

Figure 10 tries to graphically clarify the mentioned problems and propose solutions. You can see a language and its grammar on the upper-left part of the picture. The language's metamodel shall be derived directly from the grammar and some additional information. The additional information has to be written first, of course.

Once you have a grammar and a corresponding metamodel you can automatically create the compiler which parses programs and creates the appropriate model (the compiler is shown near the lower border in Fig. 10).

Similar but not identical problems exist at the backend of our compiler. In the previous section we described code generators for Java and C++. However, if we want to extend our SDL- compiler to cope with additional target languages we have to implement the corresponding code generators by hand. To avoid this work we plan to implement meta-tools which use the metamodel and the grammar of a specific language and automatically create code generators.

4   Conclusions

With ULF-Ware we propose an open framework, a methodology to build language tools based on a shared core repository with integrated languages based on common concepts. We have started to build the first example ULF-Ware pieces to prove our concept.

If successful, ULF-Ware will allow reuse among languages and among implementation of tools, independent tool development, and tools for integrated languages. This seems promising, but there are a few risky points: the idea of reusing and integrating via a common concept set is yet lacking any practical proof; the integration of languages on tool-level is useless, when there are no proper editors.

However, it is a promising and thus interesting field of research. We plan to continue to develop techniques for ULF-Ware based tools. We will prove the common concept idea with implementations to an SDL/UML integration. Reasonable languages to continue with are eODL, ASN.1, or TTCN. It is a long way to go, but ULF-Ware is a reasonable approach to unify the ITU-T language, and to provide new possibilities and means to model the telecommunication systems of tomorrow.

Even if ULF-Ware is in the first place intended to unify the ITU-T languages, its philosophy (and more importantly all research it results in) is applicable to all language development.

References

1. ITU-T Z.100: Specification and Description Language (SDL). International Telecommunication Union (2002)
2. UML: Unified Modeling Language, Version 1.5. Object Management Group (2003) formal/2003-03-01.
3. MDA: Model Driven Architecture Guide, Version 1.0.1. Object Management Group (2003) omg/03-06-01.
4. MOF: Meta Object Facility, Version 1.4. Object Management Group (2003) formal/2002-04-03.
5. Atkinson, C.: Meta-Modeling for Distributed Object Environments. In: 1st International Enterprise Distributed Object Computing Conference. (1997)
6. Fischer, J., Piefel, M., Scheidgen, M.: A metamodel for SDL-2000 in the context of metamodelling ULF. In: SAM2004 System Analysis and Modeling. LNCS 3319, Springer-Verlag GmbH (2005)
7. Fischer, J., Holz, E., Prinz, A., Scheidgen, M.: Tool-based Language Development. In: Workshop on Integrated-reliability with Telecommunications and UML Languages. (2004)
8. Martin, J., Odell, J.J.: Object-Oriented Methods: A Foundation. Prentice Hall PTR (1995) 2nd edition (1997).
9. Coad, P., Yourdon, E.: Object-Oriented Design. Yourdon Press (1991)
10. OCL: Object Constraint Language Specification (OCL). Object Management Group (1997) ad/1997-08-08.
11. Scheidgen, M.: Metamodelle für Sprachen mit formaler Syntaxdefinition, am Beispiel von SDL-2000. Humboldt-Universität zu Berlin (2004) master thesis.
12. Schröder, R., Böhme, H., von Löwis, M.: SDL Integrated Tool Environment. Web site, Humboldt-Universität zu Berlin (1997-2003) http://www.informatik.hu-berlin.de/SITE/.
13. Fischer, J., Neumann, T., Olsen, A.: SDL Code Generation for Open Systems. In: SDL2005 System Design. LNCS 3530, Springer-Verlag GmbH (2005).
14. Neumann, T., Piefel, M.: Kimwitu++. Web site and manual, Humboldt-Universität zu Berlin (2000-2004) http://site.informatik.hu-berlin.de/kimwitu++.

An Access Control Language for Dynamic Systems – Model-Driven Development and Verification

Manuel Koch and Karl Pauls

Freie Universität Berlin, Berlin, Germany
{mkoch, pauls}@inf.fu-berlin.de

Abstract. Security is a crucial aspect in any modern software system. We consider access control as a concern in the sense of Aspect Oriented Programming and present a design language for access control aspects in distributed systems, called View Policy Language. The specification of the View Policy Language for a given application is integrated into a model-driven software engineering approach to support the designer throughout the entire software process. We give a graph-based formal semantics to the design models in order to reason about model transformations. In particular, we can formally ensure the preservation of model constraints in the transformation process, and hence prove the reusability of security aspects in dynamic models for different platforms.

1 Introduction

Security is a crucial aspect in any modern software system and is usually spread across the entire system merged with functional system components. The mixture of application and security logic complicates the enforcement of policy changes and is error-prone. Aspect-oriented programming separates application code from application independent code [8, 15]. Aspects represent usually non-functional concerns such as logging, security. More specific, in adaptive programming the Law of Demeter for Concerns (LoDC) is implicitly used (that is "talk only to your friends that contribute to a common set of concerns or that share the same concerns" [14]). This has the advantage that application logic can be developed independently and aspects can be added when needed without changing application code.

We present a design language for access control aspects in distributed systems, called *View Policy Language* (VPL). The specification of the VPL for a given application is integrated into a model-driven software engineering approach to support the designer throughout the entire software process. Access control requirements can be modelled as platform independent in the VPL and are then mapped according to the mappings defined in the VPL to specific platforms. Since a platform independent model (PIM) is valid for any specific platform, it reduces the management and maintenance of one model instead of many models for each specific platform. Changes in the access control model can be done once

A. Prinz, R. Reed, and J. Reed (Eds.): SDL 2005, LNCS 3530, pp. 16–31, 2005.

in the platform independent model and the change then propagates consistently to all platform specific models (PSM).

Model Driven Development (MDD)[9] has the additional advantage that the many specification documents developed in the software development process are related and that existing dependencies are documented. Documentation of dependencies helps to take into account every change of a model or a relation necessary to guarantee consistency. One of the main drawbacks of model-driven development is the consideration of security requirements in the development process, which is not yet sufficiently supported.

Another advantage of MDD is the documentation of model transformations due to changing requirements. However, to ensure a consistent model transformation and the preservation of constraints, we give a graph-based formal semantics to the design models. In particular, we investigate how the satisfaction of access control constraints is preserved by a model transformation. We present formal results that ensure the preservation of model constraints throughout the transformation process, and hence prove the reusability of security aspects in dynamic models for different platforms. Satisfaction of all modified PSMs can be decided only on the basis of the evolution of the PIM. None of the PSMs need to be checked anymore. This reduces the check of a set of PSMs to a single check of the evolution morphism.

The remainder of the article is organized as follows: Section 2 presents the VPL as a design language for access control aspects. Section 3 concerns the integration of the design of a VPL into the model-driven software engineering process. Section 4 introduces the graph-based semantics and Section 5 concerns model transformations and results for access control constraint preservation. Section 6 concludes the article and points to future work.

2   VPL – A Design Language for Access Control Aspects

Aspect-oriented programming (AOP) separates concerns into single units called *aspects* [8]. Aspects can range from notions such as security and quality of services to buffering, caching and logging. An aspect is a modular unit of cross-cutting implementation and encapsulates behaviors that affect multiple classes into reusable modules. With AOP, each aspect can be expressed in a separate and natural form, and can then be automatically combined together into a final executable form by an aspect weaver. As a result, a single aspect can contribute to the implementation of a number of procedures, modules, or objects, so increasing reusability of the codes.

The *View Policy Language* (VPL) we propose to specify access control aspects, is based on an extended role-based access control (RBAC) model [18]. A VPL policy is written with respect to any model or interface intermediate language, which specifies operations and their parameters. Examples of such models are UML class diagrams, IDL (Interface Definition Language) or WSDL (Web Service Description Language) specifications. The VPL introduces *views* as a grouping concept for permissions to call operations. Views are assigned to roles and a subject can call an operation if it has a role with a view that contains the permission required to call the operation.

The VPL constructs are illustrated in this paper by a small conference management application [5, 3]. In the conference management system, the program committee (PC) can issue a call for papers to open a submission phase for a conference, so that authors may submit papers. The PC is responsible for the declaration of the submission deadline, which terminates the submission phase and starts the reviewing phase. The PC writes and submits reviews for the papers. The reviewing phase is terminated by the PC calling for a final decision.

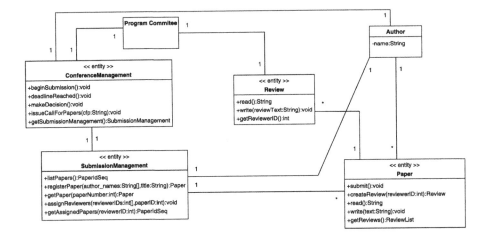

Fig. 1. The class diagram for the conference application

The VPL for this application is based on the class diagram in fig. 1: it gives the permissions to call the operations specified in the diagram. A VPL policy consists of a set of *roles*, a set of *views* and a set of *schemas*. A VPL policy starts with the keyword **policy** and a policy name. A **roles** clause specifies the roles and optionally a role extension relation between roles, role properties and an initial view assignment to roles. In the example, we have the roles `Program Committee` and `Author` which both have a property `name` of type `String`.

```
policy Conference {
    roles
        Program Committee
        Author property String name  ...}
```

Views are defined with the keyword **view**, the view name and the interface the view controls (the interface for which the view gives the permission to call a subset of the interface operations). The view *PaperBaseView* is a view on the interface `Paper` that gives the permission to call operation *read()*. View *PaperView* extends view *PaperBaseView* (specified by *extendedView:baseView*).

Therefore, *PaperView* permits calling the operations *read()* and *createReview()*. View *PaperView2* permits calling the operations *read()*, *write()* and *submit()*. Virtual views are views that do not contain operations. They are used to control the view assignment.

```
view PaperBaseView controls Paper {
    allow read }

view PaperView:PaperBaseView {        view PaperView2:PaperBaseView {
    allow createReview }                  allow write,submit }

virtual view SubmissionPhase controls ConferenceManagement
virtual view ReviewingPhase controls ConferenceManagement
```

Besides roles and views, a VPL policy specifies schemas for the dynamic assignment and removal of users and views to and from roles, respectively. The modification of the role assignments are triggered by operation calls. Each VPL schema (specified by the keyword **schema**) specifies for one interface (specified after the keyword **observes**) which operation call causes which role assignment modifications. For example, the schema *InitialState* observes the interface *ConferenceManagement* and assigns the virtual view SubmissionPhase to role Author when the operation *beginSubmission()* is called. The schema *SubmissionPhase* has a trigger operation *registerPaper()* and assigns the view PaperView2 on the registered paper to the authors of the registered paper. The keyword **result** specifies the return value of an operation (here the return value of operation *registerPaper()*, which is a paper). The condition Author.name in author_names ensures that the view PaperView2 on the registered paper can be used only by the authors of the paper (specified in the parameter author_names).

```
schema InitialState observes ConferenceManagement
{
    beginSubmission
        assign SubmissionPhase to Author ... }

schema SubmissionPhase observes SubmissionManagement
{
    registerPaper(author_names, title)
        assign PaperView2 on result to Author
                where Author.name in author_names }
```

The VPL policy is then deployed. This is done by assuming an interceptor facility as a mediator between the aspect layers and the system kernel (CORBA interceptor [16], RACCOON interceptor implementation [6], Axis handler concept [2]). This approach is different from the aspect weaving approach in which aspects are implemented separately from the application logic and is then compiled together (for example in AspectJ, JBOSS4.0).

3   Model-Driven Development of the VPL

The specification of the VPL for a given application is a difficult design task, especially since system designers are usually not security experts. Therefore, the designer should be supported in the software development process to obtain the right security requirements and their translation into a VPL policy. We present in this section a model-driven approach to develop the access control aspects in a VPL policy.

3.1   Developing the PIM for Access Control Aspects

The software process starts with the analysis stage in which use case diagrams are developed. We use the example of the conference management system introduced in section 2, and fig. 2 shows the corresponding use case.

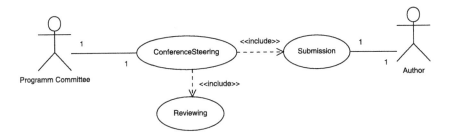

Fig. 2. The use case for the conference application

The class diagram developed on the basis of the use case diagram is shown in fig. 1. The entities model the core functionality of the system.

The use case and the class diagram already contain access control aspects. Actors in the use case diagram must have access to the use cases to perform their task. A use case is the basis for operations specified in the class diagram. Therefore we have access requirements of actors to operations of interface operations. In [4] it is shown that the access control roles can be derived from the UML actors of the use case diagram. Following the example we get the roles Program Committee and Author.

The use cases are refined in sequence diagrams using the operations of the class diagram. Sequence diagrams specify the required accesses of actors to call operations. In the sequence diagram in fig. 3 we see the required accesses of an author. An author must be able to call operation *getSubmissionManagment()* on interface *ConferenceManagement*, operation *registerPaper()* on *Submission-Management* and operations *write()* and *submit()* on *Paper*. A basic set of views are generated from the sequence diagrams, which contain the inherent access information. In each sequence diagram each of the occurring objects is considered. For each object a view is generated, which contains the operation calls on this object. For the sequence diagram in fig. 3 we get views which control interface *Paper, ConferenceManagement* and *SubmissionManagement*. The view on

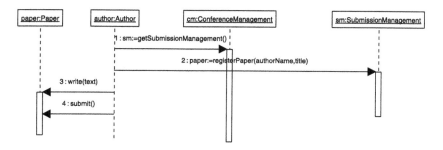

Fig. 3. The sequence diagram for the author's view

interface *Paper* permits calling the operations *write()* and *submit()*. The view on *ConferenceManagement* permits calling operation *getSubmissionManagement()*. The view on *SubmissionManagement* permits calling operation *registerPaper()*. For a more complete sequence diagram specification of the conference management application and its generation of views see [13].

The views generated from sequence diagrams are generally incomplete in the sense that they do not give a complete access control specification. This is due to the fact that sequence diagrams show only scenarios the designer is interested in. On the other hand, the views may be redundant in the sense that the same views are generated from different sequence diagrams. To sum up, not all of the access control information can be generated, and the designer uses the generated views as a basis that is refined to the final access control specification. The refinement includes also the introduction of access control roles and their initial assignment to views.

The software designer gets a graphical model containing the actors as access control roles and the views generated from the sequence diagrams. This model is refined by the designer. Figure 4 shows the refined model that the designer created on the basis of the generated views. For example, view **PaperView2** is generated from the sequence diagram in fig. 3. Views are assigned to roles by associations. For example, role **Actor** is assigned to the views *PaperView2* and *SubmissionMgmtView2*. The cardinality at the association end of the view specifies whether the view is initially assigned (value 1) or whether the view is not assigned in the initial state but can be assigned later (value 0..1). For example, the views *SubmissionMgmtView2* and *PaperView2* are not initially assigned to the role **Author**, but can be assigned dynamically during runtime. For a more detailed description of the generated model and its refinement see [13].

The dynamic assignment or removal of views to and from roles, respectively, is modeled in an activity diagram. The operation call which triggers a view change and the actual view-role relation modification are specified as edge labels in the diagram. Figure 5 shows the activity diagram of our example. The initial state is given by the assignment of views as specified in fig. 4. The protection state changes if the PC opens the submission phase by calling operation **beginSubmission**. Therefore the trigger is a call of oper-

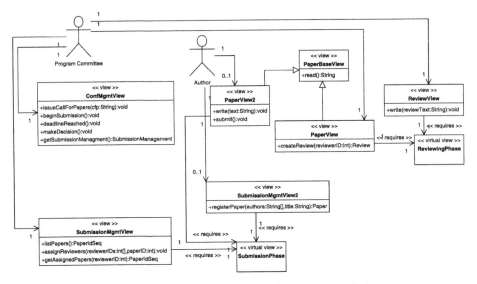

Fig. 4. Extension and refinement of the generated views

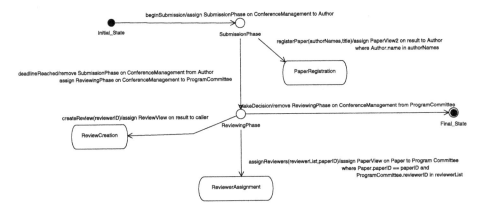

Fig. 5. The dynamic changes of the protection state

ation `beginSubmission`, whose effect is the assignment of the view *SubmissionPhase* (which is a view on class `ConferenceManagement`) to role `Author`. The new protection state is called *SubmissionPhase* in which authors are permitted to submit their articles. Authors can register papers by calling operation `registerPaper(authorNames,title)`. The effect of this operation call is that all authors of the paper get the view *PaperView2* on the registered paper. That authors have only access to their paper ensures the condition `where Author.name in authornames`. The attribute *name* of the role `Author` conveys the caller's name which must coincide with one of the authors of the paper. Calling operation `deadlineReached` ends the submission phase and starts the reviewing phase. The activity diagram specifies the view removal and assignment effects. In the reviewing phase, the operations **assignReviewers** and **createReview** cause view assignment changes. In the former case, a set of reviewers get the right to work on the assigned paper. In the second case, a reviewer gets the right to create a review for a paper. Calling operation **makeDecision** changes into the final state.

The diagrams in fig. 4 and fig. 5 can be used to automatically generate a VPL policy as introduced in section 2 and [13]. Therefore a software engineer does not necessarily have to know the VPL syntax, since (s)he works only with the graphical models integrated into the UML software process.

3.2   PSM for Web Services

After the PIM is modeled it can be mapped to specific platforms. We consider next a Web Service platform. In theory, a Web Service specific UML profile should be able to do the model-model transformation from the PIM to the Web Service PSM, but in practice it is unlikely that this can be achieved in a general form (then some design decisions must be done by the application designer). Subsequently, an arguable design decision could be the introduction of a primary, denoting a specific entity in the interfaces of the Web Service PSM entities.

We omit the detailed PSM for the class diagram and show only the PSM for the access control specification in fig. 6. Roughly speaking, the name of the entities are mapped onto Web Service endpoints (service interfaces) with the name of the corresponding entity, while the methods are enhanced by a parameter of type **String** representing the identifier (**cfMmgtID**, **paperID**, etc.). These identifiers act as a primary key denoting the specific entity to interact with via the service. The modified operations are used in the Web Service PSM in fig. 6.

4   Formal Semantics by Graph Transformation

We give next a formal semantics based on graph transformations to PIMs and PSMs. We briefly introduce the basic notions of graph transformations necessary for the remainder of this article[1] and present the representation of models and model relations by graphs and graph morphisms, respectively.

A *graph* consists of disjoint sets of *nodes* and directed *edges* $e : a \rightarrow b$ from a *source* node a to a *target* node b. Nodes and edges of a graph have a *type* used to identify graphical objects and *attributes* used to store data together with the static objects. The graphical representation of PIMs and PSMs gives a direct interpretation of these models by graphs, which we denote by $G(PIM)$ and $G(PSM)$, respectively. Consider as an example the Web Service PSM in fig. 6. The nodes of the underlying graph $G(PSM)$ are all views, virtual views and

---

[1] For the general concepts of graph transformations see [17].

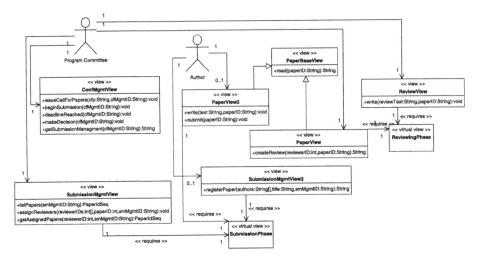

Fig. 6. Web Service PSM

actors. The edges of $G(PSM)$ are all associations. View nodes are of type `view`, virtual view nodes have type `virtual view` and actor nodes (which represent the access control roles) have type `role`. Graph $G(PSM)$ has edges of type `requires` (for associations labelled `requires`), `inherits` (for associations representing generalizations) and a (not explicitly shown) default label (for all associations without special label). The node attributes of nodes consist of a node name and (if the model element has any) a set of operations. Attributes of edges contain the multiplicities of associations.

A *graph morphism* $f : G \to H$ between two graphs G and H consists of an injective partial mapping between the nodes of G and the nodes of H and an injective partial mapping between the edges of G and the edges of H so that f respects the graph structure. This means that whenever the mapping for edges is defined for an edge e, the mapping for the source node s and the target node t of e is defined and $f(s)$ and $f(t)$ are the source and target node for the edge $f(e)$ in H. Furthermore, nodes and edges are mapped only to nodes and edges of the same type and f respects the attribution – the values of the attributes are either unchanged or they are in a previously defined relation (what is defined in the algebraic specification of the attribute type). We call a graph morphism *total* if the mappings between the node and edge sets are total.

A relation between PIMs and PSMs (or between two PIMs, or two PSMs) is represented as a graph morphism between the underlying graphs $G(PIM)$ and $G(PSM)$. Consider fig. 8 as an example, which shows four graphs and four graph morphisms. The graph PIM on top of the left-hand side is the underlying graph of the PIM in fig. 4. For the sake of readability, we omitted the operations and multiplicities of edges in fig. 8. The graph on the bottom of the left-hand

side is the underlying graph of the PSM in fig. 6. The graph PIM' on top of
the right-hand side is the underlying graph of the PIM in fig. 7 and the graph in
the right lower corner is constructed by these models (more details in Sect. 5).
The graph morphism $f : PIM \rightarrow PIM'$ maps the grey nodes of graph PIM to
the grey nodes of graph PIM' which have the same name. The white nodes of
graph PIM are not mapped by graph morphism f, i.e. f is undefined on these
nodes. The white nodes of graph PIM' have no pre-image in PIM. The graph
morphism m between graph PIM and PSM is total (i.e., each node of PIM is
mapped to a node in PSM).

5   Evolution of the PIM and Model Transformation

Due to changing requirements a PIM may be modified. If a PIM changes, however, all PSMs belonging to this PIM must be changed consistently. This section
concerns the evolution of a PIM and the succeeding transformation of all PSMs.
We show how PIM evolution is modeled and give a formal construction for the
modification of the PSMs. Furthermore, we formally prove conditions for the
preservation of model constraints in this transformation process.

The evolution of a PIM is modeled by a graph morphism $f : G(PIM) \rightarrow$
(PIM') where PIM' models the new requirements. We call the graph morphism f an *evolution morphism*. All elements of $G(PIM)$ on which f is undefined are removed, all elements on which f is defined remain unchanged
and all elements of $G(PIM')$ without pre-image in $G(PIM)$ are added. Figure 7 shows an evolution of the PIM in fig. 4. The evolution concerns the
removal of role Program Committee and the addition of the roles Chair and
Reviewer. The reviewer is responsible for the management, reviewers can only
review papers. Furthermore, the view ConfMgmtView is removed and replaced by
a new view ConfMgmtView and ConfMgmtView2. ConfMgmtView2 contains only
the operation getSubmissionManagement which is not contained anymore in
ConfMgmtView. ConfMgmtView is an extension of ConfMgmtView2. Lastly, the
view SubmissionMgmtView3 is added.

Figure 8 on top shows the corresponding evolution morphism $f : G(PIM) \rightarrow$
(PIM'). The morphism is undefined on the white nodes of PIM and defined on
grey nodes. The white nodes in PIM' are added by f.

All PSM models must be changed according to the modified PIM. For the
construction of the PSMs the categorical construction of a *pushout* is used. We
explain the construction informally and refer the reader interested into the formal
definition to [7].

Construction 1 (Pushout). *Construct the pushout graph PSM' of an evolution morphism $f : PIM \rightarrow PIM'$ and a total graph morphism $m : PIM \rightarrow
PSM$ (the PIM-PSM mapping) as follows:*

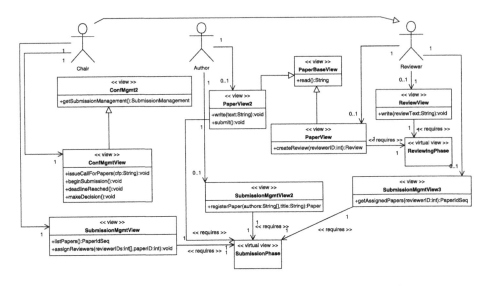

Fig. 7. Evolution of the PIM in Figure 4

1. *Take PSM and remove all nodes and edges x with x = m(y) from PSM if f is undefined for y. If there remain edges without source or target node, delete them. One gets a graph PSM^i.*
2. *Add all elements x of PIM' to PSM^i which have no pre-image in PIM. We get the graph PSM'.*

Performing the construction for morphisms $f : PIM \rightarrow PIM'$ and $m : PIM \rightarrow PSM$ we get the following diagram. The morphism f' is partial, the morphism m' is total and we have $f' \circ m = m' \circ f$ [7].

$$
\begin{array}{ccc}
PIM & \xrightarrow{\ f\ } & PIM' \\
{\scriptstyle m}\downarrow & & \downarrow{\scriptstyle m'} \\
PSM & \xrightarrow[\ f'\ ]{} & PSM'
\end{array}
$$

Figure 8 shows an example of a pushout construction. First, we remove from *PSM* the nodes **Program Committee** and **ConfMgmtView**, since *f* is undefined on theses nodes. The evolution morphism is also undefined on all edges connected to these two nodes. Therefore these edges are deleted as well. Then, the nodes **Chair, Reviewer, ConfMgmtView2, ConfMgmtView** and **SubmissionMgmtView3** and all their connected edges are added and we get the graph *PSM'*. The morphism *m'* is the embedding of *PIM'* into *PSM'*, *f'* is the partial embedding of *PSM* into *PSM'*.

By the pushout construction, we can automatically construct the modified PSMs for any evolution morphism $f : PIM \rightarrow PSM'$.

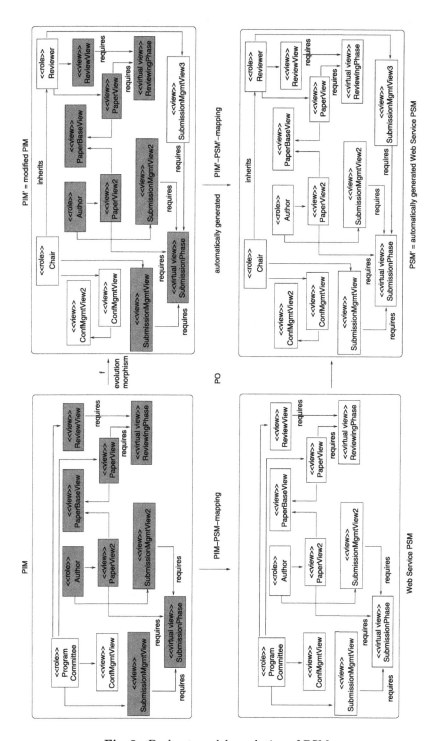

Fig. 8. Pushout models evolution of PSMs

5.1   Preservation of Access Control Constraint Satisfaction

Access control models can be extended by access control constraints to describe requirements that have to be satisfied by any configuration of the system. For example, the following access control constraints should be satisfied in the conference management system.

1. A virtual view must not have any operation.
2. There is no multiple inheritance of roles.

Constraint expression is a difficult task and existing languages are often too complex for administrators to determine whether a set of constraints really satisfies a requirement. Therefore, access control specification languages are introduced, which have a complexity understandable by administrators and expressive enough for most of the practical access control constraints [1, 10, 11]. We use the approach of *graphical constraints* presented in [11] which integrates into the graph transformation approach introduced above and which provides a formal semantics to verify the constraints [12].

Definition 1 (Graphical Constraint). *A graphical constraint is a graph C and a graph G satisfies C if there does not exist a total graph morphism $p : C \to G$.*

Graphical constraint 1) in fig. 9 specifies the requirement of operationless virtual views. The expression $(\text{operation})^+$ means that there is at least one or more operations. A system satisfies this constraint if no system state contains this forbidden structure. Graphical constraint 2) forbids a role which inherits two (or more) roles.

Fig. 9. Graphical constraints for the conference management system

In the sequel, we investigate how the satisfaction of access control constraints is preserved by an evolution morphism. The aim is to decide the satisfaction of all modified PSM models only on the basis of the evolution morphism. None of the PSM models themselves need to be checked anymore. This reduces the check of a set of PSM models to a single check of the evolution morphism.

The following is a necessary condition for the satisfaction of constraints in the modified PSM models. Only if the new PIM satisfies the constraints, can the PSMs satisfy the constraints. The proof is based on the fact that PIM' is a subgraph of PSM'.

Proposition 1. *Let $f : PIM \to PIM'$ be an evolution morphism, $m : PIM \to PSM$ a PSM mapping and PSM' be the pushout of f and m. If PSM' satisfies a graphical constraint C then PIM' satisfies C.*

The next proposition requires some further notations: We define by $G|_C$ the greatest subgraph of a graph G that contains only the nodes and edges with a type occurring in C. For example, constraint 2) in fig. 9 has nodes only of type role and edges only of type inherits. The graph $PIM'|_C$ for the graph PIM' in fig. 8 consists of the role nodes *Chair, Author, Reviewer* and the *inherits* edge between *Chair* and *Reviewer*. Furthermore, we call a constraint C *connected* if there is for each node v in C a path of edges to any other node v' in C.

The next proposition states that an evolution morphism does not violate a constraint if the evolution morphism does not add any parts occurring in the constraint. Furthermore, an evolution morphism does not violate a connected constraint if the added elements relevant to the constraint are not connected to existing elements.

Proposition 2. *Let PSM' be the pushout of an evolution morphism $f : PIM \rightarrow PIM'$ and a total morphism $m : PIM \rightarrow PSM$ so that PSM and PIM' satisfy the graphical constraint C.*

1. *If $(PIM' \setminus f(PIM)) \cap C = \emptyset$ then PSM' satisfies C.*
2. *Let C be connected and for each edge e in $(PIM'|_C \setminus f(PIM|_C))$ both the source node and the target node are in $(PIM'|_C \setminus f(PIM|_C))$. Then PSM' satisfies C.*

Proof. 1. Assume PIM' does not satisfy C (that there is a total injective morphism $p : C \rightarrow PIM'$). Then we have several cases. First, $p(C) \subseteq f'(PSM)$. This is not possible since then there is the morphism $f'^{-1} \circ p : C \rightarrow PSM$. This is a contradiction to the assumption that PSM satisfies C. Second case, $p(C) \subseteq m'(PIM')$. Since there is no overlap between C and $(PIM' \setminus f(PIM))$, $p(C) \subseteq m'(f'(PIM))$. But then there is a morphism $m \circ f^{-1} \circ m'^{-1} \circ p = f'^{-1} \circ p : C \rightarrow PSM$. This is again a contradiction.
2. Assume PSM' does not satisfy C (that there is a total injective morphism $p : C \rightarrow PSM'$). $p(C) \subseteq f'(PSM)$ and $p(C) \subseteq m'(PSM)$ is not possible since otherwise PSM or PIM does not satisfy C. Therefore, there must be a node or an edge in $m'(PIM')$ that is not in $f'(PSM)$. Assume it is a node x: since C is connected there must be a node in $f(PSM) \setminus m'(PIM')$ to which x is connected. This is a contradiction to the fact that there are no edges between elements of $(PIM'|_C \setminus f(PIM|_C))$ and $f(PIM|_C)$. Assume it is an edge e: since C is connected then also the source and target node are not in $m'(PIM')$. Then there is a contradiction analogy to the node case.

Proposition 2 can be used to verify the satisfaction of the PSMs with respect to the constraints in fig. 9 and the evolution morphism in fig. 8. PSMs satisfy constraint 1) since the evolution morphism does not add any virtual view. PSMs satisfy constraint 2) since the constraint is connected and the added roles Chair and Reviewer are not connected to the existing role Author. Or rephrased, the source and target nodes of the added *inherits* edge are both added by the evolution morphism. Therefore, we are sure that any transformation of a PSM with respect to this evolution morphism satisfies the constraints in fig. 9.

6   Conclusions

We presented the VPL as design language for access control aspects and integrated the design of a VPL policy into a model-driven software engineering process. A graph-based semantics for the models enables us to prove the preservation of access control constraints during the model transformation process.

Future work will integrate the model-driven approach into the Eclipse project including the generation of the access control model from UML diagrams. Another interesting verification approach for access control constraints is model checking. A model checker can be used to automatically check constraints and to provide counter examples for constraint violations visualized in UML sequence diagrams. Future work in this area concerns the integration of a model checker into the Eclipse-based access control development process.

References

1. G.-J. Ahn and R. Sandhu. Role-Based Authorization Constraints Specification. *ACM Transactions on Information and System Security*, 3(4):207–226, Nov. 200.
2. Apache. Axis. http://ws.apache.org/axis/.
3. G. Brose. Manageable Access Control for CORBA. *Journal of Computer Security*, 4:301–337, 2002.
4. G. Brose, M. Koch, and K.-P.Löhr. Integrating Access Control Design into the Software Development Process. In *Proc. of 6th International Conference on Integrated Design and Process Technology (IDPT)*, 2002.
5. Gerald Brose. *Access Control Management in Distributed Object Systems*. PhD thesis, Freie Universität Berlin, 2001.
6. Gerald Brose. Raccoon — An infrastructure for managing access control in CORBA. In *Proc. Int. Conference on Distributed Applications and Interoperable Systems (DAIS)*. Kluwer, 2001.
7. H. Ehrig, R. Heckel, M. Korff, M. Löwe, L. Ribeiro, A. Wagner, and A. Corradini. *Handbook of Graph Grammars and Computing by Graph Transformations. Vol. I: Foundations*, chapter Algebraic Approaches to Graph Transformation Part II: Single Pushout Approach and Comparison with Double Pushout Approach. In Rozenberg [17], 1997.
8. T. Elrad, R. Filman, and A. Bader. Aspect-Oriented Programming. In *Communications of the ACM*, volume 44, pages 28–97, 2001.
9. D. S. Frankel. *Model Driven Architecture: Applying MDA to Enterprise Computing*. John Wiley and Sons., 2003.
10. T. Jaeger and J.E. Tidswell. Practical Safety in Flexible Access Control Models. *ACM Transactions on Information and System Security*, 4(2):158–190, 2001.
11. M. Koch, L. V. Mancini, and F. Parisi-Presicce. A Graph Based Formalism for RBAC. *ACM Transactions on Information and System Security (TISSEC)*, 5(3):332–365, August 2002.

12. M. Koch, L.V. Mancini, and F. Parisi-Presicce. Conflict Detection and Resolution in Access Control Specifications. In M.Nielsen and U.Engberg, editors, *Proc. of Foundations of Software Science and Computation Structures (FoSSaCS 2002)*, Lect. Notes in Comp. Sci., pages 223–237. Springer, 2002.
13. Manuel Koch and Karl Pauls. Model-driven Development of Access Control Aspects. In *Proc. of Sicherheit 2005, 2. GI-Jahrestagung Fachbereich Sicherheit*, 2005.
14. Karl J. Lieberherr. Controlling the Complexity of Software Designs. In *Proc. of 26th International Conference in Software Engineering*, pages 2–11, 2004 2004.
15. C. Lopes. *Aspect-Oriented Software Development*, chapter AOP: A Historical Perspective. Addison Wesley, 2004.
16. OMG. *Common Object Request Broker Architecture: Core Specification V.3.0.2*, December 2002.
17. G. Rozenberg, editor. *Handbook of Graph Grammars and Computing by Graph Transformation, Volume 1: Foundations*. World Scientific, 1997.
18. R. Sandhu, D. Ferraiolo, and R. Kuhn. The NIST Model for Role-Based Access Control: Towards A Unified Standard. In *Proc. of the 5th ACM Workshop on Role-Based Access Control*. ACM, July 2000.

Non-deterministic Constructs in OCL
– What Does any() Mean

Thomas Baar*

École Polytechnique Fédérale de Lausanne (EPFL),
School of Computer and Communication Sciences, Lausanne, Switzerland
thomas.baar@epfl.ch

Abstract. The Object Constraint Language (OCL) offers so-called non-deterministic constructs which are often only poorly understood even by OCL experts. They are widely ignored in the OCL literature, their semantics given in the official language description of OCL is ill-defined, and none of today's OCL tools support them in a consistent way.

The source of the poor understanding and ill-defined semantics is, as identified in this paper, OCL's attempt to adopt the concept of non-determinism from other specification languages with fundamentally different semantical foundations. While this insight helps to improve the understanding of non-deterministic constructs it also shows that there are some formidable obstacles for their integration into OCL.

However, in some cases, non-deterministic constructs can be read as abbreviations for more complex deterministic constructs and can help to formulate a specification in a more understandable way. Thus, we suggest to integrate non-deterministic constructs in other specification languages such as Z, JML, Eiffel whose semantical foundations are similar to those of OCL.

1 Introduction

Specification languages describe properties of systems on a certain level of abstraction. System development typically requires a broad spectrum of specification languages which must be able to cope with different properties (structural, behavioral, non-functional) in different stages of development. This was the main motivation in the early 90-ies to tightly bind 7 different diagrammatic languages to the Unified Modeling Language (UML)[1].

The UML language description [2, 3] defines the integrated languages and their interconnections in terms of a meta-model that is written in MOF (a derivate of UML class diagrams) and the Object Constraint Language (OCL). The meta-modeling technique has become extremely popular in recent years and is used more and more often to define other specification and even programming languages.

---

* This work was partially supported by Hasler-Foundation, project DICS-1850.

A. Prinz, R. Reed, and J. Reed (Eds.): SDL 2005, LNCS 3530, pp. 32–46, 2005.

This development has promoted the use of OCL through the fact that well-formedness rules of the syntax in meta-model based language definitions are described by OCL constraints. Since well-formedness rules are the core of a language description, the application of OCL in meta-models requires an exceptionally deep understanding of this constraint language. Mistakes, made during the definition of a new language, will obfuscate its syntax and also its semantics and thus the purpose of the new language itself.

Widely neglected and often misunderstood are up to now so-called *non-deterministic constructs* in OCL. The most basic non-deterministic construct is the library operation `asSequence()` that expects as an argument a term of type `Set(T)`[1] and yields a term of type `Sequence(T)`. Semantically, `asSequence()` is used to turn a set into a sequence that has the same elements as the set. The construct `asSequence()` is called non-deterministic, because it imposes a non-deterministically chosen ordering on the elements in the resulting sequence which is not given for the elements of the argument set. As a second non-deterministic construct, the operation `any()` is offered by the OCL library. It expects a term of type `Set(T)` and yields a term of type `T`. Semantically, the operation `any()` can be used to select non-deterministically an element from a set. The non-deterministic selection could be simulated by turning the set into a sequence imposing an ordering on its elements and, in a second step, by taking that element which has order number 1. For this reason, `any()` can be seen as an abbreviation for `asSequence()` concatenated with `first()`, another library operation which yields the first element of a sequence if the sequence has at least one element and *undef*, otherwise.

As it is shown in section 2, there are some formidable obstacles for defining a formal semantics for non-deterministic constructs in OCL. The main argument goes as follows: The semantics of constraints attached to a system description is defined on the basis of constraint evaluations in concrete system states. For instance, a constraint attached as an invariant to the system description characterizes the allowed system states for which the constraint must be evaluated to *true*. This simple semantics, however, cannot be applied to an invariant containing non-deterministic constructs because the evaluation of the invariant in a given state might yield more than one result, for example, *true* and *false*.

The problematic semantics of non-deterministic constructs in OCL makes users understandably reluctant to take advantage of non-determinism. For example, the UML metamodel [2,3] (both documents have together 839 pages) is authored by some of the leading experts for UML, but `any()` is the only non-deterministic construct that occurs (21 times). Even more interesting, the construct `any()` is always applied on sets containing exactly one element. When applied on a singleton set, however, the construct `any()` can be seen as a deterministic operation. Thus, the whole UML metamodel contains not a single, truly non-deterministic constraint.

---

[1] `Set(T)` is a parameterized type where T is a placeholder for subtypes of the predefined type `OclAny`.

Although `asSequence()` is the more basic construct compared to `any()` this paper concentrates on the semantics of `any()` for two reasons. Firstly, the non-determinism introduced by `asSequence()` cannot be captured by an evaluation based semantics without losing other important logical properties. Secondly, the only non-deterministic construct used in practice, and this also only very rarely, is `any()` – that is, the combination of `asSequence()` and `first()`. Fortunately, a constraint using `any()` can, as we will see, often be rephrased by another constraint that has the same 'intended' meaning, but only contains deterministic constructs.

For the design of the specification language OCL, our results have two consequences. In principle, the evaluation based semantics prevents OCL having non-deterministic constructs. Thus, we propose to delete `asSequence()` from the OCL library. The construct `any()` can remain in the library with the same meaning it currently has (non-deterministic selection of one element from a set) but not as an abbreviation for `asSequence()->first()`. Instead, `any()` should be introduced as an abbreviation according to the transformation algorithm given in section 4.

The remainder of the paper is structured as follows. Section 2 points out the problems in the current semantics of OCL caused by non-deterministic constructs. A subsection illustrates how the unsolved problems have a disastrous impact on the tool support for OCL. Section 3 compares OCL with other specification languages and identify the reasons why OCL tries to offer non-deterministic constructs. This comparison will clarify what the *intended meaning* of the construct `any()` is. After the role, the construct `any()` plays in OCL, is understood, Section 4 presents two attempts to capture the intended meaning formally. Both approaches have some limits, but the limitations of the second approach based on transformation are irrelevant for practical specifications. Section 5 concludes the paper.

2   Problems with the any()-Construct in OCL

The Object Constraint Language (OCL), specified in its most recent version 2.0 in [4], is a strongly typed, term-based specification language. Terms are either atomic, for example variables, or are composed of an operation that is applied to subterms. Terms of the predefined type `Boolean` are called *constraints*.

When attached to a class diagram, the purpose of an OCL constraint is to *restrict* the allowed states of the system described by the class diagram. If a constraint is attached as an invariant, then the state of the system must always *conform* to that constraint. If a constraint is attached as a pre- or post-condition of a system operation, then the system state must conform to the constraint whenever the operation is invoked or has terminated.

The meaning (semantics) of an OCL constraint must clarify which of the possible system states conform to it and which of them do not conform. The separation between conforming and non-conforming states is implicitly given by an *evaluation function* eval that yields, applied on a concretely given state and a constraint, one of OCL's three truth-values *true*, *false*, *undef*. The function *eval* is defined in [4] by structural induction on all OCL terms.

The application of *eval* on a constraint *constr* and a state *st* is called *evaluation of constr in st*. The state *st* conforms to *constr* if and only if *constr* is evaluated in *st* to *true*. If a constraint is attached as a post-condition to the system and contains the @pre operator, then its evaluation is analogously defined on a pair of states instead of a single state.

In the OCL language description [4], any() is declared as an operation with one argument[2] of type Collection(*T*) and return type *T*. More precisely, the operation any() is used in composed terms of the form *src*->any(), where *src* has the type Collection(*T*) and the composed term is of type *T*. Most often, any() is applied to terms of type Set(*T*) (a subtype of Collection(*T*)) and, to facilitate our argument, we will assume in the rest of the paper *src* to be of type Set(*T*).

The evaluation of terms of form *src*->any() is described in the OCL language specification as a non-deterministic choice from the set that is obtained by evaluation of *src* (see [4–page A-19]). If the evaluation of *src* yields an empty set or a singleton set, the evaluation of *src*->any() yields *undef* or the single element of the singleton respectively. In these two exceptional cases, the evaluation of *src*->any() is deterministic and well-defined. In all other cases, the non-deterministic evaluation can cause serious problems as a first example illustrates:

context Foo :: foo1():Integer
post: result = Set{1,2}->any()

The term Set{1,2}->any() is non-deterministically evaluated in any state to 1 or 2. The official OCL semantics in [4] does not clarify the consequences of non-deterministic evaluation for the conformance of states to a non-deterministic constraint. Suppose, the system operation foo1() terminates in a state *st* and returns[3] for example the value 1. If Set{1,2}->any() is evaluated to 1, then *st* would conform to the post-condition but does the same state conform if 2 is non-deterministically chosen by the evaluation algorithm instead of 1? It seems the only thing that can be concluded from the OCL semantics, is, that all post-states in which foo1() returns a value different from 1 and 2 do not conform to the post-condition. It remains an open question if this indeed completely captures the meaning of that constraint.

The next example is a slight variation of the last one.

context Foo :: foo2():Integer
post: **if** Set{1,2}->any() = Set{1,2}->any()
      then result = 1
      else result = 2
      endif

---

[2] Sometimes, any() is used with a second argument of type Boolean that serves as a guard. Note, that terms of the form *src*->any(*guard*) can be rewritten to *src*->select(*guard*)->any().

[3] The return value of an operation is represented in post-conditions by the predefined variable result.

Would this specification allow a post-state where `foo2()` returns 1? One could argue 'yes', because it is possible to find among all non-deterministic evaluations for both `any()`-terms such an evaluation where the if-condition is evaluated to *true*.

Analogously, one could argue for conformance of a post-state with return value 2, because an evaluation could be found where the if-condition is evaluated to *false*. This would require that the two `any()`-terms are evaluated differently, for instance the first to 1 and the second to 2.

A conformant state with return value 2, however, would contradict the fundamental logical law that equality is a reflexive relation. Note, that the if-condition is of form $X = X$ and most logics allow to simplify this to *true*. Consequently, the `if-then-else` expression would collapse to `result = 1`, which would not allow 2 as a return value.

2.1   Current Tool Support for any()

Current tools for OCL (see [5] for an overview) have either not implemented the `any()` construct (a sign that non-deterministic constructs are not well-understood yet) or have implemented it in a way which contradicts basic and widely accepted laws in logic.

For instance, as one of the few tools that can handle `any()`, OCLE [6] evaluates the expression `Set{1,2}->any() = Set{1,2}->any()` always (!) to *true* whereas `Set{1,2}->any() = Set{2,1}->any()` is always evaluated to *false*. This contradicts the law that for a set the ordering of the elements is not important; the term `Set{1,2}` should denote the same set as `Set{2,1}`.

Probably, the authors of OCLE have understood the non-determinism of the evaluation function in OCL in such a way, that the decision, which among all possible evaluations should be chosen, can be made by the tool. But such a setting would give one tool the freedom to confirm the conformance of a state to a constraint while another tool comes to the opposite conclusion for exactly the same state and the same constraint. Finally, the meaning of an OCL constraint (the decision which of the system states conform to it), could depend entirely on the tool that is used to process that constraint!

3   Non-determinism Versus Under-Specification

In order to understand the construct `any()` offered by OCL it is helpful to concentrate on the usage of OCL as a contract specification language. A contract [7] for a system operation describes its behavior in terms of pre- and post-conditions.

3.1   Constructive Versus Restrictive Languages

Contract specification languages can be classified into two groups. The classification is based on the technique in which post-conditions are formulated (the formulation of pre-conditions is much more uniform than for post-conditions and relies always on a dialect of predicate logic).

Languages belonging to the first group, *constructive specification languages*, provide pseudo-code for the formulation of the post-condition. The pseudo-code allows specification of the operation's behavior in the form of an algorithm. In other words, the transition of the system from the pre-state to the post-state is given by the sequential, conditional (and sometimes also parallel) composition of more atomic state-transitions. The pseudo-code often resembles imperative programming languages with their basic control structures (assignment, sequential and parallel execution, if-then-else, loops). Two of the most prominent examples of constructive specification languages are Abstract State Machines (ASM) and B. The specification given in the post-condition is called *update* in the ASM terminology and *generalized substitution* in B.

Languages of the second group, *restrictive specification languages*, offer for the formulation of the post-condition basically the same formalism as for the pre-condition. In such languages, a post-condition restricts the set of possible post-states. The intention is not to describe *how* the post-state is 'constructed' from the pre-state (even if this is possible in some situations as our examples will show). Nevertheless, it is possible to specify in the post-condition how the post-state is related to the pre-state. For that reason, restrictions can be formulated on the value of the state variables in the post-state as well as in the pre-state because all such languages allow the post-condition to refer to both pre- and post-state. For example, in OCL, `att1 > att1@pre` means that the value of `att1` in the post-state must be greater than its value in the pre-state.

Well-known examples for restrictive specification languages are Hoare-Triple, Dynamic Logic, Eiffel, Java Modeling Language (JML), and Z.

Non-deterministic constructs play an important role in constructive languages, but they cannot, as seen in the last section, be naively integrated into restrictive languages. A comparison between constructive and restrictive specifications helps to uncover the intended semantics of the `any()` construct. We start with a tiny specification that is both given in B and in UML/OCL.

3.2   A Motivating Example

Figure 1 shows part of a Dispatcher-Depot scenario. A depot is a place to temporarily keep trains (e.g. during the night). For the purpose of our example, it is sufficient to know the number of trains which are currently at the depot (indicated by `no`). The task of a dispatcher is the management of depots, especially the dispatcher has to choose a depot where to place incoming trains (operation `addTrain()`). We assume a dispatcher to manage only two depots (`d1,d2`), furthermore we abstract from the fact that real world depots have a limited capacity.

Figure 1 shows in its left-hand side a formalization of the Dispatcher-Depot example written in B whereas the right-hand side formalizes the same scenario using a UML/OCL specification.

The B specification starts with the description of train depots whose states are encoded by the state variable `no` of type `Integer`. The state of a dispatcher is given by the state variables `d1` and `d2` of type `Depot`. The specification of

Machine Depot
Variables no
Invariant no $\in \mathbb{Z}$

Machine Dispatcher(Depot)
Variables d1, d2
Invariant d1,d2 $\in$ Depot
Operations
addTrain() $\triangleq$
PRE true
THEN
  IF no(d1) < no(d2)
  THEN no(d1) := no(d1) + 1
  ELSE no(d2) := no(d2) + 1
  END

```
context Dispatcher :: addTrain()
pre:   true
post: if d1.no@pre < d2.no@pre
   then d1.no = d1.no@pre + 1 and
     d2.no = d2.no@pre
   else
     d2.no = d2.no@pre + 1 and
     d1.no = d1.no@pre
   endif
```

Fig. 1. Constructive and restrictive specification in B and OCL

the operation `addTrain()` can be read as follows: It is always possible to invoke `addTrain()` (precondition is `true`) and upon termination of `addTrain()`, the number of trains in depot `d1` will be increased by 1 if `d1` had less trains than `d2` in the pre-state, otherwise the number of trains in depot `d2` is increased by 1.

The post-condition is constructive in the sense that it prescribes the behavior of `addTrain()` in an algorithmic way. Note, that the operator `:=` has to be read as assignment and thus the ordering of its arguments is crucial. In the line `no(d1) := no(d1) + 1`, the value of the state variable `no` for `d1` (left-hand side) is updated with the value of this variable in the pre-state increased by one (right-hand side). The B specification also ensures that the number of trains is increased only for one of the two depots `d1`, `d2`; the number of trains in the other depot remains the same.

In the UML/OCL formalization, the declarations of the state variables are given in form of a UML class diagram. The lower part shows a restrictive specification of `addTrain()` written in OCL. The post-condition is structured the same way as the post-condition in the constructive B specification (`if-then-else`). Both specifications only differ in the `then/else` branches:

For example, the line `d1.no = d1.no@pre + 1` is not to be read as an assignment but just as a restriction that the state-variable `no` of `d1` has in the post-state the same value (=) as in the pre-state but increased by one. Note, that in contrast to the assignment operator used in the constructive B specification, the ordering of the arguments in the equality does not matter: the line `d1.no@pre + 1 = d1.no` would have expressed exactly the same.

There is another difference between constructive and restrictive specification that is illustrated in this tiny specification: The **then**-branch of the post-condition, for instance, covers the case where a train is added to the depot d1 whereas depot d2 remains untouched. If the latter fact is important (here it is, because an implementation of addTrain() would not be correct if it would, say, increase the number of both depots) it must be explicitly mentioned in the OCL specification (d2.no = d2.no@pre) whereas this is expressed in the B specification automatically. For a deeper understanding of this problem (in literature known as the Frame problem) the interested reader is referred to [8].

3.3   Motivation for Non-determinism

The specification of addTrain() shown above is extremely detailed in the sense that for any given pre-state, the specification allows exactly one post-state. At a first glance, such specifications seem superficial because the implementation of the operation could have been given directly. This argument ignores the fact that the implementation and specification of a system usually reside on different levels of abstraction. An actual implementation for addTrain() would most likely use a much more detailed model of the system than would be derived by a refinement of the shown model. However, we use the term *implementation* in the rest of the paper as a synonym for the set of concrete pre-/post-state pairs that represent the behavior of the operation for the abstraction level given by the class diagram.

Normally, specifications are not as detailed as for addTrain() and intentionally leave more freedom to the implementations. Then, only a more liberal version of the specification would be appropriate, for example, that upon termination of addTrain() the number of trains of exactly one depot should be increased by one. This specification is less detailed because it does not prescribe which of the two depots will change its number of trains. Such a more liberal version can be easily formalized by a restrictive specification:

context Dispatcher :: addTrain ()
pre: true
post: d1.no + d2.no = d1.no@pre + d2.no@pre + 1 **and**
        (d1.no = d1.no@pre **or**
        d2.no = d2.no@pre)

This OCL specification (basically) says that the sum of no for d1 and d2 is in the post-state increased by one compared to the pre-state.

How can this be expressed in a constructive specification using pseudo-code? If the specification language would only offer the constructs known from imperative programming languages, one had to decide which depot has to be taken (as in fig. 1). In order to cope with less detailed specifications, constructive specification languages offer constructs that allow a non-deterministic choice from a set of possible executions paths. The language B, for instance, offers CHOICE-OR-END as one construct to express non-determinism. The new specification for addTrain() could be expressed as follows:

Operations addTrain() $\triangleq$
PRE true
THEN
    CHOICE no(d1) := no(d1) + 1
    OR no(d2) := no(d2) + 1
    END

The meaning of the revised addTrain() specifications is best understood by evaluating them in a given pre-/post-state pair. As an example, the state pair $(S1, S2)$ where $S1 = (no(d1) = 2, no(d2) = 2)$ and $S2 = (no(d1) = 2, no(d2) = 3)$ has been chosen.[4] Does this state transition conform to the two post-conditions?

Conformance to OCL Specification. The answer for the OCL specification is 'yes', because the state pair meets all restrictions made in the post-condition. Note, that the OCL specification would allow for the same prestate also the post-state $S2 = (no(d1) = 3, no(d2) = 2)$.
If at least two post-states for the same pre-state are possible, then the behavior of a correct implementation cannot be predicted. In such cases, the OCL constraint is called an *under-specification* of the operation's behavior.

Conformance to B Specification. The answer for the B specification is also 'yes', because the construct CHOICE allows all implementations that realize the behavior given in one of the branches of CHOICE.
As for the OCL specification, the post-state $S2 = (no(d1) = 3, no(d2) = 2)$ would also be allowed. Both state transitions are possible due to the *non-determinism* of the construct CHOICE.

3.4   Mixing Restrictive and Constructive Specification Styles

Constructive specifications (illustrated above with a B specification, but another language such as ASM could have been used the same way) use pseudo-code to specify the behavior of operations in an algorithmic way. As seen in the first example, the behavior of an operation can easily be described by a constructive specification that leaves no room for variations among the implementations of the operation. If an equivalent specification should be given in a restrictive specification language such as OCL, then the Frame problem has to be addressed, which can result in a considerable explosion of the specification size.

On the other hand, constructive languages need constructs such as CHOICE to allow variations among possible implementations. In the case of the CHOICE construct, an implementation is seen to be correct if it correctly implements one of the branches.

Restrictive specification languages can easily express variations among the implementations by a weaker post-condition; this technique is called under-specification.

---

[4] Only the relevant part of the system state is given here.

Machine Train

Machine Depot(Train)
Variables ct
Invariant ct ⊆ Train

Machine Dispatcher(Depot)
Variables d1, d2
Invariant d1,d2 ∈ Depot
Operations
sel ← selectTrain() ≜
PRE ct(d1) ∪ ct(d2) ≠ ∅
THEN
 ANY t WHERE
  t ∈ ct(d1) ∪ ct(d2)
 THEN sel := t
 END

```
context Dispatcher ::
           selectTrain():Train
pre:  self.d1.ct->
      union(self.d2.ct)->
        notEmpty()
post: result =
      self.d1.ct->
        union(self.d2.ct)->any()
```

Fig. 2. Usage of any() in OCL

The construct **any()** offered by OCL can be seen as an attempt to combine the strengths of both specification paradigms. Thanks to the **any()** construct, an OCL specification can have the same structure as constructive specifications written in B, which can make them better understandable compared to equivalent, purely restrictive specifications.

The usage of **any()** in OCL is illustrated by a slightly extended version of the Depot-example. As shown in fig. 2, the trains at the depot are represented by a state-variable **ct** (in UML represented by an association between **Depot** and **Train**). The value of state variable **no** could be computed now as the cardinality of the set of trains denoted by **ct** and is, thus, omitted.

We consider a new operation **selectTrain()** on **Dispatcher** whose intended behavior is to select one train from one of both depots. It is assumed that **selectTrain()** is only invoked in a state in which at least one depot has a train.

The B specification formalizes this informal specification in a natural way. The pre-condition encodes the availability of at least one train. In the post-condition, the return parameter of **selectTrain()** is declared by the variable **sel**. Moreover, an element t is selected non-deterministically from the set of available trains (this is done using the **ANY-WHERE** construct which is a generalized version of **CHOICE**) and then assigned to the return parameter **sel**.

The OCL specification has exactly the same structure. Instead of declaring a variable for the return parameter, OCL uses the predefined variable **result**. The post-condition states, that the value of **result** must be equal to **self.d1.ct-> union(self.d2.ct)->any()**, which can be read as a non-deterministically chosen element from the set of trains available in depot $d1$ and $d2$.

Note, that the post-condition had to address the frame problem in order to become equivalent with the specification given in B. This could be done by extending the post-condition with ... and `self.d1 = self.d1@pre and self.d2 = self.d2@pre` ... We have suppressed this part of the OCL post-condition here because it would distract us from the important part of the post-condition and our conclusions can already be drawn from the given version of the post-condition.

The semantics of both specifications is again best investigated with a concrete state transition. Let `selectTrain()` be invoked in a state where depot $d1$ has two trains $t1,t2$ and the depot $d2$ is empty. For the post-state, `selectTrain()` is assumed to return train $t1$.

This state-transition would clearly conform to the B specification. Analogously to `CHOICE`, the `ANY-WHERE` construct allow all implementations which conform to one of the given choices (the state transition has taken the choice to assign train $t1$ to variable `t`).

The conformance to the OCL specification depends on the evaluation of the equation `result = self.d1.ct->union(self.d2.ct)->any()`, which can be simplified in the current situation to `t1 = {t1,t2}->any()`. According to the official semantics of `any()`, this can be evaluated to both *true* and *false* depending on the non-deterministic evaluation of `{t1,t2}->any()` to $t1$ or $t2$.

The example suggests the following *intended semantics* of `any()`: A state (or state-transition) conforms to a constraint *constr* containing `any()` if and only if among all alternatives for the evaluation of the `any()`-subterm there can be found at least one, such that the evaluation of the *constr* would result in *true*. Such a semantics would directly correspond to the semantics of the `ANY-WHERE` construct in B.

4   Improved Semantics for any() in OCL

Despite the clarification made in the last section on the role of `any()` in OCL specifications, the fundamental problems with the formal semantics of `any()` as described in section 2 are not fully solved yet. This section describes two approaches to overcome these problems.

4.1   Turning *eval* into an Evaluation Relation

The intended semantics of `any()` could be formalized by turning the evaluation function *eval* into an evaluation relation $eval_r$. On deterministic constructs, the relation $eval_r$ is exactly defined as the function *eval*. However, when the evaluation of a non-deterministic subterm allows multiple, non-deterministically chosen variants, the relation $eval_r$ results in all variants. This is possible because $eval_r$ is a relation and not a function like *eval* which has to decide for one of the variants. A state conforms to a constraint if and only if its evaluation in that state by $eval_r$ yields at least for one variant the result *true*.

Although $eval_r$ formalizes the intended semantics of non-deterministic constructs, it has some deficiencies that prevent its adoption in practice.

$$constr(set\text{->}\mathtt{any}()^{pos})$$
$$\Downarrow$$
$$(set\text{->}\mathtt{isEmpty}() \text{ and } constr(\mathtt{undef}^{pos})) \text{ or } set\text{->}\mathtt{exists}(x| \ constr(x^{pos}))$$

Fig. 3. Substitution of any() by deterministic constructs

Firstly, the evaluation of a constraint in a given state can become exponentially complex if non-deterministic terms are nested. Note, that the evaluator had to handle all possibilities for an evaluation instead of just one result in case of deterministic evaluation.

Secondly and more important, $eval_r$ breaks with the traditional way in logic to define the semantics of specification languages. As illustrated in section 2 with the foo2() example, by adopting the $eval_r$ semantics for OCL, we would sacrifice common basic logical laws, for instance that = is a reflective relation so that expressions of form $X = X$ can be simplified to true. Consequently, we would lose the tool support gained for OCL due to the fact that OCL is based on first-order logic.

4.2   Transformational Approach

The second proposal to define a semantics for any() is in terms of a transformation from non-deterministic specifications to deterministic ones for which the official OCL semantics can be applied. Thus, the drawbacks of the $eval_r$ proposal do not apply here.

However, the transformational approach has some other drawbacks. The resulting formula is more complex than the original one.[5] A second drawback is that the transformation is not always applicable. Fortunately, this seems to be not a serious restriction in practice and the transformations can handle, for instance, all occurrences of any() in the UML metamodel.

The Algorithm. As pointed out in the $eval_r$ approach, the intended meaning of non-deterministic constructs is to take all possible evaluations into account.

Let $constr$ be a constraint that contains a term $t \equiv set\text{->}\mathtt{any}()$ at a position pos (indicated by $constr(t^{pos})$). Following the intended semantics of any() we know that $constr(set\text{->}\mathtt{any}()^{pos})$ is evaluated in a given state to $true$ if and only if there exists in the evaluation of set an element o such that $constr(o^{pos})$ is evaluated to $true$ or, in the case that set is evaluated to the empty set, that $constr(\mathtt{undef}^{pos})$ is evaluated to $true$. This justifies transformation of the constraint as shown in fig. 3.

Informally speaking, it is first tested whether set evaluates to the empty set and in this case the any()-term $set\text{->}\mathtt{any}()$ occurring in $constr$ is substituted

---

[5] This is, on the other hand, also an argument for the simplicity and readability made possible by any().

by undef or, otherwise, the any()-term in *constr* is substituted by a variable x
which is introduced outside *constr* by an exists quantifier over *set*. Note, that
the subterm *set* is moved from inside to outside of *constr*. This is only possible
if *set* does not contain any variables introduced by iteration operations such as
forAll, exists, select, etc., because the transformation would then result in
a syntactically incorrect OCL term. For example, if the transformation were to
be applied mechanically on the constraint

Set{1,2}->forAll(y| Set{y}->any() > 1)

then it would yield

(Set{y}->isEmpty() and Set{1,2}->forAll(y| undef > 1)) or
Set{y}->exists(x| Set{1,2}->forAll(y| x > 1))

what is a syntactically incorrect OCL term because the variable y in Set{y}
is not declared.

Despite the restricted applicability, the transformation defined in fig. 3 can
successfully be applied on all examples discussed in this paper.

Example foo1():

    context Foo :: foo1():Integer
    post: result = Set{1,2}->any()
               ⇓
    context Foo :: foo1():Integer
    post: (Set{1,2}->isEmpty() and result = undef) or
              Set{1,2}->exists(x| result = x)

Since the set denoted by Set{1,2} is not empty, the result of the transformation
could be simplified to

    context Foo :: foo1():Integer
    post: Set{1,2}->exists(x| result = x)

and even further simplified to

    context Foo :: foo1():Integer
    post: Set{1,2}->includes(result)

Example foo2():

The post-condition for foo2() contains two any()-terms and requires applying the
transformation twice. For brevity, the result of the transformation has already been
simplified (isEmpty() branches have been removed).

    context Foo :: foo2():Integer
    pre: true
    post: if (Set{1,2}->any() = Set{1,2}->any())
             then result = 1
             else result = 2
          endif
               ⇓
    context Foo :: foo():Integer
    pre: true
    post: Set{1,2}->exists(x1| Set{1,2}->exists(x2|
             if (x1 = x2)
             then result = 1
             else result = 2
             endif))

Note that this specification allows the implementation to return both 1 and 2. The first case is made possible by assigning x1 to 1 and x2 to 1, the latter case by assigning x1 to 1 and x2 to 2.

Example selectTrain():

```
context Dispatcher :: selectTrain():Train
pre:  self.d1.ct->union(self.d2.ct)->notEmpty()
post: result = self.d1.ct->union(self.d2.ct)->any()
```
⇓
```
context Dispatcher :: selectTrain():Train
pre:  self.d1.ct->union(self.d2.ct)->notEmpty()
post: self.d1.ct->union(self.d2.ct)->exists(x| result = x)
```
This can be simplified to
```
context Dispatcher :: selectTrain():Train
pre:  self.d1.ct->union(self.d2.ct)->notEmpty()
post: self.d1.ct->union(self.d2.ct)->includes(result)
```

5   Conclusion

Currently, the semantics of non-deterministic constructs in OCL is not clearly defined. The semantic foundation of non-deterministic constructs given in the official language description can be easily misunderstood, which leaves room for different interpretations. None of the current OCL tools is able to handle non-deterministic constructs properly, which is a sign for the poor understanding of such constructs. In practice, use of non-deterministic constructs is avoided, or they are only used in cases in which deterministic evaluation is ensured, such as the transformation of a singleton set to an object.

We have pointed out that non-deterministic constructs are very useful and even necessary in constructive specification languages such as B or ASM. The language OCL tried to adopt these constructs without paying attention to the characterization of OCL as a restrictive specification language. The comparison of OCL with constructive languages has revealed the intended semantics of non-deterministic constructs. As illustrated by examples, specifications in constructive languages using non-deterministic constructs can easily be rewritten in OCL without using non-deterministic constructs. In order to describe non-deterministic behavior, restrictive specification languages such as OCL offer the technique of under-specification.

Nevertheless, the non-deterministic construct any() allows the user to write OCL specification in a more 'constructive style'. This can make specifications more accessible for users with a strong background in programming. Since we were able to formally define the semantics of any() in terms of a code transformation, the construct any() could be easily integrated into other restrictive languages such as Z, JML, Eiffel. Such an integration could make these languages more usable and, thus, increase the acceptance of formal methods, especially for people who are used to describing the behavior of systems in a constructive way. Seen this way, OCL's often misunderstood any() construct has brought some innovation into the realm of restrictive specification languages.

References

1. Grady Booch, James Rumbaugh, and Ivar Jacobson. *The Unified Modeling Language User Guide*. Object Technology Series. Addison-Wesley, Reading/MA, 1999.
2. UML 2.0 Infrastructure Specification – OMG Adopted Specification. OMG Document ptc/03-09-15, Sep 2003.
3. UML 2.0 Superstructure Specification – OMG Adopted Specification. OMG Document ptc/03-08-02, Aug 2003.
4. UML 2.0 OCL Specification – OMG Final Adopted Specification. OMG Document ptc/03-10-14, Oct 2003.
5. Overview on current OCL tools. www.klasse.nl/ocl/ocl-services.html.
6. Dan Chiorean, Maria Bortes, Dyan Corutiu, and Radu Sparleanu. UML/OCL tools - objectives, requirements, state of the art – The OCLE experience. In *Proceedings of the 11th Nordic Workshop on Programming and Software Development Tools and Techniques NWPER'2004*, number 34 in TUCS General Publication, Turku, pages 163–180, 2004.
7. Bertrand Meyer. Applying "design by contract". *IEEE Computer*, 25(10):40–51, October 1992.
8. C. Morgan. *Programming form Specifications*. Prentice Hall, 1994.

Integrating RT-CORBA in SDL

Manuel Díaz, Daniel Garrido, Luis Llopis, and José M. Troya

Department of Languages and Computing Science,
University of Málaga, Spain
{mdr, dgarrido, luisll, troya}@lcc.uma.es

Abstract. The usage of formal description techniques (FDTs), and specifically SDL, has arisen as a promising way of dealing with the increasing complexity of embedded real time distributed systems. An important issue that must be taken into account is the predictability of the temporal behaviour of this kind of system including communications. In this sense, RT-CORBA is an interesting alternative as a middleware for real time distributed applications because, unlike standard CORBA, it guarantees predictable temporal response on particular invocations to remote objects and assures a bounded priority inversion. In order to control the predictability of the complete system we propose the design in SDL of RT-CORBA. It provides three important results: first, it is possible to include the behaviour of the communication middleware in the design of the applications and then the simulation of the whole system can be carried out; second, the implementation stage is simplified because the integration of the RT-CORBA middleware allows generation of code from the design; finally, a schedulability analysis for real time distributed systems can be included reducing the development time. In order to apply our proposal we present the design in SDL of a nuclear power plant simulator.

1   Introduction

Distributed systems are increasingly being applied for critical real-time applications, in which each task must be guaranteed a priori to meet its timing constraints. The majority of applications of this kind are embedded in distributed architectures, for example control, data acquisition, modern aircraft and car designs.

Additionally, the development of embedded real time distributed systems (ERTDSs) is regarded nowadays as a real challenge to engineers. A number of problems come together: predictable time behaviour, communication, hardware and technical system failures. In this situation a solution can be found only with the help of easy-to-use techniques and the corresponding uniform tool support covering the whole life-cycle.

Object-oriented methodologies are widely used to cope with complexity in any kind of system, but most of them lack a formal foundation that allows for the analysis and verification of designs, which is one of the main requirements

A. Prinz, R. Reed, and J. Reed (Eds.): SDL 2005, LNCS 3530, pp. 47–67, 2005.

for dealing with the complexity of concurrent and reactive systems. One of the most important advantages of the formal foundation is the improved consistency between the models of the different phases. In this sense, Formal Description Techniques (FDTs) provide the basis for an automated design process, allowing simulation, validation and automatic code generation from the specifications. One of the most widely used FDTs is SDL (Specification and Description Language) [1]. SDL is an ITU standard and it is currently well supported by commercial tools [2].

In the communication field, Real Time CORBA (RT-CORBA) middleware [3] has also simplified the development of distributed applications with timing requirements. RT-CORBA specification defines standard middleware characteristics that allow applications to allocate, schedule and control CPU, memory and networking resources necessary to ensure end-to-end quality of service support. In order to take this middleware into account in the design stage we propose a framework in SDL of RT-CORBA 2.0.

However, SDL lacks some semantic aspects (such as a priority model or a shared resource predictable access model), which are very important for the design of ERTDSs to avoid unpredictability and issues such as unbounded priority inversions. Although SDL-2000 has addressed some of these issues it has not resolved them completely. For example, SDL-2000 [4] presents a queue mechanism to avoid simultaneous accesses, but priority for the accesses must be taken into account. Additionally, the standard execution model is not predictable either. For this reason, we show how to include the RT-CORBA framework taking into account the extensions proposed for SDL in previous works [5] that assured predictability in the design level.

Including an RT-CORBA model in SDL allows us to specify the whole system at the design level and therefore:

- We can simulate the whole system at this stage. In order to do so we need to include information on the communication platform and we propose a design model of the predictable CAN communication protocol [6].
- We simplify the integration between RT-CORBA and the SDL generated code thereby reducing the time of the implementation stage.
- A schedulability analysis can be carried out at this stage.

In this paper we have modelled the main RT-CORBA characteristics: the **priority models** (*client propagated* and *server declared*), **thread pools**, **mutexes** and the **connection management**.

The paper is organized as follows: In the rest of this section some comments about related work and a summary of the main characteristics of RT-CORBA are described. Section 2 presents a review for the extension proposed in previous works and used in this paper. Section 3 presents RT-CORBA in the SDL context to design hard real time distributed applications. Finally, in section 4 we apply our proposals in a real example based on distributed simulators for nuclear power plants. This paper finishes with some conclusions and future lines of work.

1.1   Related Work

A lot of work focuses on the integration of non-functional timing aspects in SDL. In [7] an overview of the main weakness of SDL for the development of real time systems is given. Additionally, in [8] we can see proposals for extensions to include timing information in SDL. Another line of work in this context is that of supplementing SDL with load and machine models, such as those described in [9], that use queuing theory to calculate job and message queuing times and processor peak and average workloads. [10] presents another extension to SDL to describe non-functional requirements. In [11] a new approach for early performance prediction based on MSC specified systems in the context of SDL is presented.

Other lines deal with design pattern proposals. A design pattern is an SDL module, which can be used in different contexts for different applications with only minor modifications [12]. SDL patterns and examples exist for well known protocols [13]. [12] addresses how to include the timing behaviour of the communication medium for the protocols for medium access in SDL. A design pattern is proposed to allow the specification of time critical functionality such as multiplexers or Quality-of-Service (QoS) schedulers.

In [14] the use of SDL for efficient service creation is addressed. In order to provide a generic platform for the implementation of future mobile services, supporting standardized interfaces and manufacturer platform independent object [15] proposes the mapping of SDL and CORBA mechanisms.

Finally, the ITU-T Recommendation Z.130 [16] specifies the ITU Extended Object Definition Language (ITU-eODL), which is used for a component-oriented development of distributed systems. This recommendation includes an IDL-SDL mapping, but RT-CORBA is not considered.

1.2   Real-Time CORBA

CORBA is a communication middleware that allows the communication of objects developed in different programming languages and running on different hosts or operating systems in a transparent way [18]. These objects (*servers*) define interfaces with operations provided to the *clients*. *Clients* only use these operations and there is no difference between invocations to local objects and invocations to remote objects because all the communication details are managed by CORBA.

Temporal predictability is a main factor in the development of real-time applications. However, standard CORBA implementations are not suitable for real-time because they only support best-effort capacities in the communications and there are no guarantees about the temporal response on particular invocations to remote objects. So the solution is to use ORBs supporting the Real-time CORBA specification. Real-time CORBA provides mechanisms that allow configuration and control of processor resources, communication resources and memory resources. The following points show the main RT-CORBA features:

Native and CORBA priorities: RT-CORBA applications can use CORBA priorities to hide the heterogeneity of native priorities of the operating systems.

Server declared and client propagated priorities.

Thread pools: The pools allow the pre-creation of threads in such a way that a thread manages each invocation on a particular object.

Mutexes: The standard RT-CORBA synchronization mechanism that permits priority inheritance and priority ceiling protocols

Protocol properties: The underlying transport protocol used by a particular Object Request Broker (ORB) (such as IIOP - TCP/IP [18]) can be configured by RT-CORBA to benefit from special features, such as ATM virtual circuits, etc.

2   Priority Specification in SDL

In order to model real time aspects of RT-CORBA in SDL we briefly describe the extension proposed in previous works [5].

The main issue is the inclusion of the priority concept for transitions. Although, some environments [2] give extensions to incorporate priorities in the processes, we propose to assign priorities to the transitions of the processes. In this case, the process priority depends on the transition that is being executed in each time instant. Figure 1 shows how to specify this extension, adding in a comment symbol with priority x, where x is the priority level.

This extension allows us to define a predictable execution model based on a fixed priority preemptive scheduling to incorporate a real time analysis of the implementations derived directly from an SDL design. More details and the formalization of this extension can be studied in [17].

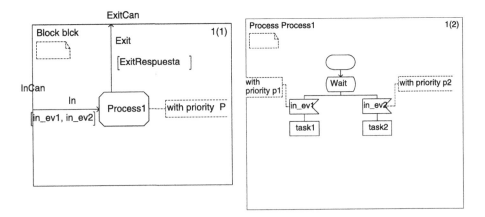

Fig. 1. Priority Specification

3   An SDL Model for RT-CORBA

In this section we present the design in SDL of RT-CORBA addressing important real time characteristics such as priority models, mutexes and thread pools.

3.1   Basic CORBA Execution Flow

In CORBA applications there are communicating objects located in different hosts. Any application can play the role of server or client depending on application requests. In this section we describe the basic execution flow of one simple client-server application.

In fig. 2 we can see the basic execution flow between a client and a CORBA object in a general request of type: `result = object->operation(args)`.

The first step for a client invocation is to obtain a reference of the target object. This reference can be obtained in different ways (Naming Service, factories, etc.) and can be performed in the first stages of the application without penalty for real-time applications. With this reference the client can perform the invocation on the target object. For this, the ORB uses a stub class instance (automatically generated) representing the target object in the client space address. This proxy has the same interface as the remote object. So, the client application does not know anything about communications and uses the methods provided by the proxy, which have the same signature as the remote object. The stub is responsible for data packaging/unpackaging and the use of ORB operations to transmit the invocation to the ORB server by using an instantiation of the GIOP protocol (such as IIOP or CANIOP) [18].

In the server space address, the invocation is caught by the ORB, which uses the information contained in the request to locate the object adapter associated to the target object, and finally the object adapter performs the invocation on the target object through a skeleton class equivalent to the stub class. If the operation has output arguments or a return value, the results are transmitted to the client using the same connection (GIOP connection are bidirectional).

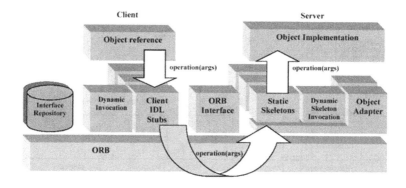

Fig. 2. General CORBA invocation

The previously described process used in standard CORBA ORBs has several problems in real-time systems related to temporal unpredictability [19]. The main inconvenience is related to the time response of the request. Standard CORBA ORBs cannot guarantee an upper limit in the invocation response time. In particular, CORBA does not define any connection policy between the server and the client and the connections can be shared with lower priority clients. So, higher priority clients can be delayed by lower priority clients, falling into priority inversions. Additionally, the connection establishment time is not bounded and on the server side perhaps there may not be resources available for the request or it may be delayed by another lower priority request.

3.2   Combining RT-CORBA and SDL

Most of these problems can be solved by using RT-CORBA, but it lacks real-time analysis methodology and tools. In previous works we have defined extensions, which enable us to perform real-time analysis in SDL systems. Our solution is based on providing an SDL model for RT-CORBA, which can be used by the user and combined with the SDL model of the user applications and communication platform. This way, the whole application can be analyzed in the first stages of the design and code can even be generated using the corresponding tools.

In fig. 3 we can see the SDL model for a generic CORBA application. This model represents a basic CORBA system with one CORBA object (contained into **Apl2**) and one client (**Apl1**). Additional SDL blocks represent the client stub

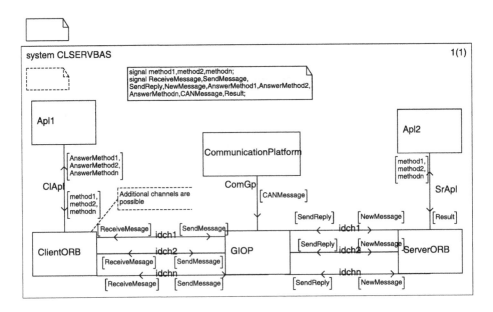

Fig. 3. RT-CORBA modelled with SDL

(`ClientORB`) and the server code (`ServerORB`) including the object adapter and skeleton. The communication platform and GIOP are other SDL blocks. All the blocks are interconnected with signals such as `methodX` for the different services or the pairs `SendMessage`/`ReceiveMessage` and `SendReply`/`NewMessage`, which are based on the CORBA GIOP protocol. This way, we can represent a CORBA-based system with SDL and we benefit from all SDL features. In particular, we can model the main RT-CORBA features, obtaining analyzable RT-CORBA systems.

When an invocation from `Apl1` is initiated (for example `method1`), the application sends a `method1` signal, which is caught in the `ClientORB` block. This block is responsible for the data packaging, sending a signal `SendMessage`, which represents an equivalent GIOP message. The `GIOP` block is now responsible for data transmission between the nodes of the application. In particular, it is responsible for the interaction with the communication platform (block `CommunicationPlatform`). Finally, the invocation is transmitted to the target `ServerORB` with the SDL signal `NewMessage`, where the unpackaging of the parameters is performed and transmitted to `Apl2`. If the invocation has a response, an inverse path is followed from `Apl2` to `ServerORB`, and from `ServerORB` to `GIOP` with the `SendReply` signal. This signal is caught by `ClientORB` and the response is transmitted to `Apl1`.

For a concrete application we only have to modify some of these provided generic blocks using some simple rules, which can be followed by the user or some automatic tool, thereby obtaining an SDL representation of the system. The modification includes the `GIOP` block, which has to be modified according to the RT-CORBA implementation used (such as TAO [21] or ROFES [22]), the communication platform to be substituted for the real ones (such as CAN-IOP [22] or ATM) and blocks `ClientORB` and `ServerORB`, which have to be adapted to the real blocks whose code is automatically generated by the IDL compiler depending on the CORBA interfaces.

We have to point out that the user or tool only has to perform small modifications to the proposed basic model such as the stub code or the name of the methods. Other blocks are provided by the environments or tools such as the RT-CORBA implementation. And other aspects such as interconnection between blocks, signals, etc. are left unchanged.

In the following subsections we show how the main RT-CORBA features (priority models, thread pools, mutexes, etc.) are modelled and we detail the CORBA-SDL mapping process for these features.

3.3   Honoring Priorities

A primary problem related to distributed real-time applications is related to the different priority schemes on different operating systems, priorities not honored in the server, etc. As we have seen, RT-CORBA provides mechanisms to overcome these inconveniences thanks to the *client propagated* and the *server declared* models. In this section we present a model of these features in the real-time extension of SDL. A considerable part of the SDL model for both (*client*

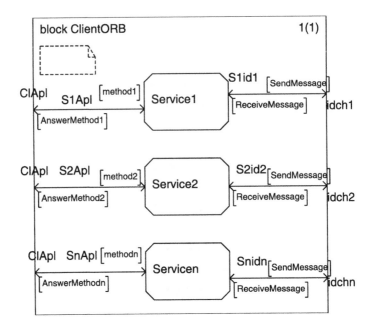

Fig. 4. Services mapping

propagated and *server declared*) is similar. So, we present the common part and then we explain the differences between them.

On the client side, the interaction between the application and RT-CORBA is performed in the ClientORB block. In this block, we use an SDL process for each CORBA service (that is methods in the interface). This way, when the application performs a request for a service, this request is caught by the corresponding SDL process through signal methodX. The result of this interaction is the creation of a new SDL signal named SendMessage, which is sent outside the ClientORB block. Signal SendMessage represents a generic CORBA message used by the CORBA GIOP protocol to start new requests. Finally, it is very possible that the requests have an associated response. So, the services have to process the signal ReceiveMessage, which contains the response to the request. The response is processed and transferred to the application via signal AnswerMethodX.

Figure 4 shows generic RT-CORBA services mapped into SDL processes. In a concrete application the generic names have to be changed (by some automatic tool) showing the names of the real services. This includes the names of the services and signals methodX and AnswerMethodX. Signals NewMessage and ReceiveMessage are generic and they are related to the GIOP protocol.

Inside the processes representing the services (Service1,...,Servicen) we have to model additional aspects such as the connection establishment or parameters packaging and we have to delegate the performing of the request to the

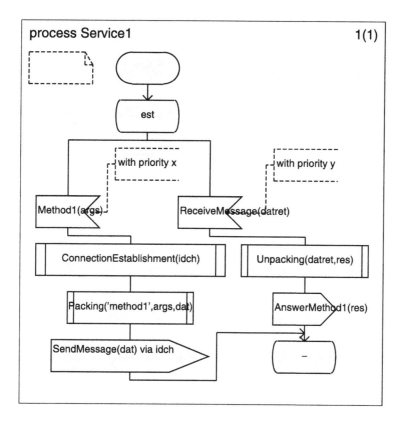

Fig. 5. Services mapping

GIOP block (via **SendMessage** signal). Also, we have to process the response to the request (via **ReceiveMessage**).

Figure 5 shows one of these services. The service process is waiting for two signals: **Method1** and **ReceiveMessage**. **Method1** is received when the application performs a new request. On the other hand, ReceiveMessage is received like a response after a request is transferred to the server.

When a new request is initiated (**Method1** received), the stub is responsible for the connection establishment. This procedure can be different depending on the RT-CORBA implementation used. After this, the data items related to the invocation are packaged and finally a new signal is generated, SendMessage, with all the required information for the successful completion of the request.

The services can wait for the signal **ReceiveMessage**. This signal is received as a response to a previous **SendMessage**. The steps are the opposite to the Method1 signal. The response is unpackaged and sent to the application via the **AnswerMethod1** signal.

The server side is more complex because we have to consider additional factors such as the object adapter (POA) and its interaction with skeleton and servant. In this case we have a process for each POA existing in the application.

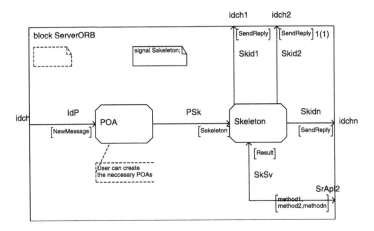

Fig. 6. Server side blocks

POAs are connected to the skeletons and they are connected to the servants representing the CORBA objects (contained in the application). Figure 6 shows these elements and the interaction between them.

The POA is waiting for NewMessage signals (received from service processes). After this, the POA identifies the target object, transferring the request to the corresponding skeleton process, which invokes the method from the servant. If the request has an associated response, this response is transmitted back to the service process through the **SendReply** signal. After the connection between the stub and the skeleton, the POA is no longer needed for the request and client and server can communicate directly.

Until this point, there are no differences between the *client propagated* model of RT-CORBA and the *server declared* model. The POA sets the difference between the two models and their mappings into SDL:

Server declared model: Invocations in this model are executed with the CORBA object priority. This model is implicitly covered by the real-time extension of SDL and we do not need modifications or extensions of the model. The SDL transitions associated to the object are executed with the object priority.

Client propagated model: In this model the priority of the clients must be honored on the server side. This priority model involves dynamic changes in the priorities from the SDL point of view and it is not covered by the previous work. The transitions associated to the different methods of the servant can be executed with different priorities depending on the client.

Thus we need some extensions to the SDL model in the *client propagated* model. In particular, we propose a new primitive: ***ThePriority***, which changes the priority associated to a signal, which enables a transition associated to a method and the priority is set to the desired value. This primitive is equivalent to the attribute Current::the_priority of RT-CORBA and this way it does not

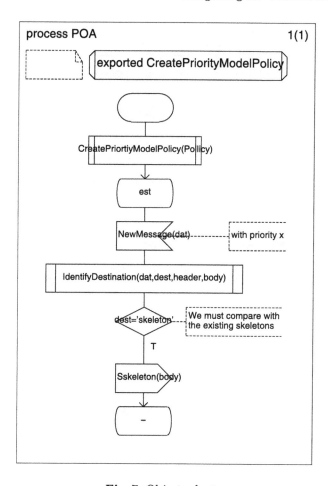

Fig. 7. Object adapter

require any change for the code when it is generated from SDL tools. That is, it follows the RT-CORBA programming model.

Figure 7 shows the SDL process associated to a POA. The change of the priority model is performed in the POA creation with the procedure CreatePriorityModelPolicy. Additional CORBA policies can be created with equivalent methods.

After this, the POA is waiting for new messages (via NewMessage signal) from the GIOP block and when some of these messages arrive, it has to locate the target skeleton delegating the request to it. The target identification is performed in the IdentifyDestination procedure and it is very dependent on the implementation. In fact, one quality factor of the RT-CORBA implementation can be found here. Thus, good implementations identify target objects in constant time while bad implementations can require lineal or polynomial times. After this identification, a signal for the target skeleton must be generated. The

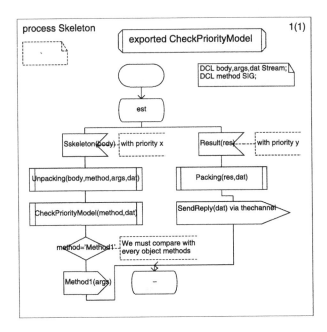

Fig. 8. Object adapter

POA must choose the target skeleton and generate the suitable signal. We must point out that the order of the NewMessage signals is not the responsibility of the POA. Instead, other blocks of our model (GIOP or communication platform) must adequately order the invocations attending to the priority of the requests. The POA only recovers these ordered signals and transmits them to the skeletons. So, at this point we can have priority inversion sources bounded by the quality of the RT-CORBA implementation.

Finally, the response to the client is not performed through the POA. Instead, the information sent to the skeleton allows us to send the response from the skeleton honoring the RT-CORBA programming model.

Skeletons (symmetric to stubs) are represented with processes waiting for new requests. Figure 8 shows a generic skeleton with two transitions. First transition (Sskeleton) is related to new requests on a servant. When a new request is received, the skeleton has to unpack the data stream. For this, it uses the Unpacking procedure (depending on RT-CORBA implementation) obtaining information such as the method to be invoked, parameters and additional information (such as client priority). The next step is to check the priority model used.

Figure 9 shows the CheckPriorityModel procedure. This procedure determines the priority model used: *server declared* or *client propagated*. If the desired model is the *client propagated* model, we have to use the *ThePriority* primitive to set the priority of the transition. For this, we use the name of the method and the priority of the client, which has been extracted in the ExtractPriority pro-

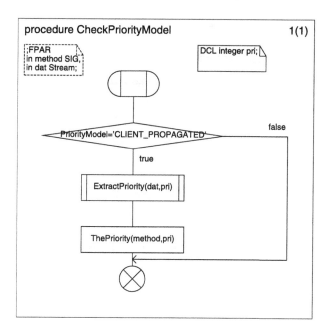

Fig. 9. CheckPriorityModel procedure

cedure. As noted before, this primitive is equivalent to the Current::the_priority attribute, so we maintain the RT-CORBA programming model.

In the case of the *server declared* model we do not need additional actions because this model is implicit in the SDL real-time extension. For our model, the CheckPriorityModel is the only difference between the *server declared* and the *client propagated* models. After checking the priority model, the skeleton selects the target method invoking it with the extracted parameters. The invocation is performed by means of a signal with the name of the method (fig. 8). The response in the skeleton is caught by the Result signal. This signal is transmitted by the servant process after the method execution. The following steps are the packaging of the response with the Packing procedure and the generation of a new signal for the response: SendReply, which is transmitted to the GIOP block and from the GIOP block to the client.

Figure 10 shows an SDL process representing a CORBA object servant. The servant process has one transition for each method of the CORBA interface. These transitions use the extension "with priority" of our model, executing the transitions with the previously established priority (*server declared* or *client propagated*). The next and most important step is the execution of the method. For analysis purposes, it is sufficient to indicate the worst case execution time of the method although it is possible to model the method itself. After the execution of the method, the results of execution are sent to the skeleton generating a Result signal.

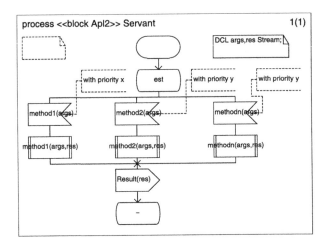

Fig. 10. Servant process

3.4   Multithread Servers

In the previous section we described the design in SDL of the RT-CORBA priority models without taking into account multithreading or shared resources. Multithreading is a necessary feature for real-time distributed systems. Furthermore, we can avoid some priority inversion sources executing higher priority requests instead of waiting for unresolved lower priority requests. On the other hand, contention resources management is an important necessity in real-time systems.

Standard CORBA ORBs follow several strategies about multithreading from ignoring it, to considering it but relying on the ORB for the number of threads to be created, priorities of these threads, etc. RT-CORBA goes further with thread pools. With the thread pools the user can completely control the multithreading behaviour of the application.

Together with multithreading we have to consider mutual exclusion between distributed objects. Once again RT-CORBA offers us mutexes, which allow us to obtain mutual exclusion in different parts of the application with bounded priority inversion.

In our model, multithreading is performed with SDL processes. On the server side of the application we indicate the maximum number of simultaneous requests that a skeleton can have. Figure 6 showed the processes associated to skeletons. So, we can have simultaneous requests ranging from 1 to n. The SDL model does not need anything else for multithreading except the blocks, processes, procedures, etc. described in the previous section.

The second issue is related to the shared resources. RT-CORBA provides mutexes with the POSIX semantics, providing three operations: lock, unlock and try_lock. In order to be modelled in SDL, shared data and resources will be encapsulated into a special kind of process. It acts as a passive server process and only uses remote procedure calls (RPC) as its communication mechanism: they are always waiting to receive RPCs from other processes.

Each of these processes has a priority ceiling assigned, which is the maximum number of the priorities among all the other process transitions where the resource is being accessed. In this way we avoid possible priority inversion in the data access, and blocking time in shared data access is predictable. Mutual exclusion is also guaranteed, since all the process transitions will be executed at the highest priority among all the processes sharing the resource.

3.5   Communication Platform

The other features of RT-CORBA are related to connection management: protocol properties, connection establishment, private connections, etc. These features are not taken into account in the client or server and they are modelled into the CommunicationPlatform block. Even the GIOP block is independent of these features and it only uses the services provided by the communication platform block. In order to get predictable real time distributed applications we need the communication platform also to have this characteristic. In this sense we propose an SDL design for the CAN protocol [6]. There are in existence RT-CORBA implementations with instantiations of the abstract GIOP protocol. Specifically, ROFES is an RT-CORBA implementation including the so called CANIOP protocol, which uses RT-CORBA on CAN.

In fig. 11 we show block Communicationsystem with the process specifying the CAN protocol. As we can see in fig. 12, busCAN is waiting for the remote call of procedure Send, and it will be executed with a ceiling priority to guarantee that it will not be preempted during the message sending. Send must build the message meeting the CAN format and send it to the processors.

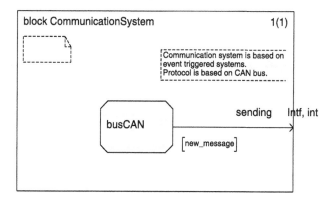

Fig. 11. Block for CAN bus protocol

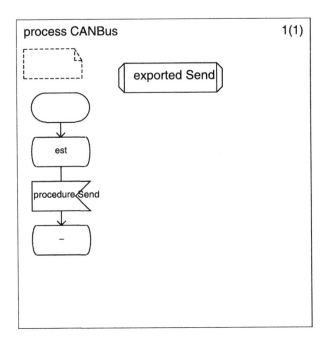

Fig. 12. Process BusCan

4   Example: Nuclear Power Plant Simulators

We have applied our proposals to distributed simulators for nuclear power plants used in different joint projects between the company Tecnatom S.A. and our research group [20]. The temporal behaviour of these simulators must be predictable providing stability, robustness, etc. In this section we present the SDL model of a part of the whole system.

Simulators are exact replicas of the control rooms, taking care of all details, from physical artefacts such as furniture, control panels, etc. to software, simulating the applications running in the control room of the power plants. The kernel of the simulators consists of simulation models with real-time constraints, which provide the values of the distinct signals and variables needed by the other hardware and software components. The main purpose of the simulators is to train the operators of the power plant, enabling them to practice different situations, ranging from standard situations such as temperature monitoring, valve manipulation, etc. to the most unusual, including emergency situations.

Tecnatom projects usually include two types of simulators that influence hardware architecture and the physical infrastructures. The first simulator type is called *Interactive Graphic Simulator SGI)*, which uses graphic applications to train the operators. The second type is called *Full Scope Simulator (SAT)*, which is an exact replica of the control room of the power plant.

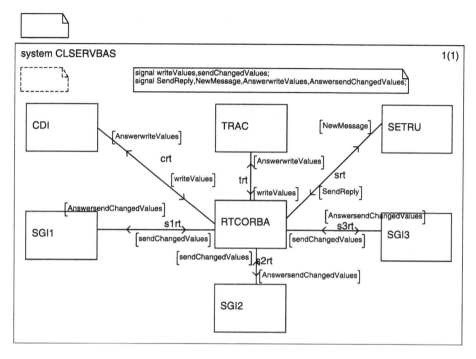

Fig. 13. Simulator system in SDL

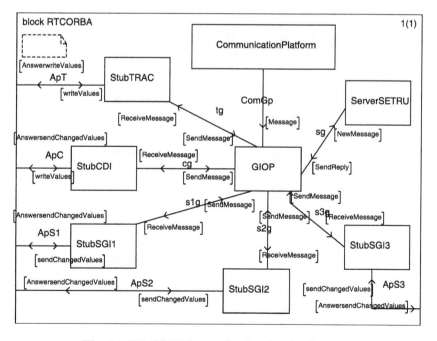

Fig. 14. RT-CORBA specification for the Simulator

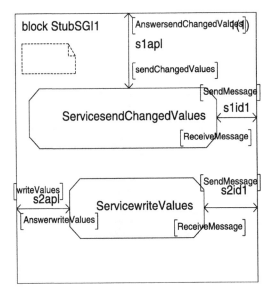

Fig. 15. Stub for SGI1

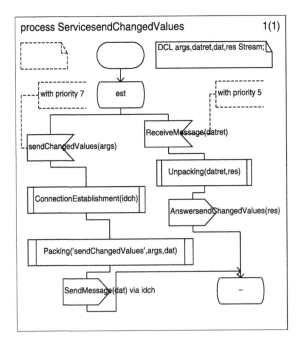

Fig. 16. ServicesendChangedValues process

4.1   RT-CORBA Model

In the modelled subset we have several software applications:

SETRU: kernel of the Tecnatom simulators, providing an execution environment for the simulation models.

Simulation models: They are responsible for the precise simulation of real physical components such as valves, sensors, actuators, etc., periodically updating simulation variables that represent the physical components. In our example the simulation model is called TRAC.

CDI: Application representing the instructor console. It allows the sending of several commands to the simulator kernel.

SGI: Sheet Displayer Application. It allows the querying of simulation variables and performs user actions over simulated physical components.

Thus, we have a CORBA server in application **SETRU**, which provides several methods to update simulation variables, query simulation variables and perform user actions. The other applications are CORBA clients using these services.

Two methods have been modelled:

1. `sendChangedValues`: This method is used by the clients to obtain modified variables. In the example, SGI applications use this method.
2. `writeValues`: This method is used to update variables in the simulator kernel. In the example, SGI, CDI and TRAC use this method to update variables and simulate user actions.

We are going to use the *client propagated* model of RT-CORBA to develop this system. Thus, SETRU creates a CORBA object into a POA with this RT-CORBA policy and the other applications invoke methods over SETRU with different CORBA priorities. Following the rules of our mapping, we can see in fig. 13 the system overview of our application. We have a block for each application and the additional `RT-CORBA` block for communication among the different parts of the system. Figure 14 shows the stub blocks and server `SETRU` together `GIOP` and the communication platform.

We show in fig. 15 the services for SGI1 with two process for the two services (see 3.3):`ServicesendChangedValues` and `ServicewriteValues`. Figure 16 shows the behaviour of process `ServicesendChangedValues`.

5   Conclusions

One important issue for distributed real time systems is the knowledge of the temporal behaviour of the communication and we think that it is necessary to include this knowledge in the design stage. In this paper we have proposed an SDL model for the communication middleware RT-CORBA. We have addressed important aspects for real time applications such as the priority models, shared resources accesses and multithreading defined in the RT-CORBA specification. We have presented an SDL model for a predictable communication protocol such as CAN. An important result of our proposal is the possibility of including a schedulability analysis in the design stage. It is out of the scope of this paper but we are currently working on it.

Although the main real time characteristics of RT-CORBA have been designed in SDL, we are extending our model. Another line of investigation is related to the development of tools to generate code compatible with the RT-CORBA specification.

References

1. ITU-T Z.100: Specification and Description Language (SDL). International Telecommunication Union (2002)
2. Telelogic TAU SDL Manuals (2004)
3. Object Management Group: RealTime-CORBA Specification, Version 2.0, 03-11-01 (2003)
4. Doldi L.: SDL Illustrated - Visually design executable models (2001)
5. Alvarez, J.M., Diaz, M., Llopis, L., Pimentel, E., Troya, J.M.: Integrating Schedulability Analysis and SDL in an Object-Oriented Methodology. SDL'99 The Next Millennium, 9th SDL Forum (1999), 241-256
6. Tindell, K., Burns, A. , Wellings, A.: Calculating Controller Area Network (CAN) Message Response Times. In: IFAC DCCS'94, Toledo, Spain (1994) 35-40
7. Bozga, M., Graf, S., Kerbrat, A., Mounier, L., Ober, I. , Vincent, D.: SDL for Real-Time: What is Missing. In: SDL and MSC (SAM00), Grenoble, France (2000)
8. Graf, S.: Expression of time and duration constraints in SDL. In: SDL and MSC (SAM2002) LNCS 2599.
9. Mitschele-Thiel, A., Müller-Clostermann, B.: Performance Engineering of SDL/MSC Systems. In: Tutorial of the 8th SDL Forum, Amsterdam, Netherlands, September (1997)
10. Spitz, S., Slomka F., Dörfel M.: SDL*- An Annotated Specification Language for Engineering Multimedia Communication. In: 6th Open Workshop on High Speed, Stuttgart, Germany, October (1997)
11. Dulz, W., Grughl, S., Kerber, L., Söllner, M.: Early Performance Prediction of SDL/MSC Specified Systems by Automatic Synthetic Code Generation. SDL'99 The Next Millennium, 9th SDL Forum (1999), 457-473.
12. Münzenberger, R., Slomka, F., Dörfel, M., Hofmann, R.: A General Approach for the Specification of Real-Time Systems with SDL: In SDL2001 Meeting UML, 10th SDL Forum (2001), 203-223 LNCS 2078.
13. Geppert, B., Gozthein, R., Robler, F.: Configuring Communication Protocols using SDL patterns. In: SDL'97 Time for Testing, SDL, MSC, and Trends. 8th SDL Forum (1997)
14. Olsen, A., Demany, D.,Cardoso, E.,Lodge, et al..: The Pros and Cons of Using SDL for Creation of distributed Services. Intelligence in Services and Networks. 1999 342-354

15. Mahimkar, A.: Modeling of software radio aspects by mapping of SDL and CORBA. In: 4th Int. Workshop on Mobile and Wireless Communications Network 2002 646-650

16. ITU recommendation Z.130: Extended Object Definition Language (eODL)

17. Alvarez, J.M., Diaz, M., Llopis, L., Pimentel, E., Troya, J.M.: An Object Oriented Methodology for Embedded Real-Time Systems. The Computer Journal, vol. 46 n° 2 2003

18. Object Management Group: The Common Object Request Broker: Architecture and Specification, 2.6 ed., December (2001)

19. Pyarali, I., Schmidt, D.C., Cytron, R.K.: Techniques for Enhancing Real-time CORBA Quality of Service. In: 8th IEEE Real-Time and Embedded Technology and Applications Symposium, California, USA, September (2002)

20. Díaz, M., Garrido, D.: Applying RT-CORBA in Nuclear Power Plant Simulators, in 7th IEEE International Symposium on Object-Oriented Real-Time Distributed Computing (ISORC 2004), IEEE Computer Society, Vienna, Austria (2004) 7-14

21. Levine, D.L., Mungee, S., Schmidt, D.C.: The Design of the TAO Real-Time Object Request Broker. Computer Communications (1998) 294-32422

22. Lankes, S., Jabs, A., Bemmerl, T.: Integration of a CAN-based Connection-oriented Communication Model into Real-Time CORBA: In IEEE International Parallel and Distributed Processing Symposium (IPDPS 2003), Nice, France, April (2003)

Component Development: MDA Based Transformation from eODL to CIDL

Harald Böhme, Glenn Schütze, and Konrad Voigt

Humboldt-Universität zu Berlin, Institut für Informatik,
Unter den Linden 6, 10099 Berlin, Germany
{boehme, schuetze, kvoigt}@informatik.hu-berlin.de

Abstract. The development of software systems in general and software components in particular becomes a more and more challenging task. The key solution for handling the complexity in the development process is the modeling of software systems and the transformation into implementation. The authors show an application of OMG's Model Driven Architecture (MDA) in the context of component development, where different languages such as eODL, SDL, CIDL and C++ are involved. The application of model transformation is based on eODL as a platform independent modeling (PIM) language and CIDL as the platform specific modeling (PSM) language. We used type based mapping rules to define the transformation. The paper shows the concrete implementation of these rules based on MOF repositories as model storage and the use of Java to perform the transformation actions. The Java technology Meta Data Repository (MDR) builds the base for an on-demand MOF repository creation in our approach. The handling of syntax based language is considered for integration purposes.

1   Introduction

The problem domain for today's software systems has broadened the scope in two dimensions. Software systems have become more complex to bridge different business areas and problems in single business fields. To cope with these new challenges different approaches were developed. Two of them are in the scope of this paper.

The component based software development is an approach for modular software development. It extends the concept of components from design and implementation, where modules are well known, to the binary software. The composition of components takes place during execution time.

Model Driven Architecture (MDA) as an initiative of the Object Management Group (OMG) centers the software development process on the models and tackles the different problems of traditional software development processes. The starting point for activities in MDA are the models, which ensures that the models are always up-to-date; back propagation from implementation change to the design model is build-in.

A. Prinz, R. Reed, and J. Reed (Eds.): SDL 2005, LNCS 3530, pp. 68–84, 2005.

With the technical specification for model storage and access, the Meta Object Facility (MOF) builds a good base for model transformation. This enables the automatic transformation of the design models into implementation (models). The gap between design and implementation known from traditional software development does not appear here.

But the successful development of new technologies cannot be independent from existing tools and methods. So the step by step integration of MDA based methods is necessary. Conventional development tools are syntax based. Therefore the integration has to be on textual syntax. This means new tools have to start with the syntactical representation of models or have to finish with it. To reach this the relation between syntax representation and repository MOF has to be resolved.

Therefore we present an example for a MDA based transformation. In the context of component based distributed software systems, the CORBA Component Model (CCM) defined by the OMG is a concrete technology for distributed software systems and can be used as a language for PSM. For the modeling of this kind of system at the abstract PIM level, this paper will use the language eODL defined by the ITU-T.

We will show the theoretical basis and appropriate languages/tools for an implementation of this kind of transformation. In the following section transformation rules at the conceptual level are introduced by an example. Section 3 gives a detailed view on MOF and model repositories usage in Java. As stated the relation between syntax representation of models and repositories has to be defined. This is done in section 4. Based on the model repositories, section 5 presents a way transformation rules can be implemented.

2   Transformation Rules – From eODL to CIDL

The complexity of developing large distributed software systems can be reduced by use of component technology and the MDA approach. By using component technology the whole system is divided into parts, which reduces the complexity. Specifying and implementing the different parts becomes easier than trying to handle the whole system at once. The overall system behavior is a constant in this process, but the process can be reduced by reusing software in terms of pre-developed software components, though MDA is not needed for doing so. The MDA approach introduces a new dimension in software reuse. With component technology alone, we are stuck to a concrete version/technology of software components in reuse. However, as we all know technology is changing over time. This leads to the situation, that at some point in the future your software system consisting out of a set of software components implemented in a certain technology, does not fit the current applied technology. Without MDA you now stop reusing your software components and are forced to redevelop the components. If we apply MDA here the transformation from the PIM design to the new component technology or platform has only to be defined.

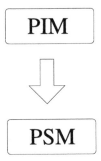

Fig. 1. Relation between PIM and PSM

2.1 Model Driven Architecture (MDA)

The MDA is a new software engineering approach developed and published by the Object Management Group (OMG). One fundamental observation in the evolution of living software systems over the years is that their basic design models are mostly unchanged. Most changes to evolving software systems take place only at engineering level, forced by the introduction of new technologies and platforms.

MDA promotes simply the usage of models for the whole software system development. To capture the problem of technology evolution MDA defines two classes of models. The first one is for abstract modelling of the software systems at the design level. This model class is called Platform Independent Model (PIM). The second class is related to specific platforms and/or technologies. It contains mainly engineering aspects of the software system and is called Platform Specific Model (PSM). Between these two classes of models, MDA defines a relation in the form of several transformations, which ensure the structural equivalence of PIM and PSM (see fig. 1).

There are three basic kinds of transformation specification:

- *Type based transformation:* Rules for transformation define a relation from concepts in the source Meta-Model to concepts in the target Meta-Model.
- *Instance based transformation:* Rules for transformation are defined on instances in the actual models: additional information for instance selection is needed.
- *Pattern based transformation:* Rules for transformation define a relation between patterns of instances in source and target model. Concepts of the Meta-Models can be used to formulate patterns.

Another key issue of MDA is a technology framework for different kinds of model handling (storage, exchange, mapping of models, etc.). The Meta Object Facility (MOF) [1] is convenient for this purpose. Historically modeling languages were defined by abstract grammars. MOF instead defines modeling languages on the base of so-called Meta-Models. Meta-Models are models (instances) of built-in MOF concepts. Using this framework the developer can focus more on the definition of mappings between models rather than having to struggle with ordinary model handling. This is due to the fact that MOF comes with a method for the definition of model classes (Meta-Models) and for the exchange of models using the XML Metadata Interchange (XMI) [2]. In addition, MOF provides mappings of Meta-Models to repository interfaces as well. Such a repository holds all necessary information about model instances.

The above argument is correct for most of today's component technology. To show the real application we have to choose concrete Meta-Models for PIM and PSM. This also leads to the selection of appropriate Meta-Models and notations for PIM and PSM. One requirement for both is the support of the component concept as a first class concept. Moreover, the Meta-Model for the PSM should be part of a well-defined and established component technology. Because the spread industrial usage is a process consuming several years, the suitable technologies have traditional syntax based languages for component definition.

2.2   eODL

eODL is a modeling language, which contains components as a first class concept. Other key concepts are interface, module, signal, data type and concepts for the description of distributed environments and deployment. Even though eODL utilizes the data type part from IDL (Interface Definition Language of OMG) it is not restricted to CORBA based platforms. The data type part from IDL is here used as an abstract data definition part, which has to be mapped for different platforms.

The definition of eODL is based on a Meta-Model utilizing MOF. The defined concepts are structured on two dimensions: first, packages are used to group the concepts according to their origin, so all concepts taken from IDL are in one package; second, structuring is more on logical level. Inspired by Open Distributed Processing (ODP) [3], in eODL all concepts are assigned to one of the following view points:

- *computational view point,*
- *implementation view point,*
- *deployment view point,*
- *target environment view point.*

Some view points are used here in the same way as in ODP, but eODL also identifies other view points. They are defined around the development cycle of software components. So the concepts from *deployment view point* are only meaningful for implemented software components and not for CO-Types in the design stage.

2.3   CCM and CIDL

The CORBA Component Model [4] is a standard published by the OMG. It provides the Meta-Model for CORBA components and the technology and runtime environment for components developed using that Meta-Model. It is based on mature CORBA technologies like the GIOP protocol[1] and language bindings for implementation languages.

The component model of CCM defines two kinds of interactions for components: there is a RPC-like interaction with request/response, and a signal-like interaction with events. For each of these interaction kinds components can declare the usage or the provision.

For the notation of models, CCM extends the IDL2[2] syntax by rules for components. CCM also contains a mapping from IDL3 (IDL2 + components) to the older IDL2. This was introduced for a compatibility with older, not component-aware CORBA clients.

But IDL3 covers only the computational aspects of components, which are first class concepts here. For the description of some implementation aspects, the Component Implementation Definition Language (CIDL) was published by OMG. CIDL is a superset of IDL3 and therefore it contains all computational concepts. Furthermore it introduces the grouping of interfaces for implementation purposes.

2.4   Apply MDA

After the identification of the development domain (distributed software components) we apply the MDA approach. This includes the full specification of computational objects and software components at the PIM level. But eODL only covers the structural aspects for this kind of specification. The full picture of involved model classes and languages is shown in fig. 2. Here we see that in addition to eODL, SDL is used to provide a mechanism for behavioral specification. It also illustrates the transformation between eODL and SDL models (see **a** in fig. 2).

Here CCM as a platform technology is the target technology for the final software system. The model class for structural aspects of software components is therefore CIDL. Also, the aspects from an implementation viewpoint in eODL can be mapped to corresponding concepts in CIDL (**b** in fig. 2). Only the behavioral aspect (which is expressed in the SDL model) cannot be transformed into the CIDL model, because there are no suitable concepts. The final goal of the development process is a running system and this means executable software. Most technologies defined by OMG are neutral regarding implementation language and base their mapping to implementation languages on existing mappings. CCM/ CIDL is no exception to this rule, and the regular mapping from IDL2 can be applied here.

In this paper we will not focus on the full set of model classes involved in the development process, but rather on the technical realization of one transformation. Therefore we narrow the process to the **b** transformation (see fig. 3).

---

[1] The General Inter ORB Protocol defines the exchange of requests and replies for RPC interaction.

[2] IDL2 is the 2.x version of the Interface Definition Language standardized by the OMG.

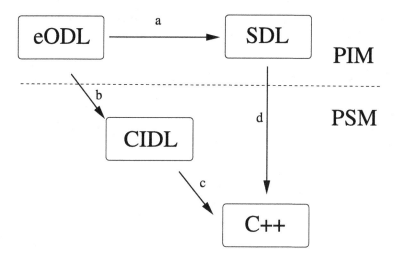

Fig. 2. Models and related transformations

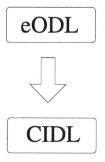

Fig. 3. Focus on technical realization of the transformation

A more detailed description of the whole development process shown in fig, 2 can be found in [5].

2.5 Example for a Rule

The transformation from eODL models to CIDL models is defined by using natural language. Unfortunately there is no well-established formalism[3] for transformation definition. In the natural language we establish a relation between concepts of source and target Meta-Model. Pure type based transformation rules are not possible in most cases. Only if the concept structures of source and target Meta-Model are nearly the same, can this happen.

---

[3] The RFP for Query/View/Transformation of models in MOF 2.0 is still under progress at OMG.

In the following example rule we show a mixture of type based and pattern based definition. The example uses this *font* for concepts in the Meta-Models and this *font* for attributes of concepts.

> **Rule:** For each **SignalDef** in the eODL model, there exists an **Event-Def** in the CCM model with same name. Each pair of name and data type associated in **CarryField** from the eODL model is mapped to a **Value-MemberDef**, which is defined in the scope of the current **EventDef**. All created **ValueMemberDef**s are public visible (*isPublicMember==true*).

The example rule transforms the concept **SignalDef** from the source Meta-Model in the concept **EventDef** of the target Meta-Model. This part of the rule is purely type based. But to transform the signal based interaction from eODL to CIDL we also need the correct relation between signal and signal parameters. The structure of the Meta-Models differs here and we have to use a "pattern" as an instrument.

3   MOF Based Repositories in Java

In this section we explain the relation between MOF and tools in the Java environment. This starts with a short overview of MOF and continues with related Java standards.

3.1   MOF

MOF (Meta Object Facility) is a standard for modeling data on different levels of abstraction. MOF provides a framework that supports all kinds of metadata. The architecture of MOF is based on the four layers as shown in fig. 4.

M3: The Meta-Meta-Model defines a language (MOF) with/by which the underlying Meta-Models are specified. For example: Meta-class, Meta-attribute, Meta-operation.

M2: The Meta-Model is an instance of the Meta-Meta-Model and it defines the language for the models. For Example: class, attribute, operation.

M1: The Model is an instance of the Meta-Model and it defines the language for the domain. For example: class:book, class:author, operation:setAuthor (for class:book).

M0: The Data are instances of the Model. For example: instance of the class:book with name "cook-book".

The MOF specification describes an abstract language for managing platform independent Meta-Models. For example: the Unified Modeling Language (UML), the Common Warehouse Metamodel (CWM) and the MOF itself.
The MOF-specification contains:

– a specification of the MOF Meta-Meta-Model, thus an abstract language for the specification of MOF Meta-Models

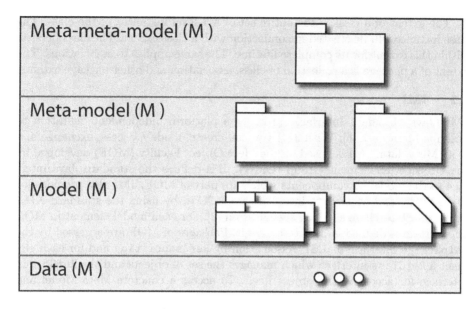

Fig. 4. Four-layered architecture

- a mapping of MOF Meta-Models to CORBA IDL (Interface Definition Language)
- a set of CORBA IDL interfaces for managing Meta-data, independent from the Meta-Model
- the XMI mapping (XML Metadata Interchange) for exchanging Meta-Models

A repository is a storage place in general. In this case we store all the data and Meta-data in the repository. Any repository object has an identity, a unique ID called MofID. That means that every repository element can be identified and accessed explicitly by its MofID.

Extents. In the MOF specification, statements about object locations have no place. Therefore the MOF assumes a concept of context in many areas:

- The classifier-scoped features of an M2-level Class are notionally common to "all instances" of the Class.
- Mapping typically allows a client to query over "all links" in an Association instance.

It is not feasible to define "all instances" or "all links" as meaning all instances or links in the known universe. For that reason, the MOF specification defines logical scopes of M1-level instances that are the base of these and other "for all" quantifications. These scopes of M1-level instances are called extents.

Every class instance belongs to precisely one class extent. These extents are part of package extents, depending on the structure of the Meta-Model. This means that extents are strictly hierarchical. Extents are related to the intrinsic container semantics of Meta-Objects.

The extent of a class is the entire set of M1-level instances of the class. The class instance will be created in connection with a class extent. The class persists within this extent for its complete lifetime. The same applies to associations. The extent of a package is a collection of class, association and other package extents.

3.2 JMI

JMI (Java Metadata Interface) provides a platform independent definition to describe Meta-data [6]. With JMI you can create, modify, access, exchange and store Meta-data. JMI is based on the Meta Object Facility (MOF) developed by the Object Management Group (OMG). JMI defines the standard Java interface to the modeling components which are part of MOF. JMI also provides for Meta-Model and Meta-data interchange via XML by using the standard XML Meta-data Interchange (XMI) specification [2]. For each model element in MOF an interface is defined in JMI to access it. Packages of MOF are accessed by the `Refpackage` interface of JMI, Association by `RefAssociation` and for each element a `RefClass` interface which manages the set of objects and the `RefObject` interface for access to the object itself. To access a concrete Meta-Model and instances of it the interfaces have to be specialized. That means that each interface for the specific model elements is a specialization of the Ref-interfaces named according to the model element. For the instances of the MOF-class, two interfaces are created, one named according to the model elements name plus class and the second uses only the name. With the use of JMI as a mapping from MOF onto Java, the implementation of a Meta-Model based mapping in Java is facilitated.

3.3 MDR

The repository we used for our implementation is called MDR (Meta Data Repository) [7]. It is written in Java and developed by the netbeans community. It contains an implementation of the MOF repository, including the persistent storage mechanism for storing the metadata. The interface of the MOF repository is based on and fully compliant with JMI [6]. The MDR provides the generation of JMI interfaces and an XMI Reader and XMI writer facility as well. It allows instantiation of any MOF compliant Meta-Model and models in the Meta-Models. We chose MDR as a repository because it is a Java and JMI based free available implementation and because of its built-in features. Besides netbeans MDR, there are also existing other JAVA based repositories. Two of them are Mod-Fact [8] and openMDX [9]. Both support JMI and are fully MOF compliant, but ModFact is still under development and considered Beta and therefore not stable. We chose MDR instead of openMDX because it is widely-used, stable and our previous experience in working with MDR.

4 Syntax Based Languages and MOF Repositories

Our aim was to enable the transfer of textual notated eODL-programs to the MOF repository. Why do we want to transfer eODL source code files to the repository? On the one hand, thus we have another possibility of input apart from model input via XMI, on the other hand we achieve a high integration, because there are tools, which create textual eODL notation from graphical eODL notation.

In this chapter we describe how textual notated programs in eODL can be transferred to the MOF repository. Here programs are the eODL source code files. eODL is a syntax based language. Its grammar is defined in Z.130. In the following part we give a short introduction to ANTLR which is the compiler generator tool we used. Apart from ANTLR we used MOF and JMI. Both are described in section 3.

4.1   ANTLR

We used ANTLR (ANother Tool for Language Recognition) [10], a compiler generator tool, to manage the lexical and the syntactical analysis process and to construct the objects in the repository by means of semantical actions.

ANTLR is developed by Terence Parr. It constructs recursive descent parsers from LL(k) grammars, for $k > 1$.

ANTLR integrates the specification of lexical and syntactical analysis. A separate lexical specification is unnecessary. Lexical regular expression (token descriptions) can be placed in double quotes and used as normal token references in an ANTLR grammar.

ANTLR accepts grammar constructs in EBNF (Extended Backus Naur Form) notation. It provides facilities for automatic abstract syntax tree (AST) construction and modification.

ANTLR allows each grammar rule to have parameters and return values. It converts each rule to a Java function; a rule parameter is simply a function parameter. Additionally, ANTLR rules have multiple return values.

4.2   From Syntax to Model Creation in MOF Repository

As we used ANTLR for building the parser, we had to change some things concerning the grammar of eODL. For example, we eliminated the optional usage of a meta symbol which is optional itself. After we had made the corrections the parsing of eODL-source files was possible.

Beside the parsing the source code in the first pass, we also generated an abstract syntax tree (AST). By contrast, to generate code (as we would do for building an usual compiler) we had to create model elements in the repository.

We used local symbol tables for each node in the AST, so we could manage and resolve container-content relations. We have to transfer these relations to the repository.

We also built up two global symbol tables realized with two associative containers, meaning two hashmaps:

- The first hashmap contains the names of the types already found associated with the created model elements.
- The second one contains elements with missing references.

At this point we can start to create instances of Meta-Model-elements in the repository. We demonstrate this technique with the following example. It is an extract from Dining Philosophers shown in listing 1.

```
module DiningPhilosophers {
    CO o_Philosopher{};
    CO o_Fork{};
    interface i_Fork;
    interface i_Philosopher;
    interface i_Observer;
    exception ForkNotAvailable {};
    exception NotTheEater {};
    enum e_ForkState { UNUSED, USED, WASHED };
    enum e_Pstate { EATING, THINKING, SLEEPING, DEAD, CREATED, HUNGRY };

    interface i_Fork {
        void obtain_fork ( in o_Philosopher eater )
                raises ( ForkNotAvailable );
        void release_fork ( in o_Philosopher eater )
                raises ( NotTheEater );
    };

    artefact a_ForkImpl {
        obtain_fork implements supply i_Fork::obtain_fork;
        release_fork implements supply i_Fork::release_fork;
    };

    CO o_Philosopher {
        implemented by a_PhilosopherImpl with Singleton;
        supports i_Philosopher;
        requires i_Fork, i_Observer;
        use l_observer observer;
        use i_Fork left;
        use i_Fork right;
    };

    valuetype Pstate {
        public e_PState mystate;
        public string name;
        public i_Philosopher philosoph;
        factory create ( in e_PState mystate, in string name,
                in i_Philosopher philo );
    };

    signal PhilosopherState {
        PState carry_pstate;
    };

    interface i_Observer {
        consume PhilosopherState pstate;
    };
};
```

Listing 1. Extract from Dining Philosophers

In the given source code (listing 1) line 13, there is the following declaration:
        void obtain_fork (**in** o_Philosopher eater)
(within **interface** i_Fork).

Each element, which is to be associated with other elements are created in the repository. We also look up in the first hashmap, whether the hashmap contains the element. If this is true, the element is associated. If not, the element have to be inserted in the second hashmap.

Types we find in the AST, we create in the MOF repository. Also they will be inserted in the first hashmap. As we find o_Philosopher while traversing the AST, we have to look up in the first hashmap, whether o_Philosopher already exists in the model. If not, we have to insert o_Philosopher in the second hashmap. For every type we find, at first we take a look at the second hashmap: if there is an item, which needs to be associated with the type we have found (this type has to be inserted in the first hashmap as a matter of course), we can complete the model element creation in the repository. In this case we have to delete all these items from the second hashmap. If we have traversed the whole AST and the second hashmap is empty the Model is transferred completely to the repository and we can work with the Model. If not, an error occurred.

5   Implementing Rules in Java

5.1   Introduction

This section describes the concrete implementation of the mapping rules with MDR using JMI. The whole project is called etoc standing for eODL to CIDL. The transformation is based on the principle of recursive descent and the technique of the Fluxbox. etoc is implementing the mapping between an eODL extent and a CIDL extent: first, the given extent is transformed into a new CIDL extent; second, it is walked to produce a syntax based output into an IDL and CIDL file. Both parts of the mapping and walking respectively are using the recursive descent principle. In contrast to traditional compiler technology, there is no need for a symbol table or AST (abstract syntax tree). Each element could be identified through its MOF-id. Using the knowledge of these properties allows an easy to understand and straightforward implementation.

5.2   Architecture of etoc

The whole transformator consists of two parts due to the split process of transformation. There is the Z130ComputationalViewTransformator responsible for the walking of the eODL model in respect to the computational view of eODL. Also, here is the Z130ImplentationalViewTransformator for walking the implementational view, allowing a split and selectional transformation. For further generation of syntactical output there is the CcmModelWalkerfor walking the transformed model and generating the output. Besides these components the FluxBox has to be used for transformation.

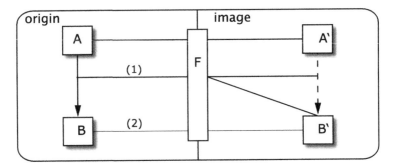

Fig. 5. Fluxbox technique

5.3 One Pass Transformation with the Fluxbox

As for the problem of relating two objects in MOF without knowledge of the existence of the other one, a concept is introduced named Fluxbox.[4]

Assume we have two objects named A and B as you can see in fig. 5, and F is representing the Fluxbox. Both are connected through a directed association. The intention is to map A on A' and B on B' and to establish an association between A' and B'. While browsing the model within the repository an instance of A has to be handled. The first step is creating the instance A' with the corresponding properties, the second is to relate A with B. While browsing the first time (1), one cannot ensure if B is existing, so it would be impossible to associate with a nonexistent object. The Fluxbox allows creation of an instance of B using the origin objects MOF-id for uniqeness and reference, without specifying B any further. The Fluxbox's base is creating a placeholder element, that can be accessed and changed by demand. By giving the Fluxbox the meta object defined by JMI for creating the image object paired with the key of the original object, the image element is created and returned. In further model walking, the element B is found (2), so B' is again accessed through the Fluxbox using the MOF-id of B and specified according to the mapping from B to B'. The Fluxbox is a container, to be more precise a `Hashmap` with the original objects MOF-id as the key and the image model element as the contained element.The Fluxbox's only operation is getting the object according to the given key. If there is no object associated with the given key a new one is created, else the existing object is returned for manipulation. Thus the Fluxbox solves the problem of possible not existing objects and simplifies the whole process of transformation by giving the possibility of one pass transformation.

5.4 Transforming the Model

The Transformator `etoc` supports two possible inputs, syntax based input files (parsed by the eODL parser and model injector as described in section 4) or

---

[4] It was originally developed by Markus Scheidgen (scheidgen@informatik.hu-berlin.de) for handling of such problems.

the XMI representation of the eODL model. Both methods result in an eODL extent within the repository, the first one by creating the eODL extent directly while parsing, the second by using the built-in XMI-Reader of MDR passing the extents target location as an argument while calling. Because OCL is not fully supported in MDR the formulated constraints are not considered, so it is possible to add them at any time. The concepts which are not supported by the mapping like *MediaDef* or the *deployment view* are not considered in the implementation. Despite that approach ,they are read and included within the repository. This preserves the implementation's future extensibility.

Having instanced the model in the repository, further actions are necessary. First a CIDL extent is created and named uniquely according to the given extent of eODL. Second, the given eODL extent has to be walked recursively for transforming the model. The key for transforming the model is the use of two techniques: the *container-content* relation, and t the Fluxbox using the MOF-id. Because of the *container-content* association, the model is presenting itself in a tree structure, meaning each model element is connected to his container. Therefore the entry points for walking can be determined by getting all top level objects. These elements are implicitly contained within the virtual global module forming also a container for elements. Each of these container elements forms a separate tree of containment, so the whole model is representing itself as a set of trees. Every tree is a spanning-tree, meaning it is covering all contained model elements, because of the containment restriction of eODL and CIDL respectively. This assures that every model element is reachable and can be walked. Using the Fluxbox technique bypasses the problem of "not yet existing" model elements and allows a one pass transformation. So every model element which has to be created during the process of transforming is generated out of the Fluxbox. The mapping is done in two steps: first, the cloning of the common IDL core; second, the mapping rules for the eODL specifics. Implementing the cloning follows a straightforward schema. For each common model element, the element's attributes and references are copied to the new created element. Also, the associations are copied by setting the corresponding reference objects on the new created model elements. Implementing the mapping rules is done as straightforwardly as cloning the IDL core. Because each element of eODL is mapped on one CIDL element, the Fluxbox can be used with the original element's MOF-id. This allows the assignment of the image element to the origin model element. Afterwards the repository contains the eODL model and the CIDL model resulting from the transformation, so both of the models can be accessed and manipulated on demand.

5.5   Traversing the Transformed Model

After the transformation has finished, the extent is walked by the `CcmModelWalker` to produce a syntax-based output in files. The principle of the walker is again the recursive descent using the *container-content* relation. While passing each element the corresponding code is created by converting types to strings and resolving the namespace. The walk is not obligatory because there is the possibility of writing the resulting model in an XMI file by using the built-in feature of MDR for generating XMI output.

5.6   Using JMI

This section covers the more implementational aspects of the transformation. Accessing the model is done by using JMI and MDR which is implementing the provided operations. In the following, the access is described by example. Handling of the package hierarchy of eODL and CIDL is done by providing elements of the type `RefPackage` which delivers the class proxy objects and association objects. The type `IdlPackage` grants access to all IDL model elements of eODL and the type `CCMMetamodel` to those of CIDL. Note that z130 is an instance of `Z130Package` which is the start point of the extent and therefore the extent itself.

```
ComputationalViewPackage compView =
z130Extent.getAdvancedConcepts().getComputationalView();
Iterator signalDefIterator = compView.getSignalfDef().refAllOfType().iterator();
```

Listing 2. Example for package handling

The iterator provides the browsing in the collection of instances, each of the type *SignalDef*. For each model element there are two types of interfaces granting access. The first one is a specialized element of *RefClass* representing the proxy object which is managing the set of instances. The second one is a specialized *RefObject* object providing the access to the model elements instance itself. In the following example the former *SignalDef* element is walked and named `signal`. The *EventDef* in context of CIDL is created with the Fluxbox and named `newEvent`.

```
EventDef newEvent = (EventDef)
              fluxBox.getObject(ccm.getComponentIdl().getEventDef(), signal);
newEvent.setIdentifier(signal.getIdentifier());
newEvent.setRepositoryId(signal.getRepositoryId());
newEvent.setVersion(signal.getVersion());
newEvent.setDefinedIn(setContainer(signal.getDefinedIn()));
```

Listing 3. Example for element mapping

As you have seen, the attributes were copied by using the get-function calls on the original element using their value on the set-functions of the new eventtype. The members of the signal are also traversed recursively. The setting of their Idltype is the setting of the reference object of the *TypedBy* association. Another way of handling the association instances is getting the `RefAssociation` objects allowing to add or remove instances taking part in the relation. Each association is specialized according to the related types. Besides this, it is also possible to access them by setting or getting the proper reference attributes. The code in listing 4 describes how to handle the association proxy object.

```
z130.idl.InterfaceDef interfaceBase;
ccmmetamodel.baseidl.InterfaceDef interfaceDerived;

...

InterfaceDerivedFrom derivedFromAss =
        z130Extent.getIdl().getInterfaceDerivedFrom();
derivedFromAss.add(interfaceBase, interfaceDerived);
```

Listing 4. Example for association handling

Obviously the association is retrieved through the `z130Extent`. Both interface objects are created by using the Fluxbox. Then accessed by adding the participating objects to the association. The objects also grants functions like remove, exist and so forth.

6   Conclusions

As we showed in this paper, the implementation language Java, the JMI standard and the JMI implementation MDR build a powerful combination for the realization of MDA related tools like transformers. More generally it demonstrates that MDA is a real use case for software development; all base technologies are available as products. But the transition to new standards like MOF 2.0 from OMG is not supported by current Java tools.

The developed transformation tool enables automatic translation of platform independent models of software components to CCM specific models of these software components. With the acceptance of textual syntax, input and the output of CIDL documents in textual syntax notation and integration with existing tools is simple. The usage in automatic build processes is easy, because there is no struggling with IDE or GUI.

7   Further Work

Most of the work to build an MDA based transformer can be done by using tools. The lack of formal description methods of transformations is the main obstacle here. There are some promising approaches, but no easy-to-use tooling like for MOF repositories. So the definition of such formalism has to be tackled in future. The activities in the Query/View/Transformation RFP by the OMG have great potential. But only tools for automatic implementation derivation especially in Java will support the application of MDA further.

Also, the automatic or semi-automatic integration of traditional syntax based languages in the Meta-Model centered world is a field of future activities.

References

1. Object Management Group: Meta Object Facility, Version 1.3, OMG document, formal/00-11-02 (2000)
2. Object Management Group: XML Metadata Interchange (XMI) version 1.1, OMG document, formal/00-11-02 (2000)
3. ITU-T: Open Distributed Processing, ITU-T Recs. X.901, X.902, X.903, X.904 (1997)
4. Object Management Group: CORBA Components, v3.0 full specification, OMG document, formal/02-06-65 (2002)
5. H. Böhme, J. Fischer: eODL and SDL in combination for components, in SAM2004, LNCS 3319.
6. Java Community Process: The Java Metadata Interface(JMI) Specification(Final Release), JSR-000040, (2002)
7. netbeans.org: Metadata Repository (MDR), http://mdr.netbeans.org/
8. lip6: ModFact, http://forge.objectweb.org/projects/modfact/
9. openMDX: http://www.openmdx.org/
10. ANTLR: ANother Tool for Language Recognition, http://www.antlr.org/

Service Discovery and Component Reuse with Semantic Interfaces

Richard T. Sanders[1], Rolv Bræk[2], Gregor von Bochmann[3], and Daniel Amyot[3]

[1] SINTEF ICT, NO-7465 Trondheim, Norway
`Richard.Sanders@sintef.no`
[2] Department of Telematics,
Norwegian University of Science and Technology,
NO-7491 Trondheim, Norway
`rolv.braek@item.ntnu.no`
[3] SITE, University of Ottawa, 800 King Edward,
Ottawa (ON) Canada, K1N 6N5
{`bochmann, damyot`}`@site.uottawa.ca`

Abstract. Current trends in distributed computing and e-business processing suggest that many applications are evolving towards Service Oriented Computing (SOC) with technologies such as Web services. Services are autonomous platform-independent computational elements, and we observe an increasing need for core SOC technologies for dynamic discovery, selection, and composition of services. However, such technologies are often based on syntactic descriptions of the services and of their interfaces, which are insufficient to ensure that desired liveness properties are satisfied. In this paper, we propose an approach for the description, discovery, and selection of services based on role modeling and goal expressions that enables the definition of semantic interfaces and the evaluation of liveness properties. The same mechanisms also enable component reuse. We discuss how UML 2.0 can support the modeling of both the services and the desired properties. The approach is illustrated with telephony services.

1 Introduction

Many emerging distributed applications, platforms, and architectures, such as Web services and grid architectures, attempt to take advantage of the concept of service. A *service* is an autonomous platform-independent unit of work done by a provider to achieve desired end results for a consumer. The purpose of increasingly popular Service-Oriented Architectures (SOA) is often to promote the use and reuse of application-neutral services and components, and to achieve loose coupling between the participating entities. Such architectures contain three main parts: a provider, a consumer, and a registry. Providers publish or announce their services on registries, where consumers find and then invoke them. To support such Service-Oriented Computing, several protocols and languages

A. Prinz, R. Reed, and J. Reed (Eds.): SDL 2005, LNCS 3530, pp. 85–102, 2005.
© Springer-Verlag Berlin Heidelberg 2005

have been developed to characterize, register, discover, invoke, and compose services [16].

Of particular interest is the problem of selecting a service that can interoperate with a client application and that can meet the desired goals of the collaboration. As we move toward open environments where anyone can wrap existing functionalities or create new ones and then offer them as remote services, being able to select the most appropriate service (if any) becomes imperative. Current enabling technologies are often based on *syntactic* descriptions of the services and of their interfaces. For example, the Web-Service Description Language (WSDL) uses ports, operations, and message types to define the abstract interface and protocol bindings of a service [17]. A UDDI registry catalogs such service characteristics, together with business and category information [13]. Other service discovery protocols (such as SLP, SDP, Jini, Salutation, and UPnP) describe services with identifiers, types, attributes (including some quality of service), and/or static interfaces [3]. We believe such descriptions to be insufficient to ensure that liveness properties (the collaboration goals) desired by the service customer are satisfied. A discovered service may offer the required static interface but may not be able to achieve the desired goals; it should then not be selected.

To tackle this problem, we propose an approach for the description, discovery, and selection of services based on role modeling and simple goal expressions that enables the definition of *semantic* interfaces and the evaluation of liveness properties. These mechanisms are generic enough to address the related issue of component reuse. Section 2 presents how UML 2.0 [14] can support the modeling of both the services and the desired properties. Typical usages of semantic interfaces are discussed in section 3. The approach is illustrated with telephony services, but is not limited to the telecommunication domain. Our conclusions follow.

2   Semantic Interfaces

2.1   Distributed Systems Architecture

Figure 1 suggests an architecture for service-oriented systems that is characterized by horizontal and vertical decomposition. On the horizontal axis, several computational objects (*actors*) are identified that may reside in different computing environments. This axis represents the physical and logical distribution of the system. On the vertical axis, several services are identified that are provided by the distributed systems. In the simplest situation, these services are provided independently of one another. In practice, however, there are usually constraints relating to resources of an actor that are shared by the components involved in the different services, which leads to dependencies between the different services.

The main concern in this paper is the compatibility of the different service components involved in the provisioning of a given service. (We note that

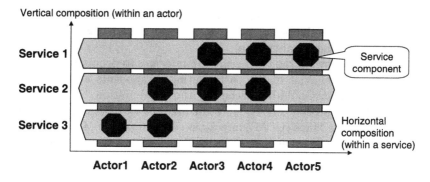

Fig. 1. Two-dimensional view of a Service-Oriented Architecture

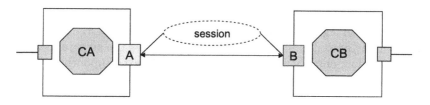

Fig. 2. Two interacting components with two interfaces each

one or several of these components may constitute a user agent). In the following, we call these service components simply *"components"*. Typically, each component interacts with several other components within the same horizontal service. For a given component, we identify a number of *interfaces*, one for each other component with which it cooperates. Figure 2 shows an example of two components, CA and CB, each having two interfaces, and where the two components interact with one another through the interfaces A and B, respectively.

The figure also indicates that messages are exchanged between these two components. What is labeled *session* in the figure, actually represents the *collaboration* between these two components. Different graphical notations have been proposed in UML for representing collaborations [14]. In this article, we consider the description of collaboration behaviors at different levels of abstraction. At the highest level, we use UML activity diagrams which only represent the order in which certain phases of the service collaboration proceeds. If we want to describe globally the messages exchanged during a collaboration, we use UML interaction diagrams. These two descriptions are not necessarily complete; they typically concentrate on certain use cases. For a complete description of a collaboration, we consider first the state machine description of the behavior of each of the components. Since such a *component behavior* description includes all interactions of the given component over all interfaces, it is more complex than required, if we are only interested in the collaboration of the component over a specific interface. Therefore we also consider the projection of the component behavior over a given interface, which we call the interface *role behavior* of the given component. It is the behavior it exhibits over the interface where it plays a particular role in the collaboration.

We use in the following the term *semantic interface* to denote a collaboration including the role behavior of the participating components and the progress goals (see below) that should be reached by the collaboration.

Note that this approach is not bound to UML: activity diagrams could be replaced with Use Case Maps (UCM), interaction diagrams with Message Sequence Charts (MSC), and state diagrams with the Specification and Description Language (SDL).

2.2   A Simple Example

We consider the following simple example from telephony in order to explain the concepts introduced in this paper. The telephony service involves two components, the user agent of the calling user, named A, and the user agent of the called user, named B. The diagram of fig. 3 shows the structural aspect of this collaboration; only the interfaces between these two components are shown, not the interfaces with their respective terminals and users. The diagram also shows a progress goal that should be reached by the collaboration: The system should reach a global state where VoiceCnt(A, B) is true, that is, A has a voice connection to B and B has a voice connection to A.

We consider that a UserCall collaboration may involve the following phases: Invite, Calling, and Busy, as shown in the activity diagram of fig. 4. This is a very basic behavior that may be enriched with more service features as will be illustrated in section 3.

The following sequence diagrams give more details about these phases. They show the overall sequencing of the phases, similar to the activity diagram above

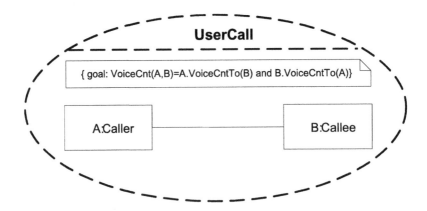

Fig. 3. The UserCall collaboration structure

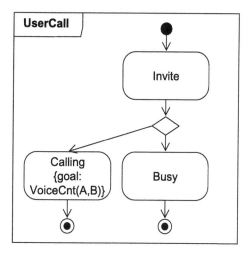

Fig. 4. Phases of the UserCall collaboration

as well as the interactions leading up to the connected state. Reaching the connected state is clearly a goal for the UserCall service, and this is represented by the goal expression goal: VoiceCnt(A,B) where VoiceCnt(A,B) is a predicate over properties of the two participating roles A and B, for instance:

$$VoiceCnt(A,B) = A.VoiceCntTo(B) \text{ and } B.VoiceCntTo(A)$$

In order to keep the example simple, we only show a basic call handling service with one feature, WaitOnBusy, in fig. 5. Using the same general approach a much richer set of features can be designed.

Finally, the two state transition diagrams in fig. 6 show the role behavior of the two collaborating components in a featureless basic call service. Since only one interface is considered for each component so far, the role behavior at these interfaces is identical to the overall behavior of these components. In these diagrams, we have omitted behavior needed to resolve conflicts in the case of initiative collisions which may occur in states with both input and output transitions (called mixed initiative states in [5, 8]). In reality, the role behaviors must be extended to include behavior for resolving such conflict situations (e.g., see the work of Gouda [9] and Floch [8]).

It should be noted here that the diagrams in fig. 6 define what we call the *semantic interface* of the UserCall collaboration. In addition to defining the static interface in terms of the signal types interchanged in each direction (not explicitly shown here), it also defines the interface behavior in terms of sequences of interactions and the goals in terms of predicates specifying properties of desirable states and events.

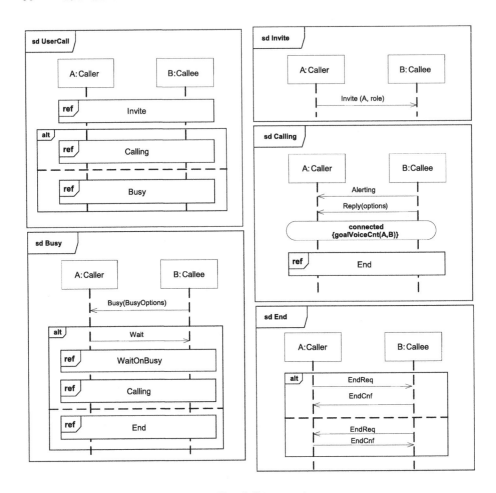

Fig. 5. UserCall interactions

2.3   Criteria for Component Reutilization and Service Discovery

To set the stage for the following discussion, we consider two situations where it is important to compare different component specifications and implementations:

1. We consider the following scenario of *service discovery* (refer to fig. 2): A component CA is given; and we are looking for a "service" that presents an interface *similar* to the one presented by component CB, such that CA and CB may perform a collaboration similar to the one described above.
2. We consider a scenario of *component reuse*, where during system design we identify a system component C with a given requirements specification S_C. Now we are looking for an existing implementation I that could be used as component C in the implementation of the system.

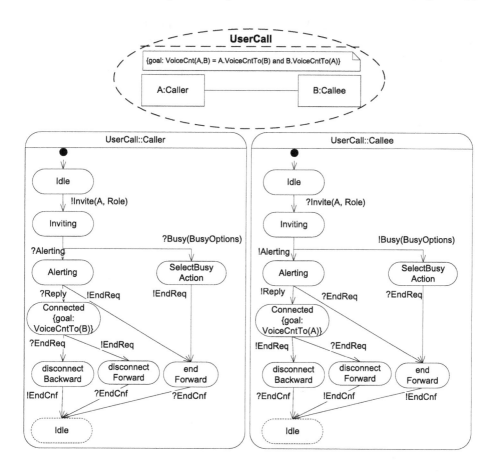

Fig. 6. A semantic interface with a goal and interface role behaviors

We assume in the following that a requirements specification S is given in the form of some logical predicate that must be satisfied by the implementation. This predicate may define a state machine, or it may be of a more general form. We also assume that each implementation I can be described by a logical predicate P_I that characterizes all the properties of the implementation. Then we have the following lemmas/definitions:

Lemma 1 (Conforming implementation). *An implementation I conforms to the requirements S if $P_I \Rightarrow S$ (logical implication).*

Lemma 2 (Specialization). *A specification S' is a specialization of another specification S if $S' \Rightarrow S$. (One also says that S' is a* subtype *of S).*

Lemma 3 (Reuse of a component). *An implementation I that conforms to the requirements S' can be reused as an implementation for a component that must satisfy the specification S, if $S' \Rightarrow S$.*

A requirement has often the form of an implication: If certain assumptions about the environment of the component are satisfied then the component will have to satisfy certain guaranteed properties [1]. We therefore assume that a requirements specification is given the form $S = (As \Rightarrow GP)$, where As represents the assumptions and GP the guaranteed properties. Then we can say that S' is a specialization of S if $(As' \Rightarrow GP') \Rightarrow (As \Rightarrow GP)$ which is equivalent to $(As \Rightarrow As') \wedge ((As \wedge GP') \Rightarrow GP) \vee (\neg(As \Rightarrow As') \wedge GP)$. This means that S' is a specialization of S if, and only if, the assumptions of S' are weaker than or equal to those of S and the guarantees of S' (when the assumptions of S are satisfied) are stronger than or equal to those of S, or the guarantees of S are satisfied independently of any other assumptions.

We note that component requirements can usually be divided into structural (static) properties and dynamic properties that relate to the dynamic behavior of the component. The following paragraphs discuss briefly the structural properties; aspects related to the dynamic behavior are discussed in the next subsection.

Definitions of interfaces (in the sense of object-oriented languages or SDL channels) represent structural properties. An interface definition states what kind of methods must be provided by a class (a guarantee provided by the component); it also states that the component may make the assumption that the environment will not try to call a method that is not defined. The latter assumption is usually checked by the compiler according to the type checking rules of the language.

The declaration of the type of a parameter in an input message for a given component specification represents the assumption that the environment will only provide input parameters of the specified type. Conversely, the declaration of the type of a parameter in an output message (or return value of a method call) represents a guarantee to be provided by the component that only values of that type should be presented in the output message. Together with the definition of specialization given above, this leads to quite general type checking rules, as for instance defined for the Emerald language [2].

2.4   Formalizing Safety and Liveness Properties of Collaborations

Subtyping of State Machines. We assume in the following that the dynamic behavior of a component is specified in the form of a (deterministic) finite state machine where each transition is either associated with an input or an output. We also assume that the specification of the static structure defines the set of input and output interactions that may occur at each of the interfaces of the component. Assuming that a state machine specification only defines safety properties of the component (we will discuss liveness properties later in this section), we interpret a given state machine specification for a component C as follows:

1. If the component produces an output, then the state machine has an output transition with this output as a label from the current state of the component. When doing the output, the component enters the new state defined

by that transition. This is in fact a guarantee that any produced output is one of those allowed by the specification.

2. If the component receives an input, it will enter a new state as defined by the transition (from its current state) labeled by this input. The specification makes in fact the assumption that only inputs that are defined for the current state in the specification will be produced by the environment of the component.

Based on this interpretation of state machine specifications, we note that a state machine specification S', which is obtained from a given specification S by adding some additional input transitions, has weaker assumptions than S and defines therefore a subtype behavior of S. Note that a new input transition may lead to an existing state or a new state; additional input and output transitions may be added from the new states while keeping the subtyping relationship. We call this form of subtyping *extension*, indicated by the label "ext" in the UML icon for inheritance (see fig. 8). The diagram in fig. 7 provides an example where the CalleeW role is an extension of the Callee role from fig. 6.

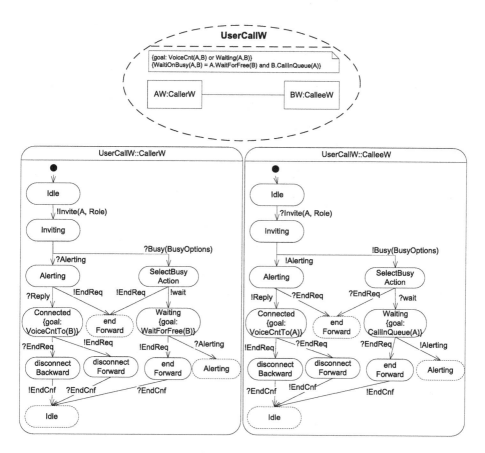

Fig. 7. Semantic interface for UserCallW: UserCall with WaitOnBusy feature added

Similarly, if S' is obtained from S by removing some output transitions, then S' defines a subtype behavior of S. In this case, some liveness properties may get lost, because the subtype restricts the interaction possibilities. We call this form of subtyping *reduction*, indicated by the label "red" in the UML icon for inheritance. (This is similar to the reduction of nondeterminism considered in [6]). As an example, the Caller role in fig. 6 is a reduction of the CallerW role in fig. 7.

Safety Compatibility Requirements for Collaborations. We now consider that a component CA should collaborate with a component CB, as shown in fig. 2. If we are only interested in the compatibility of these two components for the interactions taking place over the common interface, we first can make abstraction of the interaction of these components over other interfaces. This operation of abstraction is often called *projection* and consists of hiding all interactions that do not occur over the interface of interest. This projection operation, applied to the state machine S defining the overall behavior of the component, leads in general to a nondeterministic machine. We assume in the following that the well-known determination algorithm ([10], which is of exponential complexity) has been applied in order to obtain a deterministic state machine $Proj_{IF}(S)$ showing the behavior of the component S at the interface IF of interest.

We now consider the collaboration between the components CA and CB with specifications SA and SB, respectively. We note that compatibility between CA and CB means that CA only sends interactions to CB that CB can handle in its current state, and inversely, that CB only sends interactions to CA that CA can handle in its current state. In other words, the guarantees of $Proj_{IF}(SA)$ imply the assumptions of $Proj_{IF}(SB)$, and the guarantees of $Proj_{IF}(SB)$ imply the assumptions of $Proj_{IF}(SA)$.

We now may make the assumption that the interactions over the interface are immediate, that is, an output interaction generated by one component is immediately consumed as input by the other component, without any intermediate queuing. We call such an interface a *direct coupling interface*. Although not very realistic for distributed systems, this kind of interface is used for many theoretical models, such as Input/Output Automata [11]. It has the advantage that no cross-over of messages in opposite directions may occur over the interface.

Lemma 4. *Given a component CA with dynamic behavior $Proj_{IF}(SA)$ over the interface IF, the most general (in the sense of our specialization relation) behavior at the interface for the collaborating component CB is given by the state machine obtained from $Proj_{IF}(SA)$ by exchanging for each transition the direction of interaction (replace input by corresponding output or output by corresponding input). See for instance the work of Gouda [9] or Drissi [7].*

In the more realistic case where outputs are queued within the communication medium before they are consumed as input by the destination component, the compatibility conditions are more complex because messages may cross over within the medium and the order of inputs and outputs occurring at one component may be different from the order of the corresponding outputs and inputs at the other components. Gouda [9] and Floch [8] propose some interesting approaches for deriving a most general behavior at the interface for a component CB collaborating with a given component CA.

Considering Liveness Properties in Collaborations. While safety talks about constraints that must be satisfied for any valid execution sequence that may occur, liveness properties talk about certain progress that should be made or states that should be reached. Various approaches have been proposed for describing liveness (or progress) properties. We propose in this paper the notion of a *goal* which is a predicate on the local or global state space of the system. We say that a system satisfies a given goal G if one of the execution paths of the system leads to a state s for which $G(s)$ is true. This is equivalent to a statement in branching time temporal logic saying that there exists a branch that leads eventually to a state for which G holds. In general, the requirements of a given system may include several goal predicates that should be reachable. If a single state should be reachable that satisfies a set of goals $G_1, \ldots, G_n$ simultaneously, this can be expressed by a new goal of the form $G = G_1 \wedge \ldots \wedge G_n$.

In the example of the telephone system presented previously, the activity diagram of fig. 4 contains the mention goal: VoiceCnt(A,B) for the activity Calling. This means that the Calling phase should be reachable, while the text VoiceCnt(A,B) has no formal meaning at this point. In fig. 5, the location of this goal (within the reachable global state space) is further refined. Also, in fig. 6, the same goal is described from the point of view of one of the components participating in the collaboration; here we see that a particular state of the state machine should be reachable. The additional predicate VoiceCntTo(B) may be evaluated within the component A by referring to additional variables not shown in the diagram.

As mentioned earlier in this section, when one replaces, within a given system, a component A with behavior S by another component A' with behavior S' where S' is a subtype of S, it could be that certain global (and local) states that were reachable with S are not reachable anymore with S' (except in the case when S' is a pure extension of S). If such states are associated with goals, these goals would not be reachable anymore. We conclude that the definition/lemma (3) mentioned in section 2.3 must be revised by indicating that the relationship $S' \Rightarrow S$ implies that there is no problem for reuse as far as safety properties are concerned, but there may be a problem concerning progress, unless the subtype relationship is a pure extension. We do not know of any general rule for solving this dilemma, however, we know that the relevant progress properties may possibly not be satisfied by the replacement component S'. These progress properties should therefore be checked. This could be done by performing a reachability analysis of the collaboration in question.

We conclude this section by noting that the compatibility of two components participating in a collaboration over a given interface has two aspects: safety properties and progress properties. These properties can be checked by considering the role behavior of the components which is the behavior of the components projected onto the collaboration interface. Safety compatibility means that any output produced by one component is acceptable by the other component when it is received as input. In the case of interfaces without any message transfer delay (excluding cross-over of messages), this relationship is easily checked by comparing the respective role behaviors. In the case of message delays over the interface, the verification of compatibility is much more complex, and can for instance be solved by reachability analysis, which may, however, involve arbitrarily long message queues. The safety-oriented subtyping relationship of dynamic behaviors is useful for deciding these compatibility questions.

We introduce in this paper a notation for specifying progress properties of collaborations. It is important to note that they are not implied by the behavior specifications that are commonly represented by finite state machines or other similar formalisms. We show in this paper how progress properties can be taken into account during the definition of collaborations and for identifying components that are compatible with a given component, not only as far as safety is concerned, but also concerning the progress properties.

3   Using Semantic Interfaces

3.1   Service and System Composition

We assume now that each component type may have a number of interfaces, and that each interface is defined (typed) by referring to a semantic interface. Safety and liveness properties may be analyzed once for each semantic interface as explained in section 2. This analysis does not need to be repeated for each component, but it is necessary to check for each component type that its behavior is consistent with the role behaviors attached to its interfaces. This means to check that the role behavior is a projection of the component behavior as explained in section 2.4. When this is done, the semantic interfaces can be used to check compatibility of static and dynamic links between component instances in a service or system structure.

Traditional model checking is performed on instance structures and does not scale well when the structures change and grow. By analyzing each component type and semantic interface separately and building maps over subtype relationships, much of the computation intensive work can be done once and for all at design time and thus reduce the work needed at runtime. In this way, semantic interfaces provide an enabler for scalable, runtime compatibility checks in dynamic system structures. This is especially important in systems where new services and components may be added dynamically, as for instance in the emerging service oriented computing paradigm, but it is important in any system with dynamic link structures.

As a simple example consider the case presented in fig. 7. Here the UserCall has been extended with a WaitOnBusy feature. More precisely, the Callee role has been extended so that CalleeW $\Rightarrow$ Callee (extension). In order to fully explore this extended role behavior, corresponding output must be added to the Caller role as

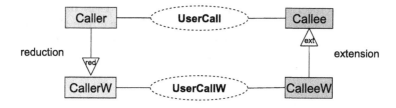

Fig. 8. Subtyping relationships for the semantic interfaces of UserCall and UserCallW

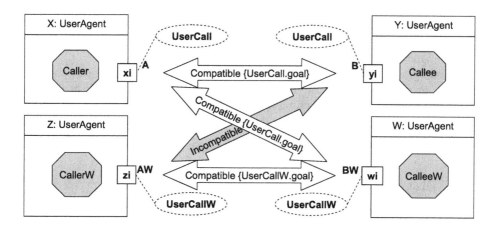

Fig. 9. Using semantic interfaces

shown in the CallerW role. As a consequence, the Caller ⇒ CallerW (reduction), as illustrated in fig. 8.

Now, consider four components that subscribe to these interfaces as illustrated in fig. 9. Obviously two components that provide dual roles of the same interface will fully satisfy safety and liveness properties when connected across the interface. In addition, components providing the Caller role may inter-work safely with components providing the CalleeW role. However, in this case the WaitOnBusy goal is not reachable. CallerW and Callee are incompatible, as indicated in fig. 9.

In service providing systems, it is quite common that links between components are dynamic. In telecommunication services for instance, the links between user agents, terminals and other objects change from call to call. The service features available at a given instant will normally depend on subscription information, user preferences, current state and available resources. Therefore, it may be necessary to check the compatibility for each dynamic link that is established. In our examples this has been omitted, but could be added as checks or possibly negotiations performed during the Invite phase.

In many telecommunication services, such as the UserCall presented here, the identity of the objects playing the service roles are important. The Caller for instance wants to reach a particular user, not just any user. In other cases the identity is not so important. The problem is to find some object that can provide a service or part of a service, in other words to find an object that can play a given role. This is a case of service discovery.

3.2   Service Discovery

Service discovery has two dimensions:

1. Finding existing component types and instances that can provide a desired behaviour across a semantic interface. This is needed when a component with a given semantic interface needs to find and connect to a compatible component over that interface. We call this *discovery of complementary components*.
2. Finding new component types and new semantic interfaces that can provide new or enhanced services, e.g., finding out if an actor can perform new or enhanced services by obtaining a new type of component. We call this *role learning*.

In the following sections we present approaches to these challenges.

3.3   Discovery of Complementary Components

Discovery of complementary components is a mechanism by which a component can determine what other component types or instances are capable of playing compatible complementary roles. This may be accomplished by specifying a desired semantic interface and role, given knowledge of collaboration roles and their subtyping relationships. An example is presented below.

Components are defined with their semantic interfaces in fig. 9. Given knowledge of the interface role subtyping relationships in fig. 8, compatibility relationships and goal opportunities can be analyzed efficiently. Interoperable, complementary components can be found with which services can be performed, while incompatible components can be avoided:

- X looks for components that are compatible with the UserCall.Callee interface. This is obviously Y, since it subscribes to that interface. It is also W because UserCallW.CalleeW is an extension of UserCall.Callee, as shown in fig. 8.
- Y looks for components that are compatible with the UserCall.Caller interface. Component X can be found, but not Z, since UserCallW.CallerW is incompatible with UserCall.B.
- Z looks for components compatible with UserCall.CalleeW. Component W can be found, but not Y, again due to incompatibility.
- W looks for components compatible with UserCall.CallerW. Z is compatible and can achieve all the goals of UserCallW. X is compatible, but can only reach the goals of UserCall that are without the WaitOnBusy feature.

Given the subtype relationships calculated at design time, one can search for components with compatible interfaces, and determine that they satisfy safety and liveness properties and therefore have the possibility of reaching service goals when interacting.

Discovery of complementary components is a static comparison of semantic interfaces of component types. It does not take the current state of components into consideration. The objective is not to discover or learn new behavior, an issue we discuss below.

Note that component interfaces can be classified as either initiating ("client" side) or offered ("server" side), depending on which interface is designed to take the first initiative in the collaboration. This can be exploited to simplify the discovery procedure, since a component is only interested in finding compatible offered interfaces.

3.4 Role Learning

Given knowledge of what interface roles are deployed in its environment, it may be desirable for an actor object to learn new behavior so that it can achieve more service goals when interacting with components towards its environment. It can for example use a lookup mechanism to search for service components that give a better match against offered roles: components that can achieve more progress.

Given a service brokering function or registry, an actor may perform a request for a component that can enable it to take part in a new service or a "better" service than previously. This will require that a new component with new semantic interfaces is downloaded. A possible collaboration pattern for this is depicted in fig. 10.

In fig. 10, a component X sends a request to component W to play a User-Call.Callee role. The role request is confirmed, since W is capable of a consistent collaboration with X. However, in the role confirmation, W supplies a description

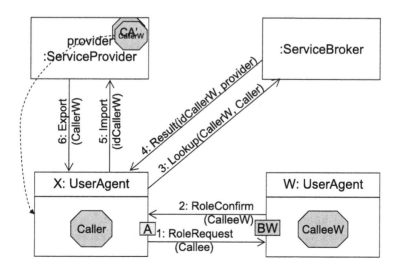

Fig. 10. Role learning pattern used to retrieve a new component

of its interface behavior CalleeW. As described earlier, CalleeW extends Callee with WaitOnBusy functionality. In step 3, X consults a service broker to check for the existence of a service component that is a better match for CalleeW than Caller, i.e., a service component that can achieve more service goals. Note that X supplies a description of its semantic interface Caller. Steps 4 thru 6 result in the service component CallerW being identified and retrieved from an appropriate service provider. X has thus improved its functional repertoire by obtaining the CallerW component.

Whether X casts away the Caller component is an open issue; remember that CallerW cannot collaborate safely with Callee components, so the Caller component may be useful in another context. The example also does not indicate what component is used in the collaboration with W. Which component to select can be decided in the Invite phase of the call. Figure 10 illustrates how this may be accomplished by replacing the Invite signal by an interaction consisting of a RoleRequest(requested-role) signal and a RoleConfirm(granted-role) signal. Compared with existing lookup services, the enhancements lie in the description of the semantic interface, and the learning factor made possible by issuing and granting role requests [4, 12].

4   Conclusions

We have described and illustrated how semantic interfaces, composed of behavior expressions annotated with goals, can be used for the selection of services and of components while satisfying the liveness properties of the collaboration. This improvement over the use of static interfaces by existing service discovery mechanisms prevents the selection of services that would lead to unsatisfactory or even dangerous behavior. Goals can be attached to behavior models at various levels of abstraction, for instance to UML 2.0 activity, interaction, or state diagram elements (or respectively to UCM, MSC, and SDL model elements). Subtyping relationships such as extensions and reductions, together with role-based projections, enable the efficient comparison between desired collaboration behavior and available services and components. Semantic interfaces can support service selection but also more advanced discovery functionalities such as role learning.

The telephony example used here illustrates in simple terms the description and selection mechanisms. However, applications for such technology are not limited to telecommunication. We anticipate practical use in many convergent services, where information technology services and telecommunication services unite (such as Web services and grid services, applied to many vertical domains).

Due to the well-defined projection relationship between component behavior and semantic interfaces, it is possible to provide tool support for deriving semantic interfaces, and for checking compatibility between semantic interfaces and component behaviors. We have developed prototype tools to demonstrate this. Rather than being an additional burden for the service engineer, semantic interfaces may be integrated into the service engineering process in ways that can support both productivity and quality. Scalability of the approach follows from the relative simplicity and compositional nature of the compatibility checks needed among component instances. These checks can be limited to checking compatibility among semantic interfaces, which may be pre-calculated for component types and interface types at design time.

Service discovery as outlined here relies on well-defined interface names and maps over inheritance relations between semantic interfaces. It also relies on a common understanding of goals and the relationship between goals, services and service features. One way to achieve this would be to define a suitable ontology over goals, services, and features, using approaches suggested in the semantic Web community [15]. In order to enable service discovery across different service providers, this ontology must be shared. We plan to investigate how emerging standards like the Web Ontology Language (OWL) [18] could improve the description of semantic interfaces and be used to allow matches across different domains.

References

1. Abadi, M. and Lamport, L.: Conjoining specifications. ACM Transactions on Programming Languages & Systems, vol.17, no.3, May 1995, 507-534.
2. Black, A., Hutchinson, N., Jul, E., Levy, H., and Carter, L.: Distribution and Abstract Types in Emerald. IEEE Trans. on Software Engineering, Vol. SE-13, no. 1, January 1987, 65–76.
3. Bettstetter, C. and Renner, C.: A Comparison of Service Discovery Protocols and Implementation of the Service Location Protocol. Proc. EUNICE Open European Summer School, Twente, Netherlands, Sept 13-15, 2000.
4. Bræk, R., Husa, K.E., and Melby, G.: ServiceFrame: WhitePaper. Ericsson Norarc, 2002.
   http://www.item.ntnu.no/lab/nettint1/ServiceFrame/ServiceFrame.html
5. Bræk, R. and Haugen, Ø.: Engineering Real Time Systems. An Object Oriented Methodology using SDL. Hemel Hempstead, Prentice Hall, 1993.
6. Brinksma, E. and Scollo, G.: LOTOS specifications, their implementations and their tests. Protocol Specification, Testing and Verification VI (IFIP Workshop), Montreal, 1986, North Holland, 349–360.
7. Drissi, J. and Bochmann, G.v.: Submodule construction tool. M. Mohammadian (Ed.), Proc. Int. Conf. on Computational Intelligence for Modelling, Control and Automation, Vienna, Feb. 1999, IOS Press, 319–324.
8. Floch, J.: Towards Plug-and-Play Services: Design and Validation using Roles. Ph.D. thesis 2003:47 NTNU, Norway, 2003.
9. Gouda, M.G. and Yu, Y.-T.: Synthesis of communicating Finite State Machines with guaranteed progress. IEEE Trans. on Communications, vol. 32, No. 7, July 1984, 779–788.
10. Hopcroft, J.E., and Ullman, J.D.: Introduction to Automata Theory, Languages, and Computation. Addison-Wesley Publishing Company, 1979.
11. Lynch, N.A. and Tuttle, M.R.: An introduction to input/output automata. CWI Quarterly, 2(3), 1989, 219–246.

12. Melby, G. and Bræk, R.: Delivery of convergent telecommunication services on J2EE platforms. Int. Conf. on Intelligence in Service Delivery Networks, ICIN, Bordeaux, France, October 2004.
13. OASIS: Universal Description Discovery & Integration (UDDI), Version 3.02, February 2005. http://www.oasis-open.org/committees/uddi-spec
14. OMG: UML 2.0 specifications. http://www.omg.org/uml
15. Paolucci, M., Kawamura, T., Payne, T.R., and Sycara, K.P.: Semantic Matching of Web Services Capabilities. I. Horrocks, J.A. Hendler (Eds.): The Semantic Web-ISWC 2002, First International Semantic Web Conference, Sardinia, Italy, June 9-12, 2002, Proceedings. Lecture Notes in Computer Science 2342, Springer 2002, 333–347
16. Singh, M.P. and Huhns, M.N.: Service-Oriented Computing: Semantics, Processes, Agents. John Wiley & Sons, 2005.
17. World Wide Web Consortium: Web Services Description Language (WSDL) 1.1. March 2001. http://www.w3.org/TR/wsdl
18. World Wide Web Consortium: Web Ontology Language (OWL). February 2004. http://www.w3.org/2004/OWL/

$ns+$SDL – The Network Simulator for SDL Systems

Thomas Kuhn, Alexander Geraldy, Reinhard Gotzhein,
and Florian Rothländer

Networked Systems Group, University of Kaiserslautern,
Postfach 3049, 67653 Kaiserslautern, Germany
{kuhn, geraldy, gotzhein, f_rothla}@informatik.uni-kl.de

Abstract. Today, simulators for the performance evaluation of networked systems are seldom integrated with tool environments used for system development and maintenance. This requires the system developer to establish and maintain separate code bases for simulation and production purposes, a tedious and error-prone task. In this paper, we present $ns+$SDL, an extension of the network simulator ns-2 to combine SDL design specifications with ns-2 network models. $ns+$SDL enables the developer to use SDL design specifications as a common base for the generation of simulation and production code. Furthermore, the same SDL-to-C code generator is used to generate this code. Both measures increase confidence that the results of the performance evaluation hold for the networked system in operation. Another important aspect is the composition of SDL systems and existing ns-2 simulation components, in particular, components implementing detailed timed models of existing communication technologies. We illustrate the application of $ns+$SDL by a simulation of DSDV, the Destination-Sequenced Distance-Vector routing protocol, over WLAN.

1 Introduction

A crucial part of any system development is the evaluation of the system's performance, for instance, by regarding throughput and delays in a variety of typical execution scenarios. This is especially relevant for the assessment and comparison of networked systems, or protocol mechanisms such as routing and quality of service provision. In many cases, performance evaluation is achieved through simulation experiments, which requires a suitable simulation tool environment.

Today, system development is based on formal design languages such as SDL [5], and tool support for the creation, maintenance, validation and automatic implementation of system designs, as in the TAU environment [8]. With these tools, the functional behaviour of the specified system can be analyzed. To assess system performance, additional tool support is used. Existing simulators such as the network simulator ns-2 [9] require the developer to extend the code base of the simulator by an implementation of the system that is to be evaluated. As these simulators are often not integrated with existing tools for

A. Prinz, R. Reed, and J. Reed (Eds.): SDL 2005, LNCS 3530, pp. 103–116, 2005.

the generation of production code from system designs, system implementations have to be hand-coded. This has the following drawbacks:

- Hand-coding for simulation purposes substantially adds to the overall development effort, and is error-prone.
- The fact that the simulation code is different from the production code reduces confidence that the results of the performance evaluation hold for the system in operation.
- System design, production code and simulation code have to be kept consistent both during system development and system maintenance, which is extremely difficult under the tight time constraints in practice.

In this paper, we present a solution that builds on SDL design specifications as a common code base for simulation and production purposes. From this code base, C code is automatically generated, using the mature SDL-to-C code generator Cadvanced of the TAU environment [8]. Since the same code generator is used for generating simulation and production code, it can be expected that the results of the performance evaluation faithfully reflect the behaviour of the system in operation.

To use this generated code for performance simulations, we have devised and implemented several extensions to the network simulator *ns*-2, a well-known and freely available simulation environment. The *ns*-2 library already contains simulation components modelling the timing behaviour of existing communication technologies, such as WLAN. If it can be assumed that the system performance is determined by its underlying communication technology so that processing capacity is not a bottleneck, the performance of higher level protocols and networked applications, functionally specified with SDL, can be studied. When combined with a suitable SDL environment package that supports the complete interface of *ns*+SDL, all system nodes may use their own configuration and log files. The SDL Environment Framework introduced in section 3 provides this capability. With this support, the effort required for performance simulations of networked systems is substantially reduced. Especially when systems are developed incrementally, the simulation support of *ns*+SDL is a valuable addition to existing tool chains.

At Humboldt University Berlin, the SDL Integrated Tool Environment (SITE) with compiler components for the target languages C++ and Java is being developed [6]. Additional tool support for the simulation of SDL systems based on code generation with SITE is described in [1]. A drawback here is that compiler components such as code generation are "not published because of stability, insufficient documentation and project-specific licensing" (see [6]). Also, only self-contained SDL systems can currently be simulated, excluding, for instance, the simulation and fine-grained control of multiple SDL systems communicating via an external network simulator, or the use of simulation components from different sources.

Recently, a tool environment for performance simulations based on SDL specifications has been developed at the University of Aachen [2, 7]. This environment consists of the SDL Performance Evaluation Tool Class Library (SPEETCL), the

SDL-to-C++ compiler SDL2SPEETCL for the generation of simulation code, and the Graphical Interactive Simulation result Tool (GIST). When applied together with the TAU environment, SDL design specifications can serve as a common code base for the generation of simulation and production code. A drawback is that since the compilers used for generating simulation and production code are different, the degree of confidence that the results of the performance evaluation hold for the system in operation is reduced.

The rest of this paper is organized as follows. In section 2, the basics of the network simulator *ns*-2 are briefly surveyed. In section 3, we present the structure and operation of *ns*+SDL, the network simulator for SDL systems. We illustrate the application of *ns*+SDL to simulate DSDV, the Destination-Sequenced Distance-Vector routing protocol, over WLAN in section 4 and present conclusions in section 5.

2 The Network Simulator *ns*-2

For the simulation of computer networks, in particular, TCP, routing, and multicast protocols over wired and wireless networks, the network simulator *ns*-2 has been developed at the Information Sciences Institute of the University of Southern California [9]. The source code of *ns*-2 is freely available under the terms of a BSD style license. *ns*-2 is an event-based simulator, consisting of a simulation framework and a set of simulation components that can be configured in a flexible way, yielding an executable simulation system. The simulation framework is structured into the *ns scheduler*, a set of configurable *ns nodes* and a library of predefined components. Figure 1 gives an overview on the structure of typical *ns*-2 simulations.

As shown in fig. 1, every *ns*-2 simulation consists of a global *ns scheduler*, multiple *ns nodes* and *ns links* between them. The typical components of an *ns node* are an *ns agent*, a simulated application, routing functionality, a link layer, and the simulated network adapter(s) (Mac/Phy Layer). Most of these compo-

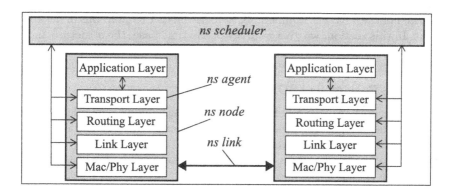

Fig. 1. Simplified structure of the *ns*-2 simulations

nents must be contained in every *ns node*; however, it is possible to implement them without any functionality, for example, if routing is not required in a given simulation. *ns-2* ships with a large library that already contains components covering a large variety of simulation scenarios.

The global *ns scheduler* controls all events during a simulation. Two types of events can be distinguished. First, there are prescheduled events, which are read from a user provided tcl script during simulation. Second, internal events such as the reception of packets from the network are generated during simulation runs. To simplify the use of the *ns scheduler* for developers of *ns components*, *ns timers* can be used to wrap the scheduler interface, providing a more flexible, object oriented interface.

Each *ns node* contains one or more protocol stacks. In the application layer, communication traffic according to specific application profiles is generated. So-called *ns agents* are responsible for providing the functionality of higher level protocols, whereas the lower layer protocols are combined into the *ns link layer*. Originally, *ns links* were introduced to model the different types of physical links between nodes in a wired network. In the case of wireless communication, a component representing the virtual broadcast medium is used instead of *ns links*.

Currently, simulator components for many possible scenarios and technologies are available, including wired and wireless LAN (IEEE 802.3, IEEE 802.11), routing mechanisms (DSDV, AODV, TORA), transport protocols (TCP, UDP), and simulated applications. By composing these components in different ways, a large variety of scenarios can be obtained. The composition is defined in a tcl script that controls the entire simulation. Besides configuring the simulation components, the tcl script also contains all prescheduled events such as movement patterns and the control of specific applications.

3   Time Base, Structure and Operation of *ns*+SDL

ns+SDL, the *network simulator for SDL systems*, is an extension of *ns-2* that enables developers to use code generated by the mature SDL-to-C code generator Cadvanced of the TAU environment [8] for performance simulations of networked systems. In this section, we give a survey of the time base, the structure and the operation of *ns*+SDL.

3.1   Time Base of *ns*+SDL

ns-2 supports both real-time and simulation-time scheduling of simulation events. Real-time scheduling is preferable when the system under simulation is incorporated into an environment that consists of real applications and/or physical communication networks. In cases where this is not feasible, for instance, if the system under simulation is too complex to be simulated under real-time constraints or a physical environment is not required, the simulation-time scheduler of *ns-2* can be used. A drawback is that *ns-2* components for the simulation of the environment (such as traffic generators or detailed simulation models) have to be supplied, which adds to the development effort and requires calibration experiments to achieve a high degree of confidence into the simulation results. On the other hand, simulation-time scheduling enables full control of simulations, which become reproducible.

As *ns*-2, *ns*+SDL offers both real-time and simulation-time scheduling, the latter being the default. The choice is made by the system developer when providing the tcl script controlling the simulation run. Since SDL assumes a global time, a common time base for all simulation components has to be supported. *ns*+SDL synchronizes the time of *ns*-2 (either simulation-time or real-time) with the time of all SDL systems that form part of a simulation. Details on how this synchronization is achieved are given in section 3.3.

3.2   Structure of *ns*+SDL

ns+SDL is an extension of the network simulator *ns*-2 that supports performance simulations of networked systems based on simulation code generated by TAU Cadvanced. This extension consists of several *ns*-2 simulation components replacing predefined simulation functionalities, an SDL kernel for the interaction between *ns*-2 and an SDL system, and an environment package for SDL systems.

Additional *ns*-2 Modules: The *ns scheduler* assumes the simulation architecture shown in fig. 1, which consists of several protocol layers with individual interfaces. In order to avoid modifications to the scheduler, we have adopted this architecture. Basically, simulation code generated from SDL design specifications can replace each of the *ns components* in each of the protocol layers. For instance, routing code generated from an SDL specification can be incorporated into the routing layer (see fig. 1). This, however, requires that for each layer, an individual interface between the *ns scheduler* and the corresponding SDL simulation code is provided.

Without loss of functionality, we have devised a different solution (see fig. 2). The basic idea is to place all SDL simulation code into the *ns agent*, and to have *ns components* in the protocol layers below. This offers the following flexibility:

- Protocol layers (routing layer, link layer etc.) may be configured from existing simulation components of the *ns*-2 library (see section 2), as usual.
- The code of the upper layers including the application (called *SDL system* in the following) may be generated from an SDL design, and, together with a suitable interface, may replace the *ns agent*.
- If routing protocols are designed with SDL, the generated simulation code can be placed into the SDL system. In this case, a routing layer without any functionality is needed as a placeholder in the actual routing layer. In a similar way, the link layer can be treated.

To implement this solution, we have developed the following *ns* modules (see fig. 2) and have added them to the *ns* library:

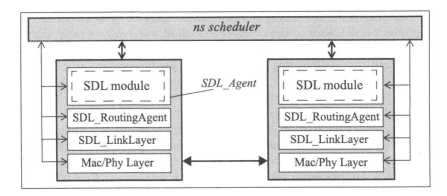

Fig. 2. Simplified structure of simulations with *ns*+SDL

- SDL_Agent: This module replaces the *ns agent* and the simulated application (see fig. 1). When triggered by the *ns scheduler*, it loads the SDL module under simulation.
- SDL_RoutingAgent: This module acts as placeholder, if the routing protocol is part of the SDL system. When triggered by the *ns scheduler* due to the reception of a packet, it forwards the packet to the SDL system.
- SDL_LinkLayer: This module acts as placeholder, if the SDL system under simulation provides a link layer protocol, and ensures that raw data are sent through the network.

The SDL_RoutingAgent and SDL_LinkLayer modules bypass *ns-2*'s strict treatment of connections. The original version of *ns-2* requires all connections to be established from within the tcl script. With the additional modules, the SDL system may set up connections dynamically. Since for *ns-2*, SDL systems appear as simulated applications, the developer may specify functionalities in SDL that otherwise would have to be implemented in C++.

We have implemented further modules that provide suitable abstractions and interfaces to *ns-2* and therefore are of interest for developers:

- Ns2_ExtPart: This module contains the generic functionality to attach external parts to *ns-2*. These external parts may be implemented using any language, as long as the message formats are observed. Currently, only SDL systems use this generic functionality.
- Ns2_ExtAgentPart: This module contains functionality that is specific for attaching external agents to *ns-2*.
- Ns2_Time: This simple module provides an interface to the *ns-2* time base, used by the Ns2_ExtPart module.
- Ns2_Timer: This is a simple *ns-2* timer that is used by Ns2_ExtPart to handle the timer requests from the external (SDL) systems.

The SDL Kernel: SDL modules are structured into an SDL kernel, an SDL environment (see the following section), and the actual SDL system that is generated from the SDL design specification (see fig. 3). The SDL kernel has the following responsibilities:

- Dispatching of SDL transitions: The SDL kernel triggers the transition scheduler, which is already part of the TAU runtime library, and dispatches scheduled transitions.
- Handling of messages between different SDL systems: Message exchange between different SDL systems is controlled by *ns*-2. As part of this message exchange, the SDL kernel provides encoding and decoding functions to and from *ns*-2.
- Handling of control messages: Control messages are exchanged between *ns*-2 and the SDL kernel to, for instance, query the system time or to return control to *ns*-2 after all pending transitions have been executed.
- Time synchronization between *ns*-2 and the SDL system: To support a global time, the time of *ns*-2 is synchronized with the time of all SDL systems under simulation.

To make simulation runs reproducible, concurrent behaviour has to be avoided, which is achieved by two measures. Firstly, the tight synchronization between *ns*-2 and the SDL kernel ensures that only one SDL system is executed at any point in time. Secondly, the *ns*-2 scheduler ensures that transitions that are fireable at the same simulation instant, for instance, due to the simultaneous expiration of SDL timers, are executed sequentially (see section 3.3).

The SDL Environment Framework: To implement open SDL systems (systems interacting with their environment), an environment interface satisfying the semantics of the SDL signalling mechanism is needed. When using the TAU tool chain, manual coding steps are required in order to supply this interface (also called *environment functions*). In general, the environment interface depends on a variety of aspects, such as the type of interaction supported by the environment (message passing, method invocation), the interaction formats, and the communication service (connection-oriented, connection-less, addressing). In [4], we have presented *APIgen*, a tool that, based on a set of SDL interfacing patterns, is capable of generating a tailored environment interface for various communication technologies (such as TCP sockets, CAN, UART/TP).

In the context of performance simulations, signal exchange among open SDL systems is via *ns*-2, possibly involving *ns*-2 components of different communication layers (see Figure 2). Instead of extending *APIgen*, we have developed a generic, specification independent environment package called *SDL Environment Framework* that is placed between the SDL system and *ns*+SDL as shown in fig. 3. On the one hand, the SDL Environment Framework supports the SDL signaling mechanism, on the other hand, it plugs into the *ns*+SDL interface. This way, SDL signals can be exchanged between open SDL systems via a network configured from *ns*-2 components. Also, individual configuration and log files for multiple SDL systems can be used, which offers the possibility to define prescheduled events on a node by node basis.

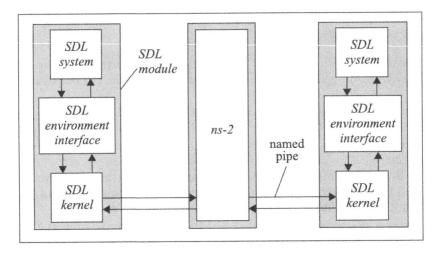

Fig. 3. Interaction between *ns*-2 and SDL systems

The SDL Environment Framework can be configured by using the TAU targeting expert to either interface to the *ns*-2, or to physical hardware. This has the advantage that code for simulation and production purposes can be automatically generated from the same SDL specification, which therefore serves as a common code base, with the same code generator, the TAU Cadvanced SDL-to-C compiler.

3.3   Operation of *ns*+SDL

Simulations consisting of multiple SDL systems and *ns*-2 components are controlled by the *ns scheduler*. A possible configuration is shown in fig. 3, with two SDL modules consisting of SDL kernel, SDL environment interface and SDL system, and the *ns*-2 consisting of *ns scheduler* and possibly further *ns*-2 components.

Loading of SDL modules, which form part of an SDL_Agent (see fig. 2), is controlled by a user provided tcl script. For each SDL module, a new memory context is created. This prevents variables (used for example as input queues) being shared between several SDL systems. However, it also requires other mechanisms for interprocess communication. We are using named pipes for the exchange of signals and commands between SDL modules and the *ns*-2, as shown in fig. 3. Alternatively, sockets could be used for this purpose, but would result in a substantially larger simulation overhead.

After an SDL module has been loaded, the SDL kernel issues a READY message to *ns*-2, signalling that the SDL system under simulation is ready to select and execute transitions. Execution control is passed between *ns*-2 and the SDL system in one of the following ways:

- A control message RUNSYSTEM_REQ is sent to the SDL kernel. This happens, for instance, when a run-command starting the SDL system is read from the tcl script, or if an external SDL signal to the SDL system has arrived (see below). After all enabled transitions have been fired, execution control is returned by a message RUNSYTEM_RSP.
- A control message TIMER_EXPIRED_REQ is sent to the SDL kernel. This happens when a timer event has been previously created by the SDL system (see below), and system time has advanced such that the timer expires. After all enabled transitions have been fired, execution control is returned by a message TIMER_EXPIRED_RSP.

While execution control is with an SDL system, further control messages between the SDL kernel and *ns*-2 may be exchanged. If, for instance, timers are set during a transition, *ns*-2 is notified to create and record a corresponding timer event. Also, signals of the SDL system under simulation to its environment are forwarded to *ns*-2 via the SDL kernel:

- querying the current system time
  Before the execution of a transition, the SDL system queries the current system time. The code for this query is automatically generated by Cadvanced during compilation of the SDL specification. To support a common time base, the request is forwarded to *ns*-2 by means of a GET_TIME_REQ message, which returns a GET_TIME_RSP message carrying the current system time. This way, global time as required by SDL is effectively realized.
- setting and resetting timer events
  After all enabled transitions have been executed, the SDL system determines the next expiration time of all currently active timers. The code for these computations is automatically generated by Cadvanced. If there is an active timer, the next expiration time is forwarded to *ns*-2 by means of a SET_TIMER_REQ message. On reception of this message, *ns*-2 creates a timer event, adds it to the event list, and returns a handle to the timer event by sending a SET_TIMER_RSP message. This handle is used by the SDL system in cases when the timer event needs to be cancelled due to a reset. Cancellation of timer events is done by a RESET_TIMER_REQ, followed by a RESET_TIMER_RSP.
- signal output to the environment
  If an SDL signal is sent to the environment, for instance, to another SDL system via a simulated network, the SDL environment forwards it to the SDL kernel. The kernel in turn issues a SIGNAL_OUTPUT_REQ carrying the signal as parameter to *ns*-2, which, after recording the signal in the event list, returns a SIGNAL_OUTPUT_RSP. Execution control remains with the SDL system until all enabled transitions have been fired. Delivery of the SDL signal is then controlled by *ns*-2.
- signal reception from the environment
  Signal events trigger the delivery of SDL signals that have previously been sent to the environment. Delivery is controlled by *ns*-2, by issuing a

SIGNAL_DELIVERY_REQ carrying the signal as parameter. The SDL kernel forwards the signal to the SDL system and returns a signal called SIGNAL_DELIVERY_RSP.

4   Application of *ns*+SDL to Evaluate the Performance of DSDV over WLAN

To illustrate the use of *ns*+SDL, we evaluate the performance of DSDV, the Destination-Sequenced Distance-Vector routing protocol for mobile networks [3], over WLAN. We start with an overview of DSDV and the structure of the SDL specification used as code base. Then, we explain the simulation scenario, and present some simulation results.

4.1   The DSDV Routing Protocol

DSDV, the Destination-Sequenced Distance-Vector protocol [3], is a routing protocol especially focused on mobile ad-hoc networks. It is assumed that each

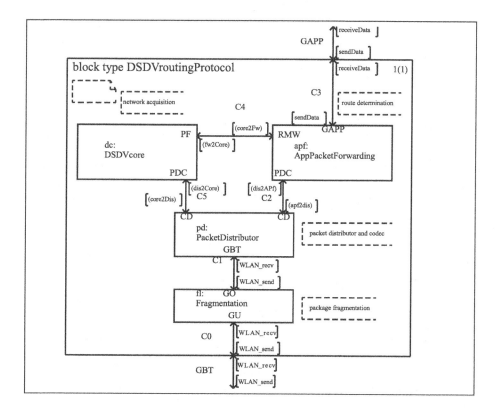

Fig. 4. SDL structure of the routing layer

mobile host, while running its applications, also serves as a specialized router. DSDV builds on an aggregated network status given by a distance vector, such as the Bellman-Ford mechanism, which is periodically shared with the immediate neighbors. Each routing entry is tagged by a sequence number that originates from the destination node (hence the name of the protocol). A mechanism based on this sequence number is used to prevent routing loops and the count-to-infinity problem.

DSDV is a proactive routing protocol, which means that the network status is determined and maintained regardless of the existence of route requests. This leads to a fixed amount of network traffic for routing management purposes. Each DSDV protocol instance periodically (for example every 15 seconds) broadcasts its complete routing table to its local neighbors (called *full dump*). Additionally, it may broadcast a subset of the routing table, for instance, new or modified entries, depending on their importance, at any time (called *incremental dump*).

As mentioned in section 2, *ns*-2 already contains a DSDV component, which may be used for performance simulations. However, to obtain a common code base, we have specified DSDV with SDL. As shown in fig. 4, we have decomposed the instances of the DSDV routing protocol into four SDL blocks. DSDVcore determines, records and maintains the network status. AppPacketForwarding sends and receives PDUs from and to the application layer. PacketDistributor performs encoding and decoding of PDUs, and associates incoming packets with SDL processes. Finally, Fragmentation segments and reassembles packets transmitted via the local network. To encode and decode data transmitted via the local network, we use ASN.1.

4.2   Overview of the System Under Simulation

In the simulation, the performance of DSDV in a lecture hall scenario with 400 students is evaluated. Each student carries his own WLAN device, forming a stationary node of the resulting network. We assume that in this scenario, all nodes are within reach of each other. DSDV is used to establish multi-hop routing within an ambient network covering a broader range, say, the university campus.

Each system node runs a DSDV protocol instance, and optionally, a simulated application. Depending on the type of a node, a CBR (constant bit rate) traffic generator or a receiving application is added on top of the protocol stack. In fig. 5, an excerpt of the system topology illustrating the different node types is shown. All nodes communicate via wireless LAN, and use DSDV for packet routing. Nodes without an application component are available for routing purposes.

The shaded parts of fig. 5 represent the SDL_Agents, i.e., those parts of the simulation that take the place of *ns agents* in the simulation (see figs. 1 and 2). Link layer, MAC layer and PHY layer are simulated by *ns components*. For the simulation of wireless networks following the IEEE 802.11 standard (WLAN), we have devised and calibrated a new *ns component*. This component is a more accurate model of the WLAN standard and has been used in the performance simulations described in the following section.

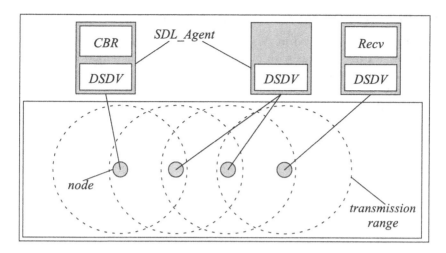

Fig. 5. Simulating DSDV: node types

```
for { set i 0} { $i < $val(nn)} {incr i} {
        # Create SDL agent
        set sdl_agt($i) [new Agent/SDL]
        $ns_ attach−agent $node_($i) $sdl_agt($i)

        # Forward all incoming traffic to the SDL agent
        set p [$node_($i) set dmux_]
        $p defaulttarget $sdl_agt($i)

        # Load the SDL system
        $ns_ at 1.0 "$sdl_agt($i) loadSDL ./dsdv_sdl"
        $ns_ at 1.1 "$sdl_agt($i) setLogFile dsdv_log_$genlog"
        $ns_ at 1.1 "$sdl_agt($i) setCfgFile dsdv_cfg_$gencfg"

        # Start the SDL system
        $ns_ at 1.2 "$sdl_agt($i) run"
}
```

Fig. 6. Sample tcl script (excerpt)

To obtain tcl scripts and traffic patterns, we have applied generation techniques. fig. 6 shows an excerpt of a tcl script, where for every node, an SDL agent is created and initialized. *ns*-2 is requested to load the SDL system dsdv_sdl. For every SDL system, a configuration file and a log file are set. After all SDL systems have been loaded, the tcl command run is executed at simulation time 1.2, passing execution control to the SDL kernel (see section 3.3).

4.3   Results of the Performance Evaluation

In the simulations discussed in this section, we have analyzed the scalability of DSDV over WLAN in areas with many visible nodes. The period for full dumps has been set to 15 seconds. To achieve an equal distribution of full dumps, we have equally spread the starting of nodes over this period.

Figure 7 shows started nodes in relation to known neighbors. All nodes broadcast their address during startup. Without bandwidth limitations, the number of known neighbor nodes should equal the number of started nodes. Figure 7 indicates that when placed on top of WLAN, the management traffic generated by DSDV quickly absorbs the available resources. The effect is that the number of known neighbors quickly falls behind the number of started nodes.

As shown in fig. 8, the amount of received data (inbytes) increases with the offered routing traffic (outbytes) for about 4 seconds, and then drops to approximately 30.000 bytes per second. This is a clear sign for an overloaded medium, an indication that DSDV is not well suited for the simulated environment. Since the network is already overloaded with the protocol traffic generated by DSDV, there are no capacities remaining for the application layer.

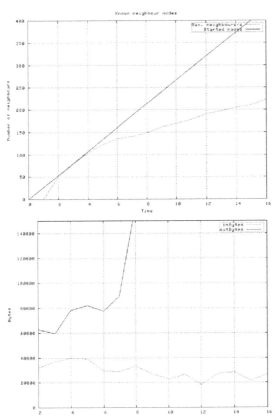

Fig. 7. Started nodes versus known neighbors

Fig. 8. Received traffic versus attempted sending traffic

5   Conclusions

In this paper, we have presented *ns*+SDL, an extension to the well-known network simulator *ns*-2 to combine SDL design specifications with *ns*-2 network models. *ns*+SDL enables the developer to use SDL design specifications as a common code base for the automatic generation of simulation and production code. This substantially reduces the effort required for performance simulations of networked systems, as hand-coding for simulation purposes is avoided. Furthermore, with TAU Cadvanced, the same SDL-to-C code generator for simulation and production code is used. This boosts confidence that the results of the performance evaluation faithfully reflect the behaviour of the networked system in operation.

ns+SDL is fully compatible with *ns*-2, since no modifications other than extensions have been made. This enables the system developer to use all features of *ns*-2 when configuring and simulating networked systems. In addition, individual protocol layers may be replaced by implementations obtained from state-of-the-practice development tools in a flexible and fine-grained way. For instance, it is possible to load and simulate multiple SDL systems, and to link them to *ns*-2 simulation components, in particular, components implementing detailed timed models of existing communication technologies. In combination with the SDL Environment Framework, all system nodes may use their own configuration and log files, to define, for instance, different network topologies, communication technologies and movement patterns (in case of a mobile network). To illustrate the features of *ns*+SDL, we have specified DSDV, the Destinations-Sequenced Distance Vector routing protocol, and made a performance evaluation on top of a simulated wireless LAN.

References

1. N. Fischbeck, M. von Löwis: Simulating SDL using SITE, 9th European Simulation Symposium and Exhibition Simulation in Industry, 1997
2. M. Lott, B. Walke: Performance Analysis of a Wireless Ad hoc Network with QoS Support, Telecommunication Systems, Vol. 16 (1–2), 2001, pp. 115–134
3. C. E. Perkins, P. Bhagwat: Highly Dynamic Destination–Sequenced Distance–Vector Routing (DSDV) for Mobile Computers, ACM SIGCOMM'94 Conference on Communications Architectures, Protocols and Applications, 1994, pp. 234–244
4. P. Schaible, R. Gotzhein: Development of Distributed Systems with SDL by Means of Formalized APIs, 11th International SDL Forum "System Design", LNCS 2708, Springer, 2003, pp. 317–334
5. SDL Forum Society, http://www.sdl–forum.org/
6. SDL Integrated Tool Environment,
   http://www.informatik.hu–berlin.de/Themen/SITE/site.html.en
7. SPEETCL, http://www.aixcom.com/Produkte/Speet/Produkt_e.php
8. Telelogic Tau Generation 1, Telelogic,
   http://www.telelogic.com/products/tau/index.cfm
9. The Network Simulator *ns*-2, Information Sciences Institute, University of Southern California, http://www.isi.edu/nsnam/ns/

Semantics of Message Sequence Charts

A.A. Letichevsky[1], J.V. Kapitonova[1], V.P. Kotlyarov[2], V.A. Volkov[1],
A.A. Letichevsky Jr.[1], and T. Weigert[3]

[1] Glushkov Institute of Cybernetics,
National Academy of Science of Ukraine, Kiev, Ukraine
[2] Global Software Group, Motorola ZAO,
St. Petersburg, Russia
[3] Global Software Group, Motorola, Inc.,
Schaumburg, Illinois, USA
thomas.weigert@motorola.com

Abstract. The language of MSC diagrams is widely used for the specification of communicating systems, the design of software and hardware
for real time and reactive systems, and other industrial applications. Often it is used as an abstraction of systems specified in SDL or UML (in
the form of sequence diagrams). In this paper, a novel representation of
the semantics of message sequence charts is described. This formulation
has been developed to enable the implementation of tools aimed at the
verification of requirements for interactive systems. Our definition of the
formal semantics of the language of MSC diagrams relies on the theory of
interaction of agents and environments. This approach helped to simplify
the definition of the semantics in comparison to other approaches based
on highly sophisticated process algebras and it brought the definition of
the semantics closer to possible implementations.

1 Introduction

The language of Message Sequence Charts (MSC diagrams) is widely used for the
development of communicating systems, and for the design of software and hardware for real time and reactive systems [1]. MSC is an asynchronous language
without an explicit notion of time. To enable the development of tools for the
verification of highly reliable systems, a formal semantics of the language which
can be easily implemented must be available. To define the formal semantics of
MSC diagrams, we relied on a new semantic approach based on the theory of
interaction of agents and environments [3, 4, 5]. This approach greatly simplified
the definition of the semantics in comparison to conventional approaches based
on highly sophisticated process algebras, such as that of Reniers [6]. In addition, the definition of our semantics is much closer to possible implementations
and thus simplifies its realization in tools. Moreover, this semantics is easy to
modify and new features can be added easily. For example, we have also developed extensions of this semantics representing timed message sequence charts
and an algorithm for checking time consistency, albeit these are not discussed in
this paper.

A. Prinz, R. Reed, and J. Reed (Eds.): SDL 2005, LNCS 3530, pp. 117–132, 2005.

Our definition is represented in the form of a calculus which defines transitions for an untimed MSC environment. In section 2, we review the theory of agents and environments. Section 3 gives the semantics of MSC diagrams. In section 4 we briefly outline the translation of MSC diagrams to MSC processes. Finally, in section 5, we give an example of computing the meaning of an MSC diagram following the presented semantics.

2   Agents and Environments

MSC diagrams describe interacting entities or *instances*. Mathematically, these entities are represented by means of labeled transition systems with divergence and termination, considered up to bisimilarity. These transition systems, which we shall refer to as *agents*, execute in an environment. *Environments* are agents supplied with an insertion function, which describes the change of the behavior of an environment after inserting an agent into this environment.

2.1   Agents

Agents are objects which can be recognized as separate from other agents and their environment. They can change their internal states and interact with other agents and their environments, performing observable actions. The notion of an agent formalizes such diverse objects as software components, programs, users, clients, servers, active components of distributed knowledge bases, or similar.

Agents with the same behavior are considered as equivalent. The equivalence of agents is characterized in terms of an algebra of behaviors $F(A)$ which is a free continuous algebra (algebra with approximation) with two sorts–actions $a \in A$ and behaviors $u \in F(A)$. The operations of this algebra are non-deterministic choice $u + v$, $u, v \in F(A)$, which is an associative, commutative and idempotent binary operation, and prefixing $a.u \in A$, $a \in A$, $u \in F(A)$. The approximation relation $\sqsubseteq$ on a set of behaviors is a partial order such that these two operations are continuous. The algebra $F(A)$ is closed relative to the limits (least upper bounds) of the ordered sets of finite behaviors. Consequentially, the minimal fixed point theorem can be used for the definitions of infinite behaviors. Finite elements are generated by three termination constants: Δ (successful termination), $\bot$ (the minimal element of the approximation relation), and the deadlock element 0.

Behaviors can be considered as states of a transition system by interpreting a transition $u \xrightarrow{a} u'$ to mean that $u = a.u' + v$ for some behavior v. Compositions described by the various kinds of process algebras (including parallel and sequential composition) can be defined through continuous functions over the behavior of agents. For example, to define parallel composition, an algebraic structure on the set of actions is leveraged to define synchronization operations in the action algebra. In this paper we shall use only interleaving for the definition of parallel composition; thus the set of actions is a flat set (without synchronizing operations).

Each behavior $u \in F(A)$ over an action algebra A can be represented in the form

$$u = \sum_{i \in I} a_i.u_i + \varepsilon$$

where a_i are actions, u_i are behaviors, the set I is a finite or infinite set of indices, and the termination constant ε is either Δ, $\bot$, $\Delta + \bot$, or 0. If all summands in this representation are different, then this representation is unique up to the associativity and commutativity of non-deterministic choice.

2.2   Environments

An *environment* E is an agent over an *algebra of actions* C with an *insertion function*. The insertion function is a function of two arguments written as $e[u]$. The first argument e is a behavior of an environment, the second is a behavior of an agent over an action algebra A in a given state u (the action algebra of agents may be a parameter of the environment, if needed). An insertion function is an arbitrary function continuous in both of its arguments. Its result is a new behavior of the same environment.

Using the notion of an environment, we define a new type of agent equivalence which is in general weaker than bisimilarity: *insertion equivalence* depends on an environment and its insertion function. Two agents (in given states) or behaviors u and v are insertion equivalent with respect to an environment E, written $u \sim_E v$, if for all $e \in E$, $e[u] = e[v]$. After the insertion of an agent into an environment, the new environment is ready to accept new agents to be inserted.

2.3   Insertion Function

To define insertion we use rewriting rules in the algebra of behaviors. Each rule has one of two forms:

$$F(x)[G(y)] \longrightarrow d.F'(z)[G'(z)]$$

and

$$F(x)[G(y)] \longrightarrow F'(z)[G'(z)]$$

where $x = (x_1, x_2, \ldots)$, $y = (y_1, y_2, \ldots)$, $z = (x_1, x_2, \ldots, y_1, y_2, \ldots)$, $x_1, x_2, \ldots,$ $y_1, y_2, \ldots$ are action or behavior variables, $d \in C$ (C is an action algebra), and F, G, F', G' are expressions of a behavior algebra, that is, expressions built by nondeterministic choice and prefixing. The first kind of rule defines labeled transitions, the second kind of rule defines unlabeled transitions. The latter are not observable; the definition of environment behavior includes the following rule

$$\frac{e[u] \overset{*}{\longrightarrow} e'[u'], \; e'[u'] \overset{d}{\longrightarrow} e''[u'']}{e[u] \overset{d}{\longrightarrow} e''[u'']}$$

where $\overset{*}{\longrightarrow}$ denotes the transitive closure of unlabeled transition. Rewrite rules must be left linear with respect to their behavior variables, that is, no behavior variable may occur more than once in the left hand side. We add the obvious rules for terminal and divergent states, as well as the following condition:

$$e[u] \xrightarrow{d} e'[u'], \ v \sqsubseteq u, \ f \sqsubseteq e, \ f[v] \nrightarrow \ \Rightarrow f[v] = \perp$$

where $f[v] \nrightarrow$ means that there are no transitions from the state $f[v]$. Under these conditions, the insertion function defined will be continuous even if there are infinitely many rules. This is because to compute the function $e[u]$ one needs to know only some finite approximations of e and u.

Rewriting rules define a non-deterministic transition relation if two different left hand sides can be matched with the same state of an environment $e[u]$ (critical pairs are allowable).

3 The Environment for MSC Diagrams

An MSC agent corresponds to a set of MSC diagrams; the insertion of an MSC agent into an MSC environment correspond to MSC references, which are the only way to transfer control of execution between different diagrams. The environment itself can be considered as an execution engine for a set of MSC diagrams. It synchronizes the interaction of the agents defined by those MSC diagrams and generates all possible traces for a given set of diagrams. Figure 1 shows a simple MSC diagram: Two instances, A and B, represented by the vertical lines, interact with each other by sending asynchronous messages, indicated by the arrows running between the lines representing the instances. A message is characterized by two events: the sending of the message, and the receiving of the message. Reduced to its bare essentials, an instance is characterized by the sequence of events that occur during its lifetime. Events on an instance line are considered to be temporarily ordered, but no ordering is assumed between events occurring on different instance lines. That is, each instance executes

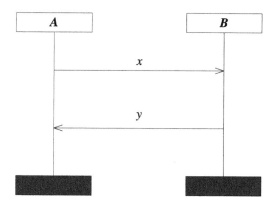

Fig. 1. An MSC diagram

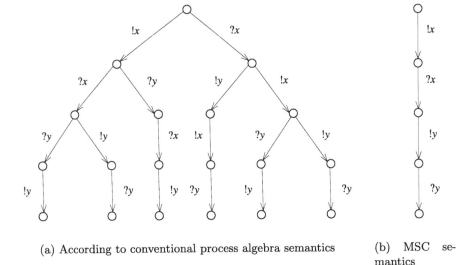

(a) According to conventional process algebra semantics

(b) MSC semantics

Fig. 2. Traces for the MSC diagram in fig. 1

each event on its instance line in the order in which it occurs on the line, from top to bottom. Each instance executes its events independently of any other instance on a diagram. If we label the event of sending message x as $!x$, the receiving of message x as $?x$, and so on, and interpret the diagram in fig. 1 based on ordinary process algebra semantics, then the traces in Figure 2(a) are induced.

However, an MSC diagram describes the transitive closure of the orderings between the events, subject to the constraints that a message must be sent before it is received. Consequentially, the explication of the semantics of MSC diagrams must yield the single trace shown in fig. 2(b) as the meaning of the MSC of fig. 1. (An MSC diagram may contain events other than message interactions, and there are special constructs which remove the ordering constraint for an instance line, which are discussed below.)

The doctoral thesis of M.A. Reniers [6] which is based on the Algebra of Communicated Processes [7] is probably the best known explication of the semantics of MSC. Reniers defined the operators of his algebra operationally in the style of [8]. He introduced the following operators to capture the semantics of MSC diagrams: Delayed choice expresses the meaning of MSC alternatives, generalized parallel composition allows to combine several instances into a diagram, generalized weak sequential composition gives the vertical composition of events on an instance line, and iteration and unbounded repetition express looping. Altogether, 41 rules are required to specify these operators (and two additional rules for constants). The result is a highly complex semantic description which is very difficult to implement; to our knowledge, no tool has been able to implement Reniers' semantics.

In contrast, our approach begins with the simple set of traces induced by conventional process algebra semantics. Taken by itself, the agent representing the MSC diagram of fig. 1 would generate the traces shown in fig. 2(a). However, we define an environment such that, when the agent is inserted into this environment, only the trace shown in fig. 2(b) is permitted. We call such environments *MSC environment*. After insertion into the MSC environment, the agent derived from fig. 1, $u = !x.?y \,.\, \Delta \,\|\, ?x.!y \,.\, \Delta$, is equivalent to a much simpler agent, $v = !x.?x.!y.?y \,.\, \Delta$. We say that u and v are insertion-equivalent.

In addition, our semantics for MSC is different from the formulation by Reniers in the use of additional synchronization for conditions, references, and in-line expressions.

3.1   The Structure of MSC Environments

To create the environment one must define both the actions of agents and environment and the insertion function. The insertion function will be described through a calculus for the transition relations of the environment. To textually express message sequence charts we rely largely on the event-oriented syntax of MSC defined in the Z.120 standard [1], as shown in Figure 3.

In Figure 3, i and j are instance names, J is a set of instance names, m is a message expression, b is an expression describing an action or condition, t is a timer expression, and z is an MSC reference expression. (The detailed syntax of the expressions is not relevant to this paper. For example: A message expression m may contain parameters describing structural components of the message. A timer expression t may contain a duration. While in MSC conditions and actions are not further interpreted, in many practical applications these are given specific meaning and syntax.) Note that the last two forms are not part of [1] and are not user-visible.

Feature	Textual syntax
Send message	$i :\ m$ **from** j
Receive message	$i :\ m$ **to** j
Local action	$i :$ **action** b
Set timer	$i :$ **set** t
Reset timer	$i :$ **reset** t
Timeout	$i :$ **timeout** t
Instance start	$i :$ **instance**
Instance creation	$i :$ **create** j
Instance stop	$i :$ **stop**
Condition	$J :$ **condition** b
Reference	$J :$ **reference** z
Local condition	$i :$ **cond** $b(J)$
Local reference	$i :$ **ref** $z(J)$

Fig. 3. MSC textual syntax

We assume, without loss in generality, that all names used in an MSC diagram are distinct. Each instance is executing in the context of an agent deriving from an MSC diagram. If i is an instance, **agent**(i) is the agent executing this instance. Each event belongs to some instance, and if a is an event, then **inst**(a) denotes the instance to which this event belongs.

Message events represent communication events in the system: Instances may receive messages, or they may send messages to other instances. The names **lost** and **found** are always-defined instance names to allow representation of incomplete events: A lost message is a message that is sent but will never be received by another instance. A found message is a message where the sender is unknown. The name **env** is always defined and refers to the environment of the instance containing this event; messages may be send to the environment or may be received from the environment.

Local events do not impact other instances. They may describe arbitrary, not further defined actions, the setting or expiration of timers, as well as timer resets.

Instance events describe the life-time of an instance. An instance may be created by another instance, and an instance may stop its execution. The start of a sequence of events belonging to an instance is indicated by the instance start event.

Control events synchronize conditions and references across a set of instances. These events are not observable from the outside environment and establish that events preceding a condition or reference on a given instance have completed. In [1], control events are represented as "multi-instance events", while we represent the occurrence of a control event on each instance as a separate event (referred to as *local condition* and *local reference* in fig. 3; the conversion from multi-instance events to local events is performed by the translation rules in section 4). The set of instances J indicates all instances that are synchronized by this control event, where each instance $i \in J$.

Due to space limitations, in the following discussion gates and causal orderings are not considered, but the corresponding extensions are straightforward.

Note that while [1] speaks of instances as comprised of a partially ordered sequence of events, in the explication of the semantics of message sequence charts we will speak of sequences of actions (to remain consistent with the terminology of process algebra). We shall use the terms "event" and "action" interchangeably, when there is no danger of confusion.

Agents are composed from actions (events) by the standard algebraic operations (such as prefixing, sequential and parallel compositions, or non-deterministic choice), considered up to bisimilarity. The transition rules for these operations are as usual, but parallel composition is interpreted as interleaving.

Using this syntax, we can express the instance A in fig. 1 as

$$A : \textbf{instance} . A : x \textbf{ to } B . A : y \textbf{ from } B . A : \textbf{stop} . \Delta$$

and the instance B as

$$B : \textbf{instance} . B : x \textbf{ from } A . B : y \textbf{ to } A . B : \textbf{stop} . \Delta$$

The environment states of an MSC environment will be represented by the tuple of functions $\langle \mathcal{O}, \mathcal{S}, \mathcal{R}, \mathcal{U} \rangle$.

$\mathcal{O}$ is a partial function of three arguments m, i, j, where m is a message expression, and i and j are instances. This function yields values in the set of positive integers. $\mathcal{O}(m, i, j) = k$ means that earlier k message events $i : m$ **to** j occurred for which there are no corresponding receiving message events pending. (If $\mathcal{O}(m, i, j)$ is undefined, there are no in message events pending.)

$\mathcal{S}$ is a partial function of two arguments y and J. The first argument is a condition or reference expression, the second is a set of instances. $\mathcal{S}(y, J)$ represents a nonempty subset of the set J. $\mathcal{S}(y, J) = I$ means that earlier a control event $i : \mathbf{cond}\ y(J)$ or a reference event $i : \mathbf{ref}\ y(J)$ had been executed, for all instances $i \in I$. The condition or reference event is attached to all instances in J. In other words, $\mathcal{S}(y, J)$ is the set of all instances which have already been synchronized by the condition or reference.

$\mathcal{R}$ is a partial function from a set of reference names. If $\mathcal{R}(x) = J$, where J is a set of instances, then the agent corresponding to reference expression x attached to the instances in J is currently executing. Several references to the same MSC diagram can be executed at the same time.

$\mathcal{U}$ is a function defined on the set of reference names. $\mathcal{U}(x) = I$ is a set of all instances active in the agent deriving from the MSC diagram denoted by reference expression x. The condition $\mathcal{U}(x) = \emptyset$ is a termination condition for the agent defined by the MSC diagram.

The states of the MSC environment are expressions $e[P]$ where e is an environment state and P is an MSC agent. The insertion function is defined so that $(e[P])[Q] = e[P \parallel Q]$. The environment in a state $e[\Delta]$ is called the empty environment if e is an environment state. Initial states are state expressions $e[P]$ where P is an MSC agent. The set of environment states is restricted to the set of states reachable from the possible initial states. This restriction is consistent with the insertion function, because if $e'[P']$ is reachable from $e[P]$ then $e'[P' \parallel Q]$ is reachable from $e[P \parallel Q]$.

3.2   Insertion Function for MSC Environments

An environment state consists of partial functions; in the following we make extensive use of partial functions transformations: Let f be a partial function, then $\mathrm{Dom}(f)$ denotes the domain of this function. For any x, we write $f(x) = \bot$ if $f(x)$ is not defined – if $x \notin \mathrm{Dom}(f)$. The operator $[x := y]$ transforms f to a new function f' such that for all z, if $z \neq x$, $f'(z) = f(z)$, and $f'(x) = y$. Note that $\mathrm{Dom}(f[x := y]) = \mathrm{Dom}(f) \cup \{x\}$, as x may or may not be in $\mathrm{Dom}(f)$. The operator $[\mathrm{Dom} \backslash E]$ deletes the set E from the domain of f, that is, it transforms f to a new function f' such that $\mathrm{Dom}(f') = \mathrm{Dom}(f) \backslash E$ where f is an extension of f'.

Suspended Instances and Actions

Let $e = \langle \mathcal{O}, \mathcal{S}, \mathcal{R}, \mathcal{U} \rangle$. Instance k is called suspended in environment state e if one of the following conditions is true, for some name y:

1. $k \in \mathcal{S}(y, J)$, where $k \in J$ or
2. $k \in \mathcal{R}(y)$

Suspended instances are synchronized by either a condition or by a reference. Action a is suspended in an environment state e if one of the following conditions is true:

1. $\mathbf{inst}(a)$ is suspended in e,
2. $i = \mathbf{inst}(a)$ and $k \notin \mathcal{R}(\mathbf{agent}(i))$.
3. for some message m and some instances i and j,
    $a = i : m \mathbf{\ from\ } j$ and $\mathcal{O}(m, j, i) \not\succ 0$.

Each reference is invoked from the main diagram or some other uniquely identifiable executing diagram (invoked through another reference). All references are executing in parallel. The following restriction must be satisfied: If an instance i is active in an executing reference x, it must be suspended in all other currently executing references. This restriction will be satisfied if each instance used in the reference is attached to this reference and if an instance that is shared by two references is attached to both.

In the rules below, the environment state for e is $\langle \mathcal{O}, \mathcal{S}, \mathcal{R}, \mathcal{U} \rangle$; the environment state for e' is $\langle \mathcal{O}', \mathcal{S}', \mathcal{R}', \mathcal{U}' \rangle$.

The necessary conditions for the existence of an environment state e' such that $e \xrightarrow{a} e'$ is that action a is not suspended in e. This condition is assumed for all rules below.

General Rules

$$s \longrightarrow e' \Rightarrow e[P] \longrightarrow e'[P] \tag{1}$$

$$e[P + Q] = e[P] + e[Q] \tag{2}$$

$$\frac{e[\Delta] \xrightarrow{a} e'[Q], \ P \xrightarrow{a} P'}{e[P] \xrightarrow{a'} e'[Q \parallel P']} \tag{3}$$

for an observable action a and

$$\frac{e[\Delta] \xrightarrow{a} e'[\Delta], \ P \xrightarrow{a} P'}{e[P] \longrightarrow e'[P']} \tag{4}$$

for a non-observable action. (An action is non-observable if it is an incomplete control action, see below, otherwise an action is observable. Note that the notion of observability depends on the state of the environment.) In rules (3) and (4), we assume that there are no hidden transitions for the environment state $e[\Delta]$. Action a' in (3) is different from a only if a is a control action. In this case, if $a = i : \mathbf{cond}\ y(J)$ or $a = i : \mathbf{ref}\ y(J)$, then the observed action $a' = J : \mathbf{reference}\ y$ or $a' = J : \mathbf{condition}\ y$, respectively.

Rules for Messages and Local Actions

For a non-suspended message action or local action a, the transition

$$e[\Delta] \xrightarrow{a} e'[\Delta]$$

is always possible. Only function $\mathcal{O}$ is changed as a result of this action, as follows:

$$
\left.\begin{array}{l}
a = i: \ \textbf{action } b \\
a = i: \ m \ \textbf{to lost} \\
a = j: \ m \ \textbf{from found}
\end{array}\right\} \Rightarrow \mathcal{O}' = \mathcal{O}
$$

$$
\begin{array}{l}
a = i: \ m \ \textbf{to } j, j \neq \textbf{lost} \Rightarrow \mathcal{O}' = \mathcal{O}[(m, i, j) := n + 1] \\
a = j: \ m \ \textbf{from } i, i \neq \textbf{found} \Rightarrow \mathcal{O}' = \mathcal{O}[(m, i, j) := n - 1]
\end{array}
$$

where $n = 0$ if $\mathcal{O}(m, i, j) = \bot$, otherwise $n = \mathcal{O}(m, i, j)$.

Rules for Instance Actions

For a non-suspended instance action a the transition

$$
e[\Delta] \xrightarrow{a} e'[\Delta]
$$

is possible under the conditions below. Only function $\mathcal{U}$ is changed by this action. Let $x = \textbf{agent}(i)$, where i is an instance, then

$$
\begin{array}{l}
a = i: \ \textbf{instance}, i \notin \mathcal{U}(x) \Rightarrow \mathcal{U}' = \mathcal{U}[x := \mathcal{U}(x) \cup \{i\}] \\
a = i: \ \textbf{create } j, j \notin \mathcal{U}(x) \Rightarrow \mathcal{U}' = \mathcal{U}[x := \mathcal{U}(x) \cup \{j\}] \\
a = i: \ \textbf{stop}, i \in \mathcal{U}(x) \Rightarrow \mathcal{U}' = \mathcal{U}[x := \mathcal{U}(x) \backslash \{j\}]
\end{array}
$$

The cases which are not covered by these conditions are forbidden.

Rules for Control Actions

Finally, consider control actions $i : \textbf{cond } y(J)$ and $i : \textbf{ref } y(J)$, where y is a name. A control action is complete in a state e if $J = \{i\}$ or $\mathcal{S}(y, J) \cup \{i\} = J$. Otherwise the action is incomplete. For a non-suspended incomplete control action a a transition

$$
e[\Delta] \xrightarrow{a} e'[\Delta]
$$

is always possible. Only function $\mathcal{S}$ is changed as follows:

$$
\mathcal{S}' = \mathcal{S}[(y, J) := \mathcal{S}(y, J) \cup \{i\}]
$$

For a complete control action $a = i : \textbf{cond } y(J)$, a transition

$$
e[\Delta] \xrightarrow{a} e'[\Delta]
$$

is always possible, and $\mathcal{S}$ is changed as follows:

$$
\mathcal{S}' = \mathcal{S}[\text{Dom} \backslash (y, J)]
$$

For a complete control action $a = i : \textbf{ref } y(J)$, the transition is

$$
e[\Delta] \xrightarrow{a} e'[Q]
$$

where Q is a new agent derived from the MSC reference expression y. The functions $\mathcal{R}$ and $\mathcal{S}$ are changed as follows:

$\mathcal{R}' = \mathcal{R}[x := J]$, where x is the name of the newly created agent Q
$\mathcal{S}' = \mathcal{S}[\text{Dom}\backslash(y, J)]$

Other functions do not change.

Terminate Reference Execution Rule

The following transition is always possible

$$\mathcal{U}(x) = \emptyset \Rightarrow e[\Delta] \longrightarrow e'[\Delta]$$

Only functions $\mathcal{U}$ and $\mathcal{R}$ are changed when this transition is executed:

$\mathcal{U}' = \mathcal{U}[\text{Dom}\backslash x]$
$\mathcal{R}' = \mathcal{R}[\text{Dom}\backslash x]$

4 Translation of MSC Diagrams to MSC Environment Expressions

Each MSC diagram in a specification is considered and translated individually. The result of a diagram translation is an expression P describing the agent representing the MSC diagram. We begin by translating all HMSC diagrams to the equivalent MSC diagrams involving in-line expressions. Then we can assume that the body of each MSC diagram contains only event definitions. We change all in-line expressions to named reference expressions introducing separate MSC diagrams for the MSC bodies. After this change, the only instance events involving multiple instances are conditions and references.

The condition $i_1, i_2, \ldots$: **condition** y attached to instances i_1, i_2, $\ldots$ is changed to the set of events i_1 : **cond** $y(J)$, i_2 : **cond** $y(J)$, $\ldots$, where $J = \{i_1, i_2, \ldots\}$ and these new events are attached to the corresponding instances i_1, i_2, and so on.

To translate a reference event $i_1, i_2, \ldots$: **reference** y attached to instances i_1, i_2, $\ldots$, where y is an MSC reference expression containing names of the MSC diagrams x_1, x_2, $\ldots$, first translate the diagrams x_1, x_2, $\ldots$ obtaining the set of MSC agents P_1, P_2, $\ldots$, and then compute the function $\mathcal{F}(y, P_1, P_2, \ldots)$ using the definitions shown in fig. 4.

After this translation a name z is used as the name of the new agent resulting from the translation of this diagram by evaluating $\mathcal{F}(y, P_1, P_2, \ldots)$ and each reference event is changed to the set of local events i_1 : **ref** $z(J)$, i_2 : **ref** $z(J)$, $\ldots$, where $J = \{i_1, i_2, \ldots\}$, and these actions are attached to the corresponding instances i_1, i_2, and so on.

The translation of a diagram x without in-line expressions containing only local events on the instances i_1, $i_2, \ldots$, is the agent $p_1 \parallel p_2 \parallel \ldots$, where p_k is a sequential composition of local events belonging to the instance i_k if there are no coregions on this instance. For coregions a parallel composition is used instead of sequential composition. Actions x : **instance** and x : **stop** are added at the beginning and the end of this agent, respectively.

$$\mathcal{F}(\mathbf{loop}\langle m, n\rangle(E), P_1, P_2, \ldots) = \mathbf{loop}(m, n, \mathcal{F}(E, P_1, P_2, \ldots))$$
$$\mathcal{F}(E_1 \ \mathbf{alt} \ E_2 \ \mathbf{alt} \ldots, P_1, P_2, \ldots) = \mathcal{F}(E_1, P_1, P_2, \ldots) + \mathcal{F}(E_2, P_1, P_2, \ldots) + \ldots$$
$$\mathcal{F}(\mathbf{opt} \ E, P_1, P_2, \ldots) = \mathcal{F}(E, P_1, P_2, \ldots) + \Delta$$
$$\mathcal{F}(E_1 \ \mathbf{par} \ E_2 \ \mathbf{par} \ldots, P_1, P_2, \ldots) = \mathcal{F}(E_1, P_1, P_2, \ldots) \parallel \mathcal{F}(E_2, P_1, P_2, \ldots) \parallel \ldots$$
$$\mathcal{F}(E_1 \ \mathbf{seq} \ E_2 \ \mathbf{seq} \ldots, P_1, P_2, \ldots) = \mathcal{F}(E_1, P_1, P_2, \ldots) \ ; \mathcal{F}(E_2, P_1, P_2, \ldots) \ ; \ldots$$
$$\mathcal{F}(\mathbf{exc} \ E, P_1, P_2, \ldots) = (\mathcal{F}(E, P_1, P_2, \ldots) \ ; 0) + \Delta$$
$$\mathcal{F}(x_i, P_1, P_2, \ldots) = P_i$$

$$\mathbf{loop}(0, 0, G) = \Delta$$
$$\mathbf{loop}(0, \mathbf{inf}, G) = (G \ ; \mathbf{loop}(0, \mathbf{inf}, G)) + \Delta$$
$$\mathbf{loop}(m, \mathbf{inf}, G) = (G \ ; \mathbf{loop}(m - 1, \mathbf{inf}, G))$$
$$\mathbf{loop}(0, n, G) = (G \ ; \mathbf{loop}(0, n - 1, G)) + \Delta$$
$$\mathbf{loop}(m, n, G) = (G \ ; \mathbf{loop}(m - 1, n - 1, G))$$

Fig. 4. Translation rules for MSC reference expressions

The names of agents are used to create the initial state e and the environment expression $e[P]$, where P is the translation of the main diagram. If there is no main diagram, the translation is $e[\Delta]$. The function **loop** used above is computed at execution time.

We use strict sequential composition instead of weak sequential composition as it was defined in Reniers' semantics. First, in engineering practice events are usually considered strictly ordered. Secondly, the computation of a weak product has high complexity and is unsolvable for recursive diagrams.

5   Examples

Consider the MSC diagram in fig. 5(a). In algebraic notation, we can express the instances A and B as

$$A = A : \ x \ \mathbf{to} \ B . \Delta$$
$$B = B : \ x \ \mathbf{from} \ A . \Delta$$

To be more precise, A and B begin with an instance start event and end in a stop event, but as these do not impact the examples they are omitted for conciseness.

The semantics of the example MSC is $P = e[A \parallel B]$, that is

$$P = e[A : \ x \ \mathbf{to} \ B . \Delta \parallel B : \ x \ \mathbf{from} \ A . \Delta]$$

We can expand this to

$$P = e[A : \ x \ \mathbf{to} \ B . B : \ x \ \mathbf{from} \ A . \Delta + B : \ x \ \mathbf{from} \ A . A : \ x \ \mathbf{to} \ B . \Delta]$$

which by rule (2) can be rewritten to

$$P = e[A : \ x \ \mathbf{to} \ B . B : \ x \ \mathbf{from} \ A . \Delta]$$
$$+ e[B : \ x \ \mathbf{from} \ A . A : \ x \ \mathbf{to} \ B . \Delta]$$

Now let a be $A : \ x \ \mathbf{to} \ B$. Since this is an output action, and a is not lost, the transition

$$e[\Delta] \xrightarrow{a} e'[\Delta]$$

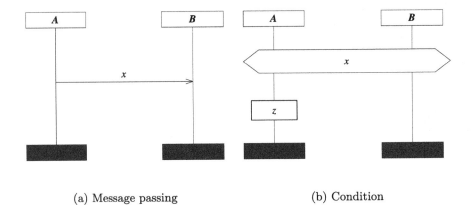

(a) Message passing   (b) Condition

Fig. 5. Two simple MSC diagrams

is always possible. Let Q be Δ, then we can apply rule (3), and obtain

$$P = A: \ x \ \textbf{to} \ B \ . \ e'[\Delta \parallel B: \ x \ \textbf{from} \ A \ . \ \Delta]$$
$$+ \ e[B: \ x \ \textbf{from} \ A \ . \ A: \ x \ \textbf{to} \ B \ . \ \Delta]$$

where e' is obtained from e by setting $\mathcal{O}' = \mathcal{O}[(x, A, B) := 1]$ as given by the rules for message actions. Using the algebraic law $\Delta \parallel P = P$,

$$P = A: \ x \ \textbf{to} \ B \ . \ e'[B: \ x \ \textbf{from} \ A \ . \ \Delta]$$
$$+ \ e[B: \ x \ \textbf{from} \ A \ . \ A: \ x \ \textbf{to} \ B \ . \ \Delta]$$

We can now apply the rule for input actions together with rule (3) and obtain

$$P = A: \ x \ \textbf{to} \ B \ . \ B: \ x \ \textbf{from} \ A \ . \ e''[\Delta]$$
$$+ \ e[B: \ x \ \textbf{from} \ A \ . \ A: \ x \ \textbf{to} \ B \ . \ \Delta]$$

where e'' is obtained from e' by setting $\mathcal{O}'' = \mathcal{O}'[(x, A, B) := 0]$. By $e[\Delta] = \Delta$,

$$P = A: \ x \ \textbf{to} \ B \ . \ B: \ x \ \textbf{from} \ A \ . \ \Delta$$
$$+ \ e[B: \ x \ \textbf{from} \ A \ . \ A: \ x \ \textbf{to} \ B \ . \ \Delta]$$

Note that x is suspended in e, as there is no $(x, A, B) \in \text{Dom}(\mathcal{O})$ such that $\mathcal{O}(x, a, b) > 0$. Therefore, there is no transition possible for the agent state $e[B: \ x \ \textbf{from} \ A \ . \ A: \ x \ \textbf{to} \ B \ . \ \Delta]$, and so $e[B: \ x \ \textbf{from} \ A \ . \ A: \ x \ \textbf{to} \ B \ . \ \Delta] = 0$. Thus we obtain

$$P = A: \ x \ \textbf{to} \ B \ . \ B: \ x \ \textbf{from} \ A \ . \ \Delta + 0$$

and by $P + 0 = P$, we finally arrive at

$$P = A: \ x \ \textbf{to} \ B \ . \ B: \ x \ \textbf{from} \ A \ . \ \Delta$$

In other words, when we insert the agent $A \parallel B$ into the MSC environment, the behavior of that agent is restricted to the one allowed by the MSC semantics: the instance A first sends message x, and then instance B receives this message. The alternative behavior of the agent $A \parallel B$, namely B receiving the message x before A has sent x, is not permitted by the environment.

The MSC diagram in fig. 5(b) is expressed in algebraic notation as

$$A = A : \mathbf{cond}\ x(\{A, B\}) . A : \mathbf{action}\ z . \Delta$$
$$B = B : \mathbf{cond}\ x(\{A, B\}) . \Delta$$

The expanded semantics of this diagram, as rewritten by rule (2) is

$$P = e[A : \mathbf{cond}\ x(\{A, B\}) . A : \mathbf{action}\ z . B : \mathbf{cond}\ x(\{A, B\}) . \Delta]$$
$$+ e[A : \mathbf{cond}\ x(\{A, B\}) . B : \mathbf{cond}\ x(\{A, B\}) . A : \mathbf{action}\ z . \Delta]$$
$$+ e[B : \mathbf{cond}\ x(\{A, B\}) . A : \mathbf{cond}\ x(\{A, B\}) . A : \mathbf{action}\ z . \Delta]$$

If we apply the rule for control actions together with rule (4) to the first summand, we obtain

$$P = e'[A : \mathbf{action}\ z . B : \mathbf{cond}\ x(\{A, B\}) . \Delta]$$
$$+ e[A : \mathbf{cond}\ x(\{A, B\}) . B : \mathbf{cond}\ x(\{A, B\}) . A : \mathbf{action}\ z . \Delta]$$
$$+ e[B : \mathbf{cond}\ x(\{A, B\}) . A : \mathbf{cond}\ x(\{A, B\}) . A : \mathbf{action}\ z . \Delta]$$

where $\mathcal{S}(x, \{A, B\}) = \{A\}$ in e'. Note that this action is not observed, by rule (4). However, now $A \in \mathcal{S}(x, \{A, B\})$, and therefore, A is suspended in environment e, and no further behavior is possible for instance A. If we instead begin with the second summand, we have

$$P = e[A : \mathbf{cond}\ x(\{A, B\}) . A : \mathbf{action}\ z . B : \mathbf{cond}\ x(\{A, B\}) . \Delta]$$
$$+ e'[B : \mathbf{cond}\ x(\{A, B\}) . A : \mathbf{action}\ z . \Delta]$$
$$+ e[B : \mathbf{cond}\ x(\{A, B\}) . A : \mathbf{cond}\ x(\{A, B\}) . A : \mathbf{action}\ z . \Delta]$$

where $\mathcal{S}(x, \{A, B\}) = \{A\}$ in e'. Note that $B : \mathbf{cond}\ x(\{A, B\})$ is complete in state e', and therefore we can transition to

$$P = e[A : \mathbf{cond}\ x(\{A, B\}) . A : \mathbf{action}\ z . B : \mathbf{cond}\ x(\{A, B\}) . \Delta]$$
$$+ A, B : \mathbf{condition}\ x . e''[A : \mathbf{action}\ z . \Delta]$$
$$+ e[B : \mathbf{cond}\ x(\{A, B\}) . A : \mathbf{cond}\ x(\{A, B\}) . A : \mathbf{action}\ z . \Delta]$$

where $\mathcal{S}(x, \{A, B\}) = \emptyset$ in e''. Now we can continue execution with the local action:

$$P = e[A : \mathbf{cond}\ x(\{A, B\}) . A : \mathbf{action}\ z . B : \mathbf{cond}\ x(\{A, B\}) . \Delta]$$
$$+ A, B : \mathbf{condition}\ x . A : \mathbf{action}\ z . e'''[\Delta]$$
$$+ e[B : \mathbf{cond}\ x(\{A, B\}) . A : \mathbf{cond}\ x(\{A, B\}) . A : \mathbf{action}\ z . \Delta]$$

leaving the state of e''' unchanged. Applying the same reasoning to the final summand, and using algebraic laws as in the example above, we determine the meaning of this MSC diagram to be

$$P = A, B : \mathbf{condition}\ x . A : \mathbf{action}\ z . \Delta$$

Again we can see that when we inserted the agent for MSC diagram P, the behaviors not licensed by the MSC semantics have been disallowed.

6 Conclusion

In [9, 10, 11] we have presented an environment to verify the consistency and completeness of behavioral descriptions expressed in the form of message sequence charts. This environment has been deployed for the verification of telecommunications applications and has enabled us to verify systems that have not been amenable to other techniques, such as model checking, due to the large state space induced by the specifications of these systems. In this environment, automated reasoning is performed over the semantic representation of message sequence charts.

In this paper, we explicated the formal semantics of message sequence charts as leveraged in our environment. The use of the semantic representation in tools imposed two constraints on the formal definition: The presentation had to be close to feasible and efficient implementations, as this makes a correct implementation of the semantics more likely. More importantly, the presentation had to be flexible to introduce variations into the semantics with relative ease. Different subject domains require variation in the interpretation of MSC diagrams to account for domain-specific differences. For example, while many telecommunication applications interact with their environment asynchronously, when specifying embedded processors or applications interacting with the system bus, communication is synchronous. While in many situations, the agents comprising a system are executing independently and in parallel, when modeling applications on an embedded operating system, these agents are executing in a sequential environment.

Our experience has taught us that reasoning about these systems is more efficient (which is crucial in light of the large state spaces) when the underlying concurrency semantics and interaction semantics are represented in a manner close to the characteristics of the subject domain. Separating the presentation of the semantics in a small but well-understood process algebra core and the insertion function allowed us to adjust the detailed semantics of a system specification to the actual behavior of the represented systems.

We have further developed a number of extensions to standard message sequence charts. We have added temporal concepts to message sequence charts, such as time intervals between events and the specific timing of events. We have further developed different communication styles between instances of message sequence charts, such as queuing behavior or bounded buffers. By specifying appropriate environments and an insertion function it was straightforward to capture the meaning of these extensions and immediately integrate them in our tools.

We believe that it would have been significantly more difficult to implement our tools on a conventional semantic model, such as the process algebra presentation by Reniers.

References

1. ITU-T. Recommendation Z.120: Message Sequence Charts (MSC). Geneva, October 1996.
2. ITU-T. Recommendation Z.120: Message Sequence Charts (MSC). Geneva, October 2000.
3. A. Letichevsky and D. Gilbert. A general theory of action languages. Cybernetics and System Analysis, 1, 1998.

4. A. Letichevsky and D. Gilbert. A Model for Interaction of Agents and Environments. In D. Bert, C. Choppy, P. Moses, editors. Recent Trends in Algebraic Development Techniques. Lecture Notes in Computer Science 1827, Springer, 1999.

5. A. Letichevsky and D. Gilbert. A Model for Interaction of Agents and Environments. In Selected papers from the 14th International Workshop on Recent Trends in Algebraic Development Techniques. Lecture Notes in Computer Science, 1827, 2004.

6. M.A. Reniers. Message Sequence Charts: Syntax and Semantics. PhD Thesis, Eindhoven University of Technology, June 1999.

7. J.A. Bergstra, A. Ponse, S.A. Smolka, editors. Handbook of Process Algebra. North-Holland, 2001.

8. G.D. Plotkin. A Structural Approach to Operational Semantics. Technical Report, DIAMI FN-19, Aarhus University, 1981.

9. S. Baranov, C. Jervis, V. Kotlyarov, A. Letichevsky, and T. Weigert. Leveraging UML to Deliver Correct Telecom Applications. In L. Lavagno, G. Martin, and B. Selic, editors. UML for Real: Design of Embedded Real-Time Systems. Kluwer Academic Publishers, Amsterdam, 2003.

10. A. Letichevsky, J. Kapitonova, A. Letichevsky Jr., V. Volkov, S. Baranov, V. Kotlyarov, T. Weigert. Basic Protocols, Message Sequence Charts, and the Verification of Requirements Specifications. Computer Networks, 47, forthcoming in 2005.

11. J. Kapitonova, A. Letichevsky, V. Volkov, and T. Weigert. Validation of Embedded Systems. In R. Zurawski, editor. The Embedded Systems Handbook. CRC Press, Miami, forthcoming in 2005.

Compositional Semantics for UML 2.0 Sequence Diagrams Using Petri Nets

Christoph Eichner, Hans Fleischhack, Roland Meyer,
Ulrik Schrimpf, and Christian Stehno

Parallel Systems Group,
Department for Computing Science,
Carl von Ossietzky Universität,
D-26111 Oldenburg, Germany
forename.surname@informatik.uni-oldenburg.de

Abstract. With the introduction of UML 2.0, many improvements to diagrams have been incorporated into the language. Some of the major changes were applied to sequence diagrams, which were enhanced with most of the concepts from ITU-T's Message Sequence Charts, and more. In this paper, we introduce a formal semantics for most concepts of sequence diagrams by means of Petri nets as a formal model. Thus, we are able to express the partially ordered and concurrent behaviour of the diagrams natively within the model. Moreover, the use of coloured high-level Petri nets allows a comprehensive and efficient structure for data types and control elements. The proposed semantics is defined compositionally, based on basic Petri net composition operations.

1   Introduction

The long-standing and successfully applied modelling technique of Message Sequence Charts (MSC) [11] of ITU-T has finally found its way to the most widely applied software modelling framework, the Unified Modelling Language (UML) [18]. In its recent 2.0 version, sequence diagrams (SD, interaction diagram) were enhanced by important control flow features. This change is one of the major differences between UML 1.x and UML 2.0 for interaction diagrams. Most importantly, sequence diagrams may now completely specify a system's behaviour, while former UML versions only provided support for describing exemplary execution sequences.

We describe a Petri net based semantics of most elements of sequence diagrams. The semantics is built compositionally according to the structure of the diagrams. Due to the use of Petri nets as a basic model, the inherent partially ordered structure of sequence diagrams can be captured explicitly in the semantics.

In this paper, time inscriptions in sequence diagrams are not handled by the semantics, neither are object-oriented data structures. However, we define a data access model and show its general capabilities. In an extended version of the semantics we will add support for time features. Additionally, we will

A. Prinz, R. Reed, and J. Reed (Eds.): SDL 2005, LNCS 3530, pp. 133–148, 2005.

equip activity diagrams and interaction overview diagrams with semantics based on the same underlying model to also express object internal behaviour and relationships between different diagrams.

Although verification of the gained semantics would be possible with standard Petri net tools (such as the PEP tool, being developed in the authors' group), the main aspect of the current development is to capture behaviour, and simulate and visualize it. In addition to the translation described in this paper, we are developing an animation environment within the P-UMLaut project [19] capable of linking together 3D objects of the simulated world and entities in the UML model. The 3D world will be animated driven by the Petri net simulation of the semantics.

2   Related Work

Semantics for SDs and MSCs have been investigated for quite a long time. Since UML did not provide a properly defined semantics, most of the early papers on semantics dealt with MSCs.

For the basic UML concepts, the reference is OMG's standard [18], but also a number of good books exists for UML 2.0 (such as [8, 12]). A discussion of the major elements from interaction diagrams can be found in [23].

A thorough examination of MSC-96 regarding all details can be found in [22]. The thesis covers all MSC elements and presents a formal operational semantics. Another approach to define a semantics for MSCs uses pomsets [14].

Due to the inherent non-interleaving semantics of MSCs and SDs, a number of authors chose Petri nets to describe MSC semantics (such as [2, 10, 9, 15]). Most of the papers, however, deal with communication structures only, and abstract from data types to allow verification algorithms to be applied. Due to these restrictions, a number of elements of MSCs become useless and are thus not examined.

A major extension of both the concept of MSCs as well as the concept of SDs has been given as Life Sequence Charts (LSC) in [4]. LSCs introduce new concepts to combine different diagrams and additional elements. The goal is to allow a complete specification of the system's behaviour as well as of system properties within the same model. Although some features of LSCs have been integrated into MSCs and SDs, many aspects of a system can be described much more comprehensively and precisely by using LSCs.

Although object-oriented features are not handled by our semantics, there are solutions for expressing object-orientation by means of Petri nets (see [1, 16]). An integration of some of these concepts into the data handling proposed in this paper will be part of further research.

3   M-Nets – An Algebra of High Level Petri Nets

Petri nets are an easy and intuitively comprehensible visual model with a strong mathematical foundation. Thus, Petri nets, and especially high level Petri nets, have been established as a commonly used model on all levels of formal software engineering and verification (for example see [13, 17, 21, 20]).

The semantics given in this paper is based on the algebra of M-nets (multi-valued nets). The benefits of using M-nets rely on the fact that any M-net is constructed from very simple nets by application of a set of well defined operators. As a consequence, modelling semantics and verification of the semantic models is comparably simple when using M-nets.

An M-net consists of a high level Petri net with the usual inscriptions governing colored token flow and additional inscriptions governing composition and synchronization of nets.

Places are classified as *entry* (no incoming arcs; labeled by $+$), *exit* (no outgoing arcs; labeled by $-$) or *internal* (no restrictions with respect to arcs; no additional label). The composition operators include sequential, choice, and parallel composition and an iteration operator. For example the sequential composition of two nets N_1 and N_2 consists of their juxtaposition, where all exit places of N_1 are combined with all entry places of N_2 using a cross product operation.

Transitions of M-nets are inscribed with a set of (parameterized) synchronous action labels and a set of (parameterized) asynchronous action labels. Synchronous action labels are used for (CCS-like) synchronization and restriction. The combined operation of synchronization followed by restriction is called *scoping* (**sc**).

The asynchronous action labels are subject to the **tie** operator, which links two transitions t_1 and t_2 by inserting a place between both, making occurrence of t_2 dependent on occurrence of t_1.

Handling of a data variable is modeled by a *data box* within the algebra of M-nets. Essentially, a data box consists of a place p containing the actual value of the variable, and a transition t for communicating the actual value or storing a new value. Occurrence of t is usually governed by transitions of the control part of an M-net via synchronization with t.

The scoping and tie operations build up the correct links between data accessing transitions and data boxes and send and receive events, respectively. The effect of applying the **tie** operator can be seen in fig. 1. The data access to variables x and y would be resolved by synchronization over actions $X/2$ and $Y/2$. This would replace a with the current value of x, thus storing a in y while discarding the old value b of y. Since application of these operators is purely

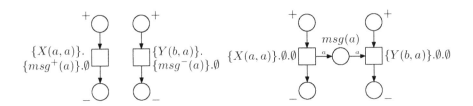

Fig. 1. Message creation with **tie**

technical, we will show throughout the paper only nets where **sc** is omitted and **tie** has already been applied.

For the translation of complete interaction fragments (see section 4.2) the algebra is extended by the new composition operator of *net concatenation*, defined as follows:

Definition 1 (Net Concatenation). *Let $N_3 = N_1 \circ N_2$ be the* concatenation *of two M-nets $N_1 = (P_1, T_1, F_1)$ and $N_2 = (P_2, T_2, F_2)$. Let ^-P be a subset of the exit places of N_1 and ^+P be a subset of the entry places of N_2. The resulting net is defined by $N_3 = (P_3, T_3, F_3)$ with*

$$P_3 = P_1 \cup P_2 \setminus {}^+P$$
$$T_3 = T_1 \cup T_2$$
$$F_3 = F_1 \cup F_2 \setminus \{(p,t) \in F_2 | p \in {}^+P\} \cup \{(p,t) | p \in {}^-P, (h(p), t) \in F_2\}$$

$h : {}^-P \to {}^+P$ *is a bijective mapping on the subsets to be connected that may be arbitrarily chosen.*

A description of M-nets theory with applications to modelling and verification can be found in references such as [3, 5, 7].[1]

4   Translation

In this chapter a mapping $PN : SD \to M-nets$ of UML 2.0 sequence diagrams to M-nets is defined. This paper does not define the semantics of time events (which are not translated in this approach due to a time-free semantical model used), some combined fragment types (which are not applicable due to the different point of view on system specification), or part decomposition. Although part decomposition offers a number of useful features for comprehensible models, and most of these features should be translatable to Petri nets, extra global fragments are intrinsically non-compositional, and thus not implementable in our semantics. An extension of the proposed semantics with non-compositional features including extra global fragments will be part of future work.

4.1   Data Types

Since the semantics given in this paper shall describe the general behaviour of systems, we do not restrict ourselves to interactions describing exemplary execution traces. Thus, parameters given to messages are not necessarily constants, but may refer to attributes and variables found within the scope of the examined interaction.

Handling of data is only sketched in this proposal due to lack of space. However, the semantics for handling data types in communication parameters and

---

[1] At http://www.p-umlaut.de/paper/mnets.pdf a brief introduction to M-nets can be found.

within conditions and invariants is described in such a way that it depends only on a proper mathematical definition of the data domain to incorporate data types other than the proposed boolean and integers.

According to the restricted data types, the syntax of conditions used in the diagrams is defined inductively by

$$cond ::= b_1 \mid b_1 = b_2 \mid x_1 = x_2 \mid \neg cond_1 \mid cond_1 \wedge cond_2 \qquad (1)$$

where b_1, b_2 are variables or values of type **bool**, x_1, x_2 are integer variables or values, and $cond_1, cond_2$ are conditions. Conditions are translated to transition guards, which ensure that firing of a transition is only possible if the condition is satisfied.

The behaviour of method calls in SDs is very similar to those in common programming languages. Each actual parameter of a method defines a variable local to the receiving instance. Such variables may be undefined and will cease to exist after the method has returned. Return values may be stored in previously defined variables and attributes of the caller's scope with UML's own shorthand definition `varname = methodname(parA, parB):RetValue`. Here, the variable `varname` is set to the explicitly given value `RetValue`, which may be a constant or an existing variable.

Thus, parameters only define the way data access has to be scoped and the way values have to be copied to different scopes. A semantics for this context has already been defined in [6, 7]. The idea is to define data boxes with a predefined scope, which handle all access to a distinct variable. While this concept does not provide for object-oriented relations like inheritance, all necessary features, such as instantiation and removal of variables, scoping, call by reference, and undefined values, are covered.

4.2   Compositional Construction

The semantics of an interaction diagram is built bottom-up: composition starts from innermost elements, and incrementally adds surrounding elements on each level of nesting.

To define the semantics, we need to define *maximal independent sets*. These sets contain partial lifelines whose elements are completely unordered with respect to all other contained elements that are not part of the same lifeline. Thus, these lifeline fragments do not need special care for sequentialization. The blocks will be later on glued together using a special concatenation operation.

Definition 2 (Maximal Independent Set). *Let* $\mathcal{L} = \{L_1, \ldots, L_n\}$ *be a set of lifelines. An* independent set *of events ordered by their causal ordering on the lifelines is a set* $\mathcal{I} = \{e_{1,1}, \ldots, e_{1,k}, \ldots, e_{n,1}, \ldots, e_{n,k_n}\}$ *of events of the different lifelines. The projection of* $\mathcal{I}$ *to a single lifeline leads to a set of consecutive elements. A* maximal independent set *(MIS)* has a combined fragment or the diagram border both at its start and at its end.

With this definition, we can find a partition of a sequence diagram into maximal independent sets. This partition is unique and groups partial traces with only messages inside, thus separating unordered parts of the diagrams from parts with orderings imposed by combined fragments.

We will define our Petri net semantics based on maximal independent sets. The resulting nets are incrementally glued together with surrounding combined fragments and other blocks until all parts are grouped into one net.

The semantics of each MIS is defined compositionally and separately for each lifeline that is part of the set. Since we only have EventOccurences inside an MIS, we can give the semantics of one lifeline as the sequential composition of elementary boxes, as defined by the semantics of send and receive events in the next section. All lifelines are put in parallel due to their independent behaviour.

Each MIS is defined such that the first and last events either border start or end of lifelines, or such that all events border the same combined fragment. Thus, the semantics of a complete interaction fragment is defined by concatenating the different blocks with respect to causal ordering imposed by lifelines.

Send and receive events as well as data access inside conditions, actions, and message parameters are only handled by inscriptions of the Petri nets, using action symbols and tie symbols of M-nets. The resulting nets have to be completed in a last step to gain explicit representations of the Petri net semantics.

4.3   Elementary Diagram Elements

Interaction Frames. A sequence diagram is denoted by an interaction frame as shown in fig. 2. The variables par_1 to par_m declared in the diagram header are parameters receiving values while instantiating the frame. Local variables are given as $local_1$ to $local_n$ below the header. They are initialized by the *Init* action which occurs at the beginning of an interaction frame, and are destroyed upon *Term* at the end.

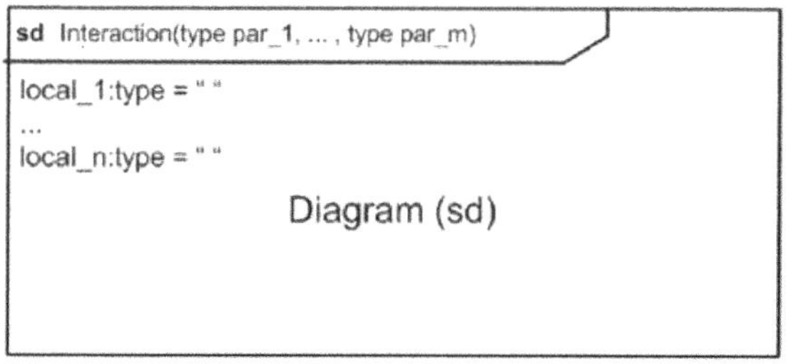

Fig. 2. Interaction frame

Messages are represented in the semantics just by their sending and receiving events. Concrete message representations are created by the **tie** operator when all such events are placed. The semantics of an interaction frame is given by

$$PN(IF) = \left(Init; PN(Diag); Term \parallel \underset{1 \le i \le m}{\parallel} DB(par_i) \parallel \underset{1 \le j \le n}{\parallel} DB(local_j) \right)$$

$$\mathbf{sc}\; act(par_1)\dots\mathbf{sc}\; act(local_n)\mathbf{tie}\; *$$

Lifelines. Lifelines denote the existence of objects during system execution. A lifeline starts with a named or anonymous object of a certain type as represented in fig. 3 (in the example with an additional creation message). Any event of the sequence diagram is connected to one or more lifelines. Lifelines themselves have no explicit semantics, but are represented by their events.

Since lifelines represent objects, object attributes have to be set up at creation time. All lifelines not generated by a creation message are initialized before the first event of each lifeline is handled. To achieve this, an elementary box is created with an initialization action for each attribute of the object. The data boxes for these variables are added to the local variables of the main frame. Initialization is only applied to the outermost interaction frame since diagrams used in reference frames only contain already existing lifelines.

In sequence diagrams new lifelines can be created by others using a *creation message*. The semantics of object creation is similar to that for lifelines starting from the beginning. The only difference is that initialization of attributes occurs when the creation message is received.

Destruction of a lifeline (STOP) is depicted as shown in fig. 4. When a destruction is reached, the corresponding object is deleted. The semantics of stop is given by an elementary box with termination actions for each attribute of the object to destroy the contents of each data box belonging to the object. Destruction of the object itself is implemented by an M-net stop box, which is put in sequence with the data boxes' termination.

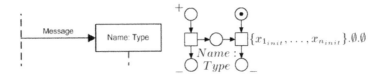

Fig. 3. Object creation

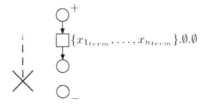

Fig. 4. Object destruction

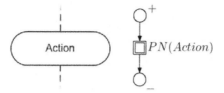

Fig. 5. Action symbol

EventOccurrences and Actions. EventOccurrences and Actions define an active part of the lifeline where (for example) calculations are done. Since these activities are arbitrarily and often not exactly specified, semantics for these elements is only vague. EventOccurrences, denoted as thin rectangles covering the part of the lifeline the activity is running, define a scope. This scope ensures the availability of parameters instantiated by a receive event as part of the EventOccurrence. Thus, local variables instantiated to hold the actual parameters of a message will be destroyed at the end of the EventOccurrence they were received in. EventOccurrences may be nested, such that subscopes may be defined. Scopes are directly related to the **sc** operation of M-nets, which hides all scoped variables. Thus, the semantics of event occurrences consists of creating proper data boxes and applying the **sc** function to all events inside the scope. The instantiation of the data boxes is described in section 4.3.

Action elements describe internal activities of one lifeline at a certain point rather than just the duration. The action need not be specified inside the diagram, but may refer to an Activity Diagram or just use natural language to describe the idea of what is happening inside. Since both alternatives are not translated into Petri nets in this paper, these actions are represented by silent transitions inside the Petri net, i.e. an elementary box without labels as shown in fig. 5. We are, however, working on an Activity diagram semantics which later on can be integrated into the semantics defined in this paper.

The only actions translated to Petri nets in the current semantics are assignments. An assignment action labelled **varname=expression** assigns the variable of the given name the value of the evaluated expression. Therefore, the variable has to be accessible from the current scope and the expression has to evaluate to a value of the data type of that variable. The semantics is defined as an elementary box with appropriate action symbols and the action as guard. For atomic actions at reception of a message, the guard is put to the receiving transition.

Messages. There are five message types in sequence diagrams: *asynchronous messages, synchronous messages, creation messages, lost messages, and found messages.* Messages consist of different parts: the sending event of a message, the sending process (denoted as a named arrow), and the receive event.

The sending event is represented by an elementary box with action symbols for each local variable accessed by the message's parameters. In addition, an export link is added, which will create the message with its actual parameters.

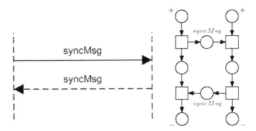

Fig. 6. Synchronous message

Thus, parameters become instantiated, such that only values and not references are sent.

The reception is modelled vice-versa, i.e. the elementary box gets an import link to receive the values of the message place. For parameters, local data boxes are created and initialized by the received values. If the message carries a return value, that value is saved to the local variable given in the assignment of the message.

The semantics of a message before and after applying the **tie** operation is shown in fig. 1. If scoping is also applied, the variables exported by the **tie** operator will be instantiated with actual values from the data boxes.

Synchronous messages, as depicted in fig. 6, consist of two messages. One message initiates the exchange, the second one is the the reply. Control flow in the initiating lifeline is halted until the reply has arrived. Thus, no event is allowed between the send event and its reply. Since this constraint is purely syntactical, the semantics for messages can be applied unchanged.

A *lost message* is a special message without a receive event. Thus, the message does not end on a lifeline. The idea is to have messages without an explicitly specified receiver. The semantics is defined analogously to normal send events. A *found message* is the dual of a lost message. Thus, having matching names, a lost message may be used by a found message's receiving event resulting in a complete message transmission. Since **tie** is applied when all send and receive events have been created, message finding is correctly implemented.

Gates are named points in an interaction frame that may be the source or target of a message. The semantics is equivalent to that of lost and found messages, except that messages are explicitly linked when formal and actual gates are merged during reference replacement.

Fig. 7. Lost and found messages

State Invariants and Continuations. *State invariants* are necessary conditions for further progress of a lifeline. They are denoted similarly to actions but labelled with formulae as defined in (1). They are part of only one lifeline, while continuations cover more than one. Continuations, on the other hand, have just a label as inscription.

State invariants check the truth value of their expression. If it is true, the execution may continue, otherwise the lifeline gets stuck, leading finally to improper termination of the interaction diagram. The semantics is defined by an elementary box with the condition as guard and appropriate action symbols to read all necessary variable values.

There exist two kinds of continuations, which always occur pairwise. A *setting continuation* defines a new global boolean variable set to true. The name of the variable is defined by the label of the continuation. All lifelines synchronize on setting the newly created variable. A non-setting continuation is the dual of a setting continuation in that the lifelines synchronize on reading the boolean value created before by a setting continuation. Only if the value has been set to true, may the lifelines proceed with their execution. The semantics of these elements is defined as the generation of a new anonymous message on a globally accessible place named such as the continuation label. This is achieved by an elementary box similar to the one shown in fig. 8. The box exports the boolean variable to global scope instead of checking a condition, is put in sequence with the end of the combined fragment. Non-setting continuations are implemented by an elementary box importing the variable (that is receiving a message) placed in sequence at the the beginning of the combined fragment.

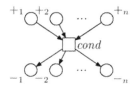

Fig. 8. Delimiting net for combined fragments

4.4   Combined Fragments

With *Combined Fragments*, high level programming constructs may be used in sequence diagrams. Combined fragments are denoted as frames with an operator in the left upper corner and sequence diagram elements inside. The semantics of the diagram depends on the operator. A combined fragment may be built of different operands: that is, separate sequence diagram fragments to which the operator is applied.

Entering a combined fragment, as well as leaving a combined fragment, is considered as an atomic event. In particular, entering a combined fragment has to be done synchronously by all lifelines in the proposed semantics. The rationale for this demand is that otherwise the change of data values might change evaluation of the fragment condition before all lifelines have entered it. Thus, in order to prevent inconsistencies caused by accessing combined fragments only by a subset of all participating lifelines there are two possibilities to interpret combined fragments:

- Either a black box semantics is applied as done in this paper, such that behaviour inside a combined fragment does not interfere with behaviour outside.
- Or the condition has to be evaluated when the first lifeline's execution enters the fragment, and that truth value has to be stored to allow consistent condition evaluation of following lifelines.

The two interpretations seem to respect all constraints of the standard, so the standard might be too imprecise in this case. Both interpretations are however implementable using Petri nets. Due to the artificial introduction of variables and implicit side-effects of the second alternative, we prefer and present the former.

Each combined fragment will thus be prefixed and postfixed sequentially by a net as shown in fig. 8. If a condition is attached to the combined fragment, this condition will be used as the guard of the transition. If more than one operand can be chosen as the first to be executed, a number of such nets might be combined as defined by the operator's semantics. The postfixed transitions do not use guards, as leaving a combined fragment is unconditional.

No semantics are given for *ignore*, *consider*, *neg* and *assert*. Mainly, these types are not considered since they are used for a different application domain of interaction diagrams. The semantics defined in this paper assumes that all behaviour is explicitly specified in the diagrams, such that the mentioned operators do not apply.

Alternative, Optional, and Break Fragments. An *alternative fragment* as given in fig. 9 may have several operands. Each operand has a condition as defined in (1). A special condition `else` can be used as a shorthand for a default operand. If a condition evaluates to true, the diagram fragment is executed and the alternative fragment has finished. If no condition is satisfied the `else` operand is processed. The semantics of an alternative fragment is defined by a choice operation over the semantics of each operand. For the alternative fragment, each operand net itself is prefixed and postfixed by a combined fragment delimiter net as shown in fig. 8. Since the `else` condition is not usable as-is in M-nets, this special condition has to be modelled using a negated disjunction of all other conditions.

In an *optional fragment* a condition indicates whether the (one and only) operand needs to be executed. Optional fragments are equivalent to an alternative fragment with empty `else` operand.

A *break fragment* tests a condition and, if necessary, processes the elements of the break fragment which in turn ends the interaction diagram. If the condition is not satisfied, the rest of the sequence diagram is executed. The semantics is equivalent to that of an alternative fragment with the contents of the break

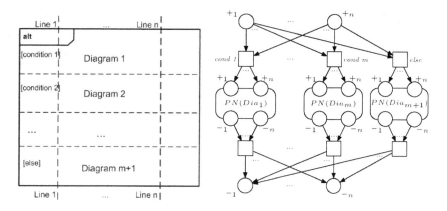

Fig. 9. Alternative fragment

fragment as one operand and all remaining elements of the diagram as `else` branch.

Loop Fragments. A *loop fragment* is given by a combined fragment with two integral parameters $0 \leq minint \leq maxint \leq \infty$ as shown in fig. 10. The diagram in the fragment is processed at least *minint* times, at most *maxint* times, and is optional as soon as *minint* is reached.

The semantics consists of an iteration part that may be executed several times, and a skip transition to bypass the loop initially. The bypass can be used if either the condition of the loop is not satisfied, or *minint* is zero such that the loop need not be executed.

To control the number of iterations, a token on an additional place named *Counter* is incremented in each execution of the loop body. Two transitions in conflict ensure that the loop is executed at most *maxint* times and is optional as soon as *minint* is reached. The loop body is inserted by transition refinement of the *loop* transition.

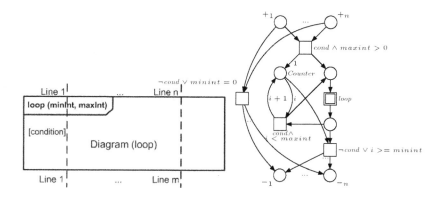

Fig. 10. Loop fragment

Parallel Fragments. Concurrent execution of operands of *parallel fragments* is modelled as shown in fig. 11. The semantics is given by the semantics of the operands composed by the parallel operator, which are sequentially prefixed by the entry transition with empty guard. *Coregions* are equivalent to a parallel fragment covering just one lifeline with each event being its own operand.

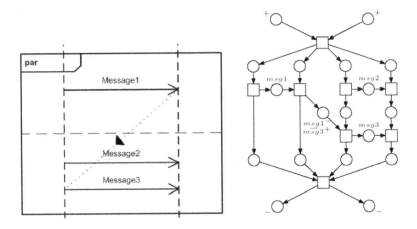

Fig. 11. Parallel fragment with general ordering

General Orderings. In parallel fragments some actions in different operands may be related, and thus need to be executed in a certain order. This is expressed by a dashed line with an arrow in the middle between the actions, called *general ordering*. The semantics is defined by interpreting the general ordering as a special kind of message between two linked events. This message makes the ordering explicit in that additional preconditions and postconditions are installed.

Sequencing. A *strict sequencing fragment* is given by a combined fragment where a strict execution order is imposed by the position of the events across all lifelines.

The semantics of a strict fragment is thus equivalent to a normal interaction diagram with general ordering applied to all events that are not explicitly ordered by messages or their lifeline. We will therefore not define a special semantics but use some preprocessing to add the general ordering.

Operands in strict fragments do not make sense since the ordering would delay the next operand until all events in the current operand are executed. Thus, removing the operand intersections does not change the semantics.

A *weak sequencing fragment* ensures a strict order inside the operands. When all actions in one operand for a lifeline have been processed, actions in the next operand for that lifeline may continue. The semantics of a weak sequencing fragment is thus defined as for strict sequencing, per operand. The different operands are then concatenated in order to execute some events concurrently, if no causal ordering is imposed.

Thus, weak sequencing defines local causality inside operands of a combined fragment, and strict sequencing defines global causality inside the combined fragment. Both operators apply only to the current nesting level, i.e. an ordering is not promoted to nested combined fragments.

Critical Sections. Some fragments of parallel executions may be executed atomically, meaning that other events of the participating lifelines are processed concurrently. This behaviour is captured in *critical sections* inside an operand of a parallel fragment.

In order to define the semantics for a critical section, we have to establish means to prohibit execution on parallel lifelines. This is achieved by an additional place for each concurrent instance of a covered lifeline, that has to be checked for an existing token each time an event of the lifeline is executed. The critical section would then collect all such tokens on entering the fragment, thus stopping all concurrent executions on the monitored lifelines. After the critical section is finished, the tokens are put back and the concurrent instances of the lifelines may continue.

Since each lifeline operates on its own "active" token, concurrency is not limited by this semantics. However, a compositional construction would need to introduce the activity token to every parallel operator, regardless of the presence of a critical section. Without loss of generality and due to enhanced readability, we introduced these concepts only at this point.

Interaction Reference. An *interaction reference* is given by a combined fragment with a name and probably with parameters. Another sequence diagram with that name has to be defined separately, with an identical set of lifelines.

The semantics of the reference is defined by replacing the reference with the actual sequence diagram, and parameters and gates replaced as needed. Since such a replacement can be done statically during compilation, no explicit Petri net semantics is needed. On the other hand, a reuse of the replacing diagram can be done if a procedure semantics is applied. Such a semantics has been defined for M-nets in [6]. Using a procedure semantics would also allow recursion to take place, while the replacement semantics (as proposed by the standard) would require infinite replacement in such cases.

5   Conclusion and Future Work

The semantics defined in this paper covers all elements of Interaction Diagrams of UML 2.0 with the mentioned exceptions. Although defining a semantics based on Time Petri nets should be possible, there has to be some further research on feasibility. The implementation of the proposed semantics has already started. The next step after finishing that implementation will be the extension of the proposed semantics to Activity diagrams and Interaction Overview diagrams.

We would like to thank all other members of the project group P-UMLaut, namely Eike Best, Eike Frost, Martin Hilscher, André Kaiser, Mark Ross, Casjen

Schnars, Tim Strazny, and Harro Wimmel for their support and fruitful discussions on the semantics. Additionally, we would like to thank Alexander Knapp and Cécile Bui Thanh for help on UML, object orientation and semantics, and Hanna Klaudel and Franck Pommereau for their M-nets introduction.

References

1. Gul Agha, Fiorella de Cindio, and Grzegorz Rozenberg, editors. *Concurrent Object-Oriented Programming and Petri Nets, Advances in Petri Nets*, volume 2001 of *Lecture Notes in Computer Science*. Springer, 2001.
2. Simona Bernardi, Susanna Donatelli, and José Merseguer. From UML sequence diagrams and statecharts to analysable petri net models. In Simonetta Balsamo, Paola Inverardi, and Bran Selic, editors, *Workshop on Software and Performance '02*, pages 35–45, Rome, Italy, 2002. ACM Press.
3. Eike Best, Wojciech Frączak, Richard P. Hopkins, Hanna Klaudel, and Elisabeth Pelz. M-nets: an Algebra of High-level Petri Nets, with an Application to the Semantics of Concurrent Programming Languages. *Acta Informatica*, 35(10):813–857, 1998.
4. Werner Damm and David Harel. LSCs: Breathing Life into Message Sequence Charts. *Formal Methods in System Design*, 19(1):45–80, July 2001.
5. Raymond Devillers, Hanna Klaudel, Maciej Koutny, and Franck Pommereau. Asynchronous Box Calculus. *Fundamenta Informaticae*, 54(1):1–50, 2003.
6. Hans Fleischhack and Bernd Grahlmann. A Petri Net Semantics for $B(PN)^2$ with Procedures. In Gul Agha and Stefano Russo, editors, *Parallel and Distributed Software Engineering*, pages 15–27. IEEE Computer Society, May 1997.
7. Hans Fleischhack and Bernd Grahlmann. A Compositional Petri Net Semantics for SDL. In J. Desel and M. Silva, editors, *Application and Theory of Petri Nets*, volume 1420 of *Lecture Notes in Computer Science*, pages 144–164. Springer-Verlag, 1998.
8. Martin Fowler. *UML Distilled*. The Addison-Wesley Object Technology Series. Addison-Wesley Longman, 2004.
9. Thomas Gehrke, Michaela Huhn, Arend Rensink, and Heike Wehrheim. An Algebraic Semantics for Message Sequence Charts Documents. In Stanislaw Budkowski, Ana R. Cavalli, and Elie Najm, editors, *Formal Description Techniques and Protocol Specification, Testing and Verification (FORTE/PSTV '98)*, pages 3–18. Kluwer Academic Press, 1998.
10. Stefan Heymer. A Semantics for MSC Based on Petri Net Components. In *SAM200*, pages 262–275, Col de Porte, Grenoble, France, 2000. VERIMAG, IRISA, SDL Forum.
11. ITU-T. *Recommendation Z.120 (11/99): Message Sequence Charts* ITU-T, Geneva, 2000.
12. Mario Jeckle, Chris Rupp, Jürgen Hahn, Barbara Zengler, and Stefan Queins. *UML 2 glasklar*. Hanser, 2004.
13. Kurt Jensen. *Coloured Petri Nets — Basic Concepts, Analysis Methods and Practical Use*, volume 1 of *EATCS Monographs in Computer Science*. Springer, 1992.
14. Joost-Pieter Katoen and Lennard Lambert. Pomsets for Message Sequence Charts. In H. König and P. Langendörfer, editors, *Formale Beschreibungstechniken für verteilte Systeme*, pages 197–207, Cottbus, June 1998. GI/ITG, Shaker Verlag.

15. Olaf Kluge. Modelling a railway crossing with message sequence charts and petri nets. In Hartmut Ehrig, Wolfgang Reisig, Grzegorz Rozenberg, and Herbert Weber, editors, *Petri Net Technology for Communication-Based Systems*, volume 2472 of *Lecture Notes in Computer Science*, pages 197–218. Springer, 2003.

16. Johan Lilius. OB(PN)^2: An object based petri net programming notation. In Agha et al. [1], pages 247–275.

17. Tadao Murata. Petri nets: Properties, analysis and applications. *Proceedings of the IEEE*, 77(4):541–580, April 1989.

18. Object Management Group. *UML 2.0 Superstructure Specification*, 03-08-02 edition, August 2003.

19. Project P-UMLaut. http://www.p-umlaut.de.

20. Lutz Priese and Harro Wimmel. *Theoretische Informatik: Petri-Netze*. Springer-Verlag, 2002.

21. Wolfgang Reisig. *Petri nets – An introduction*. Springer, 1985.

22. Michel Adriaan Reniers. *Message Sequence Charts*. PhD thesis, Eindhoven University of Technology, 1999.

23. Harald Störrle. Semantics of Interactions in UML 2.0. In *2003 IEEE Symposium on Human Centric Computing Languages and Environments*, pages 129–136, Auckland, New Zealand, October 2003. IEEE Computer Society.

SDL Design of OSPF Protocol for the Wireless Private Network

Yang Yang, Yang Lu, and Xiaokang Lin

Department of Electronic Engineering,
Tsinghua University, Beijing, 100084, China
{yy01, lu-y02}@mails.tsinghua.edu.cn,
lxk-dee@tsinghua.edu.cn

Abstract. This paper presents the design of the open shortest path first (OSPF) protocol for the wireless private network using the specification and description language (SDL). Simulations are run in many scenarios to show that our design is excellent in the aspects of both function and performance. In addition, SDL is proven to be an efficient tool in the development of communication software.

1   Introduction

Covering thousands of square kilometers, the wireless private network serves as an information exchange platform to support such integrated services as voice, video, data and so on via microwave channels. The network adopts the protocol stack of IP over asynchronous transfer mode (ATM) and accordingly the selection of IP routing protocol becomes an important issue. In this paper we only discuss the intra-domain routing protocols, which mainly include the route information protocol (RIP), the interior gateway routing protocol (IGRP) and the open shortest path first (OSPF) [1, 2]. RIP and IGRP belong to distance vector protocols, and the routing information stored in routers is dependent on each other, which may incur route flapping when there is something wrong with a given router. Compared with RIP and IGRP, OSPF is a link state protocol and has such advantages as fast convergence, robustness, scalability, security and so on. So it is selected for the wireless private network.

In the OSPF domain, all routers exchange link state information with neighbors to maintain a topology graph and calculate the optimal routes. Moreover, OSPF introduces the concept of area to decrease the traffic of protocol information. An autonomous system (AS) is divided into many areas and each one maintains its own link state database formed by the link state advertisements (LSA). To describe the link information each router will originate several types of LSAs, namely router LSA, network LSA, network summary LSA, AS boundary router summary LSA and AS external LSA. LSA instances are transmitted by the use of OSPF packets, including Hello packets, data description packets, link state request packets, link state update packets and link state acknowledgment packets. When a router starts up, it will send out Hello packets from all interfaces

A. Prinz, R. Reed, and J. Reed (Eds.): SDL 2005, LNCS 3530, pp. 149–161, 2005.

periodically to detect the neighbor routers and initiate the database synchronization, which includes the negotiation of master/slave relation, exchange of LSA database summary, request, update and acknowledgment of LSA instances, and finally both LSA databases are identical. Then the routers can use the Dÿkstra algorithm to calculate the routing tables.

Though there are many OSPF designs for public networks, they can hardly fit the special characteristics of the wireless private network. First, the system works in the wireless environment. As a result, the link bit error rate (BER) is very high and the bandwidth is limited. Second, the network scale is smaller compared with public networks. Commonly speaking, there are tens of routers in the wireless private network. In addition, the topology changes more frequently. Last but not least, the reusability and maintainability of OSPF software are the top concerns for the owner of the wireless private network. According to these characteristics, we must simplify the standard OSPF protocol to enhance the overall performance of the wireless private network. Additionally, the selection of the most appropriate tools to develop the software is also a vital issue. Considering the features of the specification and description language (SDL) [3, 4, 5], we use it to design and implement the OSPF protocol for the wireless private network. Note that SDL-based OSPF design is partly introduced in [6], but the emphasis is put on the comparison between different LSA refreshment functions. The design of the protocol itself is not given in detail.

2   SDL Development Issues

Using SDL to develop software can drastically improve the maintainability and reusability of the code. The SDL hierarchy consists of four levels: system, blocks, processes and procedures. Such a structure follows the natural functional subdivisions and facilitates the reusing of existing specifications. Based on type declarations, the object-oriented concepts of SDL also give users powerful tools for reusing. As to the working environment, we use the Telelogic Tau SDL suite 4.3 [7] on the Windows platform. The suite is designed to simplify and speed up the development work and users can efficiently produce SDL code that is free of syntactic or semantic errors.

The Telelogic Tau SDL suite also provides the simulation environment to evaluate the system in the aspects of both function and performance. According to our experience, SDL simulation can be run in two different modes: the simulator user interface (UI) mode and the command prompt mode. As to the former one, there are three methods to perform the simulations. First, we can adopt the step-by-step concept and this is very suitable in the debugging of system functions. Second, a simulation script file can be created to control the system running, which is often used to send signals from outside and simulate the bottom-layer network behavior. Last, the simulation may be run automatically. Note that the last two methods are often used simultaneously. Additionally, the corresponding message sequence chart (MSC) [8] can be enabled to clearly depict the simulation process. In the prompt command mode, all simulation commands should be typed out manually by users. Though the simulator UI mode is convenient to use, it is very time-consuming. Therefore, the command prompt mode is more suitable for the performance simulation of large scale networks, and it can speed up the simulation by a factor of 10 to 20. When the simulation finishes, we will display the simulation data and write them into a log file. Then the data may be processed and our system can be evaluated effectively.

3   Requirements Analysis of the OSPF Module

The architecture of IP routers in the wireless private network consists of the OSPF module, signaling transmission module, data transmission module, debug console, simple network management protocol (SNMP) [9] module and so on. The design targets of the OSPF module can be summarized as follows:

1. The module must implement the OSPF routing protocol. The types of interfaces include point-to-point, broadcast and non-broadcast multiple access (NBMA).
2. The module will support SNMP and command-line debugging.
3. The design should adapt to the frequent change of network topology and the bad channel conditions.
4. The protocol overhead should be as small as possible and the system configuration should be simplified to the maximum extent.
5. The software should be robust, reusable and maintainable.

4   General Design of the OSPF Module

We should firstly simplify the standard OSPF protocol to achieve the best performance. The simplifications are mainly focused on three aspects: partitions of areas, LSA types and formats, and OSPF packet formats.

The wireless private network typically consists of tens of routers and the topology changes frequently, so the standard multi-area scheme proposed by OSPF will definitely lead to low protocol efficiency. Instead, if the OSPF domain is regarded as a single area, the implementation complexity of the protocol will be greatly reduced. In addition, the configuration and management of the wireless private network can be simplified effectively. So the single-area scheme is adopted in our design. Next we can reduce the number of LSA types according to the single-area scheme. Note that both network summary LSA and AS boundary router summary LSA are related to the inter-area information exchange, so they can be discarded in our design. In addition, because the link BER in the wireless private network is high and the bandwidth is limited, the LSA formats can be simplified to decrease the protocol overhead and the OSPF packet retransmission probability under bad channel conditions. For the same purpose we can also simplify the OSPF packet formats, especially the Hello packets.

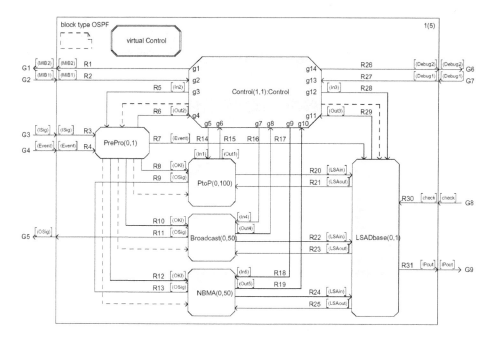

Fig. 1. General design of the OSPF module

To enhance the code reusability, we design the OSPF module in an object-oriented manner. The behavior of OSPF is specified in an SDL block type, which can be instantiated according to the particular configuration when we construct the network. Partitioning the processes in an SDL block must obey the general principle that the function of each process is fairly integrated and independent. In addition the interfaces between processes should be clear. According to this principle and our simplified OSPF protocol, we can present the general design of the OSPF module for the wireless private network with SDL as shown in fig. 1. The OSPF module is divided into six kinds of processes that are responsible for: managing the running of the module (Control), validating the incoming OSPF packets (PrePro), implementing the neighbor state machines for three types of interfaces (PtoP, Broadcast, NBMA), and maintaining the LSA database(LSADbase). In addition, LSADbase process is designed to calculate the optimal routes to all reachable destinations. There is only one instance for Control, PrePro and LSADbase in the block, respectively. For simplicity, PtoP, Broadcast and NBMA are called the neighbor processes in this paper because they are all designed to implement neighbor state machines for different types of interfaces. In our design the number of instances of the neighbor processes is decided by the corresponding interface types of the given router, and there is only one instance of the neighbor processes for each interface. Note that Control is defined as a virtual process type to facilitate the configurations for different routers. Due to the complexity of the detailed design and the space limitation, in the next section we will only informally describe the behavior and structure of the OSPF module without the corresponding SDL diagrams.

5   Detailed Design of the OSPF Module

5.1   Control Process

The Control process mainly communicates signals with debug console and SNMP module. The function of Control process can be summarized as:

1. Initiation of the OSPF module.
2. Support of network management and command-line debugging.

Initiation of the OSPF Module

When the system starts up, only the Control process is originated automatically. It will decide whether to originate the PrePro process and the LSADbase process, based on the static configuration. Because PrePro process is mainly responsible for validating incoming OSPF packets from all interfaces and sending valid packets to the corresponding neighbor processes, it is reasonable to originate the neighbor processes in PrePro process. The behavior related to the particular router configuration is not described In the specification of the OSPF block type. Instead, only a virtual state transition is given in this level. When creating the network system, we can use the subtypes of OSPF block and redefine the contents of the virtual transition. Thus the particular configurations for different routers can be implemented conveniently.

Support of Network Management and Command-Line Debugging

SNMP module can manage and configure the OSPF module dynamically. According to signals received from SNMP module, the Control process will update the entries of the management information base (MIB) and inform other processes about the changes. Then other processes can read the new configuration data via shared variables. The use of shared variables is an efficient complement to the SDL signal exchange scheme, which can avoid large amounts of signal traffic between different processes and enhance the system performance. The debug console directly monitors the running of the OSPF module by a command-line interface. For example, it can query the information of LSA databases. When receiving such commands, the Control process will communicate with LSADbase process and return the relevant data.

5.2   PrePro Process

The PrePro process mainly communicates signals with signaling transmission module and the bottom-layer hardware. Its function can be summarized as:

1. Origination of the neighbor processes.
2. Preliminary processing of incoming OSPF packets.

Origination of the Neighbor Processes
Once created, PrePro process will read the relevant configuration information
from the Control process. The information includes the list of OSPF interfaces,
router ID, Hellointerval, Deadinterval, link data of each interface and so on.
Based on this information, PrePro will originate one instance of the neighbor
processes for each router interface according to the given interface type. Additionally, the relations between SDL process IDs of the neighbor processes and
the corresponding router interfaces will be stored in an array and reported to
other processes in the module.

Preliminary Processing of Incoming OSPF Packets
Receiving the interface signals from the bottom-layer hardware, the PrePro process should send them to the corresponding neighbor processes to trigger the
interface state transitions. In addition, the validity of incoming OSPF packets
will be examined by PrePro, which judges whether the interface is in the normal
working state and decides how to deal with the packets. If the packets pass the
validation, they are sent to the corresponding neighbor process. Otherwise the
packets will be discarded. Such a scheme can effectively reduce the complexity
of the neighbor processes.

5.3   PtoP Process

The PtoP process is created for the point-to-point interface and mainly communicates with signaling transmission module. Its function can be summarized as:

1. Implementation of the point-to-point interface state machine.
2. Implementation of the corresponding neighbor state machine.

Implementation of the Point-to-Point Interface State Machine
The OSPF protocol defines seven interface states: Down, Loopback, Point-to-
Point, Waiting, DR, Backup and DRother, among which only the former three
states are available in PtoP process. Point-to-Point is the normal working state.
Down state indicates that the corresponding interface is currently invalid, and
when entering Loopback state, the interface is regarded as a virtual one to con-
duct tests, and as a result no data can be transmitted in such a state. PtoP will
ensure the normal running of the interface state machine according to received
interface events. Note that the interface state transitions may directly trigger
the change of neighbor state.

Implementation of the Corresponding Neighbor State Machine
As to the neighbor state machine, the OSPF protocol defines such states as
Down, Init, Attempt, 2-Way, ExStart, Exchange, Loading and Full, among which
Attempt and 2-Way are not be considered in PtoP process because they relate
to broadcast and NBMA networks. The nature of the neighbor state transitions
are to control the synchronization between LSA databases in neighbor routers,
as shown in fig. 2.

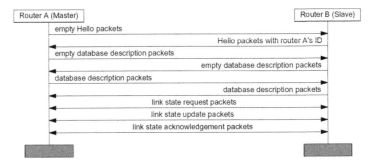

Fig. 2. Synchronization between link state databases

To maintain the adjacency between neighbors, a PtoP process must frequently access the database in the LSADbase process, so the efficiency of communications between these two processes is vital to the performance of our design. We have two schemes in the SDL environment. The first one is to use shared variables, just as we have done for the Control process, but this scheme is not suitable here because it may incur a data inconsistency problem when the shared variables are updated too frequently. So we have to use the second conventional signal exchange scheme. To effectively reduce the traffic between processes, a PtoP process only needs to maintain the LSA indexes and summaries of those instances in the LSA retransmission list. Other LSA instances are acquired from LSADbase process only when there is a neighbor router requests. In a word, LSA instances maintained by a PtoP process are only a small part of the whole data. This scheme enhances the performance of our design significantly.

5.4   Broadcast Process and NBMA Process

Compared with the PtoP process, the tasks of the Broadcast process and NBMA process are similar but more complex, and they are created for the broadcast interface and NBMA interface, respectively. Their functions can be summarized as:

1. Implementation of the broadcast or NBMA interface state machine.
2. Implementation of the corresponding neighbor state machines.

Implementation of the Broadcast or NBMA Interface State Machine
Because there is more than one neighbor for each broadcast or NBMA interface, the corresponding interface state machine is much more complex compared with the point-to-point counterpart. The interface state machine includes six states: Down, Loopback, Waiting, DR, Backup and DRother. Considering that a broadcast or NBMA network consists of several routers, a designated router (DR) should be elected to play the central part in database synchronizations. In addition, a backup DR is also elected as a substitute. Once enabled by the bottom-layer hardware, the given interface will enter Waiting state to elect the

DR and the backup DR, after which the interface state will change to DR or Backup if the router is the elected DR or the backup DR, respectively. Otherwise, the new state of the interface will be DRother.

Implementation of the Corresponding Neighbor State Machines
The neighbor state machine for the broadcast or NBMA interface is very similar to that for the point-to-point interface, but the design is more complex because there is more than one neighbor for the given interface, which means that several neighbor state machines should be implemented in each Broadcast process or NBMA process. To solve the problem, we can use SDL generators to define different arrays and store the corresponding data of each neighbor in the network. The primary data type includes the current neighbor state, the different OSPF timers, the previous sent packets, the link state request list, the link state retransmission list, the current LSA number and so on.

5.5   LSADbase Process

The LSADbase process mainly communicates with data transmission module and its function can be summarized as:

1. Maintenance of the LSA database.
2. Routing table calculation.

Maintenance of the LSA Database
All LSA instances are stored in an array that can be accessed by LSA indexes. The maintenance of the LSA database includes the origination, updating, aging and flooding of LSA instances. When originating a new LSA instance, the LSADbase process will update the database and flood the LSA instance to neighbors from all interfaces. In our design, several SDL timers are defined to control the frequency of accessing LSA database and prevent a broadcast storm in the wireless private network. As to the aging of the database, it is a primary task of LSADbase. The incrementing of each LSA's age field is controlled by an SDL timer, which expires every second. How to design the aging scheme is an important issue. The method of age box [10] is efficient for large scale networks, yet it is a little complex. Because the scale of the wireless private network is small and the number of LSA instances is consequently small, we can define a SDL array that just stores the age information of all LSA instances. The array is updated every second to realize the aging of the LSA database. By avoiding the frequent accessing of the database and the parsing of LSA instances, this method is very simple and can decrease the central processor utilization.

Routing Table Calculation
According to the link state information stored in the router, LSADbase process will use the Dÿkstra algorithm to calculate the optimal routes to reachable destinations when a change of LSA instance is detected. The routing table calculation can be divided into three stages. First, a shortest-path tree is constructed

by only considering those links between routers and transit networks. Second, the stub networks are incorporated into the tree. And finally the routes to external destinations are calculated through the examination of AS external LSAs. Note that in our design the routing table is stored in an array indexed by the destinations.

6   Simulation Analysis of the OSPF Module

6.1   Simulation Model

Based on the specification of the OSPF module, we can use the object-oriented method to perform simulations in different scenarios. According to the router architecture, the exchanges of OSPF packets are controlled by the signaling transmission module, so the OSPF blocks can't be directly connected to construct simulation networks. To solve the problem, we add the Rec and Send processes to our design. Because the scale of the wireless private network is small, it is enough to provide seven interfaces for each router in the simulation stage. The processes and the primary signal channels are illustrated in fig. 3. These two kinds of processes are responsible for realizing the basic functions of router interfaces, including the receiving and sending of packets, interface identification and so on. In addition, the Send process can add the transmission time delay and random errors to the data flows to simulate the behavior of physical links. The Telelogic Tau SDL suite provides a scheme to generate random numbers according to different distributions such as the uniform distribution, the negative exponential distribution and the Erlang distribution, which can greatly simplify the simulation. Because the five types of OSPF packets have different

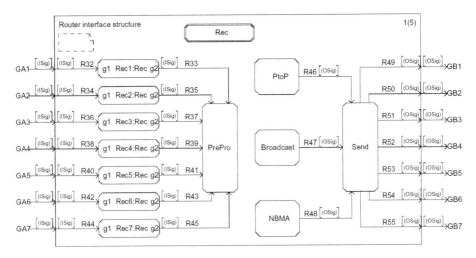

Fig. 3. Design of the router interface

formats, the corresponding SDL struct types are defined in the OSPF block to conveniently describe the protocol and each OSPF packet is a struct value. Note that all packets are transmitted in the bit string format, so conversions between the struct values and the corresponding bit string values are necessary in Rec process and Send process. Before packets are sent to neighbors, we can insert errors to the bit string flows according to the given distribution.

6.2   Function Simulation

The SDL simulator UI is suitable to perform the function simulation, and enables us to find errors more conveniently. The function simulation can be divided into two stages. First, we build the simplest scenarios to simulate the basic function. Second, larger networks (which simultaneously incorporate the point-to-point, broadcast and NBMA interfaces) can be created to give us a more comprehensive view of our design. According to characteristics of the wireless private network, the scale of the simulation network can be enlarged to 20, 40, 60 and 80, respectively.

At the first stage simulation, the function simulations are performed in three different scenarios as shown in fig. 4, because the module supports three different types of interfaces. These scenarios are simple enough and have the corresponding network features, so they are very suitable for the debugging of system functions. We will put emphasis on such aspects as LSA database synchronization, routing table calculation, reroute capability and election of the DR.

Because the broadcast network in fig. 4 is similar to the NBMA network and also supports the point-to-point interface, this scenario is very typical and as a result the corresponding simulation details are given here to demonstrate our methodology. The simulation is divided into four stages, and the duration of each one is 30 seconds. In the first and fourth stage we enable all interfaces of all routers, while in the second and third one, the interface 1 of router 1 and the interface 1 of router 3 are disabled respectively. We can see that when each simulation stage finishes, the LSA databases of all routers are synchronized and each LSA describes the latest link states, which indicates the correctness of LSA origination and flooding. In addition, the OSPF block can reroute quickly according to the topology changes. It is observed that the routing tables and the elected DRs accord with those ones in theory. Due to the space limitation, the

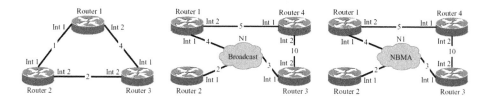

Fig. 4. Topologies of the first stage function simulations

corresponding routing tables and the simulation details of larger networks are omitted here.

6.3   Performance Simulation

To get a view of the performance of our design, here we only construct a 40-node wireless private network and perform different simulations under bad channel conditions. The simulation scenarios are summarized as follows and the simulation results are given in fig. 5.

1. STD_BER=0.007: standard OSPF protocol and BER=0.007;
2. SIM_BER=0.007: simplified OSPF protocol and BER=0.007;
3. STD_BER=0.006: standard OSPF protocol and BER=0.006;
4. SIM_BER=0.006: simplified OSPF protocol and BER=0.006.

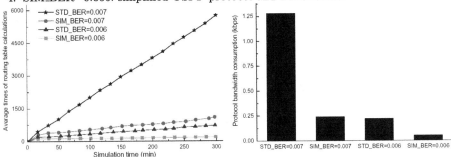

Fig. 5. Network performance in four scenarios

Compared with function simulations, in performance simulations the speed is the most important factor to be considered. So we run the simulations in the command prompt mode. Note that each scenario is simulated for 300 minutes. The performance evaluation is focused on the average times of routing table calculations per router and the bandwidth consumption of protocol packets. We can see that the results vary greatly in different scenarios, among which our design has a better performance compared with the standard protocol under the same condition. The enhancement is mainly due to the format simplifications of different LSAs and OSPF packets, which greatly reduce the events of synchronization breaks between neighbor routers. More details of the performance evaluation are omitted here.

7   Learned Experience

There are many benefits of using SDL to develop a large scale communication system, and here we summarize some points that impressed us the most in our work. First, the capability of SDL to describe systems is very strong. SDL provides generators for users to define almost any new data types they want. In our work the arrays are used frequently, and it is convenient because we can easily define different data structures which are indexed by the router ID, the IP address, the LSA sequence number, the reachable destination and so on. It is not that easy to accomplish this with other languages such as C/C++. Second, the embedding of C/C++ code in SDL diagrams facilitates the specification of the system. As to the common co-design schemes, we find that the directive #CODE can be used efficiently, yet it is not as powerful as another directive #ADT or the CPP2SDL tool, though these two schemes are more complex. Third, the use of shared variables is an essential complement to the SDL signal exchange scheme, and it is mainly used when many global values are shared by different SDL processes. Note that the prevention of data inconsistency is an important issue when using shared variables. Fourth, the object-oriented design makes the structuring and reusing easier. Based on the definition and redefining of virtual entities, we can add new transitions and specialize behavior specifications, an approach which has been used in the generation of the desired simulation scenarios in our project. Last but not least, using SDL to develop the software can ensure the code correctness and reduce the development cycle to the maximum extent. With the simulator UI provided by Telelogic Tau SDL Suite, we can conveniently perform simulations and debug the system functions. Note that it took us only four months to develop such a large communication system.

Though there are many advantages of SDL-based software development, we also encountered some problems in our work. First, the simulation speed is very slow even in the prompt mode, especially in the large scale scenarios. Note that an 80-node network simulation will run for nearly 10 days. Second, in the Telelogic Tau SDL environment the simulation networks can only be constructed manually, which is really tedious when the topologies are complex. Though this problem is partly solved in [11], the scheme introduced is not very convenient. So we suggest such an issue be considered in the development tools. Last, the C code generated automatically in our project exceeds 100000 lines and maybe the code space efficiency is a potential problem.

8   Conclusion

In this paper we present the SDL design of the OSPF protocol that fits well characteristics for the wireless private network. Function and performance simulations are performed in many scenarios, which indicate that our design can meet the system requirements very well. First, all required functions are implemented correctly and the running of OSPF module is very stable. Second, the design adapts to the frequent change of network topology and the bad channel conditions. The protocol overhead is reduced greatly and the system configurations are also simplified. In short, the performance of our design is better than the standard protocol under the same condition. Last but not least, the code is reusable and maintainable because of the formal characteristics of SDL. According to our experience, SDL is an appropriate choice for the development of communication software, especially the large scale systems. Future work will be focused on the code migration to hardware platforms.

Acknowledgments. We would like to thank Dr. Andreas Metzger, Mr. Anthony Weber, Mr. Erik Mats, Mr. Michael Andersson and Mr. Mike Rudnick for their suggestions on such issues as the generation of random numbers and the acceleration of SDL simulation. My gratitude also goes to Mr. Rick Reed and the anonymous reviewers for their valuable comments on the paper. Special acknowledgment is made to Prof. Andreas Prinz who gave me so much help in preparing for the conference.

References

1. J. Moy: OSPF Version 2, IETF RFC 2328, 1998.
2. J. Moy: OSPF Anatomy of an Internet Routing Protocol, Addison-Wesley Pub Co, Boston, USA, 1998.
3. Specification and Description Language (SDL), ITU-T Z.100, 1999.
4. A. Mitschele-Thiel: Systems Engineering with SDL: Developing Performance-Critical Communication, John Wiley & Sons Inc, New York, USA, 2001.
5. M. Song: Fundamentals of Designing Communications Software, Beijing University of Post and Telecommunication Press, Beijing, China, 2003.
6. O. Monkewich, I. Sales, R. Probert: OSPF Efficient LSA Refreshment Function in SDL, Proceedings of the 10th International SDL Forum (SDL'01), LNCS 2078, 300-315, 2001.
7. Telelogic Malmö AB: Telelogic Tau 4.3 SDL Suite Methodology Guidelines, 2001.
8. Message Sequence Charts (MSC), ITU-T Z.120, 1996.
9. J. Case, M. Fedor, M. Schoffstall, J. Davin: A Simple Network Management Protocol (SNMP), IETF RFC 1157, 1990.
10. J. Moy: OSPF Complete Implementation, Addison-Wesley Pub Co, Boston, USA, 2000.
11. A. Iselt, A. Autenrieth: An SDL-Based Platform for the Simulation of Communication Networks Using Dynamic Block Instantiations, Proceedings of the 8th SDL Forum (SDL'97), 35-49, Elsevier, 1997.

ASM and SDL Models of Geographic Routing in Mobile Ad Hoc Networks

Uwe Glässer[1] and Andreas Prinz[2]

[1] School of Computing Science,
Simon Fraser University, B.C., Canada
glaesser@sfu.ca
[2] Faculty of Engineering, Agder University College,
Grooseveien 36, N-4876 Grimstad, Norway
andreas.prinz@hia.no

Abstract. We present here an ASM view and an SDL view of the same protocol. We show how the two different modeling paradigms complement each other and that they are similar in their underlying semantic models. Our application example is sufficiently complex, including both architectural as well as non-trivial algorithmic aspects, and overall addresses an interesting problem in a demanding technological sector.

1 Introduction

In this paper, we present two conceptually different views of the same network or routing layer protocol for geographic routing in mobile ad hoc networks based on two popular and well known modeling paradigms for distributed real-time systems, namely: the SDL view and the ASM (abstract state machine) view. The motivation for our work is that we feel that the two different views complement each other in various ways. The strengths of SDL clearly are the expressive means and the methodological framework it provides for modeling behavioral and structural aspects of a functional system architecture in terms of a hierarchically defined collection of interacting system components with well defined interfaces [4]. In contrast, the ASM formalism and abstraction principles provide a precise mathematical framework for semantic modeling of complex functional requirements at high levels of abstraction (such as in early system design phases [2]). Its particular strength is the flexibility it offers for writing highly abstract and concise specifications minimizing the need for encoding in mapping the problem space to a formal model.

Our goal is to compare the two basically different views in modeling distributed real-time systems and to illustrate how they complement each other. The chosen application example is sufficiently complex but well understood, involves both fundamental architectural aspects and non-trivial algorithmic aspects, and addresses an interesting problem in a demanding technological sector. In [1], the network layer protocol that we consider here was modeled in a fairly abstract way using distributed real-time ASM. For a refined version of this

A. Prinz, R. Reed, and J. Reed (Eds.): SDL 2005, LNCS 3530, pp. 162–173, 2005.

model, various properties characterizing its efficiency and fault-tolerant behavior are proven in [5]. From the existing ASM model, we derive a refined SDL model effectively making the transition from an abstract ASM system model to an SDL system architecture that provides a basis for implementations of the protocol. Since the ASM model is already well documented, the main focus in this paper is on the comparison with the SDL architecture.

The paper is structured as follows. Section 2 gives an overview of the network layer protocol. Section 3 compares the ASM model with the SDL model using some samples. Section 4 concludes the paper.

2   Efficient Ad Hoc Routing

Mobile ad hoc networks are designed for wireless communication and do not require a pre-established infrastructure as the mobile hosts also perform the routing tasks. The high dynamics of such self-organizing networks require routing strategies substantially different from those employed in static communication networks. Besides space limitations for storing large routing tables at mobile hosts, any attempt to permanently update such tables would congest the network with administration packets very quickly.

Packet routing in ad hoc networks has received a lot of attention in recent years. There are two common routing approaches: topology-based routing and geographic routing [6]. Geographic routing protocols improve topology-based ones by using information on geographic (physical) locations of the nodes involved in the routing. It is assumed that each node can determine its physical location (at any given time) via GPS or another navigation technology. Intuitively, the physical location of the destination node is part of the destination address. Hence, the routing decision at a forwarding node depends on both the locations of the destination and the neighbor nodes of the forwarding node. To send a packet, the sender needs to know the most recent location of the destination node.

The *logical topology based location service* (LTLS) protocol [5] is specified here. The network layer is divided into two separate sublayers, one for a distributed location service, and one for a *position based routing* (PBR) between known locations. These two sublayers cooperatively implement the network layer protocol of a mobile ad hoc network. The PBR relies on the existence of a *Media Access* or MAC layer (often IEEE 802.11). In this paper, we only cover the LTLS.

Conceptually, the LTLS protocol forms a sublayer of the network layer. The idea of the LTLS is that the nodes in a mobile ad hoc network are *logically* connected by a specific topology. The connection is defined statically and used to keep the amount of information to be stored small. Each node advertises periodically its physical location to, and keeps the location information from, its logical neighbors. When a source node s wants to find the physical location of a destination node t, it sends a location request to a neighbor in the logical topology. The request is then forwarded to the next logical node until the request reaches t. On receiving the request, node t sends its location directly to s, because it now knows the receiving location. Forwarding a location request from a node to its logical neighbor as well as sending the physical position of t to s is realized by calling the position-based routing.

3   Specifying the Protocol in ASM and in SDL

The above protocol was developed by mobile ad-hoc network specialists. To formally describe the protocol, it was modeled in terms of a *distributed abstract state machine* (DASM). This is a high-level specification formalism allowing algorithms to be expressed fairly abstractly and concisely. Upon finishing the DASM specification, we realized the need for experimental validation of an executable version. We decided to use SDL-96 based on the Cinderella tool [3] for this purpose. The rationale for our choice is that the SDL view is closer to the implementation view, yet it is an abstract modeling technique. Thus, we first turned an informal specification into an abstract formal one (DASM) and then transformed this one into a formal executable model.

The DASM model facilitates discussing formal protocol aspects with developers, whereas the SDL specification allows specific application cases to be examined.

In the following, we present a comparison of the two sample specifications by way of selected parts of the protocol description. In order to simplify the comparison, we have identified corresponding parts with matching names.

3.1   Layered Communication Model

In both models, nodes send and receive packets consisting of two logically separate parts: 1) a packet *header*, and 2) the *payload* carrying the actual data. Abstractly, packets are represented as elements of a dynamic domain PACKET. We uniformly model the payload in terms of an abstract type DATA with an access operation *data* defined on packets. The information contained in a packet's header, however, is essential for the network layer protocol and requires special attention. A header consists of several descriptors specifying: the sender node *sndr*, the destination node *dest*, the next receiver node *rcvr* (that is, the next hop on the way to *dest*), and the packet type *type*. Each of the descriptors in a packet header forms a node reference consisting of the node's address *nadr* and its geographic location *npos*. Node references are represented by the elements of a dynamic domain NREF.

In SDL, PACKET is a **struct** with fields data, sndr, dest, rcrv, type, nadr and npos. Node references in SDL are represented by Pids.

One can distinguish three basically different packet types: a) *detection packets* are meaningful for the position-based routing only; b) *discovery packets* are meaningful for the distributed location service only; and c) *data packets* (see also fig. 1). For detection packets, we further distinguish between *neighbor requests* and *neighbor replies*. Similarly, for discovery packets, we distinguish between *location requests* and *location replies*. All other packets are uniformly treated as

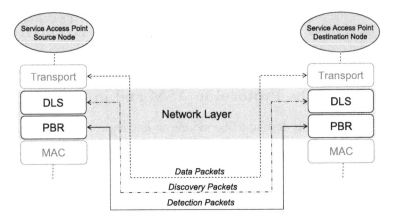

Fig. 1. Layered communication model

data packets. In SDL, we have defined three separate packet types that include the corresponding upper layer packet type. The DASM specification abstracts from this structural information on the data types.

3.2   Specifying the Structure

Within the DASM model, the mobile hosts are represented by a static domain NODE = $\{n_1, ..., n_N\}$, where N is a parameter of the communication network. Each node has a unique ID or address within a global address space. This address is given by a static mapping *address* from nodes to an abstract domain ADDRESS. A monitored unary function *position*, defined on nodes, assigns to each $n_i, 1 \leq i \leq N$, a coordinate $position(n_i)$ from a static domain POSITION of physical locations on the plane provided by some location system.[1] Since nodes move, their physical locations change over time.

We model the network layer protocol by identifying the protocol entities of the LTLS and the PBR with DASM agents. With each node we associate two agents as identified by a unary dynamic function *node* defined on DASM agents. These agents execute the program *LocationService* and *PositionBasedRouting*, respectively. Thus, the domain AGENT is formed by the disjoint union of two sets of agents to which we refer as LTLS agents and as PBR agents.

The DASM model describes the system in fairly abstract terms leaving many structural aspects subject to implementations. In particular, all the distribution and location aspects are abstract in the ASM model. In fact, the ASM model only describes how a single agent works and leaves the communication between

---

[1] Please note that according to the ASM common memory approach based on a globally shared state, all data is in principle visible to all agents. However, the position information is understood to be private in the protocol and is repeated in other agents upon receiving this information by a message. Thus, it is guaranteed that each node keeps only the position information of its logical neighbors.

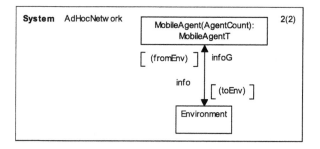

Fig. 2. SDL System level description

the agents open. In SDL, we model the network protocol through a system AdHocNetwork describing the mobile entities as well as the environment. In this model, the location and distribution aspects are part of the environment agent as shown in fig. 2.

Figure 2 shows the top-level view of the system in SDL. The mobile agents are given as blocks (containing processes) representing autonomously operating units that are connected to an environment (described in SDL)[2]. Depending on the communication layer (transport, LTLS or PBR), the environment provides different connection facilities as given by the layered communication architecture (such as direct transfer on the transport layer or position-dependent sending for the PBR). The physical location system is also included in the environment.

To describe a protocol hierarchically, SDL-96 provided the concept of a *block substructure* in addition to process specifications [4][3]. In SDL-2000 we could have made use of agent types with redefined parts, but we have chosen to use block substructures because this allowed us to execute the different alternatives without recompilation.

At the first level of the mobile agent, we just specify the transport layer. On the next level this transport view is extended by relaying the transport signals via the LocationService process. The next level of refinement refines the LSBlock to include the PBR protocol in a similar way. We have defined a complete SDL system featuring all these levels and can simulate this system on any of the layers.

Specification using SDL-96 requires all data to be encapsulated into processes and does not allow cross-process access to data. Therefore, some data items of the DASM specification that were globally visible have to be made local in SDL. An example is the physical location information, that is shared between PBR

---

[2] The SDL-96 standard does not allow block instance sets as given here, but in Cinderella this is allowed as a step towards SDL-2000.

[3] Combined block specifications express alternative views when looking at a block from different perspectives, such as the transport view versus the LTLS view. Structurally, both views of a combined block specification share the same external interfaces, but there are no other language constraints to ensure behaviour equivalence.

and LTLS in the DASM model, but that is stored only within LTLS in the SDL specification.

3.3   LTLS Protocol Description

We first give an outline for the main functions of the LTLS protocol.

Initialization: Each node in the network maintains a dynamic routing table identifying its logical neighbors in terms of a set of node references given by a function *logicalNeighbors*. The routing tables of all the nodes jointly yield the logical network topology. For each logical neighbor, the address is pre-assigned while the physical location (initially undefined) is updated dynamically. Each node broadcasts its physical location to all other nodes in the network by the PBR defined previously.

Position advertising: Each node periodically sends its present physical location to its logical neighbors. Each node has a timer for each of its logical neighbors. If a node has not received any location information from a logical neighbor when the timer expires, then the node sets the location of this neighbor temporarily to undefined.

Location request: When a node s wants to send a location request to a node t, s selects a path in the logical topology, sends the location request to the logical neighbor in the selected path, and sets a request timer, denoted as *reqTimer*. If s receives the location reply from t before the timer expires, s completes the location request process; otherwise, s considers the request as lost and selects alternative paths from s to t, retransmits the location request via the selected paths, and sets *reqTimer*. Retransmissions of location requests are counted by a sequence number, denoted as *seqno*. If s can not get the location reply from t after all available paths have been tried, s decides that t is not reachable (see [5] for details).

Location reply: On receiving a location request from s, node t replies by sending its physical location directly to s using the PBR protocol.

Recover from failure: When a node recovers from failure, it broadcasts its present location to all nodes in the network.

We now model the LTLS protocol formally in terms of a DASM. With every node u in the network the logical topology associates a non-empty set of logical neighbors of u as identified by a static function *logicalNeighbors*(u). The set of logical neighbors of u is statically defined in terms of node references. If a neighbor of u is unreachable, the related node reference in *logicalNeighbors*(u) is invalidated by resetting its position information to undefined. Initially and after each recovery, the location information for the logical neighbors may be undefined or invalid.

$logicalNeighbors :$ NODE $\rightarrow$ NREF-set

In SDL, we use an array of PIdstrings (NREF-set) indexed by Pids (nodes).

```
dcl logicalNeighbors PIdStringArray;
newtype PIdString String (PId,'') endnewtype;
newtype PIdStringArray Array(PId,PIdString); endnewtype;
```

The request timer in DASM is a function returning a time value, and the sequence number yields a value from a domain SEQNO.

$$reqTimer : \text{LTLS} \times \text{ADDRESS} \to \text{TIME}, \quad seqno : \text{LTLS} \times \text{ADDRESS} \to \text{SEQNO}$$

The request timer is of course modeled as an SDL timer. This way, we do not need the LTLS parameter of the $reqTimer$ function because this information is implicit in that the timer is local to a process. Moreover, the sequence number is given as a variable in the process, effectively avoiding to store it as a complete function. In fact, as the sequence number is used only in handling resend operations, it is simply stored within the corresponding $reqTimer$.

```
timer reqTimer(PId, Integer):= delta_req;
```

3.4   LTLS Protocol Dynamics

The below DASM program *LocationService* defines the behavior of LTLS agents in several steps, where *self* refers to an LTLS agent executing this program. Complex operations are subject to stepwise refinements and thus have the form of subrules expressed by means of parameterized rule macros.[4] Communication between the LTLS layer and the transport layer, respectively the PBR layer, is modeled by packet receive events of the form *OnPacketFromLayer(Agent)*

$LocationService \equiv$
   let $node = node(self)$ **in**
     if $devicestatus(node) = on$ **then**
       $BroadcastLocationInformation(node)$
       $CheckLocationUpdates(node)$
       forall $a \in \{x \in \text{ADDRESS} \mid reqTimer(self, x) \leq now(self)\}$
       // handle location request timeouts
         if $seqno(self, a) < maxTry(node)$ **then**
         $GenerateLocationRequest(node, a, seqno(self, a) + 1)$
         $seqno(self, a) := seqno(self, a) + 1$
         $reqTimer(self, a) := now(self) + \delta_{reqTimer}$
           // set location request timer
        else // node is unreachable
         $NotifyTransport(a, "unreachable")$
           // notification of failure to transport layer
         $reqTimer(self, a) := \infty$// reset location request timer
       $OnPacketFromTransport(node)$
       $OnPacketFromPBR(node)$

On the top level, the *LocationService* only describes the handling of the $reqTimer$. In SDL, the *LocationService* is represented by the main body of the LTLS process, including the $reqTimer$ handling and all the other events that are handled

---

[4] Note that the various subrules of a complex ASM rule are executed in parallel rather than sequentially since a sequence of ASM rules logically defines a parallel composition of rules forming one single rule.

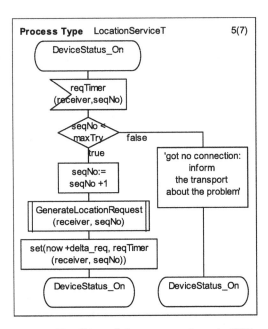

Fig. 3. Handling of the request timer in SDL

in the various subrules of the DASM description. The corresponding SDL representation is given in fig. 3. Please note that the part of communication back to the transport is not given here because it is not formally shown in the ASM.

3.5   Broadcast Location Information

For any node u, $BroadcastLocationInformation(u)$ periodically broadcasts the current position of u as controlled by a location update timer $locTimer$. Additionally, it broadcasts its position whenever u is activated (initially or after failure recovery). In the rule definition below, $SwitchedOnEvent(u)$ holds if node u has been (re-)activated in the current state. For brevity, packet header initialization is specified by a subrule referred to as INITPACKET.

$BroadcastLocationInformation(node : \mathrm{NODE}) \equiv$
  if $SwitchedOnEvent(node)$ **or** $locTimer(self) \leq now(self)$ **then**
    $locTimer(self) := now(self) + \delta_{locTimer}$ // set location timer
    forall $nref \in logicalNeighbors(node)$
      extend PACKET **with** p // generate location packet
      $InitPacket(p, location)$
      if $SwitchedOnEvent(node)$ **then**
        // location information for neighbors is invalid
        $nadr(dest(p)) := broadcast$
      else // location information for neighbors is valid
        $dest(p) := nref$
      $\mathrm{Packet\_to\_PBR}(p)$

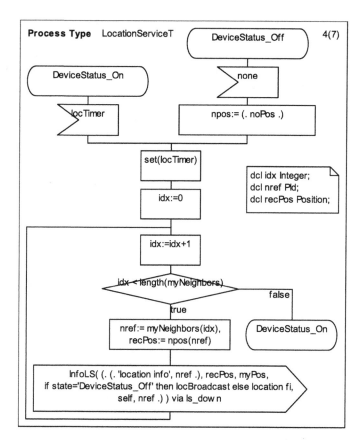

Fig. 4. BroadcastLocationInformation handling in SDL

Location requests require a retransmission mechanism that chooses alternate paths when a timeout occurs. A dynamic function *pathselect* computes a subset of the node references of the logical neighbors of u depending on the address of u, the address of the destination v, and the sequence number i of the retransmission attempt. Basically, an increasing number of redundant requests will be generated to compensate node failures in a network with reduced connectivity until all paths have been explored.

The DASM specification of *BroadcastLocationInformation* amounts to the handling of alternative input signals in terms of SDL.

For the broadcast of the location information shown in fig. 4, we have chosen to represent the switching-on event with a spontaneous transition from the 'Off'-state to the 'On'-state as we do not handle explicitly which events reactivate a node. The actual handling is very similar to the one in the ASM description. Please note that the cycle handling of DASM is far simpler than the SDL handling because in SDL the cycle has to be implemented directly as opposed to the DASM **'forall'**-mechanism. Please do also note that in SDL the creation of the signal is easily described as a creation of the corresponding data structure, whereas the ASM model uses a separate function to fill in the data. This is due to the fact that in SDL one has a complete description of the data contained in the signals, whereas in ASM the data items are attached to packets using functions. This way the data can be extended incrementally.

3.6   Handling Location Requests

When receiving a location request, the LTLS first checks the address of the final destination which is encoded into the data part of the discovery packet. In response to a location request, a location reply returns the most recent position of the destination node. Forwarded location requests are not subject to retransmissions performed by intermediate nodes; only the requesting node initiates retransmissions on failure.

$$HandleLocationRequest(node : \text{NODE}, p : \text{PACKET}) \equiv$$
$$\textbf{if } address(node) = data(p) \textbf{ then } // \text{ return node position}$$
$$GenerateLocationReply(node, sndr(p))$$
$$\textbf{else } // \text{ compute next logical hop and forward packet}$$
$$\textbf{let } \{nref\} = pathselect(address(node), data(p), 0) \textbf{ in}$$
$$dest(p) := nref$$
$$\text{Packet\_to\_PBR}(p)$$

As this is a second level subrule in the DASM description, it is captured as a procedure in the SDL description. Since the descriptions in ASM and SDL are very similar here, there is no need to consider such rules further. Please find the SDL description for *HandleLocationRequest* in fig. 5.

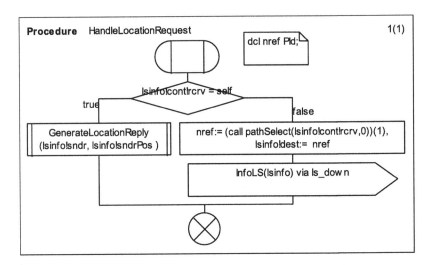

Fig. 5. Handling of location request in SDL

Please note that the assignment for *nref* has to be a selection in SDL, whereas this is done abstractly in DASM.

The above definition of retransmission led to problems in the simulation, because it is not checked if the request has already been sent by the same node, such that the request is sent in a cycle between some nodes without reaching the final destination. In practice, the protocol has to take this into account.

3.7   Handling PBR Packets

The communication with the PBR layer is modeled by the rule defined below.

$$OnPacketFromPBR(node : \text{NODE}) \equiv$$
if Packet_from_PBR(p : PACKET) **then**
　　if $type(p) = locreq$ **then**
　　　$HandleLocationRequest(node, p)$
　　if $type(p) = location$ **then**
　　　$HandleLocationReply(node, sndr(p))$
　　if $type(p) = data$ **then**
　　　$Packet\_to\_Transport(p)$

In SDL, the handling of packets coming from PBR is given as signal inputs as shown in fig. 6. The SDL signal input gives a clear indication of what is happening compared with the rather blurred description in ASM.

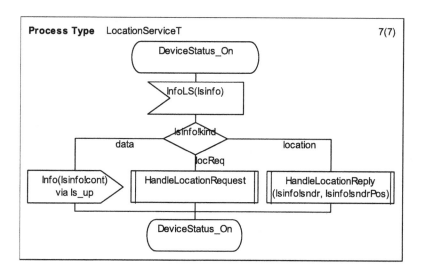

Fig. 6. Handling of packets from PBR in SDL

4   Concluding Remarks

Starting from an ASM model of the network layer protocol for geographic routing in mobile ad hoc networks, we have devised an executable SDL model; this also reveals a better understanding of the architecture. It seems natural that we have identified a few problems and errors in the ASM model, becoming visible due to the better structure modeling capabilities of SDL and the executability of the model. A typical example is the location of the positioning device: while the ASM model can access it from everywhere, the SDL model requires placing it in a definite location. Another typical problem is the communication between transport and LTLS layers, which was not specified in the ASM model. We also found a problem in the execution model: the broadcast and location requests have to be protected against transmission cycles.

In comparison with ASMs, the following features of SDL proved to be particularly beneficial: built-in timer mechanism, built-in communication via signals, explicit specification of the system structure, locality of variables, explicitly defined content of signals. On the other hand, SDL has problems where ASMs have advantages: abstract specification of variable types, abstract cross-layer connection, conciseness of representation with minimal encryption, easy handling of collections of items (**forall**).

Both modeling paradigms allow specification of the algorithm on a fairly abstract level and to perform analyses on it. Due to the high level of abstraction and the use of tools, they both produce flexible and easy to change models. Overall, none of the two paradigms is superior over or can replace the other one; rather they complement each other so that one can actually expect real benefits from a combined use. Therefore, it would be most desirable to have a methodological framework providing guidance for an effective combination. This is subject of our future work.

References

1. A. Benczur, U. Glässer and T. Lukovszki, *Formal Description of a Distributed Location Service for Ad Hoc Mobile Networks*, in E. Börger, A. Gargantini, E. Riccobene (Eds.): Abstract State Machines — Advances in Theory and Applications, vol. 2589 of LNCS, Springer Verlag, 2003.
2. E. Börger and R. Stärk, *Abstract State Machines: A Method for High-Level System Design and Analysis*, Springer, 2003.
3. Cinderella home page, URL: www.cinderella.dk.
4. J. Ellsberger, D. Hogrefe and A, Sarma, *SDL — Formal Object-oriented Language for Communicating Systems*, Prentice Hall Europe, 1997.
5. U. Glässer and Q.-P. Gu, *Formal Description and Analysis of a Distributed Location Service for Mobile Ad Hoc Networks*, Theoretical Computer Science, Elsevier, May 2005.
6. M. Mauve, J. Widmer and H. Hartenstein, *A Survey on Position-Based Routing in Mobile Ad-Hoc Networks*, IEEE Network, 15(6): 30-39, 2001.

Modeling Route Change in Soft-State Signaling Protocols Using SDL: A Case of RSVP

Constantin Werner, Xiaoming Fu, and Dieter Hogrefe

Telematics Group, University of Göttingen,
Lotzestrasse 16-18, D-37083 Göttingen, Germany
{werner, fu, hogrefe}@cs.uni-goettingen.de

Abstract. Soft state signaling protocols install and maintain states in network nodes, expiring without receiving refreshes. These states require proper reparation when the flow path changes, especially in case of link or node failures. As the specifications usually do not describe in detail how to handle these failures, we present insights by developing SDL models for RSVP on this issue.

1 Introduction

For the last decade, a group of protocols have been designed using soft state for state maintenance. In contrast to hard state, a soft state itself expires if no periodical refreshes are received. Soft state protocols are expected to have less protocol complexity in state maintenance operations especially with extreme network situations. However, as far as we know, rigorous investigations have rarely been performed on modeling these behaviors, especially for multi-hop soft state signaling protocols such as the Resource Reservation Protocol (RSVP) [1]. RSVP was the first soft state signaling protocol for Quality of Service (QoS) resource reservation developed by the Internet Engineering Task Force (IETF). RSVP specifications provide necessary message formats and processing rules for establishing and maintaining a state along a flow path. However, in common with most of the follow-up soft state signaling protocols, the RSVP specification does not describe in detail how a link failure is detected and circumvented.

This paper presents a formal model based on the Specification and Description Language (SDL) [7] of soft state signaling protocols. We investigate the RSVP protocol as a case study and particularly with respect to route changes. The model is built on a simplified IP layer model for RSVP message routing. Different from existing modeling approaches, our model allows an easy change of the analyzed network scenario without the need of any re-specification of the SDL router blocks. There is no centralized entity that responsible for routing, avoiding the necessity of re-specification for any new network topology. We show how the RSVP state recovery is verified and validated. We believe this modeling approach will be useful for the validation, modeling, and analysis of soft state protocols in general.

A. Prinz, R. Reed, and J. Reed (Eds.): SDL 2005, LNCS 3530, pp. 174–186, 2005.

The remainder of this paper is organized as follows: in the following subsections, we summarize existing studies on soft state protocols, and give a short introduction to RSVP and the formal process. In section 2, we describe the network layer model used for IP routing and route re-establishment in case of link failures. In section 3, we show the formal analysis of the RSVP soft state maintenance in the normal case and in the case of link failures. In section 4, we discuss formal description techniques versus textual description used by the IETF. We outline where ambiguities arise through unclear descriptions in the RSVP standard. Finally, we discuss the conclusions and give an outlook of the further work for formal modeling soft state protocols in SDL.

1.1   Studies on Soft State Protocols

System designers argue soft state is "better" than hard state, and using soft state the handling of network condition changes is "easy" [9, 10]. However, these claims have been more based on intuitive, high-level thoughts and explanations, instead of formal, exhaustive modeling and analysis. In contrast to the original expectations, soft state protocols developed so far are still far from being simple, especially when coupled with channel reliability, multicast sessions or traffic control models. Soft state protocols developed so far can be categorized into two types: end-to-end protocols and hop-by-hop protocols.

The former only involves certain types of state in an end-to-end way, without bothering any other nodes in between; examples of this type include RTCP and SIP. On the other hand, hop-by-hop protocols (such as RSVP and NSIS [12]) involve state in one or more router(s) in between, in addition to state in the communicating ends. The latter is more representative and more comprehensively demonstrates the soft state operations, so we choose this as the example for general discussions of soft state. Given the particular importance of soft state protocols, there have recently been a few efforts on their modeling and analysis: Raman and McCanne [10] presented a model for the soft state notion based on Jackson queuing networks, and a performance study of hard state and soft state signaling protocols was performed by Ji et al. [8]. However, more detailed formal modeling and validation is still missing. A general formal soft state protocol analysis has been presented in [6] but a concrete analysis of an existing soft state protocol is missing as well.

1.2   Overview of RSVP

RSVP aims to provide end-to-end quality of service (QoS) signaling for application data streams. Hosts use RSVP to request a specific QoS from the network for a particular application flows. Routers use RSVP to deliver QoS requests to all routers along the data path. RSVP can also maintain and refresh states for a requested QoS application flow. RSVP carries QoS signaling messages through the network, visiting each node along the data path. If the reservation succeeds, the RSVP module sets parameters in a packet classifier and packet scheduler to obtain the desired QoS. The design of RSVP distinguished itself in a number of fundamental ways, particularly: soft state management, two-pass signaling message exchanges, receiver-based resource reservation and separation of QoS signaling from routing [11]. Because the flow of delivery paths might change during the life of an application flow, RSVP takes a soft state approach in its design, creating and removing the protocol states (Path and Resv states) in routers and hosts. RSVP sends periodic refresh messages (Path and Resv) to maintain its states and to recover from occasional message loss. In the absence of refresh messages, the RSVP states automatically time out and are deleted. RSVP is not a routing protocol, but rather is designed to interoperate with current and future unicast and multicast routing protocols. While routing protocols are responsible for choosing the routes to use to forward packets, RSVP consults local routing tables to obtain routes and is responsible only for reservation setup along a data path.

1.3   Introducing Formal Process into the IETF Protocol Development

Traditionally, IETF protocols in the Request for Comments (RFC) documents are specified in a textual, informal format. A formal description using SDL of such a protocol can help to clearly and unambiguously specify the functional operation, because it allows easier detection of protocol anomalies or design errors such as deadlock or livelock situations. Previous studies such as [2, 4, 5] presented analysis and validation of several IETF protocols using formal description techniques. However, their analyses were limited to a single or only very few fixed use cases and applied only to protocols operating in an end-to-end fashion or using hard state in principle. None of them investigated any soft state signaling protocol, nor considered randomly chosen link failures. We argue it is important to guarantee the proper protocol operations in dynamic environments, especially that soft state signaling protocols are error-free and also precisely presented for

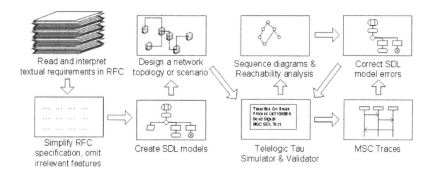

Fig. 1. The formal process. After the interpretation of an RFC, the SDL models are specified and a network scenario is created. An integrated SDL development tool, *Telelogic Tau 4.6*, is used for the formal verification and validation of the created model

the correctness of implementations. In this paper, we show a modeling approach that proves that despite the interactions between the possibly dynamic chain of intermediate hops and random link failures, the correctness and robustness in soft state protocols can still be proven by way of formal description and validation.

Figure 1 shows the formal process flow which we used in our modeling, starting with reading and interpreting the RFC. RSVP features which do not relate to route change detection and recovery were chosen to be omitted to reduce complexity. A network topology was created which is assumed to be sufficiently complex to show the route re-establishment functionality of RSVP. Due to the decentralized IP network layer architecture, additional network topologies can be created and analyzed without the need to re-specify the SDL models.

2   SDL Modeling of Message Routing in IP Networks

To the best of our knowledge, formal models focused on IP based networks developed so far either model end-to-end protocols (which are formally specified for their special purpose), or simply three entities are assumed: a sender, a recipient, and a general transport block as a centralized entity for routing, forwarding and packet loss modeling (see [2, 4, 5]). These approaches have the disadvantage that for each new network topology the central routing entity or intermediate nodes have to be re-specified and adapted to the new network configuration. Additionally, link failures are hard to emulate. Multi-hop protocols with route failures cannot be modeled using a centralized entity or fixed formalized nodes for message transport.

We propose a formal decentralized network layer architecture, which automatically learns its neighboring entities and reachable destinations by itself. However, modeling of IP based communication protocols in dynamic network topologies can suffers from some SDL shortcomings and limitations of Telelogic Tau. SDL does not offer a dynamic number of channels connected to a block, therefore, our router models have a fixed amount of three channels (network links) available. Furthermore, SDL does not provide native support of IP addresses, so we use SDL process IDs (*Pid*) for addressing of nodes in the topology instead. We believe that this is no drawback of our model if small network topologies without the need for special routing are required. The signal *myPID* is used to announce the destination node's address (process IDs) to other nodes. In reality, this is defined by the user or user's application.

Our routing algorithm is inspired by *Distance Vector Routing* protocols like the *Routing Information Protocol* (RIP) [3]. To reduce complexity, the periodically broadcasted distance vector updates are replaced by signals that trigger distance vector updates between neighboring routers. This feature is especially useful in not being confused by minor relevant network layer messages if the upper layer's soft state protocol messages are to be analyzed and validated. Furthermore, this is required for formal analysis using the Telelogic Tau Validator. The Validator does not include signals from the environment if any transitions are still scheduled. While the routing tables are updating, the system converges to a stable state. Some more enhancements and simplification have been undertaken to bypass known Distance Vector Routing problems (such as the *count-to-infinity* problem [13]). We do not discuss them here in detail, since this is not the scope of this paper. Note that our model of RSVP is intentionally not bound to any specific IP routing protocol, so the use of a modified routing protocol here does not violate any RSVP requirement.

The IP routing layer is modeled as a block consisting of a *forwarding* and a *routing* block. The basic operational principle is the following: The *forwarder* receives *datagrams*, which is an SDL structure consisting of the variables *Source* (sender of this packet), *Destination* (destination for this packet), *Phop* (previous hop), and a payload *msg* from the upper layer – RSVP messages in this case. If the *forwarder* receives a datagram, it queries the *routing* block for the address of the next hop and forwards the *datagram* to this hop. Routing table updates

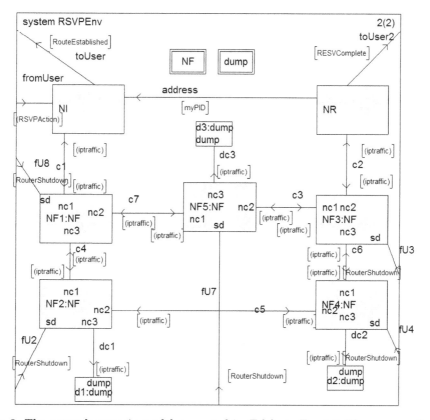

Fig. 2. The network scenario model generated in *Telelogic Tau 4.6*. The message flow used in this scenario is from NI down to NR via several NFs and vice versa. Note that the shortest route between NI and NR is via NF1, NF5, and NF3. After a possible shutdown of NF5, an alternative route is established via NF1, NF2, NF4, and NF3

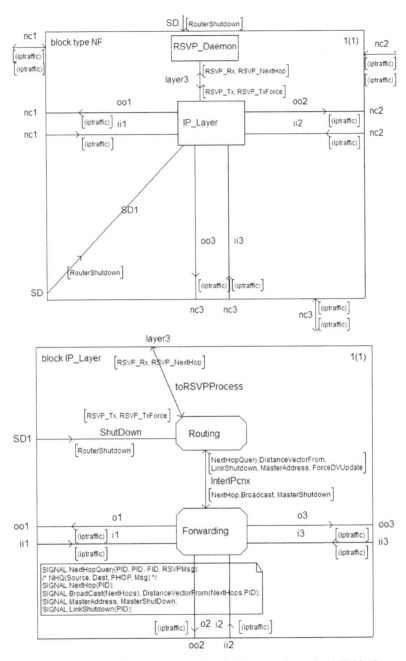

Fig. 3. The internal network structure block of all NF nodes. The NF block consists of a layered block structure which is the IP layer with routing functionality and a higher layer which is the RSVP daemon here. The *forwarding* block is responsible for the receiving and forwarding datagrams. The *routing* block selects the next hop for a received datagram and maintains its local routing table. RSVP messages are sent to the RSVP daemon block by the *routing* block if received

are received by a special signal *Distance Vector* containing the routing table of the neighbor's routing layer. This information is used by the *routing* block to update its local routing table.

Figure 2 shows the SDL system for the described network topology. The investigated scenario consists of one *NI* (network initiator), multiple *NF*s (network forwarder with routing functionality) and one *NR* (network receiver). The NI is the entity, which generates RSVP messages and tries to establish a reservation state along the path from NI via multiple NFs down to the receiving NR. Every single hop on the path establishes a requested RSVP state. All NF nodes have three connectors available for creating a network scenario. Unconnected signal channels have to be connected to *dump* blocks that silently consume all signals they receive.

All routing layers feature an external *Shutdown* signal from the environment, which allows the user to shutdown any or multiple instances freely. If a routing layer is triggered by such a *Shutdown* signal, it announces shutdown by sending a *LinkFailure* signal to all its neighbors. Note that this is one modification to Distance Vector routing protocols, which detect a node failure by the absence of the failed node's routing table updates. Because periodic routing table update messages add avoidable communication complexity to the scenario, the *LinkFailure* signal has been introduced.

All neighboring hops are now trying to update their routing tables with new routing information and request table updates from their neighbors as well. The routing layer, once being shutdown, is no longer operational from now on and only consumes each signal or message silently which it receives. The whole entity cannot operate any more. This allows the analysis if the soft state timing is able to maintain its state even if refresh messages are lost at the non-operational hop until the new route is established. See fig. 3 for an overview of the IP routing and RSVP block.

3   Formal Analysis of RSVP State Maintenance with Link Failure

We analyzed with our models and Telelogic Tau how RSVP can restore a valid path after a link failure. When the simulation was started, the system announces via a special signal that it is ready for operation and all routing tables are built up to allow a complete routing between all nodes. The NI accepts three different signal triggers from the environment: *RSVPStart, RSVPTeardown,* and *RSVPStop.* RSVPStart begins creating a path state and resource reservation along the path down to the NR. The NI periodically sends new path messages to keep the RSVP soft state alive. The RSVPTeardown signal triggers the NI to stop sending refresh messages and to send a *PathTeardown* message towards the NR. All nodes in-between delete the associated states from this reservation and forward the teardown message to the next hop (*Explicit Teardown*). The RSVPStop signal just stops the NI from sending new state refresh messages

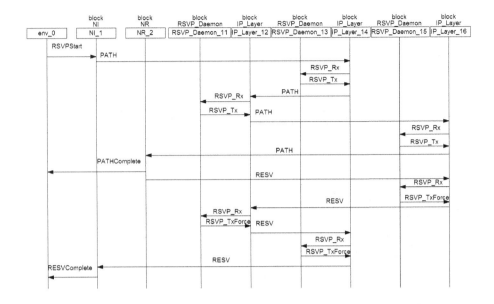

Fig. 4. Message flow of a RSVP resource reservation. The *Path* message is sent downstream from the NI hop-by-hop to the NR. The corresponding *Resv* message is sent upstream from the NR hop-by-hop to the NI. Message parameters and process states are not shown for clarity

towards the NR. This leads to a state timeout at all hops and the states are deleted after the state lifetime expiry.

In fig. 4 a default RSVP *Path* and *Resv* message refresh flow is shown. The message exchange in this MSC is shown from the NI via N1, N5, and N3 down to the NR. This is the shortest path. Notice the internal message exchange between the IP Layer and the RSVP instances. The RSVP daemon is notified of the reception of RSVP messages by the *RSVP_Rx* signal and itself sends a RSVP message using the *RSVP_Tx* or *RSVP_TxForce* signal. While the RSVP_Tx signal allows the IP layer to select the next hop, the RSVP_TxForce explicitly addresses the next hop. The Telelogic Tau SDL simulator is being used to trace the correct establishment of *RSVP_Established* states in all RSVP intermediate hops and the NR.

Next, a router shutdown is triggered. In this scenario, NF5 is selected as the failure hop. By doing this, an alternative route has to be established by the IP routing layer. After NF5 has been shutdown, it announces its imminent death by sending a *LinkFailure* signal to all its neighbors. Because of this signal, they try to update their local routing tables with their neighbors as well. See the following fig. 5 for an MSC which shows the message exchange in case of the NF5 shutdown. While the routers try to update their information, a newly created RSVP message is lost while being routed, visible at the signal marked with the dotted arrow.

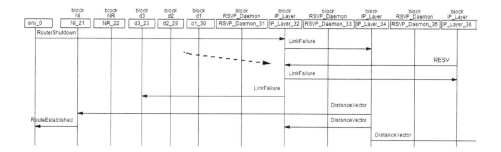

Fig. 5. Initial message exchange after router shutdown. After the router is shutdown by a *RouterShutdown* signal (top left in the MSC) all neighboring routers try to update their local routing tables. Note that the *Resv* message which was already on the way up to the NI is discarded by the link failure and is lost (marked by a dotted arrow)

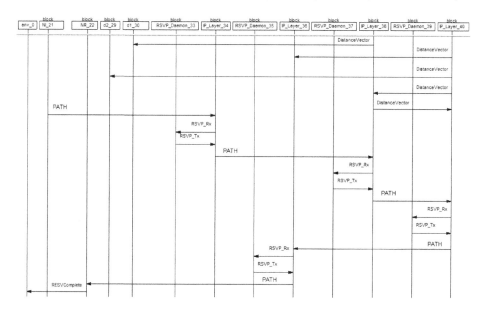

Fig. 6. New route and state establishment. This MSC is the time continuation of the MSC shown in fig. 5. Some routing table update messages and inactive instances are skipped. The RSVP message (*Path*) is delivered via the alternative route NF1, NF2, NF4, NF3 down to the NR. This is accomplished using normal path state recovery initiated by the next refresh message from the NI

Most of the messages shown in fig. 5 are routing table updates used for the establishment of the new path between NI and NR. So we do not discuss them in detail here. The next RSVP refresh message is due shortly after the new route has been established and is shown in the following fig. 6. One can see that the message is correctly routed through the new hops of the alternative

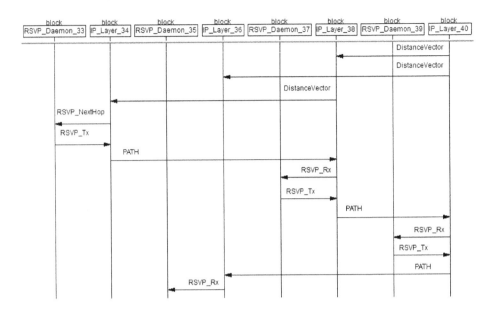

Fig. 7. A cut-out of the new route establishment using *Local repair*. This MSC is another time continuation of the MSC shown in fig. 5. Some routing table update messages and inactive instances are skipped. The new RSVP message (*Path*) is delivered via the alternative route NF1, NF2, NF4, NF3 down to the NR. Note that a *Path* message is sent triggered by the routing table update by receiving the *Distance Vector* signal. The RSVP process gets notified of the route change by the *RSVP_NextHop* signal

route. The SDL simulator confirms that all new hops are able to establish a correct *RSVP_Established* state. The RSVP soft state operation continues with correct behavior. This is caused by the detection of the route change if the previous hop of the new RSVP message differs from the one which has been recorded on previous RSVP messages. The same detection applies on changes of the next hop which is decided by the IP routing layer. This operation has been validated using the built-in Validator of Telelogic Tau using exhaustive state space exploration.

Note that our RSVP model does not include RSVP features like multicast, and the admission and policy modules, since these are not particularly interesting for route re-establishment. RSVP multicast adds a high level of complexity to the protocol design and multicast support (actually one of its succeeding IETF efforts, NSIS, has decided to remove multicast from basic signaling support), thus it is not considered here. Therefore, all multicast related operations like merging and styles processing are not considered. *Local repair* has been implemented, which improves route recovery by immediately sending *Path* and *Resv* messages towards the previous and next hop if a route change is detected. Figure 7 shows an MSC with local repair action triggered by routing table updates.

4   Formal Description Techniques Versus Textual Description

The RSVP standard is not very clear in its route change detection specification and handling. The *Local Repair* section of the RSVP document describes how route changes are detected by evaluating the previous hop field and being informed by the routing layer of the outgoing interface selection. Unfortunately, a precise formalism of how route changes are detected and handled is not present.

As an example, it is stated in the *Local Repair* section of the RSVP specification: "*[. . .] To provide fast adaptation to routing changes without the overhead of short refresh periods, the local routing protocol module can notify the RSVP process of route changes for particular destinations. The RSVP process should use this information to trigger a quick refresh of state for these destinations, using the new route. When routing detects a change of the set of outgoing interfaces for destination G, RSVP should update the path state, wait for a short period W, and then send Path refreshes for all sessions. [. . .] When a Path message arrives with a Previous Hop address that differs from the one stored in the path state, RSVP should send immediate Resv refreshes to that PHOP.*"

From this description it is unclear for the reader whether the routing layer is responsible for the route change detection (and just notifies to the RSVP process) or the RSVP process has to query the routing module for each RSVP packet transmission. Additionally, the description about the case of *previous hop detection* does not explicitly state how RSVP handles this case. That is, detailed interactions are missing in the specification. How does the routing protocol know that there is a routing change? Does it save the next hop node for all outgoing RSVP messages and processes or does it notify the RSVP process of the outgoing interface or next hop which was taken for the most recent RSVP message and it is up to the RSVP process to detect that the next hop has changed? When does an action have to be taken? The same thing applies for the previous hop detection.

Besides, how the RSVP process is able to instruct the routing layer to send a message hop-by-hop using the previous hop is not specified. The RSVP specification gives information saying in the *RSVP messages* section: "*[. . .] These Path messages store 'path state' in each node along the way. This path state includes at least the unicast IP address of the previous hop node, which is used to route the Resv messages hop-by-hop in the reverse direction. [. . .]*". We have to make the assumption that RSVP looks up the previous hop information in the path state according to a matching between the flow identifier (however, this can be some other metric) and the path state, and then sets the IP header of the Resv message as the previous hop's IP address. However, due to the ambiguity of the specification, even ignoring the looking up metric, one can also interpret the Resv message to be encapsulated with a routing header where destination addresses are the flow sender's address (inner IP header destination field) and previous hop's IP address (direct IP header destination field). We have developed a concrete communication model which allows the RSVP process to explicitly specify the outgoing hop. See fig. 3 for an overview of this model. Our communication model allows the RSVP process to receive the RSVP message received by a previous hop, and to transmit a message implicitly by specifying the destination but the next hop decision is up to the routing layer. The RSVP process is able to get a notification of the next hop address which has been selected by the routing layer when routing table updates have occurred. Additionally, the RSVP process is able to explicitly specify the next hop which is required to send RESV messages upstream on the same path.

We have shown a precise, formalized way how the RSVP process can detect and handle such extreme situations. We modeled the previous hop and next hop change detection in the RSVP process so that there is a clearly defined interaction needed between the RSVP process and the routing layer. The RSVP process gets a notification of the next hop address via the *RSVP_Nexthop* signal shown in fig. 3 chosen by the routing layer. It can compare this with the stored next hop address from previous RSVP messages. The RSVP process detects previous hop changes by evaluating the previous hop field in the RSVP message. The *RSVP_Nexthop* signal may be send asynchronously, which means that the signal can be transmitted at any time from the routing layer to the RSVP process.

In our model and particularly with this investigated scenario, this approach was able to build up the reservation state in the alternative route and to maintain the state in hops which were already involved in the prior resource reservation.

5   Conclusions and Future Work

It is often argued that soft state protocols are "better" but these claims have been more based on intuitive, high-level thoughts and explanations, instead of formal, exhaustive modeling and analysis. This calls for a detailed formal modeling and validation. A general formal soft state protocol analysis has recently been done but a concrete analysis of an existing soft state protocol is still missing.

In this paper, we presented an SDL model of a concrete, existing soft state protocol, namely the RSVP resource reservation protocol developed by the IETF. Because this protocol relies on IP routing, an IP routing layer was also implemented in SDL which performs the message routing. We focused on the modeling of a typical soft state operation caused by a link failure and the RSVP route re-establishment through an alternative route. The studied scenarios consisted of one initiator, one responder and a dynamic amount of intermediate nodes. In this paper, we only considered one single scenario where the shortest route between the initiator and responder is broken by a link failure and an alternative route is established. We showed the message exchange in normal operation, with local repair and the route and state recovery after a link failure has occurred in MSC diagrams. RSVP operations especially under route change situations were simulated and validated using the tool Telelogic Tau 4.6.

The RSVP standard lacks a detailed and formalized description of how route changes are detected and handled. Although a description can be found about this in the RFC document, it is unclear which process is responsible and how it is achieved in detail. Our model proposes a way to detect a route change and handling within the RSVP process. We have shown that a formal description and analysis of an existing soft state protocol and its state maintenance operations under various network conditions is possible using formal description techniques.

The RSVP model used in this paper was simplified. Some features of RSVP were left out: multicast support, detailed presentations for reservation flows and sessions, admission control and policy control. Though most of these RSVP features are not relevant for this operation and link failure analysis, the actual flow and session presentations, and admission control are important towards a more realistic modeling of RSVP. These features are not irrelevant in route change modeling because some new reservations may be rejected on alternative paths which we did not consider here. In future versions of this model, we want to integrate these modules into our SDL model of RSVP. Additionally, we want to analyze multiple sessions between multiple initiators and responders. Currently, we support multiple intermediate hops but only with a single initiator and responder, which create a resource reservation along the path hop-by-hop.

References

1. Braden, R., Zhang, L., Berson, S., Herzog, S., and Jamin, S.: Resource ReSerVation Protocol (RSVP) – Version 1 functional specification. RFC 2205, IETF (1997)
2. Monkewich, O., Sales, I., Probert, R.: OSPF Efficient LSA Refreshment Function in SDL. In: Reed, R., Reed, J. (eds.): SDL 2001, Lecture Notes in Computer Science, Vol. 2078, Springer-Verlag, Berlin Heidelberg New York (2001) 300–315
3. Malkin, G.: RIP Version 2 – Carrying Additional Information. RFC 1723, IETF (1994)
4. Chan, K. Y., v. Bochmann, G.: Modeling IETF Session Initiation Protocol and its services in SDL. In: Reed, R., (ed.): SDL 2003, Lecture Notes in Computer Science, Vol. 2708, Springer-Verlag, Berlin Heidelberg (2003) 352–373
5. Cavalli, A., Grepet, C., Maag, S., and Tortajada, V.: A Validation Model for the DSR protocol. ICDCS 2004 (2004)
6. Fu, X., and Hogrefe, D.: Modeling Soft State Protocols with SDL. To appear in: Proceedings of IFIP International Conference on Networking, Waterloo, Canada (2005)
7. Ellsberger, J., Hogrefe, D., and Sarma, A.: SDL – Object Oriented Language for Communication Systems. Prentice Hall (1997)
8. Ji, P., Ge, Z., Kurose, j., and Towsley, D.: A comparison of hard-state and soft-state signaling protocols. In: Proc. of SIGCOMM 2003, Karlsruhe, Germany (2003)
9. Sharma, P., Estrin, D., Floyd, S., and Jacobson, V.: Scalable timers for soft state protocols. In: INFOCOM'97, Kobe, Japan (1997)
10. Raman, S. and McCanne, S.: A model, analysis, and protocol framework for soft state-based communication. In: Proc. of SIGCOMM 1999, Cambridge, MA (1999)
11. Zhang, L., Deering, S., Estrin, D., Shenker, S., and Zappala, D.: RSVP: a New Resource Reservation Protocol. IEEE Network (1993).
12. Hancock, R., Karagiannis, G., Loughney, J., and v. d. Bosch, S.: Next Steps in Signaling: Framework. Internet draft, work in progress, IETF (2004)
13. Tanenbaum, A.S.: Computer Networks. 4th Edition, Prentice Hall (2002)

Experiences in Using SDL to Support the Design and Implementation of a Logical Link Layer Protocol

Laila Daniel, Matti Luukkainen, and Markku Kojo

Department of Computer Science, University of Helsinki, Finland
{ldaniel, mluukkai, kojo}@cs.helsinki.fi

Abstract. We have used SDL to support the design and implementation of SLACP, a novel logical link layer protocol to enhance the performance of TCP over wireless WAN links. The protocol was modeled in SDL and successive refinements of its design were carried out based on feedback obtained from using the validation facilities of Telelogic Tau 4.4 SDT.

1 Introduction

Transmission Control Protocol (TCP) [1] is the dominant transport protocol in the Internet. TCP performs well in wired networks where packet losses occur mainly due to congestion. Unfortunately TCP performance suffers in wireless networks where packet losses due to link errors and handoff are predominant [2]. We have designed a link-aware protocol called Satellite Link Aware Communication Protocol (SLACP) to improve TCP performance over wireless WAN links such as satellite links[1].

We use SDL [3] to support the design and implementation of SLACP based on a *validation-oriented design approach*. In this approach an initial abstract executable model that covers the basic functionality of the protocol is developed. In the abstract model the number of data elements (both in signals and in processes) is kept to a minimum. We then validate the internal consistency and functionality of the abstract model. Subsequently we add details to the basic model in an incremental manner by specifying additional elements such as signal parameters, error handling and validate the enhanced model. This step is iterated until all the elements of the protocol have been added to the model. This incremental design approach helps in controlling the complexity of the protocol and in evolving a design that could be validated. This approach is facilitated by modeling SLACP in SDL and using the feedback obtained from the validation facilities provided by Telelogic Tau 4.4 SDT [4]. The SDL model of SLACP is the basis of the implementation of the protocol in Linux [5, 6].

---

[1] This work was done as a part of Transat project sponsored by European Space Agency.

A. Prinz, R. Reed, and J. Reed (Eds.): SDL 2005, LNCS 3530, pp. 187–197, 2005.

The rest of the paper is organized as follows. Section 2 gives an overview of SLACP. Sections 3 and 4 are devoted to the modeling of SLACP using SDL. Section 5 deals with SLACP validation and section 6 compares the SDL model with the actual implementation of the protocol. In section 7 we discuss the conclusions of the paper.

2   Satellite Link Aware Communication Protocol (SLACP)

SLACP is a full-fledged logical link layer protocol which provides data transfer, error recovery and a Quality of Service (QoS) mechanism for enhancing TCP and other Internet protocol performance on wireless WANs. A detailed description of the protocol with performance results is given in [5, 6]. We briefly describe the salient features of SLACP needed to understand the design of the protocol.

The main goal of SLACP is to reduce the errors perceived by TCP. SLACP uses selective repeat sliding window mechanism [7] for data transfer. Error recovery is done using a combination of Automatic Repeat reQuest (ARQ) and Forward Error Correction (FEC). SLACP provides flow control mechanisms between the Internet Protocol (IP) layer and the satellite Medium Access Control (MAC) layer. SLACP performs a QoS mapping in which all packets belonging to an IP QoS class are directed to a SLACP channel with appropriate QoS parameters. SLACP supports several logical channels with independent choice of QoS parameters and error control schemes.

SLACP frames are of two types, *control frames* and *data frames*. Control frames carry the signals to setup, disconnect and reset a channel besides providing information regarding acknowledgments, packet loss and flow control. Data frames carry the IP packets. Frames transmitted over each logical channel are delivered independently of the frames sent over the other channels. A single high priority channel, called *control channel*, allows timely delivery of time-critical frames such as retransmitted data frames, acknowledgments and control frames. The frames sent through the control channel are FEC encoded to make them robust against errors. By default all original data frames are sent without FEC encoding as the satellite and other wireless channels are relatively error free most of the time and FEC encoding consumes additional bandwidth.

A problem with the link layer recovery is that it may interfere with the TCP recovery if the link level recovery takes a long time. We designed SLACP to minimize the link recovery delay by providing a high priority channel for the time-critical frames, by using acknowledgments with selective repeat information (SACK blocks), by setting the ARQ persistence level to one, together with employing FEC-encoding to protect retransmissions, and by introducing special frames such as nothing_to_send frame and rxmtpkt_loss frame. SLACP can recover lost frames readily if the loss occurs at the beginning or in the middle of a burst of frames, because the loss can be detected immediately with the first successfully arriving frame. If the tail of a burst is lost, depending on the idle time until the next burst begins, SLACP might need to rely on a timer generated nothing_to_send frames getting through to trigger selective acknowledgment telling which frames were lost. Once this selective acknowledgment arrives, retransmissions take place as usual. When the SLACP receiver gets the signal rxmtpkt_loss from the sender indicating the permanent loss of a frame, it knows that the sender is not going to retransmit the frame again and that it can send all frames up to the lost frame in its buffer to the IP layer.

SLACP implements FEC encoding using Reed-Solomon codes. FEC encoding and recovery is done in a novel way to protect the frames from error bursts that tend to completely corrupt several consecutive frames. Therefore, the FEC-encoded redundancy is not added separately to each frame as usual. Instead, the frames to be FEC protected are organized as FEC blocks. Each FEC block consists of actual frames and redundancy frames. The FEC-encoded redundancy is added to the redundancy frames by computing the Reed-Solomon codeword vertically so that the ith octet of each frame in a FEC block comprises a codeword. As soon as a predetermined amount of actual frames deserving FEC protection has been sent or a threshold timer expires, a proper amount of FEC-encoded redundancy frames are computed to complete the FEC block and are transmitted. If no actual frames in a FEC block are lost, the redundancy frames are not used at all at the receiver. If some actual frames are lost, the SLACP receiver waits till the last redundancy frame of that FEC block or a frame belonging to any of the later FEC blocks is received. If at least a minimum number of redundancy frames are present in an FEC block the lost actual frames can be recovered. This minimum number depends on the parameters of the error correcting code in use. Under the minimum number, lost frames cannot be recovered by error correcting.

3   Modeling SLACP Using SDL

The link layer model also includes its interface to the layers above and below it. So in modeling SLACP we model the interface between SLACP and IP layer as well as the interface between SLACP and the Media Access Control (MAC) layer. The modeling of the IP and MAC layers allows us to see the flow control mechanisms between IP and SLACP and between SLACP and MAC. The MAC layer is also needed to model the delay and link losses in the satellite and wireless links.

The SLACP protocol engine consists of both the SLACP sender and receiver. The first question is whether to model the SLACP protocol engine (the combination of the SLACP sender and receiver) as a single entity and have two such engines as the communicating peer entities. This approach is the usual way of implementing a protocol and it helps to test the full duplex operation of the protocol. Since we are designing the protocol from scratch we model the protocol in a simple way by separating the sender and the receiver and testing the functionalities of the sender and the receiver separately. This results in a model where the SLACP sender receives packets from the IP layer and sends them to the SLACP receiver via the MAC layer. As SLACP is not concerned with the processing of the received data by the higher layer, it is not necessary to model

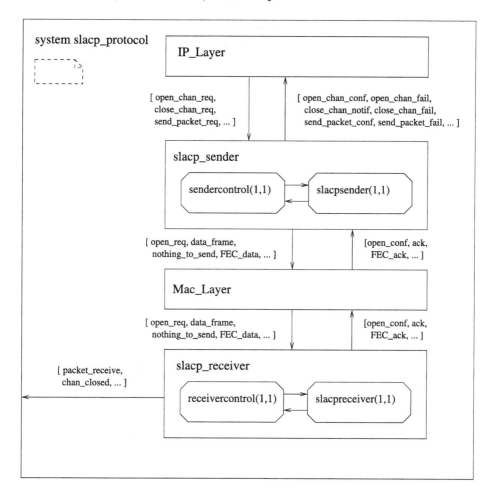

Fig. 1. SDL model of SLACP protocol

the IP layer at the receiver side, so in the SDL model the SLACP receiver sends
the received packets to the system environment.

Thus the SDL system model of SLACP consists of the blocks *IP Layer,
SLACP Sender, MAC layer and SLACP Receiver* (see fig. 1).

SDL allows us to define the system model in a top down manner. This helps
to define processes for special functionalities inside each of the blocks above.

The data structures provided in SDL are convenient to model the various queues
and frame types used in the protocol. Since the MAC buffer has different kinds of
frames, the MAC frame is modeled using SDL choice construct. We use the SDL
timer facility to implement the different timers associated with the protocol.

In the following sections we describe briefly the different blocks of the SDL
model of SLACP. We only describe in words the implementation ideas behind

the various blocks. As the entire protocol model consists of roughly 100 pages of SDL code, no concrete SDL code is shown here.

3.1   IP Layer

The main functionalities at the IP layer are to generate the signals for SLACP channel establishment, channel reset and channel disconnect. The IP layer also generates data packets to be sent to the SLACP layer. The IP layer handles the flow control signals coming from the SLACP sender and the notifications from the SLACP sender to be given to higher layer protocol entities. The layers above IP are modeled as system environment. When the IP layer gives a packet to the SLACP sender it is assumed that the packet is given to the correct queue according to the QoS requirement.

The IP layer block consists of a *packet generator* process and a *signaling* process. The packet generator process handles the functionality associated with packet generation and the signaling process deals with opening, resetting and closing of the channel. The signaling process also gives signals to the packet generator process; for example, when it sends a signal to the SLACP sender to close the channel, it also signals the packet generator to stop generating packets.

Initially both the SLACP sender and receiver are in the idle state. When the sender gets a request from the IP layer to open a channel, it sends a corresponding SLACP frame open_req to the receiver, and both the sender and the receiver negotiate the parameters of the connection. If they agree, they go to the connected state and the SLACP sender sends an open_chan_conf packet to the IP layer. The SLACP sender and receiver remain in the connected state until a channel reset or a channel close request comes from the IP layer. If the opening of the channel between the sender and the receiver has failed, the SLACP sender sends a open_channel_fail to the IP layer. Closing of the channel is modeled using a timer called channel_close_timer at the IP layer and when it expires the signaling process issues a close_chan_req to the SLACP sender.

After the connection establishment, the IP layer issues a send_packet_req to the SLACP sender for each outbound packet to which SLACP sender replies with the status of the buffer. If the buffer is available at the SLACP sender, the IP layer sends packets to the SLACP sender. The SLACP sender also informs the IP layer whether a packet was successfully delivered to the receiver. The packet generator process controls the generation of packets using the information it receives from the SLACP sender regarding the buffer status. Thus flow control is modeled between the IP layer and the SLACP sender.

3.2   SLACP Sender

In principle there are n senders for the n different logical channels but as senders are independent it is adequate to model one sender. The SLACP sender consists of two processes, *sender* and *sendercontrol*. The sender process represents the entity carrying out the processing of signals for ordinary data channel and sendercontrol represents the entity carrying out the processing of signals in the control channel. We model SLACP sender for a particular choice of QoS and ARQ-FEC parameters.

After connection setup, when the SLACP sender receives a packet from the IP layer it adds a header and a trailer to it to form a frame and enqueues the frame in the buffer. As SLACP is a sliding window protocol the sender always ensures that only a limited number of unacknowledged frames can exist at a time. The maximum number of unacknowledged or outstanding frames is called the the window size at the sender. If the window is not full, the sender process sends the SLACP frame to the MAC layer if the MAC buffer is free and updates the scoreboard data structure. The scoreboard records the information regarding the frame such as its sequence number, its address in the SLACP buffer and whether it has been retransmitted or not. The scoreboard data structure is used to implement the selective repeat mechanism. If the MAC buffer is not free the sender process keeps the data frame in its buffer. This way the SLACP sender controls the flow between the MAC and IP layers.

The sendercontrol gets the FEC encoded acknowledgment (ACK) frames from the SLACP receiver and it forwards the ACK frames to the sender process. If the data frame has been received correctly, the frame is dequeued from the sender buffer, otherwise it is retransmitted. When the sender receives a selective acknowledgment (SACK) from the SLACP receiver, it retransmits the lost frame to the sendercontrol. The details of the lost frame are obtained from the scoreboard. The sendercontrol forwards the FEC encoded retransmitted frames in an FEC block. SLACP is not meant to be a fully reliable link protocol and in the normal operation the ARQ persistence is set to one. If a retransmitted frame is lost, the SLACP sender sends a packet_loss_notification to the IP layer and also a rxmtpkt_loss to the SLACP receiver. When the SLACP sender has no data to send it sends a nothing_to_send frame to the receiver.

When the SLACP sender gets a request from the IP layer to close the channel it sends a data frame with no data to the SLACP receiver to indicate the closing of the channel. After receiving the ACKs for all the data sent to the receiver, the SLACP sender sends a close_channel_notif to the IP layer and goes to the idle state.

3.3   MAC Layer

The MAC Layer pictured here is the part of the MAC layer as seen by SLACP. So we abstract from the segmentation and reassembly at the MAC layer. The MAC layer has to perform the function of delivery of frames between SLACP sender and receiver. It also gives flow control information to both the SLACP sender and receiver. The MAC layer queues all the frames it receives from the SLACP layer and sends a frame to the SLACP layer when a link timer expires. The timeout of the link timer represents the delay in the wireless link. The MAC layer is also modeled to drop frames to simulate the behavior of frame losses due to bit corruption on the link. This is an important feature in order to validate the error recovery functionality in the SLACP protocol. We used a simple modulo based counter to determine which packet is to be dropped, though one can use random number generation to drop frames in an arbitrary manner.

3.4   SLACP Receiver

The SLACP receiver consists of two processes, namely *receiver* and *receivercontrol*. The receiver process represents the entity carrying out the processing of signals for ordinary data channel and the receivercontrol process represents the entity carrying out the processing of signals in the control channel.

SLACP receiver checks whether the frame received is a frame within the receiver window. The lower edge of the window represents the sequence number of the next frame to be received or the frame expected. When the frame received is the frame expected, the receiver process sends the received packet to the system environment. If the frames are received out of order within the window, the frames are kept in a reassembly queue. When the receiver process receives a number of data frames equal to an acknowledgment threshold value or when it receives an out of order frame, it sends an ACK frame. The ACK frame carries both a cumulative ACK sequence number and the SACK block. The SACK block indicates any out of order frames received after the cumulative ACK sequence number. The SLACP sender constructs an FEC block to retransmit all frames indicated as lost in the SACK block.

When the receivercontrol process receives an FEC block it sends an FEC_ACK to the sendercontrol process. Similar to the ACK frame, the FEC_ACK frame also has a cumulative ACK and an FEC-SACK block. The receivercontrol decodes the FEC block when it arrives and forwards the correctly received frames to the receiver process. Instead of using FEC coding to compute redundancy frames, each actual frame in the FEC block is duplicated as a redundancy frame. If a duplicate for a lost actual frame is present among the redundancy frames, it simulates the recovery of the frame.

4   The SDL Model as an Aid to the Design of SLACP

We develop the SDL model of SLACP in an incremental manner by successively refining the protocol design at each stage. Initially the protocol skeleton is built by including all the blocks and processes with minimal functionality in the blocks and processes. This helps to establish the basic interaction patterns between the processes and the blocks. Initially the functionalities for opening and closing a channel are included to build the basic model. We select these functionalities first since they are basic for communicating processes and in our model they involve all the protocol blocks in fig. 1. With this choice we could model the basic signaling mechanisms and see the patterns of interaction between the various design elements. The interactive mode of use of SDT helps to exercise the preliminary design by suitable choice of the parameters such as those for opening and closing a channel. For example, closing of a channel can be simulated by setting the duration of the channel_close_timer to a small value. After opening the channel, the IP layer will send a close_chan_req to the SLACP sender and this in turn closes the channel. From the Message Sequence Charts (MSC) generated we can see that the basic model is working.

In the second level of modeling the objective is to ensure that the data transfer can take place in the simplest possible setting. So we build enough additional functionality into the model to enable a single packet to be transferred from the sender to the receiver when there are no losses due to errors and there is no flow control. At this stage we extend the model with functionalities necessary for generating a packet at the IP layer, and delivering it to the SLACP receiver. This scenario is simulated by the IP layer opening the channel and sending a single packet to the SLACP sender and then closing the channel.

The third level of modeling is to include the flow control between IP and SLACP layers as well as between SLACP and MAC layers. We enhance the model from the previous stage by adding functionalities for queuing the frame at the SLACP sender and MAC buffers and for flow control mechanisms based on the buffer availability. The composite model is tested by setting the size of the SLACP sender buffer and MAC buffer to small values.

At the fourth level of modeling we incorporate ARQ-FEC error control schemes. We add the SACK mechanism, buffering and timer features to handle FEC coding. As it is not necessary to choose the actual FEC encoding in the model, we use a simple frame replication instead. The FEC recovery scheme follows the description in section 2.

In order to examine the working of the error recovery scheme we send several data frames to the receiver of which only the first data frame is lost. This helps to isolate the errors if they are present. Once we find that the model is able to recover from a single frame loss, we can simulate the loss of several frames at the MAC layer and check that the model works for different error scenarios.

At this point we have essentially built the SLACP model with all the features of the protocol included in it. As we build the model cumulatively, and at each stage make use of the functionalities at the earlier levels as well in extending the model, we have confidence in the basic correctness of the design.

The next phase deals with testing and simulation. We exercise the protocol model using the test scenarios and observe its working. Having gained confidence about its working, we begin the validation phase. The SDL model of SLACP is about 100 pages long and it took about 3 man months to develop and validate the protocol.

5   Validation of SLACP Using SDL

Telelogic Tau 4.4 SDT tool is used for validating SLACP. We formulate the following validation scenarios which represent the protocol operations. The scenarios correspond to the different levels of modeling described earlier.

– Opening / Closing a channel
– Sending and Receiving a frame without frame loss
– Sending and Receiving a frame without frame loss and flow control
– Sending and Receiving frames with frame loss (using ARQ and FEC)
– Sending and Receiving frames with frame loss and flow control
– Resetting the channel

Each of the above test scenarios is validated using the automatic validation methods available in SDT. In automatic state space exploration SDT builds a reachability graph for the system model. The state space is the set of all the states of the system that can be reached from its initial state by systematically exploring all the transitions. A number of general properties of a protocol such as deadlock freedom, absence of unspecified signal reception and unreachable code can be verified by exploring the state graph. As exhaustive state space verification becomes infeasible with a large state space, alternatives such as bitstate exploration and random walk methods that explore a large fraction of the state space are used [8]. By choosing as small a value as possible for the sizes of data frame, SACK block and buffers, we can reduce the complexity of the state space to some extent.

The validation reports point to the errors encountered in the state exploration. This is especially valuable as it examines scenarios that are unlikely to be considered in the test suite. For example, consider the following scenario: the SLACP sender sends a frame and the frame is lost; the receiver asks for a retransmission and the sender retransmits it; this FEC encoded retransmitted frame gets delayed and arrives at the receiver at a later time; by that time the receiver might have sent the frames in the reassembly queue to the higher layer assuming that this frame is lost. Such a delayed frame may create problems if we do not have the sanity check at the receiver to see whether the frame received is within the receiver window. It is difficult to create the above situation manually but the exhaustive state space exploration can readily set it up. Automatic validation also helps to exercise the scoreboard and the various queues.

The SDT option to display the execution trace that leads to an error state is useful to detect errors and fix them. The flexibility of the tool to show the path of error both in the SDL graphs and in the MSC supports debugging.

Automatic validation helps to ensure that the special frames such as nothing_to_send and rxmtpkt_loss perform as intended in the protocol design.

6   SLACP-SDL Model Versus SLACP Implementation

After validating the SDL model, we implemented the SLACP protocol in C for the Linux operating system. The C implementation closely followed the SDL model. However, there are some differences between the SDL model and its implementation in addition to those differences discussed earlier (FEC encoding/decoding not modeled, only a single SLACP channel modeled). In the following we highlight some of these more or less subtle differences.

In the SDL graphs, explicit flow control signals exist between the SLACP and IP layer. In the Linux implementation these signals are implicit as the SLACP protocol engine accepts a packet from the IP underbelly interface only when buffer space is available at the SLACP layer, effectively implementing the flow control between the layers. In addition, the flow control details between the SLACP and MAC layer in the Linux implementation depend on the link technology and device in use. Therefore, an abstract model of the SLACP-to-MAC flow control can be used in the SDL graphs.

In the SLACP implementation the SACK block in the ACK frame is implemented as a bit map. Each bit in the SACK block together with the cumulative acknowledgment sequence number of the ACK frame represents whether a frame has been successfully received (bit set to 1) or not (hole, bit set to 0). Since bitmaps and their operations are not easy to represent in SDL, each bit in the SACK block is actually a structure with a field for the corresponding sequence number and a boolean value indicating whether the frame was successfully received or not. The code for iterating through such a structure to check whether the SACK block is empty is clearly not as trivial as the simple check for zero bit map in C. Therefore, an additional field indicating whether a SACK block is empty was added in the SDL model.

In the automatic validation of SLACP, the symbol coverage was 94.99 %. If the symbol coverage is not 100%, the validation cannot be considered finished without a clear understanding of the missing coverage. We analyzed the uncovered symbols in the SDL graphs. Most of them were either invalid end states or conditions that do not occur. In the Linux implementation there are even more invalid states as a real protocol implementation has to test for many error conditions that do not occur except in some very exceptional conditions such as in case of broken or otherwise misbehaving implementation of the peer. Achieving 100 % symbol coverage with such sanity checks included into the SDL model would require that any such misbehavior is implemented and enforced in the peer protocol engine. Therefore, we decided to exclude most of these checks in the SDL model.

7   Concluding Remarks and Future Work

In this paper we have described the design and development of SLACP protocol using SDL modeling. A validation oriented approach to protocol design was employed to develop the protocol in a hierarchical stepwise refinement manner. This helped to control the complexity of the design and to better understand the interaction of the protocol components. The SDL model was used as a basis for the implementation of the protocol in Linux.

We found that the SDL model developed in this approach was convenient to adapt by incorporating implementation specific details such as FEC encoding scheme using Reed-Solomon codes. With hindsight we observe that this ability to adapt the SDL model to actual implementation is quite valuable as the design is not encumbered with implementation specific aspects. We believe that the approach to SLACP design can be used for general protocol design.

The SLACP protocol validation has no doubt increased the quality of the produced protocol implementation. However, we still cannot say that the protocol model has been formally verified: a 100% guarantee that the protocol works as intended in all possible cases has not been yet achieved. Partly this is because the SDT validator tool does not really support all possible kinds of behavioral properties that we would like to verify from the system. For example a property such as "*a channel open in IP-layer will in all cases either lead to channel establishment or to channel open failure signal*" is simply not expressible within SDT validator. Another thing that limits the reliability factor of our validation is the fact that our protocol model is huge in terms of size of reachability graph and since the SDT validator does not really have any sophisticated state space reduction algorithms, we have to rely on approximate methods such as bit state hashing. For these reasons we consider starting a follow-up project where we are planning to do a full fledged formal verification of SLACP with Spin model checker [8]. Partly this will be a challenge to the Spin tool itself: it will be interesting to see how a state of the art verification tool can treat a complex real world protocol.

References

1. Transmission Control Protocol. RFC 793, Internet Society, Sep 1981.
2. A comparison of mechanisms for improving TCP performance over wireless links. *IEEE/ACM Transactions on Networking*, 5(6):756–769, 1997.
3. *Recommendation Z.100 - CCITT Specification and Description Language.* ITU, 1993.
4. *Telelogic Tau 4.4 Manual* . Telelogic, 2002.
5. Enhancing TCP Performance Over Satellite Networks - A Link Aware Approach. Technical Report C-2004-50, University of Helsinki, Department of Computer Science, August 2004.
6. Improving TCP Performance Over Wireless WANs using TCP/IP-Friendly Link. In *1st International Conference on E-Business and Telecommunication Networks (ICETE)*, August 2004.
7. *Data Networks: 2nd edition.* Prentice Hall, 1992.
8. *The Spin Model Checker.* Addison Wesley, 2003.

Modeling, Verifying and Testing Mobility Protocol from SDL Language

Francine Ngani Noudem and César Viho

IRISA-Université de Rennes I, Campus de Beaulieu,
F-35042 Rennes Cedex, France
{fngani, viho}@irisa.fr

Abstract. This paper deals with mobility protocols specification, validation and testing using a formal approach. A well suited SDL model is proposed to handle the component-based nature of Mobile systems. Two solutions are proposed to derive automatically TTCN-3 test cases from the SDL model.

1 Introduction

Mobility is one of the increasing demands in the telecommunications area. Mobility systems are complex, as they are composed of several distributed, heterogeneous and obviously mobile components. Thus, there is an important need to develop methodologies that help to specify, to validate and to test the components efficiently. This paper deals with this need using formal approaches. Indeed, it is widely recognized that formal methods are suitable for specifying complex systems. Moreover, they help in verifying and validating the standard specifications as well as easing the test case generation and maintenance [1].

It has long been known that automatic test case generation is improves the correctness and the quality of test cases [11]. Moreover, it allows fast test generation at a lower cost [16]. Therefore, it appears obvious to study how appropriate the automatic test case generation could be for testing mobility protocol.

Several approaches based on automatic test case generation from formal approaches already exist [11, 12, 17]. The formal description languages generally used are SDL (Specification and Description Language) [9] and MSC (Message Sequence Chart) [8]. The produced test cases are written in TTCN-2 (Tree and Tabular Combined Notation version 2) language [7]. Recently, the European Telecommunication Standard Institute (ETSI) proposed TTCN-3 (Testing and Test Control Notation version 3) [5] language. TTCN-3 is a test specification and implementation language for testing reactive and distributed systems. Thus, it offers a framework for distributed systems as mobility system. In order to take advantage of TTCN-3 features and to benefit of formal approaches, it appeared adequate to address TTCN-3 test case generation from formal approaches.

Other work regarding specification, validation and test case generation of mobile protocols using formal approaches has been carried out (such as [2, 13]) but to our knowledge, there is no work dedicated to the specific case of mobility

A. Prinz, R. Reed, and J. Reed (Eds.): SDL 2005, LNCS 3530, pp. 198–209, 2005.

management. This leads one to suppose that the work presented here is one of the first dedicated to TTCN-3 test generation from formal specification for the new MIPv6 protocol.

The paper is structured as follows. Section 2 gives a short description of the Mobile IPv6 (MIPv6) protocol [10]. The main issues of MIPv6 protocol specification and the main results obtained during verification and validation of MIPv6 protocol are also presented. Section 3 describes the proposed test architecture and the two approaches suggested for TTCN-3 test cases generation from a SDL model. The problems encountered and MIPv6 TTCN-3 test cases produced using these two approaches are presented. The paper ends with conclusion and future work in section 4.

2   Specification and Validation of MIPv6 Protocol

In the Internet community, the Mobile IPv6 (MIPv6) is the mobility support in the new version of the Internet Protocol called IPv6. As a new protocol, it is important to verify that it does not contain inconsistencies and ambiguities.

2.1   Short Overview of MIPv6 Protocol

MIPv6 is defined by IETF (Internet Engineering Task Force) in the Request For Comments RFC 3775 [10]. It enables a node to remain reachable while moving from its *Home Network* to other networks called *Visited Networks*.

MIPv6 protocol is described in shape of three main components. The *Mobile Node (MN)* represents any node able to move through the Internet network while maintaining its communications. The *Home Agent (HA)* is an access router of the home network that manage the accessibility at anytime to the MN independently of its localization. The *Correspondent Node (CN)* is any node which communicates with the MN.

Validation and testing mobility management in MIPv6 consists in ensuring that the three following main procedures (detailed in [10, 14, 15]) are correctly implemented: (1) *Movement Detection:* all procedures performed by the MN to detect movement, (2) *IPv6 address auto-configuration:* all procedures allowing the MN to obtain a consistent IPv6 address, and (3) *Location Update:* all procedures allowing the MN to maintain its communications.

2.2   Specification Step: Main Issues

As the ultimate purpose of this work is to generate automatically test cases from formal specification, the main issue in the specification step is to build a model that will facilitate test generation. On the other hand the model has to be well suited for verifying the three main mobility procedures described above. The SDL (Specification and Description Language) language [9] is used to write a precise and rigorous specification.

Two approaches were studied to specify MIPv6 mobility management:

1. *MIPv6 model with MIPv6 components:* Only the three main MIPv6 components are represented in the model. The main problem of this approach is that there are no representation of the mobile node movement. Thus, it is not possible to check mobility procedures. The MIPv6 components are viewed as fixed components which exchange messages.

2. *MIPv6 model with environment and access router views:* In order to take into account mobility, the main question is which components trigger and take part in the execution of mobility? Two main concepts are important:

   (a) Mobile node environment: the MN detects movement when an awaited message from its current access router is not received. It is due to physical moving of the MN or to any other event of the environment that intercepted the message.

   (b) Different views of the access router by the MN: when the MN moves, it is successively connected to several access routers. These routers have the same behavior but are perceived in a different way by the MN. Indeed, they can be a Current Access Router (CAR), or a New Access Router (NAR) or an Other Access Routers (OTHAR).

Thus, the environment and the way the MN perceives an access router must be taken into account to model mobility in a suitable way. As a consequence, seven new components are integrated into the model as shown on fig. 1:

- Three access router processes (AR1, AR2 and AR3 on fig. 1) related to the three views of access router are defined. A single Access Router (AR) process could have been defined to represent at the same time CAR, NAR and OTHAR. In this case, these three processes would be created during simulation. However, the issue would be the management of mobility during simulation. For instance, it will be difficult to manage successive connections of the MN to various access routers while preserving the uniqueness of the connection to a single access router.

- Three environment processes (AR1MNEnv, AR2MNEnv and AR3MNEnv on fig. 1) related to the three access router processes are defined. According to the mobility context established, these environment processes intercept the messages exchanged between the MN and the access routers. The mobility context defines the access router which is reachable by the MN (the CAR).

- One Controller of environment (Controller on fig. 1) is defined to establish a consistent mobility context.

Figure 1 shows an SDL system of MIPv6 protocol (mipv6_sys) and the SDL block access router (AccessRouter). The three MIPv6 components are represented as well as the seven additional mobility components. The signals exchanged between components are also specified, as described in the RFC 3775 [10].

To allow a suitable description of mobility, this choice of modeling gives a global sight of the mobile system. Moreover, it highlights the behavior of a specific component and its interactions with other components.

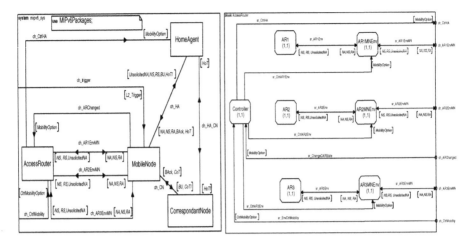

Fig. 1. SDL model: MIPv6 System and AccessRouter block

Another issue was to specify *multicast*. Multicast allows a MN to discover a new access router. The access router is unknown and a message is sent to the multicast router address. The difficulty is that the multicast message sending is not intended to a known entity but to the entity that having a specific data value. In SDL, the receiver of message must be explicitly defined through the keywords to, *via* and *via all*. The chosen solution consists to send to all processes (via all) the multicast message. According to the mobility context established by the controller process, only the reachable process, thus the current access router of the MN, will receive the message.

2.3   Verification and Validation Step: Main Results

Verification and validation are made through respectively interactive and exhaustive simulations. Based on the obtained MIPv6 model, several simulations were performed using the ObjectGeode 4.2 tool [18]. Through GOAL (Geode Observation Automata Language), ObjectGeode allows a better definition of properties. The MSC (Message Sequence Charts) language [8] is used to describe the behavior generated during simulations.

Figure 2 shows partly the MSC model generated from an interactive simulation of MIPv6 model. Some significant messages are in bold font. This MSC describes a scenario obtained when the mobile node leaves its home network to AR1 network. First of all, the Controller of environment (PROCESS controller(1) in the figure) modifies the mobility context by sending mobility messages (mobilityoption()) to indicates that only the AR1 router is reachable. Upon reception of mobility trigger (l2_trigger), the MN performs movement detection procedures (exchange of neighbor solicitation (ns()) and neighbor advertisement (rs()) messages) and detects unreachability to its home agent. The MN then performs address auto-configuration procedure (exchange of router solicitation (rs()) and router advertisement (ra()) messages followed by location update pro-

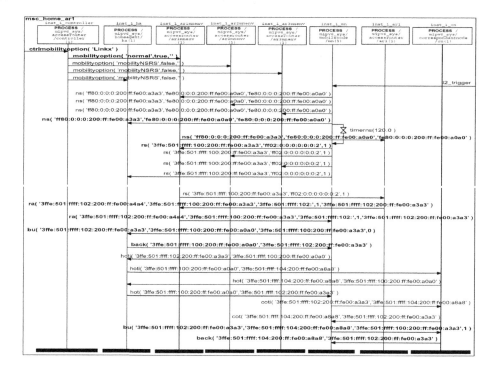

Fig. 2. Generated MSC: Mobile Node leaves home network to the AR1 network

cedure (exchange of binding update (bu()) and binding acknowledgment (back()) messages).

Different properties were checked, here are the main groups:

- *Neighbor Unreachability Detection:* checking that reachability to the current access router is always carried out when the MN receives a mobility trigger.
- *Address Auto-configuration:* verifying that address configuration is always carried out when the MN changes network.
- *DAD (Duplication Address Detection):* checking that DAD procedure is always performed before any address configuration.
- *Home registration:* verifying that binding Update with Home Agent is always carried out when MN changes network.
- *Return Routability:* verifying that return routability procedure is always carried out before the correspondent registration procedure.
- *Correspondent Registration:* verifying that correspondent registration procedure is carried out only when the MN changes network.

The results allow verification that the mobility procedures were specified as described in the RFC 3775 [10]. Moreover, the results obtained during simulation did not reveal any inconsistencies. To certain extent, it confirms that the MIPv6 mobility procedures are stable.

We can also notice that, due to integration of MIPv6 components in the same model, interactive and exhaustive simulations of a component-based model

(MIPv6 in our case) allows checking and validation of the behavior of each component and the interoperability between all components of the model. Indeed, validation of one component requires the validation of its interactions with other components.

3   Test Suite Generation

The ultimate purpose of this work is to generate test cases for the MIPv6 protocol. Because it improves the correctness and quality of test cases [11] and it allows fast test generation at a lower cost [16], automatic test case generation from formal specification is chosen for testing mobility protocol.

3.1   Test Architecture

As usual, before test generation, the test architecture must be defined. It consists in determining the Implementation Under Test (IUT) and its interfaces, the Test System (TS) and its Points of Control and Observation (PCOs), together with the environment through which the TS and the IUT will interact.

Due to the components-based structure of the model, the definition of the test architecture becomes more flexible. Indeed, depending on the aspects one may want to focus on, the IUT can be any component in the system or the whole system. The chosen model supports test architectures for both conformance and interoperability testing. It also allows a distributed approach for testing.

Test Architecture for Conformance and Interoperability Testing

Defining an architecture for conformance testing, consists in choosing the IUT among the components of the model and to consider the remaining components as part of the test system. Figure 3(a) shows a test architecture for conformance testing. The IUT chosen is the mobile node (MobileNode). The home agent, the correspondent node and the access router are considered as part of MIPv6 test system. Seven PCOs are defined between IUT and MIPv6 test system.

Defining an architecture for interoperability testing consists in choosing the components for which interoperability has to be tested. The remaining components correspond to the test system.

Distributed Test Architecture

Due to the component-based and distributed nature of MIPv6, it is possible to consider a distributed test architecture. An example of distributed test architecture for conformance testing of MIPv6 mobility management is shown in the fig. 3(b). The IUT chosen is the mobile node. The MTC (Main Test Component) is represented by Access Router with mobility controller. The MTC communicates with two PTCs represented by the home agent and the correspondent node. The PCOs and CPs (Coordination Points) are also indicated in the fig. 3(b).

Notice that during test deployment, a really distributed test architecture can be easily configured because the PTC and the MTC simulate the behavior of the components which are really distributed in practice.

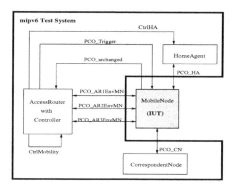
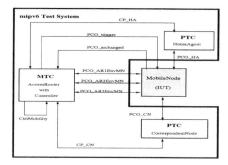

(a) Conformance testing architecture   (b) Distributed testing architecture

Fig. 3. Architecture for conformance testing and distributed testing architecture

3.2   TTCN-3 Test Cases Generation Based on Formal Approach

Different approaches based on automatic test generation from SDL languages already exist [11, 12]. In these approaches, the test cases generated were written using TTCN-2 (Tree and Tabular Combined Notation version 2) language [7]. Recently, TTCN-3 (Testing and Test Control Notation version 3) [5] has been proposed. In order to take advantage of TTCN-3 features and to benefit from formal approaches, it appeared adequate to address TTCN-3 test cases generation from formal approaches. To our knowledge, there is no methodologies or tools to automatically generate TTCN-3 test cases from a formal approach. In the following, we propose two approaches for this purpose.

TTCN-3 Test Case Generation by Combining Existing Approaches

In this approach, the TTCN-2 test cases are first generated automatically from SDL [17, 18]. Then, the obtained TTCN-2 test cases are translated into TTCN-3 test cases using TTCN-2 to TTCN-3 Converter tools.

This approach was applied for MIPv6 mobility management testing. The validation steps were performed as described in section 2.3. The TestComposer tool [18] is used to automatically generate TTCN-2 test cases. For this purpose, a test architecture and the SDL test purpose are defined. The test architecture (IUT, PCOs, Lower Tester, Upper Tester, alias, . . .) is appropriately modified to generate conformance and interoperability test cases. Telelogic TAU TTCN [18] suite is used for TTCN-2 test case syntactic and semantic analysis. The DANET Converter [3] is used to translate the obtained TTCN-2 test cases into TTCN-3. Finally, the DANET TTCN-3 toolbox is used to update the TTCN-3 test cases. The fig. 4 shows a TTCN-2 test case automatically generated with TestComposer. The defined IUT is the Correspondent node. This TTCN-2 test case corresponds to correspondent registration procedure detailed in Sections 5.2.5 and 5.2.6 of mobility support [10].

Test Case Dynamic Behaviour

Test Case Name	: mipv6_1
Group	:
Purpose	:
Configuration	:
Default	: def
Comments	: Generated by test oriented simulation of the test purpose chungeidirit_back of file obe_testback.obe
Selection Ref	:
Description	:

Nr	Label	Behaviour Description	Constraints Ref	Verdict	Comments
1		connecthacn !hoti START TAC	hot_3		
2		connecthacn ?hot CANCEL TAC, START TWAIT	hot_4		
3		connectcn !coti START TAC	coti_6		
4		connectcn ?cot CANCEL TAC	cot_7		
5		connectcn !bu START TAC	bu_8		
6		connectcn ?back CANCEL TAC	back_9	(P)	

Detailed Comments :

Default Dynamic Behaviour

Default Name	: def
Group	:
Objective	: Generalized default behaviour. Checks for OTHERWISE and TIMEOUT
Comments	:
Description	:

Nr	Label	Behaviour Description	Constraints Ref	Verdict	Comments
1		?TIMEOUT TAC		F	No response
2		?TIMEOUT TWAIT		F	No synchronization
3		connecthacn ?OTHERWISE		F	
4		connectcn ?OTHERWISE		F	

Detailed Comments :

Fig. 4. Tabular TTCN-2 test case: Correspondent Registration procedure

```
 1 module mipv6_1
 2 {import from Mipv6_ASN1module { type Hoti }
 3  import from Mipv6_ASN1module { type Coti }
 4  ...
 5  type Hoti hoti;
 6  type Coti coti;
 7  ...;
 8  type port t_ch_ha_cn message {inout all}
 9  type port t_ch_cn message     {inout all}
10  type component MyTestComponent
11  {timer dummytimer := 0.0;
12   port t_ch_ha_cn connecthacn;
13   port t_ch_cn connectcn;
14   timer TAC := 6.0; ...}
15   type component MyTestSystemType {
16   port t_ch_ha_cn connecthacn;
17   port t_ch_cn connectcn;
18  }with {display componenttype
19   {comments := {connecthacn ::= "Lower Tester"};...}; } ...;
20  group ASN1_StructuredTemplates
21  { template hoti hoti_3 := {
22   p1 := "3ffe:501:ffff:100:200:ff:fe00:a3a3",
23   p2 := "3ffe:501:ffff:104:200:ff:fe00:a8a8",
24   p3 := ...}
25   ... }
26  altstep def() runs on MyTestComponent
27  { [] TAC.timeout {
28       setverdict(fail); stop; }/*No response*/
29    [] TWAIT.timeout {
30       setverdict(fail); stop; }/*No synchronization*/
31    [] connecthacn.receive {setverdict(fail); stop; }
32    [] connectcn.receive {setverdict(fail); stop;}
33  } /* end default def */
34  testcase mipv6_1() runs on MyTestComponent
35  system MyTestSystemType
36  {var default MyDefaultVar0 := activate(def());
37   map(self:connectcn , system:connectcn );
38   map(self:connecthacn , system:connecthacn );
39   connecthacn.send(hoti:hoti_3);TAC.start(6.0);
40   connecthacn.receive(hot:hot_4);TAC.stop ;TWAIT.start(6.0);
41   connectcn.send(coti:coti_6); TAC.start(6.0);
42   connectcn.receive(cot:cot_7); TAC.stop ;
43   connectcn.send(bu:bu_8); TAC.start(6.0);
44   connectcn.receive(back:back_9); TAC.stop ;
45   setverdict(pass); } /* end testcase mipv6_1 */
46  control { execute(mipv6_1()); }
47 }/* end module mipv6_1 */
```

Fig. 5. TTCN-3 test case: Correspondent Registration procedure

Figure 5 shows the TTCN-3 test case obtained after translation of the TTCN-2 test case. One can identify the two parts of the module: the declaration part from line 2 to 45 and the control part at line 46. In the declaration part, one can identify TTCN-3 concepts: the ASN.1 type declarations, the test configuration (one test component, a test system interface, and port types), the group of templates, the default dynamic behavior and the test case behavior.

This approach has the advantage that it allows a fast TTCN-3 test case generation when TTCN-2 test cases are available. As an automatic approach, it allows fast TTCN-3 test cases generation. Indeed, generating a new TTCN-3 test case just consists in the definition of a new test purpose. However, this approach forces the production of TTCN-2 test cases before obtaining any TTCN-3 test cases. As a consequence, it is limited by the weaknesses of TTCN-2 language. For instance, the definition of the distributed test architecture is difficult to automatically derive into TTCN-3. Moreover, this approach is entirely dependent of different manufacturers tools. That increases the risk of losing information during translations and tool migrations.

TTCN-3 Test Generation Based on MSC Generated by Simulation
This approach produces TTCN-3 test cases directly from SDL and MSC specifications. It is inspired by recent work proposed by Ebner [4] on translation of MSC elements into TTCN-3 statements. Contrary to the Ebner approach where the MSC is obtained from UML (Unified Modeling Language) sequence chart, we propose to automatically generate MSC by simulation of the verified and validated SDL model. Our approach is performed through three steps:

Step 1: Based on valid SDL model, automatically generating MSC during interactive and exhaustive simulations. The MSC generated during interactive simulation allow for specific scenarios and components of the system, whereas the MSC generated during exhaustive simulation is used to test the whole scenarios and components of the system for a specific test purpose. The property defined for exhaustive simulation represents the test purpose for which test case has to be generated.

Step 2: Based on a test architecture, translate generated MSC into MSC test cases by defining the corresponding test elements (IUT, PCOs, ...).

Step 3: Translating MSC test cases into TTCN-3 test cases.
Three levels of translation must be considered:

TTCN-3 Data Types: We propose to re-use existing tools such as TTCN-Link [18] to automatically generate TTCN declarations from the SDL specification.

TTCN-3 Test Configuration: For TTCN-3 distributed test configuration, we propose to map SDL elements into TTCN-3 statements:
1. Choose the IUT among the SDL blocks (or processes).
2. Select one or several SDL blocks as the MTC. Each of remainder SDL blocks becomes the PTC. Consequently, the SDL channels between SDL blocks (other than the selected IUT) are defined as TTCN-3 CPs and belong to Test System (TS). Whereas the SDL channels between the SDL blocks selected as IUT and remaining SDL blocks are defined as TTCN-3 ports and belong to the TTCN-3 Test System Interface (TSI).
3. Define SDL signals carried by SDL channels as TTCN-3 input/output messages exchanged through TTCN-3 ports.

TTCN-3 test case behavior: To produce TTCN-3 test case behavior, we suggest to map MSC test case to TTCN-3 test case as proposed in [4]. For distributed test, we firstly need to add condition state to the MSC test case in order to specify the beginning and end of each PTC function, and synchronization between test components. This idea was already suggested to generate concurrent TTCN test cases from SDL specifications and MSC test purposes [6].

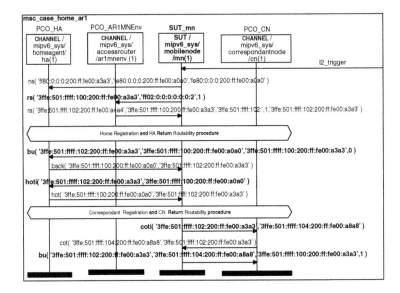

Fig. 6. An MSC test case

This approach was applied for MIPv6 mobility management testing. Several simulations both interactive and exhaustive were carried out in order to generate MSC. Figure 6 shows an MSC test case obtained by translation of generated MSC (on fig. 2). The distributed test architecture on fig. 3(b) is used. The corresponding TTCN-3 test case obtained is illustrated on fig. 7. This TTCN-3 test case corresponds to the MIPv6 mobility procedure described in Sections 11.5 and 11.7 of the mobility support RFC 3775 [10].

This approach has the main advantage that it does not need to first derive the TTCN-2 test cases. It thus allows advantage to be taken of the new TTCN-3 features as distributed test configuration. However, this approach should be tested more, in particular the PTCs synchronization notions. In addition, a mapping into TTCN-3 of the MSC *lost message*, frequently used in mobility management to detect mobile node movement, must be studied. A drawback of this approach is that the mappings of MSC and distributed test architecture into TTCN-3 test cases is still manual. Implementation of the mapping in a tool will allow automatic generation of TTCN-3 test cases from SDL specifications.

```
 1   module mipv6mobility
 2   {/*    Data Types Declaration part */
 3    import from Mipv6-ASN1module {inout all}
 4    /*   Distributed Test configuration     */
 5    type component PTC-CorrespondentNode
 6    {port MNCNPortType PCO-CN;
 7     port MTCCNPortType CP-CN;
 8     timer ReplyTimeOut := 30.0;
 9    }
10   type port MNCNPortType message
11   {        in      Mipv6-BU-PacketType,
12                    Mipv6-CoTI-PacketType,
13            out     Mipv6-BAck-PacketType ,
14                    Mipv6-CoT-PacketType ;
15   }
16   type port MTCCNPortType message {...}
17   type component PTC-HomeAgent {...}
18   type component MTC-AccessRouter {...}
19   type component mipv6-TSI
20   {        port MNHAPortType PCO-HA;
21            port MNCNPortType PCO-CN;
22            port MNARPortType PCO-AR1EnvMN;
23            port MNARPortType PCO-AR2EnvMN;
24            port MNARPortType PCO-AR3EnvMN;
25   }
26   /* Test Case Behavior
27   function HomeRegistration() runs on PTC-HomeAgent{
28    PCO-HA.receive(bu:bu-1);
29    PCO-HA.send(back:back-1);
30    PCO-HA.receive(hoti:hoti-1);/* HA ReturnRoutability */
31    PCO-HA.send(hot:hot-1);
32    setverdict(pass);
33   }
34   function CorrespondentRegistration() runs on
35            PTC-CorrespondentNode{
36    PCO-CN.receive(coti:coti-1); /* CN ReturnRoutability */
37    PCO-CN.send(cot:cot-1);
38    PCO-CN.receive(bu:bu-2);/* Binding Update */
39    setverdict(pass);
40   }
41   testcase case-home-ar1() runs on MTC-AccessRouter
42            system mipv6-TSI
43   {/* Map, connect and declarations
44    ... ,
45    PCO-Trigger.send(12-trigger); /* Checking reachability */
46    PCO-AR1EnvMN.receive(rs:rs-1); /* Configure new address */
47    PCO-AR1EnvMN.send(ra:ra-1);
48    ptc-ha.start(HomeRegistration());
49    ptc-ha.done;
50    ptc-cn.start(CorrespondentRegistration());
51    ptc-cn.done;
52    setverdict(pass);
53   } /* end testcase case-home-ar1() */
54   control { execute(case-home-ar1()); }
55   } // end Module
```

Fig. 7. TTCN-3 Test case: the MN leaves home network to the AR1 network

4   Conclusion

In this paper, we propose a suitable model to handle the component-based nature of Mobile systems. The results obtained during simulation of the MIPv6 model appeared good enough to verify and validate the specification. Due to judicious choices made after modeling, we showed that verification and validation of a component-based model allows simultaneously verification and validation of a specific component and of interoperability between components. We also show that this modeling choice allows flexibility and easy definition of test architecture. Both conformance and interoperability testing are then possible. Two approaches are proposed to derive TTCN-3 test cases from SDL. Future work concerns execution of obtained TTCN-3 test cases for conformance and interoperability testing as well as deployment of distributed test architectures.

References

1. D. Amyot, R. Andrade, L. Logrippo, J. Sincennes, and Z. Yi. Formal Methods for Mobility Standards. In *IEEE Emerging Technology Symposium on Wireless Communication & Systems - Testing of communicating systems XIV. Application to Internet Technologies and Services*, Texas, USA, April 1999.
2. A. Cavalli, A. Mederreg, and F. Zaidi. Application of formal testing methodology to wireless telephony networks. In *IEEE International Information and Telecommunication Technologies Symposium (I2TS'2003)*, Brazil, October 2003.
3. DANET. Danet. http://www.danet.de.
4. M. Ebner. TTCN-3 Test Case Generation from Message Sequence Charts. In *Workshop on Integrated-reliability with Telecommunications and UML Languages (ISSRE04:WITUL)*, France, November 2004.
5. ETSI. Methods for Testing and Specification (MTS); The Testing and Test Control Notation version 3; Part 1: TTCN-3 Core Language. ETSI Standard 201 873-1 v2.2.1, ETSI, February 2003.
6. J. Grabowski, B. Koch, M. Schmitt, and D. Hogrefe. SDL and MSC Based Test Generation for Distributed Test Architectures. In *SDL Forum SDL'99*, June 1999.
7. ISO/IEC. Information Technology; Open Systems Interconnection; Conformance Testing Methodology and Framework; Part3: The Tree and Tabular Combined Notation (second edition). International standard 9646-3, ISO/IEC, 1998.
8. ITU-T. Message Sequence Chart (MSC). Recommendation Z.120, ITU-T, November 1999.
9. ITU-T. Specification and Description Language (SDL). Recommendation Z.100, ITU-T, August 2002.
10. D. Johnson, C. Perkins, and J. Arkko. Mobility Support in IPv6. RFC 3775, IETF, June 2004.
11. A. Kerbrat, T Jéron, and R Groz. Automated test generation from sdl specifications. In Rachida Dssouli, Gregor von Bochmann, and Yair Lahav, editors, *SDL '99 The Next Millennium, 9th International SDL Forum*, pages 135–152, Montréal, Québec, Canada, June 1999. Elsevier.
12. B. Koch, J. Grabowski, D. Hogrefe, and D. Schmitt. Autolink - A Tool for Automatic Test Generation from SDL Specifications. In *IEEE International Workshop on Industrial Strength Formal Specification Techniques, (WIFT'98)*, Boca Raton, Florida, USA, October 1998.
13. M. Mackaya and R. Castanet. Modelling and Testing Location Based Application in UMTS Networks. In *IEEE Contel 2003, 7th International Conference on Telecommunications*, Zagreb,Croatia, June 2003.
14. T. Narten, E. Nordmark, and W. Simpson. Neighbor Discovery for IP version 6 (IPv6). RFC 2461, IETF, December 1998.
15. T. Narten and S. Thomson. IPv6 Stateless Address Autoconfiguration. RFC 2462, IETF, December 1998.
16. R. L. Probert, H. Ural, and A. W. Williams. Rapid generation of functional tests using mscs, sdl and ttcn. *Computer Communications*, 24(3-4):374–393, 2001.
17. M. Schmitt, M. Ebner, and J. Grabowski. Test generation with autolink and testcomposer. In *Proceedings of the 2nd Workshop of the SDL Forum Society on SDL and MSC (SAM'2000), Grenoble (France), June, 26 - 28, 2000*, june 2000.
18. Telelogic. TAU Generation 1, TAU Generation 2 and ObjectGeode 4.2. http://www.telelogic.com.

Cinderella SLIPPER: An SDL to C-Code Generator

Yosef Rauchwerger[1], Finn Kristoffersen[2], and Yair Lahav[3]

[1] NDS Israel, 5 ShlomoHalevi Street, Har Hotzvim, Jerusalem, Israel
YRauchwerger@ndsisrael.com
[2] Cinderella ApS., Moselodden 5, 2750 Ballerup, Denmark
Finn@cinderella.dk
[3] 3 Hatavor St., Ganei Tikva 55900, Israel
Yair.Lahav@Adimos.com

Abstract. Cinderella SLIPPER is a C-code generator that generates C code from SDL and ASN.1 models defined in Cinderella SDL. The code generator has been designed to produce compact readable C code, as one of the major obstacles of using generated code from design specifications is that software developers are inhibited by difficulties to understand the generated code.

1   Introduction

Clarity and comprehensibility of generated code are considered as major parameters of the code generation tool for the practicing software engineers [4]. It is crucial for the software engineers to easily read and understand the generated code to support the integration with other software components. SLIPPER has been designed using software patterns to ensure a code generation that is clear and easy to read.

Code clarity is essential also for the integration of the generated code with other software components. Another key demand for generated code is its immediate correspondence to the SDL specification (design model) structure and entities from which the code is being generated.

SDL is an object-oriented language while C is not. Nevertheless, the generated code has to preserve the encapsulation of software object internal behavior and data. It is achieved by creating sets of operator functions for each data type. These sets allow implementation of the most sophisticated data types created by means of the SDL.

SLIPPER currently supports SDL-92, and generates code only for the instances of SDL entities (finalized) but not for SDL entities defined as types. This is done to prevent the creation of an excessive amount of unused code and to simplify understanding of the generated code.

To show the capabilities implemented in the SLIPPER code generator we use examples from a model of a new standard, Digital Mobile Radio (DMR) [1, 2] that is being developed in ETSI. Although the SDL model of the DMR protocol

A. Prinz, R. Reed, and J. Reed (Eds.): SDL 2005, LNCS 3530, pp. 210–223, 2005.
© Springer-Verlag Berlin Heidelberg 2005

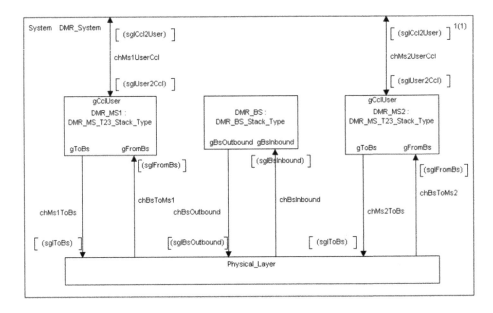

Fig. 1. The SDL example model of the DMR system

stack has been developed primarily for validation and testing purposes it still can be used to demonstrate how SLIPPER code generation is used in the software development process.

Example SDL Model. The DMR system defines a new private mobile radio standard that enables a large variety of different Private Mobile Radio systems to be implemented. This includes both systems based on direct mode (mobile station to mobile station) as well as systems including one or more repeater stations (Base station). In this paper we will use examples from an SDL model of the two lower layer protocols in the terminals and in the base stations. The model developed covers the layer 2, Logical Link control (LLC) and the layer 3, Call Control Layer (CCL). The system model overview is shown in fig. 1.

2   Code Generation Principles

The code generated using SLIPPER is based on an imperative mapping [6] from the SDL model to the C code. Also, the aim has been to generate code based on patterns that are easy for a software developer to read and understand. So the SLIPPER tool does not specifically support configuration of the code generation, for example to improve performance of the generated code as in [3] and [5].

Code generation from SLIPPER is organized in a way that resembles the structure of the SDL model. The SDL model structure and behavioral entities are preserved in the generated C-code as described in this section.

2.1   Code from SDL Behavioral Constructs

For each SDL behavioral entity such as a process and service, SLIPPER generates the following C modules:

- A "C" source code file that contains the code for the data flow and setup functions.
- An "H" file that includes definitions of data types and references to the C functions that implement data type operator functions. The data types are declared in the scope of the enclosing entity (SDL diagram).
- A "C" file that includes data type operator functions.
- An "H" file that includes type definitions for the signals and the timers, which are defined in the scope of the SDL behavioral entity.

2.2   Source Code Organization of Structural SDL Entities

The file structure of the generated code reflects the hierarchy of the SDL specifications. The code, generated for the SDL agent entity, is placed into its own unique directory. The name of the directory coincides with the name of the SDL agent. Separate directories are created for the following SDL entities:

- System
- Package
- Block
- Process
- Service
- Procedure

There exists a direct mapping from the SDL diagrams to the directories created by code generation. Thus a System diagram is always the root directory in the hierarchy of the directories tree except for directories built for packages referenced in the same diagram as the system itself. A diagram may include references to enclosed agents. The directory of such a diagram will include the sub-directories corresponding to contained referenced entities.

Two additional directories are created on the system directory hierarchy level. The code placed in these directories supports simulation and it should be substituted by user code when implementing a target code application:

- The "kernel" directory contains code that includes data for the kernel that simulates a Real-Time Operating System (RTOS).
- The "code simulation" directory includes code that simulates external system signals and provides tracing of code simulation sessions.

At least one file containing executive C code is built for each SDL agent entity included in the SDL specification. For the container type agents (system or block) the files will include setup functions generated for the entities referenced in the context of the system or block diagram. The setup code file name is constructed from the name of the corresponding SDL agent, a unique identifier derived by SLIPPER from the tree representation of the SDL model and as the last part

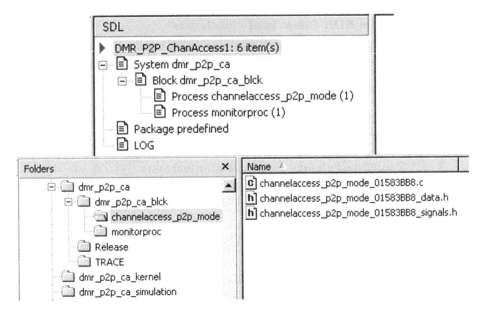

Fig. 2. An SDL model structure and the structure of the generated C-code from the model

of the name "_setup". This naming scheme allows discrimination between files built for the container agents and files comprising code for the active agents.

For the active SDL agents, whose behavior is defined by the state graph, the code file will include a number of C functions generated to implement the agent flow diagram. The file name is constructed from the agent name and its unique identifier.

Additional C and H files built for the agent entity will include the agent name, its unique identifier, and an additional name part specifying the functionality of the code in the generated software system, such as references, data types definitions, operator functions.

The hierarchy of the directories and the naming scheme allow an easy and convenient access to the units of the generated code and mapping of the generated code to the constructs of the source SDL specification. The hierarchy of directories of the generated code is congruent to the hierarchy of the SDL specification as illustrated in the example in fig. 2.

Each file that contains executable code includes references to the data type and signal definition files which are generated for the SDL entities encompassing the SDL entity for the code of concern. This ensures the correct scope for signals and data types in the generated C code.

2.3   Structural Entities and Software Setup Functions

SDL structural entities such as system and block are actually containers that define visibility scope of the enclosed entities, e.g. procedures, signals and data types and the context in which processes are enclosed (blocks). SDL-92 does not define any dynamic semantics for system or block entities. These entities are static. Nevertheless, the generated C code modules that correspond to the system or block entities are actively involved in the setup and initialization that eventually launch process instances contained in these entities. The system setup function includes calls to the Kernel API functions. The implementation of these API functions depends on the Operating System. Kernel API functions serve as an interface to the specific Operating System and adapt data of the generated code to the OS standard data structures needed to implement SDL Finite State Machine (FSM) as a task or as a thread, depending on the specific OS architecture. The realization of the inter-process signaling and timers also depends on the specific OS and demands involvement of the Kernel API functions to link the generated code to the OS. The Kernel implementation may substitute the OS functionality in cases when no OS is used on the target microprocessor.

2.4   Process Data Space

The process instance is a dynamic object that may be created and terminated during the program execution. Its status is changing from time to time as a result of inter-process signal exchange. Code generated for a process instance contains two types of variables: *implicit variables*, generated for the realization of the process FSM and *explicit variables*, generated from variables explicitly declared in the process diagram. When created, memory is allocated for each process instance. The amount of allocated memory depends on the size and number of variables defined in the process diagram. When the process terminates, then the allocated memory is freed. The process instance identifier (Pid) serves as a key to the process data space. The functions that implement the process FSM receive a pointer to the process data space as a parameter when they are activated by the Operating System via the Kernel API interface functions. The implicit variables include Process Id, FSM state, etc.

2.5   Process Finite State Machine Implementation

For each SDL process specification four C functions are generated: process creation, process initialization, process FSM, and process deletion.

The Process Creation function is called either by the Block Setup function generated for the enclosing block diagram or by the code generated for the parent process. The Process Creation function takes as a parameter, the memory allocation for its data space, and a Process Id from the Kernel API. The Process Creation function starts a task or thread for the FSM function and issues the Process Initialization message to the created task / thread. The Process Creation function gets a value of the parent Process ID as a parameter from the calling entity. The Process Creation function returns a Process ID assigned to the created instance.

The Process Initialization function is called on the reception of the message issued by the Process Creation function. This message will be the first event received by the Process FSM function in the span of its existence. Actually,

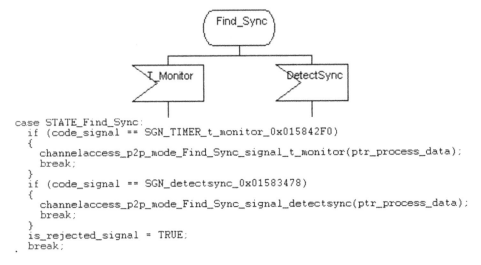

```
case STATE_Find_Sync:
    if (code_signal == SGN_TIMER_t_monitor_0x015842F0)
    {
        channelaccess_p2p_mode_Find_Sync_signal_t_monitor(ptr_process_data);
        break;
    }
    if (code_signal == SGN_detectsync_0x01583478)
    {
        channelaccess_p2p_mode_Find_Sync_signal_detectsync(ptr_process_data);
        break;
    }
    is_rejected_signal = TRUE;
    break;
```

Fig. 3. Part of an SDL process graph and the corresponding generated code for this construct

Process Initialization is an implicit state of the process. It contains code corresponding to the sequence of actions defined in the initial transition from the "start" symbol to the first state symbol of the process. The Process Initialization Function gets a pointer to the process instance data space as a parameter.

The Process Deletion function includes a call to the Kernel API functions to delete the task or the thread that was launched for the process execution and to free the data space allocated to the process instance. The Process Deletion function gets a pointer to the process instance data space as a parameter.

The Process FSM function can be easily mapped to the SDL process diagram from which the C code is derived. The bulk of this function consists of a C switch case construct reproducing the SDL process state machine. The Process FSM function gets a pointer to the process instance data space as a parameter. The function returns a value that may be used by the Kernel API. The returned value notifies if the incoming signal was accepted and processed or if it was saved or discarded (not handled in the receiving state).

In fig. 3 an example of the code generated for part of a process graph is illustrated. The TIMER signal T_Monitor and the signal DetectedSync that can both be handled from the state Find_Sync, and introduce two separated entries in the generated code. The variable is_rejected_signal is used to signal to the calling entity that an unexpected signal was received in the specified state.

3   SDL Procedure Finite State Machine Implementation

A procedure that includes states is an FSM driven by inter-processor signals or by timers. A procedures that does not include states is handled as a procedure with its FSM reduced to one initial state. Kernel API functions provide calling to the Procedure FSM function on signal reception by the process that has called to the procedure from within its scope. Both stateless and FSM procedures are recursive. No global or static variable is generated for procedures. API functions provide an access to the task identifier (VxWorks) and the thread data and thus obtain signal reception points for the FSM procedures. The generated code is independent of the specific implementation of the signal exchange.

Three C functions are generated for an SDL procedure specification:

– Main Procedure function – called from within the body of a process, service or other procedure.
– Procedure Initialization – called from within the body of the procedure itself.
– Procedure FSM – created only when the procedure contains states.

Unlike processes and services, procedures are not provided with their own data space via the "malloc" function. Procedure data space is realized as a local variable (structure) in the Main Procedure function. The Initialization and FSM procedure gets a pointer to the data space as a parameter when called.

The call to the Main Procedure function is generated to match corresponding SDL actions, a procedure call in a task symbol or a procedure call action. The function contains definition of local variables and series of calls to the Procedure Initialization function and to the Procedure FSM function (when it exists). The Procedure Initialization function is called by the Main Procedure function and it takes a pointer to the procedure data space as a parameter. The Procedure FSM function is similar to FSM functions that are generated for processes and services.

3.1   Transition Functions Triggered by the Signal Reception

For each sequence of actions performed on the signal reception by the FSM a special function is built. It means that a function will be generated for every combination of the input signal and the state that may receive this particular signal. The function is called when the signal is received by the process that resides in the state corresponding to the unique combination described above.

Signaling. A structure type definition construct is generated for each SDL signal. The generated code is placed in the include H file and the structure type definition will be accessible for all objects that correspond to the SDL objects included in the scope of the diagram containing the signal definition.

Each signal structure includes at least the following 4 fields:

– Signal ID. This code is unique and serves as a signal identifier.
– Source Process Identifier. Process ID of the function that issues the signal.
– Destination Process Identifier.
– Result of Send Signal Transaction.

The signal structure may include additional fields to carry the data from the sender process to the receiver process. Generated structures serve as parameters for the Kernel API functions that provide support for the inter-process signaling. The Kernel activates an FSM function of the receiving process using the Destination Process Identifier. The pointer to the input signal data is set by the Kernel and stored in the process data space.

Timers. The header of timer type definition structures is similar to the header of regular signal structures described in the previous paragraph except one additional field - timeout duration field that sets a time to expire. On the timer expiration a signal will be issued. All operations that are defined for the timers are performed by the Kernel functions: Set timer, Reset timer, and Check if timer is active.

Time variables are assigned through API functions, which are OS dependent. So the value of the SDL time tick is not defined in the generated code but in the API code developed in the context of the specific OS.

3.2   Data Types

Most of the basic SDL data types are easily translated to similar restricted C data types as shown in Table 1.

SDL operators defined for these data types coincide with C operators defined for the matching C data types. C code that is generated from SDL expressions is entirely transparent because the data operation symbols are identical in both of the languages.

The C code is generated for SDL "Charstring'', "Array" generator, "String" generator and user defined data types defined by the SDL Newtype construct. In C++ these data types may be more easily matched by the classes that include operator functions retaining the same SDL operator symbols. However, for the C code generation it is not a viable task to reach such similarity between the source SDL code and the generated C code.

The problem is solved in the following way:

– For each SDL data type that has no match in the C data types, a structure type definition is created. The structure may include members of another SDL data type.
– Variables of such SDL data types are accessed via a pointer to memory allocated for the variable. The memory is allocated by the variable create

Table 1. SDL basic data types and their corresponding C data types as implemented in SLIPPER

SDL data type	C data type
Integer	Int
Character	Char
Natural	unsigned int
Boolean	C enumeration type
Pid	unsigned int
Real	Float

function generated for the SDL data type. Create variable function returns a pointer to the variable that will be used in all operator functions generated for the SDL data type.

– For each operator defined for the SDL data type a function is generated. This function returns a value of the type defined by the operator. Parameters of the operator function conform to the members of the SDL operator expression. SDL operator expressions are substituted by the function calls in the generated code.

C structure data types and references to the data type operator functions are included into the H file that is placed in the directory built for the SDL diagram in the scope of which the data type is defined. A data type container C file that comprises the operator functions described above is placed in the same directory. Data type definitions are accessible for each function generated for agents included in the scope of the diagram in the body of which the data type is declared.

SLIPPER imposes some restrictions for basic types such as Integer and Real. Maximal value of the C "int" variables depends on the compiler that is always oriented to the specific processor. The size of the processor word (2 bytes, 4 bytes and more) defines maximal value of the int variables. But the user may define Newtype data types and necessary operators when there is a need to work with very large numbers. Conceptually unbounded SDL variables are bounded by the realities of the target platform.

ASN.1 Data. The principles of the code generation developed for SDL data types (including SDL NEWTYPE specifications) have been applied to the C code generation for the ASN.1 data types and variables.

The following ASN.1 types are supported:

– Sequence
– Sequenceof
– Choice
– Bit
– Bitstring
– Octet
– Octetstring
– Character String

Code generation for ASN.1 Sequence variables is similar to SDL Struct data type implementation, but it necessarily includes some additional features to support constructs such as Optional Fields. For each Optional Field an additional structure member is generated, a BOOLEAN field <variable>present. This field is set TRUE when the Optional Field is assigned a value.

The SDL Sequenceof data types maps to the **array data types** in the C language. The Sequenceof data type implementation is similar to implementation of the String data type.

```
/* 7.1.1: Group Voice User LC PDU */
Grp_V_Ch_Usr_PDU_Type ::= SEQUENCE
{
  serviceOptions ServiceOptions_Type,
  reserved2 Integer( 0..255),
  groupAddress GroupAddress_16Bit_Type,
  sourceAddress SourceAddress_Type
}
```

```
// DATA TYPE STRUCTURE

typedef struct st_grp_v_ch_usr_pdu_type
{
    struct st_serviceoptions_type * serviceoptions;
    sort220 reserved2;
    groupaddress_16bit_type groupaddress;
    sourceaddress_type   sourceaddress;
} st_grp_v_ch_usr_pdu_type;

typedef st_grp_v_ch_usr_pdu_type * grp_v_ch_usr_pdu_type;
```

Fig. 4. An ASN.1 struct definition and the corresponding generated C-code data type definitions

For the Choice data type corresponding **C union** type definitions are generated. Implementation of ASN.1 Choice variables is obtained by a structure that includes present field and the union C construct. The name "present" shall not be used as a name of a union member. Cinderella SDL creates an implicit Enumerated data type that provides unique identifiers for the Choice fields. SLIPPER generates identifier names based on this implicit Enumerated data type generated particularly for the specific Choice data type.

ASN.1 Character String is treated as the SDL Charstring type. The function set that provides implementation of operations on SDL Charstring variables serves also to support ASN.1 Character string data type.

ASN.1 Bit variables are implemented in the generated code as **unsigned char C** variables. When a Bit variable is set to 0 then the value of the generated C variable is 0 and if the Bit variable is set to 1 then the value of the generated C variable is 1.

SLIPPER creates a special structure for each Bitstring and allocates a data space to store the unsigned char array corresponding to the Bitstring variable. The structure type definition is included into the standard SLIPPER include files. The structure contains 2 fields: **bitstring size** and a pointer to the Bitstring data space. SLIPPER standard libraries include a set of functions to back the Bitstring C realization.

A C unsigned char variable matches an ASN.1 Octet variable in the output code.

SLIPPER includes special library functions to support the Octetstring operations. The structure corresponding to the Octetstring variable is defined in the

SLIPPER standard include files and is similar to the Bitstring implementation structure already described.

In fig. 4 a Layer 3 PDU data type is defined in ASN.1 in the DMR SDL model and the corresponding generated C code are shown. As can be seen there is a clear correspondence between the ASN.1 Struct data type definition and the generated C code. Note however, that for unnamed subrange data type definitions (such as "Integer(0..255)") SLIPPER generates a unique data type name ("sort220" in this case). In addition to the generated data type definition, functions to perform operations on the data type are generated such as structure assignment functions.

4   Simulation of Generated Code

The major component of the simulation code provided by the SLIPPER package is the SLIPPER KERNEL software library. The library includes a number of the system API functions supporting the process execution, the signal exchange between the processes, the timers and the simulation session trace. The references to the kernel functions are included into the SLIPPER System include files.

Kernel SW is initialized in the very beginning of the simulation session. During the Kernel initialization the following actions will be performed:

– Pid space allocation
– Process event handles are initialized.

A process is created by a call to the function:

```
Pid scgK_processRegistration(ST_SCG_PROC_HDR * ptr_process_data)
```

This function gets a Pid that coincides with the number of the thread running the process instance. Afterwards, memory is allocated to the process signal queue and to the process data space that comprises the explicit process variables (defined in the SDL specification) and the implicit variables needed for the support of the process state machine. The allocated memory and the Pid value will be freed on the Process Deletion request. Deletion is performed by the call to the API function void scgK_processDelete(pid Pid). Implementation of the API functions is dependent on the OS. For example, a reasonable solution for the Pid definition is to use the task identifier value returned by VxWorks when the task is created. Processes will be managed by the task under VxWorks and by the thread under Windows. A VxWorks user will be obliged to define task priorities while it is not required for the SW evaluation under Windows. Nevertheless, there is no need for OS specific API functions.

Signals are sent via API function:

```
STATUS scgK_sendSignal(ST_SGN_HDR * ptr_signal,
                       unsigned int size_signal)
```

and save signal operation is obtained via API function:

```
STATUS scgK_saveSignal(ST_SCG_PROC_HDR * ptr_process_data)
```

Signal send or save operations should be implemented as operations on the signal queues for the VxWorks OS. SLIPPER simulation uses event handlers to wake the thread in the simulation kernel code. Under VxWorks it will be achieved using signal queues and corresponding signal queue functions.

Also timer functions are OS dependent. Simulation timers are based on 100 ms time sample cycles. That is satisfactory enough for the simulation but it may not suit all the Real Time applications. Nevertheless, simulation timer functions fully implement basic principles of the Timer management.

The code necessary to enable simulation of the generated system implementation is placed in two separate directories, <system name>_kernel and <system name>_simulation. These directories are created at the same hierarchy level as the system directory. The directory <system name>_kernel includes two C files: <system name>_kernel.c and <system name>_kernel_data.c.

<system name>_kernel.c module includes references to the thread functions run by the kernel. The minimal number of thread functions is defined as a sum of maximal number of process instances defined by the SDL specification. The number of the thread functions, generated for the process with the unlimited maximal number of instances, must not exceed 128. The kernel calls a thread function when a signal is sent to a process. <system name>_kernel_data.c module includes an array of Process Identifier structures comprised of the unique process identifier and an index of the first registered instance. The kernel uses this information to manage the process instances.

The simulation code is saved in the directory <system name>_simulation, where two C files are generated:

<system name>_simulation.c and <system name>_simulation_data.c.

The <system name>_simulation_data.c file contains the list of external signal names, and names and identifiers of the process states. These lists are used for signal and FSM state tracing during simulation and for the external signals menu generated for the purposes of the software simulation. The <system name>_simulation.c file includes menu routine (run within a separate thread). The menu routine allows choosing which external signal should be sent to the simulated system. If there are data parameters carried by the signal the additional menu routine will be generated for each of the signal parameters.

5 Using MSC Diagrams for the Tracing of Simulation

The user may select the MSC Trace option from the SLIPPER option dialog box to generate code including MSC trace functions to produce MSC diagrams for the documentation and verification of the system simulation sessions. The output MSC diagrams present signals sent and received by the processes, process states and timer set/reset operations. The diagrams are built by the Cinderella MSC editor whose API functions are used by the MSC trace functions.

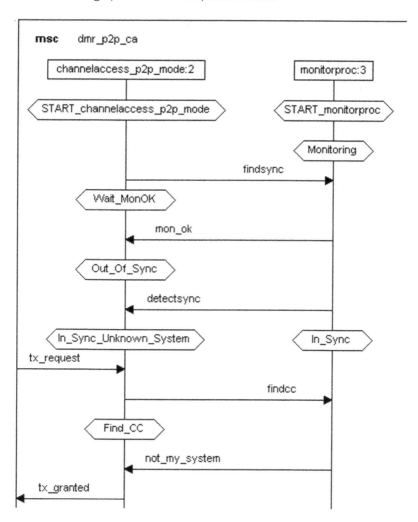

Fig. 5. A simulation MSC trace illustrating a successful DMR MS request for transmission

Figure 5 is an example of a successful channel access scenario for a direct mode DMR Mobile Station (MS) when initiating a transmission. The MSC diagram is the result of a simulation of the code generated from the SDL model of an MS channel access procedure. MSC diagrams generated by simulation from the code may be used to validate that the system requirements specified in MSC diagrams are preserved in the transformation to target code.

6   Conclusion

We have illustrated how the SLIPPER C code generator supports the software developer in the further integration of the generated code and how the SLIPPER code linked with other components in the Cinderella tool set can improve the development process. We have also shown how the linking of the SLIPPER kernel and generated code with the Cinderella MSC may also be useful for validation of system requirements.

The SLIPPER code generator is a first release of the tool and further extensions are planned to support software development processes based on automatic code generation from SDL. This, among other features, will include support for adding user defined C-code in the SDL model that will be preserved during code generation.

References

1. ETSI TS 102 361-1, "Electromagnetic compatibility and Radio spectrum Matters (ERM); Technical Requirement for Digital Mobile Radio (DMR); Part 1: Air Interface (AI) protocol", 2005, v.0.0.12.
2. ETSI TS 102 361-2, "Electromagnetic compatibility and Radio spectrum Matters (ERM); Technical Requirement for Digital Mobile Radio (DMR); Part 2: Basic Services and Facilities", 2005, v.0.0.3.
3. Sanders R.: Implementing from SDL, Telektronikk 4, 2000.
4. Mansurov N., Chernov A., Ragozin A; "Industrial Strength Code Generation from SDL"; SDL'97, Eds.: A. Cavalli and A. Sarma; 1997.
5. Langendoerfer P., Koenig H., "COCOS – A configurable SDL Compiler for Generating Efficient Protocol Implementations", SDL'99; Eds.: R. Dssouli, G.v. Bochmann, Y. Lahav.; 1999.
6. Mansurov N., Ragozin A.; "Using declarative mappings for automatic code generation from SDL and ASN.1"; SDL'99; Eds.: Eds.: R. Dssouli, G.v. Bochmann, Y. Lahav.; 1999.

Model-Driven Development of Reactive Systems with SDL

Edel Sherratt

Department of Computer Science,
University of Wales Aberystwyth,
Penglais, Aberystwyth,
Ceredigion SY23 3DB,
Wales UK
eds.aber.ac.uk
http://users.aber.ac.uk/eds

Abstract. Ubiquitous computing and communications services are the focus of intense current research and development. These systems are essentially asynchronous reactive systems of independent agents. However, there is little evidence of recent use of visual formalisms like SDL in their development. This represents a challenge and an opportunity.

1 Introduction

Recent developments in sensing, communication, and software have brought visions of intelligent, context-sensitive buildings, roads, vehicles, and even clothing tantalizingly close. Research in pervasive and ubiquitous computing is intense [1, 2, 3], prototypes have been demonstrated [4], and 'the disappearing computer' is close to full realization [5].

At the heart of these visions lie systems of intelligent, reactive agents that respond to sensor data, and communicate with each other in an asynchronous way to achieve coordinated results. Development of asynchronous reactive systems is non-trivial, and modeling and simulation are critical to providing evidence of their feasibility and reliability [6]. Indeed, it is reasonable to say that reactive systems is one area where the model driven architecture [7] *is* SDL [8, 9, 10], which when combined with UML [11, 12, 13] using the SDL UML profile [14, 15, 16] provides a basis for robust model-driven development of ubiquitous systems.

However, despite the availability of formalisms and automatic support for engineering systems of reactive agents, both the literature and anecdotal evidence suggest that ad-hoc development is the norm in ubiquitous and pervasive computing.

Examples illustrating recent ubiquitous prototypes are briefly reviewed below. Common themes, requirements and solutions are explored, and the merits of SDL-2000 for developing these new kinds of system are discussed. Challenges are summarized, and opportunities identified.

A. Prinz, R. Reed, and J. Reed (Eds.): SDL 2005, LNCS 3530, pp. 224–233, 2005.

2   Ubiquitous Systems and Reactive Behavior: Some Examples

Evolution of SDL is driven by the need to model new kinds of communications and computing systems. Such examples motivate and provide a basis for evaluating new SDL revisions [17].

The following sections briefly review a few of the many ubiquitous, context-aware, reactive systems to be found in the literature, as well as technologies to support them. These systems and technologies reveal key themes to be addressed by modeling and simulation formalisms.

2.1   IST Project ParcelCall

ParcelCall developed and demonstrated real time tracking and tracing in transport and logistics applications. Active tags equipped with sensors and radios supplied real time information about the status and location of goods via wap-enabled mobile telephones and ordinary web browsers. Trials in a live environment demonstrated the feasibility of the approach to tracking goods on journeys across several European countries [18].

Modelling proved challenging, and limitations of the UML for this kind of modeling work were identified [19].

2.2   Context-Aware Computing in Hospital Work

Well researched designs for a context-aware pill container and a context-aware hospital bed were reported by Bardram [20]. The context-aware hospital bed has an integrated computer and display, as well as sensors that can identify the patient, recognize when a nurse is attending to the patient. It can be used by the patient for internet access and television, and by clinicians for access to the patient's records.

The work yielded useful knowledge about the nature and uses of context awareness, as well as an awareness infrastructure and an applications programming interface.

2.3   Resource Aware Visualization Environment

A resource aware visualization environment (RAVE) [21] is one of the projects of the Welsh e-Science Centre [22] RAVE is currently investigating the use of grid technology (Globus 3 [23]) and agents implemented in Java^{TM} to enable collaborative visualization on a variety of platforms, from fully immersive platforms through PCs and even PDAs. It allows clients to share rendering services, and rendering services to share data services, with delivery of appropriate graphical representation depending on available resources.

2.4   System Development for Interactive Light Control (SILICON)

System development for interactive light control (SILICON) [4] concerns a building with offices, a hallway and several installations. The offices have light groups and sun blinds that can be controlled by switches. The hall lights can be controlled by switches, and are also automatically triggered by a motion sensor.

Starting from requirements for a distributed lighting system [24], SILICON went on to implement and demonstrate a physical model [4]. Development followed a model driven approach using an existing SDL toolset enhanced by a specialist tool, APIgen, that generated interfaces for a variety of communication technologies.

2.5   EgoSpaces, Supporting Coordination Between Agents

EgoSpaces [25] supports coordination between agents operating in mobile and ad-hoc environments. This technology supports ubiquitous applications by allowing them to control the data to be included in their operating contexts.

EgoSpaces applications make use of views, reminiscent of views on a database, but with the ability to update views dynamically and to react to the presence of data, derived for example, from a sensor or by way of a signal from another agent. This emphasis on management of potentially large amounts of sensor data contrasts with the large body of literature which focuses on the behavioral and methodological aspects of reactive systems.

3   Key Themes and Their Implications for Specification and Modeling

The above examples share common elements of autonomy, reactivity, context awareness, and structure. Requirements implied by these characteristics, and the extent to which SDL meets those requirements, are explored below.

3.1   Reactive Systems of Autonomous Agents

Reactive systems are driven by external events and conditions [6]. They allow for intermediate observation, and not merely observation at start-up and termination [26]. Their complexity stems from the patterns of triggers and reactions within the system, and from the concurrency and timing issues that result from their responsiveness to events. Further challenges are posed when agents form ad-hoc networks in an environment that is itself subject to change.

Complex patterns of reactions can be understood and controlled by modeling and simulation. The behavior of individual agents is described using executable visual formalisms like SDL diagrams [8] or statecharts [6, 11] for behavior of individual agents or objects, while Message Sequence Charts [27] and sequence diagrams [11] trace inter-object behavior.

Timing issues and scheduling constraints are the subject of current research [28, 29]. Further work is needed to solve these problems, but formalisms like SDL and MSC with appropriate tool support represent a clear improvement over the ad-hoc approaches currently prevalent in ubiquitous computing.

SDL-2000 allows specification of agent types that can be instantiated and destroyed, and whose instances have autonomous behavior defined by state machines. To this extent, dynamicity and autonomy are supported. However, an

SDL system as a whole is statically defined, as is the pattern of events and triggers that can be generated and recognized. This limits modeling of context awareness.

3.2   Context Awareness and Context Limitation

The behavior of a ubiquitous service is triggered by events or signals identified by its constituent agents from the physical or logical context in which those agents find themselves. In the simplest case, an active sensor broadcasts signals that can be picked up by any agent within range. A combination of agent state, physical location and logical connectivity together determine event handling.

For instance, the context-aware hospital bed [20] responds to the approach of a nurse by enabling automatic login, while the active tags in ParcelCall [18], sense the location of packages as well as the temperature, humidity and other characteristics of their container.

As well as responding to ambient signals, some agents actively seek out characteristics of their environment. For example, RAVE [21] discovers and responds to remote services as well as reacting to the characteristics of local display facilities.

Context limitation entails restricting the ambient signals recognized or accepted by an agent. This is necessary to protect agents from data overload, and to ensure ambient signals only reach their intended recipients. For example, patient privacy must be maintained despite ambient availability of patient data in the case of of the context-aware hospital bed [20], and protection of agents from data overload motivated much of the EgoSpaces [25] development.

SDL is explicitly intended for modeling agents that generate and respond to signals. This means that agents can respond to their modeled environment and can also query their environment.

Signal sets on SDL gates allow static specification of the interface between an agent and its context, and thus provide some control over context awareness [8, 10]. The gates on an agent type specify exactly the signals that agent instances can accept, and thus the kind and degree of context awareness the agent has. This also ensures that only intended recipients can act on signals.

However, as a static definition, the signal set on an SDL gate not only prescribes the behavior of an agent type, but also the behavior of the environment in that the environment must generate signals accepted by the agent and must accept signals generated by the agent.

This contradicts the idea of an autonomous agent which is capable of exploring an unknown environment, and dynamically reconfiguring the signals it accepts and its own responses to those signals in the context of the new environment.

3.3   Event Sharing

Ambient and broadcast communications imply event sharing and the potential for conflict in an environment where multiple agents can react to an event.

Intuitively, if an event is discernible in an environment, then every agent that can respond to the event should be able to sense the event. This is reflected in the semantics of Harel statecharts as described in [6, 30], where every transition that can be triggered by an event is triggered when the event occurs.

However, this is not the default semantics for UML 2.0 [11, 12] statecharts (although it is a semantic variation point). There, unless otherwise specified, if several behaviors contend for an event, then only one of those actions is taken [11] and the event is consumed.

In SDL-2000 [8] also, in the case of conflicting transitions, which are triggered by the same event, only one transition is actually fired by the event. SDL-2000 differs from UML 2.0 statecharts in that the transition to be fired is uniquely determined; that is, it is the innermost transition in a composite state that accepts the event, where state partitions in a state aggregation are required to have disjoint signal sets.

Both kinds of semantics have their merits. The statechart semantics of [6, 30] provide for the kind of concurrency that would intuitively be expected where independent agents all recognize a particular event in a given location. For example, in a hospital scenario it could well be essential that several different agents all responded to a patient event.

On the other hand, although further removed from this intuitive view, the deterministic semantics of SDL-2000 leads to very robust solutions to this kind of problem. It is reasonable to assume that the different agents that must respond to a patient event must respond in a coordinated fashion, and so it makes sense to combine those agents in a state aggregation, whose containing agent reacts to the initial patient event by controlled triggering of the state partitions. This is analogous to an approach recommended for UML 2.0 sequence diagrams in [31].

The default semantics of UML 2.0 statecharts exhibits a worrying level of non-determinacy for situations like the patient-event scenario. However, it is absolutely appropriate for describing a single-queuing mechanism for allocating tasks to duplicate resources (such as printers), any one of which could handle the event.

3.4   Composition and Structure

Composition and structure are used to model agent combination in part-whole relationships, and also agent cooperation to achieve particular results, in possibly temporary collaborations. Compositions can be static, existing throughout the life of a system, or dynamic, allowing agents to join and leave. They can also be physical or logical.

For example, in ParcelCall [18], a consignment can be composed of several logically related elements, whose active tags could, in principle, communicate with each other to provide coordinated data about the status and location of the composite package. Alternatively, the consignment might consist of physically nested packages.

SDL 2000 supports composite types, which means that structured agents can be modeled. It also supports dynamic communications structures by allowing creation and destruction of agent instances [8]. This has a well-defined and robust semantics; containing agents remain in a stopping condition until all their contained agents have terminated, so no agent is left without a container.

4   Model Driven Development with SDL

Model driven architecture (MDA) has been promoted [7] as a way to raise the level of abstraction at which software engineers work, and to increase automation of software development processes. Model driven development entails using well-defined models to specify systems with varying levels of dependency on programming languages and platforms. Models are managed and transformed with the help of tools that preserve consistency between the models.

The term MDA as used in [7] applies to software and systems development using models whose consistency relationships are defined in terms of the OMG meta-object facility (MOF) [32].

However, the use of fully automated visual formalisms, comprising systems of models in verifiable relationships was fully realized in the area of reactive systems long before UML 2.0 and MDA existed. SDL was formally defined in the 1980's, and sophisticated tools to support modeling, simulation and code generation have been available for more than 20 years. A textbook detailing an object-oriented, model-driven approach to development of real-time systems using SDL was published in the early 1990's[33]. Similarly tools to support model based development using statecharts have been in use for almost as long.

It is therefore hardly surprising that some of the most complete examples of model driven architecture have emerged from the SDL-UML and TINA communities [4, 34, 35, 36]. These studies go far beyond generation from object models of instance variable declarations with associated setters and getters to simulation, testing and generation of fully working systems.

5   Challenges

Although SDL has long proved to be an excellent formalism for specifying, modeling and developing reactive systems [33, 37], and despite the recent explosion of interest in ubiquitous services, there is little evidence of recent use of SDL in creating or prototyping these services. Literature searches yield numerous articles on ubiquitous computing, and on state machine modeling, but very few in which the two are combined[1].

Some technical challenges to the use of SDL are listed below.

- **Tool support:** Although some excellent tools are available, still more are needed, but SDL 2000 presents substantial technical challenges to tool developers. This, of course reflects the essential tension between demands for

---

[1] Searches were conducted using ISI Web of Science, Citeseer, OCLC FirstSearch, the ACM digital library and SpringerLink.

language expressiveness and implementability. Target language constraints may discourage some tool users, while costs deter others.

- **Timing and scheduling:** The problems are a subject of ongoing research, and their solution will enhance the attractiveness of the SDL family of formalisms.
- **Signal sets on gates:** These prescribe behavior of agents in a static way, and make it difficult to model agents that adapt to new environments; moreover, they also prescribe the behavior of the environment itself.
- **Event sharing:** Between independent agents, where multiple agents *all* respond to an ambient event, event sharing cannot be modeled without adding clutter to an SDL specification.

The greatest non-technical challenge concerns the general level of awareness of SDL within the ubiquitous computing community. Although SDL has kept pace with or outstripped advancements in ubiquitous computing and in model-driven development, demonstrations showing this do not make for novel research. This means that new players in ubiquitous computing remain largely unaware of the benefits of SDL 2000 with its agent-oriented features. This problem is compounded by the use of different vocabularies to describe the same concepts in the state machine modeling and ubiquitous computing communities. If SDL is to become a formalism of choice in that community, new demonstrations of its benefits will need to be made available.

6   Conclusion

Ubiquitous systems involving elements of communication and computing are rapidly becoming a fact of modern life. These systems are composed of ad-hoc combinations of autonomous agents, which exhibit asynchronous reactive behavior, responding to various environmental factors, including the presence or absence of other agents.

Best practice in development of reactive systems indicates that visual formalisms, involving diagrammatic yet semantically rigorous diagrams, should be used for specifying these systems. Amongst the many established and emerging visual formalisms, SDL and MSC are extremely well positioned to serve as the modeling formalisms of choice for development of ubiquitous systems. As well as possessing technical strengths, the manner in which their evolution is agreed amongst interested parties serves to ensure that independently developed models can readily be interchanged and combined, and that engineers' skills are applicable in a range of domains.

The emergence of the SDL UML profile [15] together with supporting tools to facilitate simulation, play-in/play-out, and model transformation serve to combine the advantages of UML's large and diverse user base with the semantic strength of SDL.

However, technical and non-technical challenges remain. The principal non-technical challenge it to raise awareness of the benefits of SDL and particularly of SDL 2000 within the rapidly growing ubiquitous/pervasive computing community. Technical challenges include:

- provision of further tool support (such as an extensible toolkit aimed at users with limited budgets);
- continued research into timing and scheduling problems (few of which are adequately addressed in current ubiquitous prototypes);
- development of intuitive models of event sharing in the presence of ambient signals;
- development of dynamically reconfigurable gates (so that agents can adapt their behavior to new environments without needing to carry information about all possible environments).

These challenges are formidable, but the rising enthusiasm for ubiquitous computing, coupled with the discovery by the wider IT community of model driven architecture, presents an excellent opportunity for SDL and its related formalisms.

References

1. Reconfigurable Ubiquitous Networked Embedded Systems,
   http://www.ist-runes.org/introduction.html
2. Eric Chung, Jason I. Hong, James Lin, Madhu K. Prabaker, James A. Landay, and Alan Liu: Development and Evaluation of Emerging Design Patterns for Ubiquitous Computing. In Proceedings of Designing Interactive Systems (DIS2004), August 2004, ACM 2004
3. Tony Houghton: Ubiquitous Services and Applications: Focus on what customers think, not what they say Eurescom Summit 2005, to appear
4. Philipp Schaible, Reinhard Gotzhein: Development of Distributed Systems with SDL by means of formalized APIs, In: Rick Reed and Jeanne Reed (Eds.): SDL 2003: System Design, Lecture Notes in Computer Science, Vol. 2708 Springer-Verlag, Berlin Heidelberg (2003) 55–76
5. Communications of the ACM, Special Issue: The Disappearing Computer, 48(3), March 2005,
6. David Harel, Yishai Feldman: Algorithmics: the Spirit of Computing, Pearson Education Limited, 2004
7. Jishnu Mukerji, Joaquin Miller (Eds.): MDA Guide Version 1.0.1 OMG omg/03-06-01, June 2003, available from http://www.omg.org/cgi-bin/doc?omg/03-06-01
8. ITU-T Recommendation Z.100 (08/02): Specification and Description Language (SDL), ITU-T (2002)
9. Rick Reed: SDL-2000 for New Millennium Systems, Free for download at http://www.itu.int/itudoc/itu-t/com17/tutorial/78255.html
10. Laurent Doldi: SDL Illustrated: Visually design executable models, Laurent Doldi 2001, ISBN 2-9516600-0-6, available from http://www.tmso-systems.com, or can be ordered in bookshops.
11. UML 2 working documents, OMG 2004, available from the OMG website http://www.omg.org/technology/documents/modeling_spec_catalog.htm#UML
12. Hans-Erik Eriksson, Magnus Penker, Brian Lyons, David Fado: UML 2 Toolkit. Wiley Publishing Incl, Indianapolis, Indiana; OMG Press (2004)

13. Laurent Doldi: UML 2 Illustrated - Developing Real-Time and Communications Systems, Laurent Doldi 2003, ISBN 2-9516600-1-4 available from http://www.tmso-systems.com, or can be ordered in bookshops.
14. ITU-T Recommendation Z.109 (11/99): SDL combined with UML, ITU-T (1999)
15. ITU-T Recommendation Z.109: SDL combined with UML, ITU-T (2005), to appear
16. Morgan Björkander: Graphical Programming using UML and SDL, IEEE Computer 2000
17. Edel Sherratt: SDL in a Changing World in Daniel Amyot, Alan W. Williams (Eds.): System Analysis and Modeling: 4th International SDL and MSC Workshop, SAM 2004, Ottawa, Canada, June 1-4, 2004, Revised Selected Papers, LNCS 3319, 2005
18. Birgit Kreller, Jens Hartmann The Field Trial Scenario Of An Inter-Modal, End-To-End And Real-Time Tracking And Tracing System. 8th World Congress on Intelligent Transport Systems, Sydney, Australia, October 2001, available online at http://www-i4.informatik.rwth-aachen.de/parcelcall/
19. Massimo Felici, Juliana Küster Filipe: Inter disciplinary approaches to the design of dependable computer systems: Limits in modelling evolving computer-based systems, Proceedings of the 2002 ACM symposium on Applied computing, March 2002
20. Jakob E Bardram: Applications of Context-Aware Computing in Hospital Work – Examples and Design Principles, Proceedings SAC'04, ACM, March 2004
21. Resource Aware Visualisation Environment http://www.cs.cardiff.ac.uk/user/I.J.Grimstead/RAVE
22. Welsh e-Science Centre/Canolfan e-Wyddoniaeth Cymru: http://www.wesc.ac.uk/
23. S. Tuecke, K. Czajkowski, I. Foster, J. Frey, S. Graham, C. Kesselman, T. Maguire, T. Sandholm, P. Vanderbilt, D. Snelling (Eds.): Open Grid Services Infrastructure (OGSI) Version 1.0. Global Grid Forum Draft Recommendation, 6/27/2003.
24. E. Börger, R Gotzhein (Guest Eds.): Requirements engineering: the Light Control Case Study, Journal of Universal Computer Science, 6(7), Springer 2000
25. Christine Julien and Gruia-Catalin Roman: Active Coordination in ad hoc Networks, R. de Nicola et al. (Eds.): COORDINATION 2004, LNCS 2949, 2004
26. C.A.R. Hoare and He Jifeng: Unifying Theories of Programming, Prentice Hall Series in Computer Science, Prentice Hall Europe, 1998
27. ITU-T Recommendation Z.120 (04/04): Message Sequence Chart (MSC), ITU-T (2004)
28. Susanne Graf, Ileana Ober: A Real Time Profile for UML and how to adapt it to SDL, In: Rick Reed and Jeanne Reed (Eds.): SDL 2003: System Design, Lecture Notes in Computer Science, Vol. 2708 Springer-Verlag, Berlin Heidelberg (2003) 55–76
29. F. Khendek, C. Lohr, L.X. Wang, X.J. Zhang, T. Zheng: Early validation of deployment and scheduling constraints of MSC specifications, in Daniel Amyot, Alan W. Williams (Eds.): System Analysis and Modeling: 4th International SDL and MSC Workshop, SAM 2004, Ottawa, Canada, June 1-4, 2004, Revised Selected Papers, LNCS 3319, 2005
30. David Harel, Amnon Naamad: The STATEMATE Semantics of Statecharts, ACM Transactions on Software Engineering and Methodology, 5(4), October 1996
31. Ingolf Krüger, Wolfgang Prenninger, Robert Sandner, Manfred Broy: Development of Hierarchical Broadcasting Software Architectures Using UML 2.0, H Ehrig et al. (Eds.): INT 2004, LNCS 3147, 2004

32. Manfred R. Koethe: MOF 2.0 XMI Convenience document OMG ptc/04-06-11, June 2004, available from http://www.omg.org/cgi-bin/doc?ptc/04-06-11
33. Rolf Bræk, Øystein Haugen: Engineering of Real Time Systems, Prentice-Hall, 1993 (ISBN 13-034448-6)
34. Harald Böhme and Joachim Fischer: eODL and SDL in combination for components in Daniel Amyot, Alan W. Williams (Eds.): System Analysis and Modeling: 4th International SDL and MSC Workshop, SAM 2004, Ottawa, Canada, June 1-4, 2004, Revised Selected Papers, LNCS 3319, 2005
35. Jörg Dorsch, Anders Ek, Reinhard Gotzhein: SPT – the SDL Pattern Tool in Daniel Amyot, Alan W. Williams (Eds.): System Analysis and Modeling: 4th International SDL and MSC Workshop, SAM 2004, Ottawa, Canada, June 1-4, 2004, Revised Selected Papers, LNCS 3319, 2005
36. Andreas Metzger, Stefan Queins: Model-based generation of SDL Specifications for the Early Prototyping of Reactive Systems, in: Edel Sherratt (Ed.): Telecommunications and beyond: The Broader Applicability of SDL and MSC. Lecture Notes in Computer Science, Vol. 2599. Springer-Verlag, Berlin Heidelberg (2003) 158–169
37. M. Toeroe, J. Zhu, V. C. Leung: SDL specification and verification of universal personal computing with ObjectGEODE, Proceedings IFIP 1997, Chapman Hall

A UML-Compatible Formal Language for System Architecture Description

Matteo Pradella[2], Matteo Rossi[1], and Dino Mandrioli[1,2]

[1] Dipartimento di Elettronica ed Informazione, Politecnico di Milano
[2] Consiglio Nazionale delle Ricerche – Istituto di Elettronica e di Ingegneria dell'Informazione e delle Telecomunicazioni (CNR-IEIIT-MT)[1]
[1,2]via Ponzio 34/5, 20133 Milano, Italy
{pradella, rossi, mandrioli}@elet.polimi.it

Abstract. This paper presents ArchiTRIO (*Architectural TRIO*), a new temporal logic language which combines a subset of the UML notation with a precise formal semantics inspired from the authors' experiences. ArchiTRIO allows developers to use standard UML 2.0 notation to describe non-critical aspects of systems, but it also offers a complementary formal notation, fully integrated with the UML one, to represent those system aspects that require precise modeling.

1   Introduction

Nowadays, UML is the *de facto* standard for system modeling in industrial practice. Its popularity derives from a number of factors such as simplicity, ease of use and a certain degree of intuitiveness and flexibility in the notation, which reduce the effort needed to be able to write UML models to a minimum. UML is evolving, and its 2.0 incarnation introduces some new constructs (such as component, connector, port) crucial for describing system architectures that were previously missing [11]. Alas, as with the previous versions, UML's lack of formality hampers its applicability to critical systems, where precise and rigorous designs are of the utmost importance for the correct development of the application. To overcome these deficiencies, a number of approaches use existing formal languages to give some chosen UML constructs, typically statecharts and sequence diagrams, a precise semantics (see [8, 9]).

Our experience with the TRIO and TC (TRIO-CORBA) languages [2] led us to develop the ArchiTRIO language, which ArchiTRIO follows a lightweight approach to the problem of formal modeling [17] to better suits industrial practices. ArchiTRIO is based upon a few selected UML 2.0 constructs especially suited for describing architectures, it gives them a formal meaning, and precisely defines their composition. It differs from the aforementioned formal approaches to UML in that it exploits a logic-based approach, which (given a UML 2.0 composite structure diagram [14]) allows one to define at a high abstraction level the dynamic properties (including possible temporal constraints) of the system components and their mutual interactions. ArchiTRIO adds expressive power

A. Prinz, R. Reed, and J. Reed (Eds.): SDL 2005, LNCS 3530, pp. 234–246, 2005.

to UML diagrams, rather than replacing or modifying any of them. Therefore a user, who at first does not need full-blown ArchiTRIO, can start by drawing bare UML composite structure diagrams. ArchiTRIO-specific notation can be introduced later, when the need arises for clarity and precision (especially for what concerns critical system temporal constraints).

Given the formal nature of the language, from an ArchiTRIO model a number of developments are possible:

- an obvious one is to apply formal verification techniques to check the correctness of the design against high level requirements (similar to the experience of TC [16]);
- another is to move from a high-level architectural design to a lower level closer to implementation – we envision the possibility of translating ArchiTRIO formulas into operational notations such as Statecharts or SDL diagrams [1, 12, 18].

The ultimate goal of our research, in fact, is to support the full life cycle by allowing the developer to move smoothly and safely from the high phases of requirements analysis and specification down to final implementation and verification. Thus, an operational version of architectural system design can be further refined into an executable implementation possibly exploiting a (semi)automatic code generator such as [18].

To provide tool support to ArchiTRIO, a plugin of the TRIO-based TRIDENT integrated development platform is currently being developed. To fully support the above methodological approach, TRIDENT will allow the user to import a "pure UML document" produced through any UML tool and to augment it with the appropriate level of formality expressed in terms of ArchiTRIO.

This paper is structured as follows: section 2 presents the ArchiTRIO approach to system development, which combines informal UML models with precise temporal logic formulas; section 3 presents the ArchiTRIO language through a running example, and briefly hints at its formal semantics; section 4 describes the tool being developed to support the aforementioned language and methodology; finally, section 5 presents a selection of related works and draws some conclusions.

2   Overview of the Approach

In this section, we sketch our approach, along with a simple running example: an access control system for a building divided into areas having different security levels. Our methodological trip starts from the high level system description, written in natural language and pure UML, and goes through the architectural design, by means of the ArchiTRIO language. This section stops right before actually presenting ArchiTRIO concepts – this is the purpose of section 3.

Our aim is to offer a methodology and tools that, starting from standard UML, may include a formally sound temporal logic-based technique. Ideally, our methodology follows the following route: a user would start by drawing a UML diagram (at present, we take into account class diagrams, and leave behavioral diagrams out of the picture), and then refine/specialize/complete it until a complete specification/architecture is obtained, consisting of Composite Structure diagrams and their ArchiTRIO semantics, possibly augmented with exclusively ArchiTRIO concepts, on which formal verification can be carried out.

Let us now consider the example system. The Access Control System is used in one or more corporate buildings having three different security levels: *low*, *medium*, and *high*. The building may contain zero or more areas of a given security level. The access control is enforced through essentially two kinds of entities: a local mechanism based on the concept of *security gate*, and a *central control* connected to a user database.

As in current UML-based industrial practice, we start by drawing a class diagram, in which we depict the relations among these higher-level entities (see fig. 1).

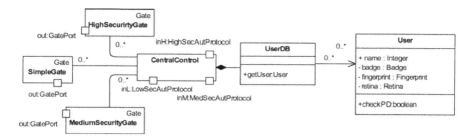

Fig. 1. Access Control System: the high-level class diagram

The diagram in fig. 1 depicts a `CentralControl` class, the main entity which enforces the prescribed security policy for user access; `UserDB` – a database containing users' data and their actual security clearance; and three kinds of `Gate` classes: `SimpleGate`, `MediumSecurityGate`, and `HighSecurityGate`, in charge of managing the local access to areas with low, medium, and high security level, respectively.

UML 2.0 introduces the useful concept of port, which is essentially an interface container. In this example ports are used to define the protocols used by the `CentralControl`, to get from, send data to, and manage gates. In fig. 1, every gate has a port of type `GatePort`, while `CentralControl` has three different ports, `LowSecAutProtocol`, `MedSecAutProtocol`, and `HighSecAutProtocol` that will be used to communicate with `SimpleGates`, `MediumSecurityGates`, and `HighSecurityGates`, respectively.

Moving in a top-down fashion, we now define the internal class structure of the gates (see fig. 2). As the reader can see, the low security gate is the simplest one, and it is depicted on the left part of the diagram. A `SimpleGate` is an entity having one or more `BadgeReaders` (a subclass of `IdRecognizer`), managed by a local controller `LC_SimpleGate`. Communication between `BadgeReader` and `LC_SimpleGate` is based on the interface `LocalControl`, implemented by the latter.

The medium security level gates are described in the central part of the diagram. A MediumSecurityGate is based on a more sophisticated IdRecognizer, a fingerprint reader (class FingerprintsReader), and has an entry sensor (class EntrySensor). In the typical usage scenario of a medium security gate, the user approaches the gate and his/her fingerprints are scanned; his/her data is then sent to the central control to be checked. If everything is ok, the gate remains open either for a short fixed time interval, or until the entry sensor actually detects the user getting in. This scenario could typically be described in UML by a sequence diagram, not reported here. Analogously to the simple gate, a medium security gate is supervised by a local controller, LC_MedSecGate, and communication between the local controller and the sensors is based on the interface LocalControl.

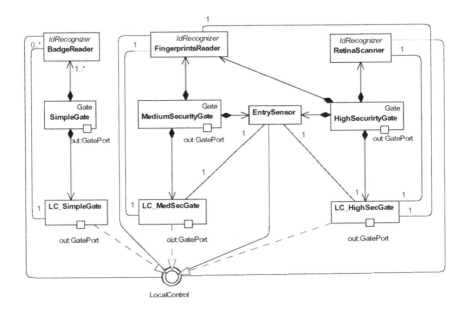

Fig. 2. Access Control System: the local-level class diagram

The most complex type of gate is the HighSecurityGate, on the right side of fig. 2: it consists of two kinds of IdRecognizers, a FingerprintsReader and a RetinaScanner; an EntrySensor; and a local controller LC_HighSecGate. Its behavior is basically analogous to the medium security level one, but for the retina scanner: the access control has to check both the user's fingerprints and retina to open the gate.

To move towards the high-level system architecture, we have now to describe how instances of the classes sketched in the previous diagrams are actually interconnected and structured. As far as UML is concerned, the new composite structure diagrams, a welcome addition in UML 2.0, are quite useful. Let us consider for instance a high security gate (fig. 3).

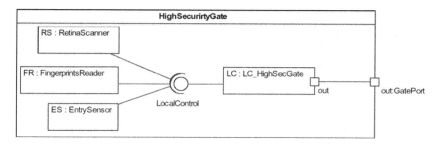

Fig. 3. Composite structure diagram of a high security gate

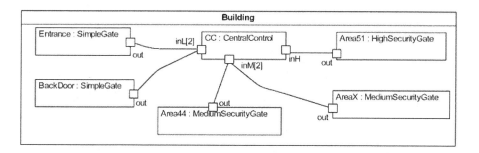

Fig. 4. The building structure: the high-level system architecture

A high security gate consists of a retina scanner (RS), a fingerprints reader (FR), an entry sensor (ES), and a local control (LC). Every one is an instance of the corresponding class; LC exchanges data with the sensors by implementing the interface LocalControl, while communication with the remote central control happens through a replicated port of type GatePort. Details of this aspect will be provided in the next section.

Last, we consider the system high-level architecture (fig. 4): our example building is made of a central control (CC); two low security gates (Entrance and BackDoor); two medium security areas and their corresponding gates (AreaX and Area44); finally, a high security area reachable through a high security gate (Area51).

This concludes a first simple architectural description of the system, based exclusively on UML constructs. As we said in the introduction, UML *per se* does not precisely define many of the constructs we used for describing our system here. For instance, in our brief description above, a precise definition of timeouts management and local control behavior is nowhere to be found. More generally, we would like to be able to precisely express a critical property and possibly to verify it. In our example an unwanted behavior like the following should not be possible: Alice has clearance to enter Area51 and authenticates herself at the gate, at the same time a malicious Bob is waiting for her authentication behind a corner nearby, trying to enter into the restricted area right behind her. On one hand it is easy to correctly model the local control by using behavioral diagrams (such as statecharts or SDL). On the other hand however, stating and verifying general properties (such as "the entry sensor must signal a single entrance after a valid authentication, and it must occur not before k ms and not after $k+n$ ms") is almost impossible if one uses pure UML, even taking into account OCL. OCL *per se* has a limited aim and has been designed to express static constraints like guards and pre-/post-conditions on operations without side-effects. We will consider OCL and some of its proposed variants later.

It is at this point that the designer of a critical system could need something more than plain UML to seamlessly incorporate desired properties and system requirements into its architecture. So ArchiTRIO appears in the picture: the designer needs a solid formal description of the used concepts (class, instance, interface, port, operation, connection, and so on) to state something more and more precisely about the system, well before implementing it.

3   The ArchiTRIO Language

The basic ArchiTRIO concepts mirror a subset of the elements one can find in UML 2.0. The core of the language is the *class*. A class defines *operations* and *attributes*, and can provide and require *interfaces*; *ports* are groups of required/provided interfaces, and can be used to define protocols. Classes can have *composite structures*, whose parts are connected by *connectors*.

Next to these UML elements, however, ArchiTRIO also includes concepts derived from temporal logic, which allow users to precisely define the behavior of a system modeled with ArchiTRIO. In fact, every UML element featured in ArchiTRIO is given a formal semantics in terms of the temporal logic (HOT, Higher-Order TRIO [5]) on which ArchiTRIO is founded. This, in turn, allows one to attach a precise meaning to the formulas describing the dynamics of the components (taken separately or as a whole) of the system being modeled.

Let us now illustrate some of the most significant syntactic features of ArchiTRIO through the example system shown in section 2. Section 3.1 will briefly hint at the semantics of some of the elements shown here, without pretending to be exhaustive.

The graphical representation of those concepts that are common to both ArchiTRIO and UML is the same as in UML. However, every ArchiTRIO element (UML-derived and logic-derived ones alike) is also given a textual representation detailing its ArchiTRIO-specific features. For example, class LC_HighSecGate introduced in fig. 2 provides interface LocalControl and has a port of type GatePort; interface LocalControl defines two operations, incomingData and personEntered. The corresponding textual declaration of fig. 5 defines that, in addition to the aforementioned UML port and interface, class LC_HighSecGate includes three logic items, inGate, lastUser and gate_open. Item inGate is time-independent (TI, meaning that its value is constant over time), and represents the identifier of the Gate to which the controller belongs; item lastUser is time-dependent (TD, that is its value depends on the time instant at which the item is evaluated) and models the data corresponding

class LC_HighSecGate	items:
temporal domain: real;	TI inGate : GateId;
	TD lastUser : User;
provides LocalControl ...	state gate_open;
ports:	constructors:
out : GatePort; ...	LC_HighSecGate(GateId g) : inGate = g;
	axioms:...
	end

Fig. 5. Sketch of the textual declaration of class LC_HighSecGate

to the user who had either his/her fingerprints or his/her retina scanned; item gate_open, instead, is a state (which means that it is true/false in intervals of non-null duration), and models the intervals in which the gate is open. Notice that the temporal domain clause defines that temporal variables range over real values (that is, time is dense).

As we will show later through some examples, in addition to the logic items explicitly declared in the class signature, an ArchiTRIO class includes a number of built-in items, which model the most significant features of the UML elements of the class (for example the parameters of an operation, an operation invocation, etc.). Then, the axioms of class LC_HighSecGate are formulas that predicate over the logic items (explicitly declared or built-in) of the class to define its precise behavior.

Axiom dataRelay shown below, for example, states that when an invocation of operation incomingData (exported through interface LocalControl) is received by the controller and the value of the rawData parameter is pd, within T time units in the future the controller will invoke (an instance of) operation sendPersData (see fig. 6 for its signature) on port out, passing pd and the value corresponding to item inGate as parameters.

```
vars: iD  :  incomingData
      sPD :  sendPersData
      pd  :  PersonalData
dataRelay:
  iD.inv_rec(pd)  ->
    ex out.sPD(WithinF(out.sPD.invoke(pd, inGate), T);
```

In axiom dataRelay, iD and sPD are variables ranging over all possible *invocations* of operations incomingData and sendPersData, respectively. Then, ex out.sPD means that "there exists an invocation of operation sendPersData (within the scope of port out) such that...". inv_rec and invoke are built-in logic items (more precisely *events*, that is predicates that are true only in isolated time instants) modeling significant events of an operation invocation; in particular, event iD.inv_rec is true when invocation iD of operation incomingData is received by the local controller; similarly, event out.sPD.invoke is true when the controller issues invocation sPD on port out. WithinF is a temporal operator taken from the TRIO formal language [2] (it stands for *within the future*). Finally, pd is a variable of type PersonalData, where PersonalData is an ArchiTRIO

interface AccessControl	interface FromAccessControl
operations:	operations:
User sendPersData(in PersonalData rawData,	openGate();
in GateId gate)	end
raises UserNonExistentException;	
enterPerson(in User user, in GateId gate)	
raises UserNonExistentException;	
end	

Fig. 6. Declaration of interfaces AccessControl and FromAccessControl

class, not shown here for the sake of brevity, modeling either the badge, or the fingerprints, or the retina of a user.

As another example of an ArchiTRIO formula, let us focus on axiom gate_open_Def below, which defines precisely when the controller leaves the gate open, thus allowing a user to enter. gate_open_Def states that, in the current instant, the gate is open if and only if there is another instant, within the past Topen time units (where Topen is a system-dependent constant), in which the controller received an invocation oG of operation openGate from port out, and no invocation of operation personEntered has been received since (see [2] for the precise definition of temporal operators Since and WithinP).

```
vars: pE   :personEntered;
      oG   :openGate;
gate_open_Def:
  gate_open  <->
    Since(not ex pE(pE.inv_rec,  ex out.oG(out.oG.inv_rec))  &
    WithinP(ex out.oG(out.oG.inv_rec), Topen);
```

Notice that as a consequence of axiom gate_open_Def the gate cannot stay open longer than Topen time units if the openGate command is not refreshed (that is received again from the central controller); in fact if, after Topen time units from the last openGate, no person has yet entered (a personEntered command has not been received), subformula WithinP(ex out.oG(out.oG.inv_rec), Topen) does not hold any more, thus gate_open becomes false (the gate closes).

Let us now focus on the concept of *port* in ArchiTRIO. Syntactically, a port is just a collection of provided and required interfaces. From a semantic point of view, instead, a port can be used to define a *protocol*, intended as a combination of invocations of operations that can be received (from a provided interface) or issued (to a required interface). Then, an ArchiTRIO port can contain axioms defining the corresponding protocol in terms of the involved operation invocations.

Consider, for example, port HighSecAutProtocol mentioned in fig. 1. It provides interface AccessControl, and requires one instance of interface FromAccessControl (the details of the operations defined by the two interfaces can be found in fig. 7).

```
vars: sPD1, sPD2 : sendPersData;
               oG : openGate;
openGate_SC:
  ac.sPD1.reply(u) & ac.sPD1.rawData = rd1 & ac.sPD1.gate = g &
  ex ac.sPD2(WithinP(ac.sPD2.reply(u) &
                     ac.sPD2.rawData = rd2 & ac.sPD2.gate = g,
                     Tprot)) &
  (type(rd1, Fingerprints) -> type(rd2, Retina)) &
  (type(rd2, Fingerprints) -> type(rd1, Retina))
  ->
  WithinF(ex fac.oG(fac.oG.invoke), T);
  ...
end
```

Fig. 7. Axiom openGate_SC of port HighSecAutProtocol

The port defines the authentication protocol for gates that require that a user authenticates him/herself through both a fingerprint and a retina scan. More precisely, the two scans can occur in any order, but always within a maximum delay one from the other for the authentication to be successful (where success means for controller allows the user to enter by opening the gate through an openGate command).

Figure 7 shows axiom openGate_SC of port HighSecAutProtocol defining a sufficient condition for the openGate command to be sent to the gate through interface FromAccessControl. Formula openGate_SC states that if there are two invocations (sPD1 and sPD2) of operation sendPersData of interface AccessControl (ac) that are completed successfully within a maximum delay of Tprot time units one from the other, and such that

- the gate input parameter is the same for both and
- the rawData input parameter has type Fingerprints for one of them and Retina for the other,

then operation openGate is invoked on interface FromAccessControl (fac) no later than T time units after the instant in which the second invocation (represented in the formula by sPD1) ended.

Finally, the textual declaration of a composite ArchiTRIO class defines the elements composing each instance of the class, and how they are connected with each other (for example which part provides the interface required by another part, and so on).

3.1   ArchiTRIO Semantics (Hints)

From a semantic point of view, ArchiTRIO is founded on a higher-order temporal logic, Higher-Order TRIO (HOT for short [5]). The choice of a higher-order logic was dictated by the need to allow an easy representation of mechanisms such as the passing of parameters of complex types (to be precise, of parameters that can be ArchiTRIO/UML objects).

In HOT terms, a class is a *type*. An *object* in HOT is an instance of a class, that is a *value* of a type. ArchiTRIO is based on the same concepts: an ArchiTRIO class is a HOT class, so it defines a type; an ArchiTRIO object is an instance of the class.

An ArchiTRIO operation also corresponds to a HOT class. All operations share a core group of features (built-in items and behavior), which is modeled by a HOT class `Operation`. This class introduces the logic items modeling the relevant features of an operation invocation (such as the `invoke`, `inv_rec` and `reply` events presented above), and the axioms defining the behavior that is common to all invocations.

A specific operation (such as `incomingData`) is also defined as a class. For example, a class `IncomingData` defines the semantics for the corresponding operation. Class `IncomingData` is a subtype of class `Operation`: in short, if a class `S` is a subtype of a class `P` then `S` inherits all the elements of `P`, and all axioms of `P` are still valid in `S`. Every instance `i` of class `IncomingData` (that is every value of type `IncomingData`) is an invocation of the corresponding operation.

An ArchiTRIO interface is just a HOT class exporting operations. A class providing an interface, from a semantic point of view, is a subtype of that interface. An ArchiTRIO class requiring an interface `I` is a HOT generic (that is parametric) class with respect to a parameter of type `I`. A connection between a provided and a required interface (like the one between modules `LC` and `RS` of fig. 3, for example) corresponds, semantically, to a parameter instantiation (in the case of fig. 3, the parameter of type `LocalControl` of module `RS` is instantiated with object `LC`).

Finally, since a port is a collection of provided and required interfaces (plus a set of axioms), an ArchiTRIO class that has a port of type `P`, which provides interfaces `PI1...PIn` and requires interfaces `RI1...RIm`, also provides and requires the same interfaces. In addition, a class that has a port `P` includes the axioms of `P`.

4   Tool Support

Our experience of several decades with the TRIO language brought the construction of a long series of prototypical tools, every one with a different slight variant of the language, and different verification or editing capabilities. From this situation came the decision of a couple of years ago to build up an industrial-strength integrated tool for supporting our methodologies and languages.

TRIDENT (short for *TRio Integrated Development EnvironmeNT*) is a tool for the development and analysis of time-critical systems based on the TRIO formal language. TRIDENT is implemented on the Eclipse platform [3], and is currently being developed jointly by Politecnico di Milano and CEFRIEL.

As typical with Eclipse-based tools, TRIDENT is plugin-based, so it is by itself an open and evolving product. The environment is still in a prototypical stage, so many of the intended features are still incomplete.

Some of the most notable present features of the tool are the ability to edit complex TRIO specifications and *histories* (these are execution traces that may be used as test cases), and check their mutual compatibility.

More recently, a plugin for supporting model-checking of TRIO specifications has been implemented [13]. This plugin, also called TRIO-PROMELA, is based on the well-known model-checker SPIN, and uses a novel translation technique based on alternating automata. We intend to use this very same technique for model-checking modular and mixed logic/operational specifications (having components written in some automata-based notation, say for example SDL), but this feature is not yet implemented.

As far as ArchiTRIO is concerned, currently there is an advanced-stage prototypical plugin, which supports class and composite structure diagrams editing, and some of the basic ArchiTRIO characteristics. In addition, a prototype plugin capable of partially transforming XMI files into TRIDENT objects has been developed and should be available in the TRIDENT distribution in a short time.

5   Related Works and Conclusions

In this paper we presented a formal language, ArchiTRIO, suitable for describing system architectures. It combines a subset of the UML 2.0 graphical notation with a higher-order temporal logic, which allows users to precisely express both the structural (static) and the behavioral properties of the modeled system. ArchiTRIO is designed to let users draw models in a subset of the usual UML notation (to be precise, using class diagrams and the new composite structure diagrams) and then, if and when necessary, add precise details about the behavior of the target system using a temporal logic-based formalism.

ArchiTRIO combines UML and formal languages to provide a powerful means to model system architecture and, as a consequence, is related to a number of works that have appeared in the literature in recent years. Let us briefly analyze how our work on ArchiTRIO differs from previous ones.

UML prior to version 2.0 if taken by itself is shown by [11] to lack concepts that are necessary for modeling system architectures, and [11] proceeds to introduce profiles for a pair of Architecture Description Languages (ADLs) to cover for these deficiencies. The approach of [11] presumes that users will then use these profiles, and the ADL-specific concepts they define, to model architectures. The ArchiTRIO approach, instead, does not introduce any new graphical notation to UML 2.0: the user who does not need the full expressiveness of ArchiTRIO can still use the plain UML notation and ignore the underlying logic altogether; the user in need of rigor and precision, on the other hand, can seamlessly introduce formal definitions of the behavior of the system in his/her model, without altering the original UML description.

How to add formality to existing UML is a widely acknowledged problem. In this regard, a number of works in the literature have proposed an approach based on *translating* UML behavioral diagrams (especially statecharts and sequence diagrams) into an existing formalism (see [8] or [10], and many others not listed here for the sake of brevity), or, alternatively, into an ad-hoc model [9]. With ArchiTRIO there is no translation into any other language; on the contrary, it is a formal language *integrated* into the UML 2.0 notation, which allows one to precisely describe both the structure and the behavior of a system, of its components and their interactions, with particular attention to their temporal constraints.

Indeed, UML already has an associated logic language, the Object Constraint Language (OCL), for which temporal extensions have been proposed [4]. However, OCL, and RT-OCL in particular, is a language with limited scope, as its intended use is mostly for expressing constraints on behavioral diagrams such as statecharts. On the contrary, the ArchiTRIO approach is a comprehensive one, which aims at supporting the whole system specification and design process by modeling all aspects of a system architecture, both structural and behavioral.

Finally, [7] presents an approach to the analysis of system architectures based on a subset of UML 2.0 concepts and a formal semantics for time-annotated statecharts. Again, with respect to this work, the scope of ArchiTRIO is wider, as it is intended for use in the whole system design phase, from modeling to verification. In fact, one could see the techniques presented in [7], and associated notations, as a target model, to be obtained through a suitable method from an ArchiTRIO design to perform subsequent verification.

This work opens the way to a variety of future developments.

- First and foremost, we will complete the development of the tool sketched in section 4, which we plan to release for free use by both academic and industrial communities.
- Secondly, we will investigate verification techniques (to be supported by the tool-set mentioned above) to complement the modeling features presented in this paper. In this regard, the semantics of ArchiTRIO in terms of HOT suggests a fairly straightforward encoding of ArchiTRIO classes into the higher-order logic of a theorem prover such as PVS, along the lines already followed for the TRIO language [6]. Other approaches will also be explored, for example translating ArchiTRIO classes into automata-based formalisms (like those used in [7] for example) to exploit model checking techniques.
- Finally, we plan on developing a method that allows one to move from the pure logic notation of ArchiTRIO to an operational formalism closer to implementation such as SDL [12] (as mentioned in section 4, techniques to translate TRIO temporal operators into Promela communicating processes have already been explored in [13], and many concepts of Promela can also be found in SDL). This would open up the possibility of using existing tools (such as [18]) to perform automatic generation of code that complies with the properties and the behavior precisely defined by an ArchiTRIO model (and, in particular, by the axioms contained in its classes).

References

1. Sergio Cigoli, Philippe Leblanc, Salvatore Malaponti, Dino Mandrioli, Marco Maz-zucchelli, Angelo Morzenti, Paola Spoletini: An Experiment in Applying UML 2.0 to the Development of an Industrial Critical Application, Proceedings of the UML'03 workshop on Critical Systems Development with UML, San Francisco, CA, October 21 2003.
2. Coen-Porisini A., Pradella M., Rossi M., Mandrioli D., A Formal Approach for Designing CORBA based Applications, ACM TOSEM, vol. 12, n. 2 (2003) 107–151
3. Eclipse Foundation, http://www.eclipse.org
4. Flake, S., Mueller, W. Formal Semantics of Static and Temporal State-Oriented OCL Constraints, Software and Systems Modeling, vol. 2, n. 3, Springer (2003) 164–186.
5. Furia, C. A., Mandrioli, D., Morzenti, A., Pradella, M., Rossi, M., San Pietro, P., Higher-Order TRIO, Technical Report 2004.28, Dipartimento di Elettronica ed Informazione, Politecnico di Milano (2004).
6. Gargantini, A., Morzenti, A., Automated Deductive Requirements Analysis of Critical Systems, ACM TOSEM, vol. 3, no. 3, (2001) 225–307.
7. Giese, H., Tichy, M., Burmester, S., Flake, S., Towards the compositional verification of real-time UML designs, Proc. of ESEC/FSE 2003, Helsinki (2003) 38–47
8. Lavazza, L., Quaroni, G. Venturelli, M., Combining UML and formal notations for modelling real-time systems, Proc. of ESEC/FSE 2001, Vienna (2001) 196–206
9. Li, X., Liu, Z., Jifeng, H., A Formal Semantics of UML Sequence Diagram, Proceedings of the 2004 Australian Software Engineering Conference, (2004) 168–177
10. McUmber, W. E., Cheng, B. H. C., A general framework for formalizing UML with formal languages, Proceedings of the 23rd ICSE, (2001) 433–442
11. Medvidovic, N., Rosenblum, D. S., Redmiles, D. F., Robbins, J. E. Modeling Software Architectures in the Unified Modeling Language, ACM TOSEM, vol. 11, no. 1, (2002) 2–57
12. Mitschele-Theil, A., System Engineering with SDL – Developing Performance-Critical Communication Systems, John Wiley (2001)
13. Morzenti, A., Pradella, M., San Pietro, P., Spoletini, P., Model-checking TRIO specifications in SPIN, 12th Int. FM Symposium, LNCS 2805, Pisa (2003) 542–561
14. Object Management Group, UML 2.0 Superstructure Specification, Technical Report, OMG, ptc/03-08-02 (2003).
15. Object Management Group, UML 2.0 OCL Specification, Technical Report, OMG, ptc/03-10-14 (2003).
16. Rossi M., Mandrioli D., A Formal Approach for Modeling and Verification of RTCORBA-based Applications, ISSTA, Boston (2004) 263–273
17. Saiedian, H., Bowen, J. P., Butler, R. W., Dill, D. L., Glass, R. L., Gries, D., Hall, A., Hinchey, M. G., Holloway, C. M., Jackson, D., Jones, C. B., Luts, M. J., Parna, D. L., Rushby, J., Wing, J., Zave, P. An Invitation to Formal Methods. IEEE Computer, vol. 29, no. 4, (1996) 16–30
18. Telelogic Tau Generation2 Tools, http://www.telelogic.com/products/tau/tg2.cfm

UCM-Driven Testing of Web Applications

Daniel Amyot[1], Jean-François Roy[1], and Michael Weiss[2]

[1] SITE, University of Ottawa, Ottawa, Canada
{damyot, jroy}@site.uottawa.ca
[2] School of Computer Science, Carleton University, Ottawa, Canada
weiss@scs.carleton.ca

Abstract. Despite their apparent simplicity, Web applications are surprisingly difficult to develop, if our aim is to build applications that behave correctly under regular conditions as well as adverse circumstances like out-of-order requests and race conditions. In this paper, we describe our experiences deriving customer-oriented acceptance tests for Web applications by modeling the essential capabilities of such applications with Use Case Maps (UCMs). Abstract test purposes are generated from a UCM model using scenario definitions and scenario extraction tools. These test purposes are then converted interactively to test cases in the FitNesse acceptance testing framework, which is popular in the Extreme Programming (XP) community. The test cases are used to validate a Web application where several typical but non-trivial bugs were planted. Challenges in the automation of the process are also discussed.

1 Introduction

Web applications can be surprisingly difficult to develop because they need to support a wide variety of expected usage scenarios. Moreover, we want these applications to be robust, that is, we want them to behave correctly under unexpected or adverse circumstances. Due to the strict time-to-market requirements imposed on Web development projects, modeling and testing are often considered too time-consuming and lacking significant payoff [11]. More significantly, though, their general lack of robustness is due to the "openness" of Web applications and to concurrency issues.

Openness is most often associated with security concerns. In a recent survey [14], more than 90% of Web applications were found to be vulnerable to common hacking attacks such as cross-site scripting, parameter tampering, and cookie poisoning. These problems are usually caused by a failure of the Web application to properly validate user input. However, this is but one way that Web applications are "wide open" to unexpected use, or malicious exploitation.

Unlike in a "closed" desktop application, or even a distributed application with a tightly controlled API, requests can be sent in any order to a Web application. Expecting the input pattern to follow the designed navigational structure may lead to subtle design errors in developing the Web application. For example, a user could bookmark a page, and resubmit the request associated with it

A. Prinz, R. Reed, and J. Reed (Eds.): SDL 2005, LNCS 3530, pp. 247–264, 2005.

later. Furthermore, Web applications can be accessed by different types of clients (browsers, robots, etc.), not just those they were designed for.

Other common errors are caused by race conditions. Web applications have been plagued by these from the beginning. A famous example is the multiple order problem caused by repeatedly clicking "Place Order" on a checkout page. The culprit here is the delay caused by processing the payment information, which may cause the user to think that their request has not been received. The actual error is that the developer forgot to check (or properly model) the state of the Web application before processing the additional order confirmations.

In this paper we describe our experiences deriving customer-oriented acceptance tests for Web applications by modeling the essential capabilities of the application as Use Case Maps (UCMs). Our hypothesis is that this scenario-based, lightweight level of modeling is more accessible to Web developers than heavyweight formal methods. We also try to tie in the existing methodologies and tools used in the Web application development community. In particular, we use the notion of *acceptance tests* as customer-driven tests, as defined in the Test-Driven Development (TDD) approach [4] in Extreme Programming (XP). Our tests run on the popular FitNesse acceptance testing framework [18].

Section 2 presents related work. In section 3 we describe the Web application for an online store used as a case study to demonstrate our approach. A UCM model capturing the essence of this application is presented in section 4. In section 5, we introduce the FitNesse-oriented testing environment used for our experiment. Test generation and results are discussed in section 6, followed by our conclusions and an outlook on future work.

2   Related Work

Although there are many commercial tools available for testing Web applications, their scope is often severely limited. Most of these tools are designed to assess the compatibility of a Web application with different browsers and operating systems, its ability to deal with large numbers of concurrent users (stress testing), and that the application is free of dead links (link testers) [8]. However, these tools do not provide facilities for structural and functional testing.

Recently, several approaches have been developed that do not only consider the externally visible behavior of the Web application, but also its internals. Kung [17] models the state-dependent behavior of interacting components in a Web application (client pages, server pages, and software components) as hierarchical, communicating state machines. In another paper [9], Di Lucca models the behavior of a Web browser as a statechart to generate test cases which can account for out-of-order messages caused by interactions with the browser buttons. Wittevrongel [24] outlines a scenario-based approach for testing Web applications in which test cases are automatically derived from sequence diagrams. Probert [19] suggests the use of an object-oriented extension to TTCN for (manually) defining various types of tests targeting Web applications.

Use Case Maps have been used to model the dynamics of complex systems in such domains as telecommunications and e-business process modeling [1, 6, 23]. They are being considered for standardization as part of ITU-T's User Requirements Notation [13, 22]. From the perspective of modeling Web applications, two prior approaches are of particular relevance. Kaewkasi [16] uses Use Case Maps to model object-oriented Web applications in his Web Application Modeling (WWM) approach. Gordijn [10] models business processes with Use Case Maps as part of his e^3-value approach for analyzing value creation and exchange in e-business models.

Several UCM-based testing approaches have been developed in recent years. Three main families have been compared in [3]: testing patterns (manual), scenario definitions (semi-automated), and translations to formal specifications (more automated). Among these three, scenario definitions [2] proved to be practical in many contexts as this approach is scalable, it prevents the generation of incorrect test purposes, it is supported by tools, and it generates test purposes in an XML format amenable to further transformations (to sequence diagrams or TTCN test skeletons, for example). However, it requires human intervention for the (simple) definition of the scenarios leading to test purposes, and to add data information to test purposes in order to convert them to real test cases. In this paper, this approach will be explored in a new context where we attempt to generate concrete test cases for a Web application.

3   Web Application Case Study

The system under test (SUT) is a Web application for an online store (named widgets.com) where users can purchase license keys for software components (or *widgets*). It has enough non-trivial behavior to be interesting from a testing perspective, but is no more complex than necessary to exhibit several planted bugs used to validate our approach. It implements the four use cases shown in Figure 1: *Browse Catalog, Checkout, Process Payment,* and *Download*.

Browse Catalog comprises selecting categories, selecting products to request product detail, adding products to a shopping cart, and editing the cart. *Checkout* includes signing in for an account, building an order summary, and confirming the order. *Process Payment* involves asking the bank to process the payment information associated with the account. *Download* comprises going to a download area, and downloading the purchased licenses. Actors include customers and a bank. Figure 1 also shows the normal flows for the two key use cases, *Browse Catalog* and *Checkout*. The full model also includes their variants.

The application follows a standard Model-View-Controller Model 2 architecture with a main controller, and subcontrollers (request handlers) and associated views (renderers) for each use case that do the actual work [7]. The application is implemented as a Java servlet, and executes in a servlet container (in our case the Tomcat servlet engine [20]). In the case study we did not make use of a specific Web application framework such as Struts or J2EE. While such frame-

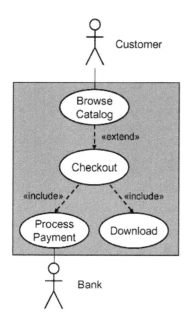

Browse Catalog

1. Customer navigates to the *widgets.com* home page.
2. System responds with a listing of categories.
3. Customer selects a category.
4. System displays a listing of all widgets in this category.
5. Customer selects a widget.
6. System responds with a product detail page for the widget.
7. Customer adds the widget to the cart.
8. System displays the updated cart.
9. Customer proceeds to checkout (see *Checkout*).

Checkout

1. Customer requests checkout.
2. System prompts the customer for his account number.
3. Customer enters account information.
4. System builds a summary of the order with totals.
5. Customer confirms the order.
6. System processes the payment (see *Process Payment*).
7. System displays invoice.
8. Customer proceeds to download area (see *Download*).

...

Fig. 1. Use case diagram for the `widgets.com` online store with two use cases

works can simplify the development of large Web applications, their use might also make our approach framework-specific, and thus less general.

Figures 2 to 4 show three typical screenshots of the online store application. In the first one, the left column of the page contains a list of available widget categories, and its center shows the contents of the shopping cart after a number of items have been added by following the *Browse Catalog* use case. Selecting "Proceed to Checkout" will terminate *Browse Catalog*, and initiate the *Checkout* use case. In that use case, the first screen (Figure 3) requires the customer to input a valid account number. Once the order is confirmed, the payment done, and the invoice displayed (not shown), the customer proceeds to the *Download* use case, where the bought widgets and license keys are available for download (Figure 4).

4   UCM Model and Scenarios

Use Case Maps (UCM) are a notation for modeling scenarios. Unlike use cases, UCMs allow us to model the dynamic behavior of an application. UCMs also allow us to model concurrency within a scenario. A single UCM can furthermore show multiple scenarios at once, and therefore allows us to study the interaction between scenarios, or multiple instances of the same scenario. However, unlike other scenario-modeling notations such as UML sequence diagrams or Message Sequence Charts (MSCs) [12], UCMs do not require an early commitment of scenarios to messages or to components.

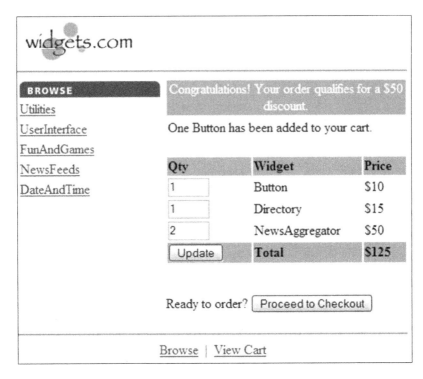

Fig. 2. Web application screenshot: Cart content while browsing

Fig. 3. Web application screenshot: Signing in with an account number

4.1   Use Case Map Model

A *scenario* is a partially-ordered set of *responsibilities* (activities, tasks, functions) that a system performs to transform inputs to outputs while satisfying certain pre- and postconditions [1]. The basic notational elements for modeling scenarios with UCMs are responsibilities (X's), paths (curved lines), start points (black dots), and end points (bars). Scenarios progress along *paths* from start to end points. Paths can fork to represent alternatives and concurrency, and also

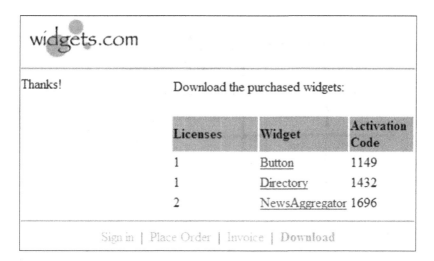

Fig. 4. Web application screenshot: Downloadable widgets with license keys

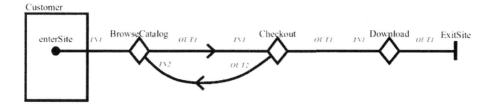

Fig. 5. Root map for the `widgets.com` online store

join. Responsibilities can be allocated to *components* by placing them within the boundaries of that component (rectangle). Figure 5 shows the root (top level) map for the `widgets.com` applications introduced in the case study.

The UCM notation also provides a hierarchical abstraction mechanism in the form of *stubs* (diamonds) and *plug-ins* (sub-maps). Each hierarchy of maps has a *root map* that contains stubs where lower-level maps can be plugged in. Figure 5 shows the root map for the `widgets.com` applications introduced in the case study. It contains three stubs, one for the *Browse Catalog*, one for the *Checkout*, and one for the *Download* use case. Figures 6 to 8 show the plug-ins for the BrowseCatalog, Checkout, and Download stubs from Figure 5.

These stubs correspond approximately to the initial use cases and to major phases of the online store application under study. Several start and end points of the plug-ins are connected to their parent stub's input and output segments, as indicated by the corresponding labels between curly braces (IN1, OUT2 and so on). This binding relationship ensures the continuity of scenarios across different levels of maps. Note that UCM plug-ins can be nested at many levels. The Checkout map contains another stub where a ProcessPayment plug-in (corresponding to the *Process Payment* use case, but is not shown here) needs to be bound.

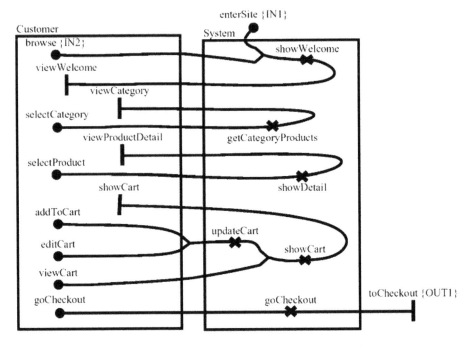

Fig. 6. Plug-in for BrowseCatalog stub in the root map of Figure 5

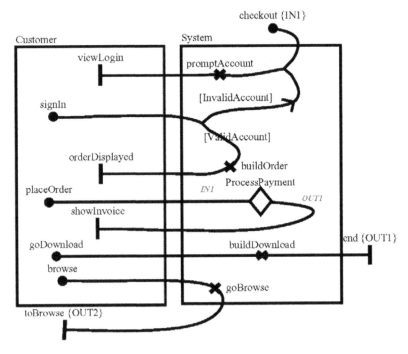

Fig. 7. Plug-in for Checkout stub in the root map of Figure 5

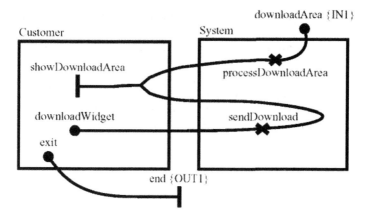

Fig. 8. Plug-in for Download stub in the root map of Figure 5

In this model, the start points in the **Customer** component correspond to events (such as hyperlinks and buttons) that customers can trigger. The end points correspond to page updates visible to the customers. Several responsibilities have been identified for the system, but none is assigned to its actors.

4.2   Scenario Definitions

In order to support scenario definitions, as defined in [2, 22], the basic UCM path model needs to be augmented with a simple data model. Several Boolean variables, described in Table 1 were created in order to formalize guarding conditions (at branching points), preconditions (in start points), and initial contexts and post-conditions in scenario definitions themselves.

Preconditions were added to many start points to reflect the situations under which they can be triggered. For instance, the preconditions for the start points

Table 1. Global Boolean variables used in the UCM model

Variable	Description
CanAddProd	Products can be added on this page.
CanGoDownload	Can go to the download area.
CanPlaceOrder	An order can be placed on this page.
CanSignIn	The customer can sign in.
CartAvailable	The cart is visible.
CategoryAvailable	Categories can be selected on this page.
InBrowser	In the browser page.
InCheckout	In the checkout page.
InDownloadArea	In download area.
ProductsDisplayed	Products are displayed.
SuccessfulDownload	The download was successful.
ValidAccount	The customer account is valid.

Table 2. Start point preconditions and parameters for the BrowseCatalog map

Start Point	Precondition	Parameter
enterSite	–	–
browse	InBrowser	–
selectCategory	InBrowser ∧ CategoryAvailable	Category
selectProduct	InBrowser ∧ ProductsDisplayed	Product
addToCart	InBrowser ∧ CanAddProd	–
editCart	InBrowser ∧ CartAvailable	Product
viewCart	InBrowser	–
goCheckout	InBrowser ∧ CartAvailable	–

Table 3. Variables modified by responsibilities in BrowseCatalog map

Responsibility	Modifications (T for True, F for False)
getCategoryProducts	ProductsDisplayed ← T
goCheckout	InBrowser ← F, CartAvailable ← F, CategoryAvailable ← F
showCart	CartAvailable ← T, CanAddProd ← F, ProductsDisplayed ← F
showDetail	CanAddProf ← T, ProductsDisplayed ← F
showWelcome	InBrowser ← T, CartAvailable ← F, CategoryAvailable ← T

in the BrowseCatalog plug-in map are described in Table 2. Several responsibilities in this UCM also modify the content of these variables. Table 3 shows, for the same map, how these variables are updated by the responsibilities.

Several *scenario definitions* were then added to our UCM model. Each such definition consists of a name, initial values for the variables, a list of start points to be triggered, and an optional post-condition expected to be satisfied at the end of the execution of the scenario. Scenario definitions can be combined to a path traversal algorithm in order to highlight specific scenarios in a complex UCM model, or to transform them to other representations. Details of the various algorithms used here can be found in [2, 22]. In a nutshell, the algorithm uses a depth-first traversal of the graph that captures the UCMs' structure and generates scenarios where sequences and concurrency are preserved, but where alternatives are resolved using the Boolean variables. If conditions cannot be satisfied or evaluated during the traversal (e.g., in a precondition or in guarded branches), then the algorithm stops and reports an error.

In our model, we created a non-exhaustive collection of scenario definitions to cover the interesting functionalities offered by the system, as well as all the UCM path segments in the model. Although scenarios extracted from a UCM can be used for many reasons (model understanding, scenario highlight, generation of MSCs, etc.), our goal was to explore the generation of several typical test purposes for testing our Web application. In Table 4, the first four scenarios represent four normal and expected usages of the Web site whereas the last three target specific types of faults in the implementation.

Table 4. Scenarios for the `widget.com` UCM model

Scenario name	Description
BaseCase	Primary scenario where customer buys one widget and everything works.
SecondThoughts	The customer goes back to the browsing mode while checking out, in order to review the cart.
ManyProducts	Several widget products are bought by the customer.
InvalidAccount	Checks that the customer cannot download widgets without a valid account.
RemoveWidgetOnCart	The customer edits the shopping cart where a widget has been added, and sets its quantity to 0.
DiscountOnOrders	Checks whether the discount is correctly applied when widgets are removed.
MultipleOrdersTwoCustomers	Checks that two customers with the same login (from the same company) can order widgets at the same time.

Table 5. BaseCase scenario definition

Initialization	ValidAccount ← T
Start points	enterSite, browse, selectCategory, selectProduct, addToCart, goCheckout, placeOrder, goDownload, downloadWidget, exit
Post-condition	SuccessfulDownload = T

As an example, the scenario definition of **BaseCase** is presented in Table 5. All the other scenarios are constructed in a similar way.

The UCMNav tool [21] was used to model this UCM and define and explore these scenarios. Each produced scenario was also automatically exported to an XML file, which uses the format described in [2]. Although these files are too verbose to be included in this paper, the result of the **BaseCase** scenario is shown as a MSC in Figure 10(a). Note that such MSCs were not used in this study; this one is included here to better visualize the scenario generated.

5   Test Environment

As explained in the previous sections, UCMNav was used to create a UCM model, with variables and scenario definitions, for the target Web application. This tool was also used to generate an XML file for each scenario, hence providing the desired test purposes. Figure 9 illustrates the remaining steps of our approach. We created a small conversion application (in Perl) called UCM2FIT (section 5.2), which converts the XML test purposes to FitNesse test cases, provided some additional information (a configuration file and user-selected values). The tests are automatically installed in the FitNesse test environment (described in section 5.1), which requires an adaptation layer composed of *fixtures* to run them on the SUT and produce test results.

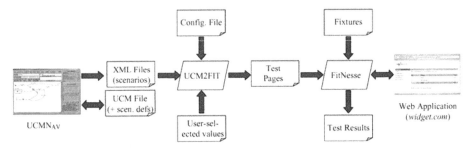

Fig. 9. Overview of the testing process used in the case study

5.1   FitNesse Framework

FitNesse is a tool popular in the Extreme Programming community [18]. It provides an environment for authoring and executing acceptance tests from within a Web browser. It is itself based on two subsystems: a Wiki clone and FIT (Framework for Integrated Test). Wiki can best be described as a Web-based, collaborative editor. FIT is the core framework for executing acceptance tests.[1] FitNesse provides a Java-based implementation of Wiki that incorporates FIT, and can be run without a Web server. Partial support for .NET is also available.

The combination of FIT and Wiki can best be described as a "literate programming" environment for tests. Not only are documentation and tests kept in the same place, but tests can be defined in a very simple way by creating a table or a spreadsheet, which can even be edited in Excel and copy-pasted into Fit-Nesse. The first row of each table defines the type of *fixture* to use for the test, and the remaining rows specify the test data to be interpreted by the fixture. A fixture is the Java or C# class that FitNesse calls to process the contents of the table.

FitNesse provides a set of standard fixtures. Most relevant in our context is the *action fixture*, which allows one to emulate a user interface. It provides three types of actions to interact with an application: **press**, **enter**, and **check**: **press** simulates pressing a button, which is mapped to invoking a method on the fixture; **enter** is used to set a value in the fixture; **check** tests if invoking a method of the fixture results in a given expected result. The rows of an action fixture contain a "script" for the class specified in the second row.

For testing Web applications we created a special type of action fixture. The methods supported by the **WebFixture** are shown in Table 6. This fixture was implemented with the help of the jWebUnit framework [15]. This framework provides a high-level API for navigating Web applications. It includes navigation via links, form entry and submission, validation of table contents, etc. Behind the scenes it uses the well-known HttpUnit unit testing framework.

WebFixture can be used on any Web application that uses HTTP. However, in order to support the testing of a specific application (**widget.com** in our case),

---

[1] Both Wiki and FIT have, incidentally, been developed by Ward Cunningham, who is also known as the father of CRC cards, and a well-known pattern and XP guru.

Table 6. Operations supported by `WebFixture`

Loading Web pages	
base(url)	Set the base URL for relative URLs
begin(path)	Set a relative URL
Setting bookmarks	
getLocation()	Get the current URL
setLocation(url)	Request the page with the given URL
Checking page attributes and contents	
title()	Get the page title
contents()	Get the content of a page
contains(text)	Check if text is present on a given page
contains(id,text)	Check if text is present in a page element with given id
matches(pattern)	Check if the page content matches a given regular expression
Clicking links	
link(id)	Click a link with a given id
linkWithText(text)	Click a link with a given anchor text
linkWithImage(path)	Click a link in an image given its file path
button(id)	Click a button with given id
Submitting form data	
form(id)	Set the working form given its id
formElement(name,value)	Set the value of a field given its name
submit()	Submit a form
submit(button)	Submit a form by pressing the given button
reset()	Reset a form

one can extend `WebFixture` and add methods that provide an adaptation layer which can interpret the abstract events in the test purposes to check the SUT. We hence created `WidgetFixture`, which contains a short Java method for each start point in our UCM model. They can be more or less complex depending on what information needs to be provided on a given Web page. For instance, selecting a category of widgets (start point selectCategory) on the Web page and providing an account number (start point signIn) are implemented as follows:

```
public void selectCategory(String category)
{
  linkWithText(category);
}

public void signIn(String accountNumber)
{
  form("sign-in");
  formElement("account", accountNumber);
  submit();
}
```

5.2   UCM2FIT

As introduced in Figure 9, the goal of UCM2FIT is to convert an XML scenario file generated by UCMNav into a FitNesse test case. However, this cannot be done entirely automatically. Part of the information that needs to be added to the test purposes can be provided in advance, for instance in a configuration file, but the information related to the selection of values is currently provided interactively by the tester, during the transformation.

The configuration file (also in XML) contains the following information:

- The target directory of the test suite, in a place where FitNesse can find it automatically.
- Test setup information (e.g., path to FitNesse and fixture classes)
- Data types (e.g., categories, products, and account numbers), together with sample values. These correspond to items that the tester can select interactively when requested by UCM2FIT.
- For each end point in the UCM, a list of text items (information) to be checked on the Web page.

As an example of information associated to an end point, what is specified for viewWelcome is a page title and a well-known text pattern that does not appear on the other pages:

```
<endpoint name="viewWelcome">
    <check type="title" value="widgets.com"></check>
    <check type="pattern" value="Welcome to widgets.com"></check>
</endpoint>
```

This information is used to generate appropriate verification code in the FitNesse tests each time an end point is mentioned in the test purposes.

When UCM2FIT gets to a start point with parameters in a test purpose (see Table 2), the human tester is interactively asked to provide a value of that type among those proposed in the configuration file. For instance, for start point selectCategory, the value NewsFeeds could be selected. Care must be taken to select appropriate values so that the test purpose can progress. For instance, if the test purpose presupposes that the account number to be provided will be valid, then the selected value must be consistent with this assumption.

Similarly, several end points have been supplemented with output parameters in the UCM model (something new for this experiment). For example, the end point showCart has a parameter that corresponds to the cost of the selected product, which needs to be input by the tester. This cost is checked against the one displayed on the Web page.

This process is performed once for each test purpose, and it is usually a matter of seconds to produce one test. The output is a collection of executable tests coded as (textual) Wiki pages and understandable by FitNesse, together with an index that corresponds to a test suite. This test suite enables FitNesse to check all the test cases, in batch, and to provide a summary of the results.

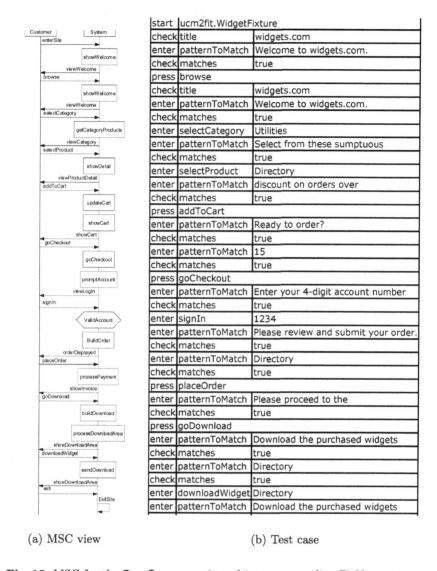

start	ucm2fit.WidgetFixture	
check	title	widgets.com
enter	patternToMatch	Welcome to widgets.com.
check	matches	true
press	browse	
check	title	widgets.com
enter	patternToMatch	Welcome to widgets.com.
check	matches	true
enter	selectCategory	Utilities
enter	patternToMatch	Select from these sumptuous
check	matches	true
enter	selectProduct	Directory
enter	patternToMatch	discount on orders over
check	matches	true
press	addToCart	
enter	patternToMatch	Ready to order?
check	matches	true
enter	patternToMatch	15
check	matches	true
press	goCheckout	
enter	patternToMatch	Enter your 4-digit account number
check	matches	true
enter	signIn	1234
enter	patternToMatch	Please review and submit your order.
check	matches	true
enter	patternToMatch	Directory
check	matches	true
press	placeOrder	
enter	patternToMatch	Please proceed to the
check	matches	true
press	goDownload	
enter	patternToMatch	Download the purchased widgets
check	matches	true
enter	patternToMatch	Directory
check	matches	true
enter	downloadWidget	Directory
enter	patternToMatch	Download the purchased widgets

(a) MSC view   (b) Test case

Fig. 10. MSC for the BaseCase scenario and its corresponding FitNesse test

Note that multiple test cases could be generated from one test purpose by selecting different combinations of values (however, this was not done for this experiment).

Figure 10(b) presents the test case generated from the BaseCase test purpose (see Table 5), in a tabular form displayed by the Web browser. Note how the **press** actions correspond to the start points and how the **enter** and **check** operations are used to verify that the output from the SUT is correct. A recurring pattern is that an **enter** method specifies an expected value (the **patternToMatch**), and a subsequent `check` asserts whether the actual value should (or should not) correspond to (`matches`) the expected value.

UCM2FIT is currently implemented with standalone, command-line Perl scripts and a `XML::DOM` parser. However, this functionality could be integrated into FitNesse itself in the future.

6   Test Execution and Results

As a measure of the effectiveness of our tests, a number of bugs were "planted" into the Web application. These are all major functional errors that affect the function of the application in a significant manner. For example, if a user account was charged for a widget that they did not order, we consider this a major error. Minor errors are errors that lead to locally incorrect behavior, but do not significantly impact the execution of the application. For example, entering a non-digit as an account number may cause an exception to be thrown, but it does not lead to an inconsistent state. Below is the list of planted errors:

1. Edits to the shopping cart are not properly updated.
2. Discount ($50 when the total is greater than $100) is incorrectly applied.
3. Race condition: Only the most recent order is shown in the download section.
4. State-/Timing-related: Can add widgets to the cart for free.

Two of these bugs (#3 and #4) require a fault model where many customers, or many sessions (of the same customer) are active at the same time. In UCM terms, this means that the same start point (enterSite) can be triggered multiple times in order to simulate multiple widget buying sessions. This is also supported by our approach based on scenario definitions.

The results generated by our test suite are reported in Figure 11, which shows the summary produced by FitNesse. In the summary table, tests that completed without failures are shown in light grey (pass), while those with failures are shown in black (fail). As expected, the first four tests from Table 4 did not reveal any problem in the SUT. These tests validate the intended functionalities of the application, without looking for subtle types of errors.

UcmAcceptanceTest

SUITE RESULTS

Suite	Test Pages: 4 right, 3 wrong, 0 ignored, 0 exceptions Assertions: 132 right, 3 wrong,
Edit	15 right, 0 wrong, 0 ignored, 0 exceptions BaseCase
Properties	25 right, 1 wrong, 0 ignored, 0 exceptions DiscountOnOrders
Versions	10 right, 0 wrong, 0 ignored, 0 exceptions InvalidAccount
Search	30 right, 0 wrong, 0 ignored, 0 exceptions ManyProducts
Refactor	21 right, 1 wrong, 0 ignored, 0 exceptions MultipleOrdersTwoCustomers
	11 right, 1 wrong, 0 ignored, 0 exceptions RemoveWidgetOnCart
	20 right, 0 wrong, 0 ignored, 0 exceptions SecondThoughts

Fig. 11. Summary of FitNesse test results

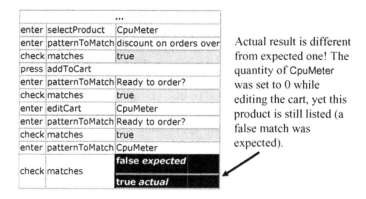

	...	
enter	selectProduct	CpuMeter
enter	patternToMatch	discount on orders over
check	matches	true
press	addToCart	
enter	patternToMatch	Ready to order?
check	matches	true
enter	editCart	CpuMeter
enter	patternToMatch	Ready to order?
check	matches	true
enter	patternToMatch	CpuMeter
check	matches	false *expected* / true *actual*

Actual result is different from expected one! The quantity of CpuMeter was set to 0 while editing the cart, yet this product is still listed (a false match was expected).

Fig. 12. Extract of the RemoveWidgetOnCart test result

However, the last three tests of Table 4 revealed three of the four planted bugs. RemoveWidgetOnCart showed that when the quantity of a product is set to 0 while editing a cart, then this quantity is not updated correctly (bug #1). In FitNesse, such an error is reported as a violation of an assertion. Figure 12 shows how FitNesse displays the test detailed test results for RemoveWidgetOnCart. Correct assertions are shown in light grey while incorrect ones are displayed in black together with the expected and actual values.

The test DiscountOnOrder adds items to the cart in excess of $100, and then removes an item. It revealed that when the total cost of the products in the cart gets over $100, the $50 discount is correctly applied but, as widgets are subsequently removed, the discount is (incorrectly) not recomputed. As a result, a discount may be applied, although the actual total may no longer be above $100. This state-related *stuck at fault* corresponds to bug #2.

The last test, MultipleOrdersTwoCustomers, checks the situation where two customers sharing the same account number try to order widgets simultaneously. Unfortunately, the implementation suffers from a race condition problem (bug #3) and the content of only one of the carts is shown for download to the customers. This scenario is interesting because it required the multiple triggering of the initial start point, enabling two orders to evolve concurrently.

Bug #4 was not revealed by our test suite. In fact, we could not produce a UCM-driven test case for it with the current environment. A more sophisticated fixture supporting forking seems required, and our UCM model needs to be able to simulate out of order messages more easily (for example, "add to cart" after "place order"). Such improvements are left for future work.

7   Discussion and Conclusions

In this paper we have described an innovative and lightweight approach for generating acceptance tests for Web applications from a Use Case Maps (UCM) model. Through a case study, we demonstrated that this approach is capable of detecting subtle design errors that often go unnoticed using conventional acceptance testing techniques such as *extended use cases* [5]. We believe that this is the first paper to introduce UCM-based testing in this emerging domain. Another contribution of the paper is to show how abstract test sequences generated from UCMs can be transformed into test cases in the FitNesse testing framework.

The UCM model presented here uses an unconventional style where many start points, capturing almost one-to-one the possible user events (hyperlink, form, or button), are at the source of disjoint paths. Preconditions ensure that they can only be triggered when the application should allow it. This is a benefit of the emphasis on the UML data model, but this is also a drawback because, from a testing point of view, we would also like to test scenarios where such events are provided in an *incorrect* or unanticipated order, as one would do using the back or forward buttons on a browser, bookmarks, or direct URLs. This is also a limitation of other Web testing approaches, including [8]. A tool like UCMNAV could be extended to allow some flexibility in the checking or bypassing of these preconditions during scenario generation.

One of the main issues to be addressed in the future relates to how best to provide suitable data values during the transformation from abstract test purpose to concrete test case. At the moment, one would need to input such values each time a scenario is modified. Some of these values could be inferred from the scenario preconditions (e.g., a valid account number when ValidAccount is true), others could come from predefined equivalence classes where the values correspond to the ones the SUT would expect (e.g., using some shared database for the test setup). Previous choices of values could also be stored independently and reused whenever possible.

This experiment also raised a few interesting points related to the UCM notation. It seems that being able to provide formal parameters to start points and end points is very beneficial in a testing context. Also, current scenario definitions focus solely on start points, whereas there might be a need for intermediate assertions of end point values in the middle of a scenario, and not just at its end.

Another area for future research is a closer integration of UCMs with Extreme Programming (XP), given their relatively lightweight nature compared to "heavier" approaches such as MSCs, which require an early commitment to messages or components. Also the extension of the current fixtures for testing more generic types of Web applications should be investigated in the future.

References

1. Amyot, D.: Introduction to the User Requirements Notation: Learning by Example. Computer Networks, 42(3), 285–301, June 2003.
2. Amyot, D., Cho, D.Y., He, X., and He, Y.: Generating Scenarios from Use Case Map Specifications. Third Int. Conf. on Quality Software (QSIC'03), Dallas, USA, Nov. 2003, 108–115.
3. Amyot, D., Logrippo, L., and Weiss, M.: UCM-Based Generation of Test Purposes. To appear in Computer Networks, 2005.
4. Beck, K.: Test-Driven Development By Example. Addison-Wesley, 2004.

5. Binder, R.: Testing Object-Oriented Systems: Models, Patterns, and Tools. Addison-Wesley, 2000.
6. Buhr, R.J.A., and Casselman, R.S.: Use Case Maps for Object-Oriented Systems. Prentice Hall, 1996. http://www.usecasemaps.org/pub/UCM_book95.pdf
7. Burke, E.: Java and XSLT: Embedding XML Processing into Java Applications. O'Reilly, 2001.
8. Di Lucca, G., Fasolino, A., Faralli, F., and de Carlini, U.: Testing Web Applications. 18th Int. Conf. on Software Maintenance (ICSM), 2002, 310–309.
9. Di Lucca, G., and Di Penta, M.: Considering Browser Interaction in Web Application Testing. 5th Int. Work. on Web Site Evolution, 2003, 74–81.
10. Gordijn, J., and Akkermans, H.: Designing and Evaluating E-Business Models. IEEE Software, July/August 2001, 11–17.
11. Hieatt, E., and Mee, R.: Going Faster: Testing the Web Application. IEEE Software, March/April 2002, 60–65.
12. ITU-T – International Telecommunications Union: Recommendation Z.120 (04/04) Message Sequence Chart (MSC). Geneva, Switzerland, 2004.
13. ITU-T – International Telecommunications Union: Recommendation Z.150 (02/03), User Requirements Notation (URN) – Language Requirements and Framework. Geneva, Switzerland, 2003.
14. Jacques, R.: Web Applications Wide Open to Hackers. vnunet.com news, http://www.vnunet.com/News/1152521, Feb 5, 2004.
15. jWebUnit: http://jwebunit.sourceforge.net
16. Kaewkasi, C., and Rivepiboon, W.: WWM: A Practical Methodology for Web Application Modeling. 26th Int. Computer Software and Applications Conf. (COMPSAC), 2002, 603–609.
17. Kung, D., Liu, C., and Hsia, P.: An Object-Oriented Web Test Model for Testing Web Applications. 24th Int. Computer Software and Application Conf. (COMPSAC), 2000, 537–542.
18. Martin, R., and Martin, M.: FitNesse Web Site, http://www.fitnesse.org
19. Probert, R.L., Xiong, P., Stepien, B.: Life-Cycle E-commerce Testing with OO-TTCN-3. M. Núñez, Z. Maamar, F.L. Pelayo, K. Pousttchi, F. Rubio (Eds.): Applying Formal Methods: Testing, Performance and M/ECommerce, FORTE 2004 Workshops The FormEMC, EPEW, ITM, Toledo, Spain, October 1-2, 2004. Lecture Notes in Computer Science 3236, Springer 2004, 16–29.
20. Tomcat: http://jakarta.apache.org/tomcat
21. UCM User Group: UCMNav 2, http://www.usecasemaps.org/tools/ucmnav/
22. URN Focus Group: Draft Rec. Z.152 – Use Case Map Notation (UCM). Geneva, Switzerland, September 2003. http://www.UseCaseMaps.org/urn/
23. Weiss, M. and Amyot, D.: Business Process Modeling with URN. International Journal of E-Business Research, 1(3) 63-90, July-September 2005.
24. Wittevrongel, J., and Maurer, F.: SCENTOR: Scenario-Based Testing of E-Business Applications. Int. Workshop on Enabling Technologies: Infrastructure for Collaborative Enterprises, 2001, 41–46.

Network Element Testing Using TTCN-3: Benefits and Comparison

G. Bhaskar Rao[1], Keerthi Timmaraju[1], and Thomas Weigert[2]

[1] Motorola India Electronics Ltd
Hyderabad, India
{bhaskarraog, keerthi.t}@motorola.com
[2] Motorola Inc.
Schaumburg, Illinois
thomas.weigert@motorola.com

Abstract. As testing often consumes over 40% of the typical project development effort, there is great need for optimizing the testing effort. In addition, as the cost of fixing defects is dramatically lower when fixing those close to where they were introduced, finding defects in the early life-cycle phases is critical. TTCN-3 (Testing and Test Control Notation), developed at ETSI and standardized by the ITU-T, enables testers to specify test cases for the various types of testing, and supports reuse of test artifacts. We have used TTCN-3 as a complete test solution in the development of network element software. This paper presents the benefits we have observed during system development and provides a comparison with other testing practices deployed in our organization.

1 Introduction

Testing consumes typically over 40% of the total software engineering effort in telecommunication system development. A typical breakdown of the total test effort is shown in Table 1, as based on our experience in developing telecommunication systems (the data in this table represents our base line of expected effort as averaged from a reasonably large number of similar development projects). These development projects traditionally have used languages such as C, Perl, or Tcl to specify test suites and implement test environments. From this table, it is apparent that most of the effort is spent on developing the environment for carrying out the overall test activity, followed by the development of the test cases. It is also clear that most of the effort is spent in activities other than testing of the system under test. Test teams typically use or develop different tools and environments for integration testing, performance testing, conformance testing, and load testing, with minimal reuse between them, or no-reuse at all. When a defect is detected, it takes considerable time to associate this defect with the appropriate aspect of the system under test due to the hand-crafted test environment, difference in environments, different test scripts, and the manual effort of tracing tests to requirements, de-

A. Prinz, R. Reed, and J. Reed (Eds.): SDL 2005, LNCS 3530, pp. 265–280, 2005.

sign, or code artifacts. It is plain that development projects could save significant efforts were they to spend time only on test objects by using standard test environments, which have the capability to support different types of testing activities, rather than developing custom environments every time again.

The results of an earlier pilot project in protocol implementation encouraged us to rely on TTCN-3 and supporting tools for the development of a major release of a telecommunication system. This system required, of course, unit testing, and integration testing. As the developed network elements were performance critical, we also needed to perform rigorous performance testing, conformance testing, load testing, and reliability testing. We wanted to rely on a single environment that could support these testing needs in a transparent manner and would allow us to reuse as much of the test artifacts as possible. In addition, some of the network elements were developed using a new development methodology (UML 2.0 and supporting tools), and thus, testing also involved profiling the system under test to obtain performance measures such as message queuing times, message processing times, timer delays, etc., under different call load scenarios, in order to obtain insights about the adequacy of this methodology.

Table 1. Effort Distribution in conventional testing

Test Activity	Effort Spent
Test architecture	7%
Test design	10%
Test case identification	8%
Test case development	20%
Cost of Quality of Test System	7%
Communication, encoders and decoders	8%
Test Environment (Logging, Tracing, Defect detection support, Validation, Regression testing, other support activities)	25%
Test Management (Test case Organization, description, communication with customer, etc.)	7%
Other (Learning, procurement, setup)	8%
	100%

This paper summarizes our experiences and the benefits observed of leveraging TTCN-3 in this development project. Section 2 highlights the features of the TTCN-3 language and the supporting tools we deployed. This section also overviews our testing approach and our test architecture. The sample test case in section 3 illustrates various features of TTCN-3. Section 4 describes our development project. In section 5, we give a comparison of the traditional test development approach relying on programming languages such as C, Perl, or Tcl with the TTCN-3 approach. We conclude with a summary of the impact TTCN-3 had on our testing efforts.

2   TTCN-3

Recent efforts at ETSI have led to the introduction of a common general purpose testing language for the industry: TTCN-3 (Testing and Test Control Notation). While its precursor TTCN-2 was mainly used for communication and network system or subsytem testing, TTCN-3 has a rich set of features which make it suitable for other domains also, such as automotive or telematics applications [5], as well as for different types of testing activities. We believe that TTCN-3 addresses most of the issues raised in section 1.

2.1   TTCN-3 as a Test Solution

The following features of the TTCN-3 language make it suitable for the testing of communication and network systems as well as for other domains.

- Synchronous and asynchronous communication mechanisms help in testing of procedure based and message based systems.
- Data and signature templates with corresponding matching mechanisms provide flexibility to the user to reuse these templates across various test cases.
- The user is able to specify the expected messages with all applicable message parameters required to determine that a test case has passed.
- Separation of test case specification from execution control. The same test case can be executed in a loop at specific time intervals, or it can be grouped with other test cases, or it may be sequenced for stress testing, and so on. Each test case can thus be independently controlled.
- Dynamic concurrent testing configurations provide the user with a flexible option to simulate the behavior of unavailable components (for example, components that are still under development). This feature also helps in writing the test case in a more realistic scenario in the presence of concurrent components.
- Encoding information can be specified along with the test case. Note that at times the same message has to be encoded or decoded differently, depending on the context.
- Test cases may be written in programming languages (such as C), MSC notation, or the tabular format familiar from TTCN-2.
- External code integration provides the flexibility to integrate legacy encoders or decoders, code libraries, transformations, etc.
- Regular expressions greatly simplify the specification of expected messages
- Extensions to implement automatic configuration of the system under test (SUT) using SUT operations.
- Finally, TTCN-3 is a standardized language supported by commercial tools, such as Telelogic Tau Tester or Testing Technologies TTThree.

2.2   Overview of Tau Tester

Telelogic Tau/Tester is a tool for designing, creating, and executing TTCN-3 test suites. It includes editors for TTCN-3, ASN.1, and text. The tool provides build facilities, an integrated MSC viewer, and a log file creator. The major features of Tau/Tester are as follows.

- Support for TTCN-3.
- Support for ASN.1 PER (aligned and unaligned) and BER (definite and in-definite) encoding and decoding rules.
- TTCN-3 encoding/decoding must be written manually.
- Integrated development environment.
- On-line help.
- C code Generator.
- Support for TRI and PL (proprietary) integration mechanisms.
- Provides logging, document generation, and recording of the test execution.

2.3   Test Environment Architecture

The typical test system architecture and components/tools involved in testing are shown in fig. 1. TTCN-3 files which comprise the test system architecture, its behavior, data and control, along with the adaptation code (encoder/decoders and communication between test system and SUT), are processed by the TTCN-3 tool which generates code, produces a makefile, and compiles the test system. Test cases can be controlled by the user through the execution control UI. The communication between test system and SUT can be implemented using standard TCP/UDP communication links or proprietary protocols.

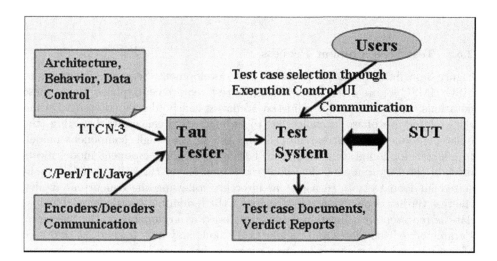

Fig. 1. Test Environment Architecture

2.4   Test System Architecture

Figure 2 shows the components of the executable Test System. TTCN-3 generated code executes on top of the runtime system libraries that implement the abstract constructs of the language. The runtime system controls the execution, it encodes/decodes messages using appropriate codecs, and logs system events via the log management system. Communication with the SUT is through the communication system.

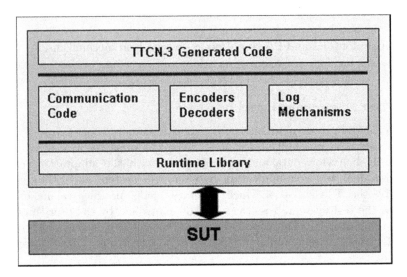

Fig. 2. Test System Architecture

2.5   Test Development Process

Figure 3 outlines the major phases of test development. Sequence Diagrams or MSC/HMSC [6] are often used during the test requirements phase. Using these notations, both valid and invalid test scenarios can be described easily. During the architecture phase, a choice has to be made between multi-threading (the multi component/concurrent model) and the simple/single component model. In general, for integration or system testing, a single component model meets most of the requirements. The concurrent model, on the other hand, is well-suited for load testing. In a test architecture following the concurrent model, the test verdict depends on the verdicts for the individual components. The test data is represented using templates and passed as arguments to the messages. Parameterized templates and regular expressions may help to increase the reuse of test data and test cases. The test cases can be called in sequence to form an integration suite.

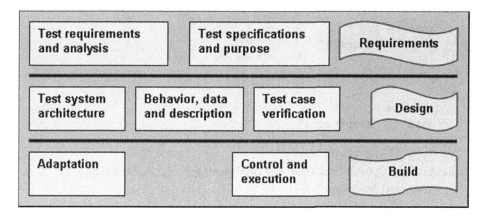

Fig. 3. Phases in test system development

3   Sample Test Case

From the example test case [1] below we can easily see the the various aspects of a TTCN test: architecture, behavior, and control. The detailed test description can be seen from the sequence diagram and objectives table in fig. 4.

```
module sampleTC_valid
{
  // Data Definitions
  type record    Packet
  {
        integer    info,
        charstring data
  }
  type port  DataPort message
  {
     inout all;
  }
  // Test Component declaration PTC
  type component MyTestComponent
  {
     port DataPort  CompPort;
     timer TCWaitTimer:= 100.0; //seconds
  }
  type component SystemComponent
  {
     port DataPort SysPort ;
  }
  // template definitions
  template Packet send_message :=
```

```
{
   info := 1,
   data := "Connect"
}
template Packet expected_message :=
{
   info := *,
   data := "Response 1"
}
/*  test case TC_01 */
testcase TC_01() runs on MyTestComponent // defines MTC
system SystemComponent
{
   log("Start test case execution for TC_01");
   map(mtc: CompPort, system: SysPort);
   CompPort.send(send_message);
   TCWaitTimer.start;
   alt
   {
        [] CompPort.receive(expected_message){
              TCWaitTimer.stop;
              setverdict(pass)
      }
        [] any port.receive{
              TCWaitTimer.stop;
              setverdict(fail)
      }
        [] MaxTimer.timeout{
              setverdict(fail)
      }
   }
   unmap(mtc: CompPort, system: SysPort);
}
control  /* control part of the module */
{
   execute (TC_01 ());
}
} /* end of the module */
```

The architecture part of this module begins by declaring a simple message data structure referred to as a packet, comprised of an **info** integer field followed by the **data** characterstring. Then a simple port type able to convey arbitrary bidirectional messages is declared. We then describe two components, the test driver and the component representing the SUT. These communicate via the identified ports.

Then two templates for messages are defined: A message to be sent to the SUT, and the expected reply message. The latter defines the pattern a message received from the SUT has to satisfy to be recognized as a reply. In this particular case, a reply message may have an arbitrary info field, as indicated by the ∗ (wildcard) symbol, but must have **Response 1** as data. In the control behavior section, a simple test case is defined. Upon invocation, the connection between test driver and SUT is established, the first message above is sent to the SUT, and a timer is started. The test component now is waiting for one of three events: Either the defined reply message is received at the appropriate port, upon which the timer is stopped and the test case is considered to have passed. If any other message is received on any port, or the reply message is received on any other port, the timer is stopped and the test case is considered to have failed. Similarly, if the timer expires without the reply message having been received, the test case is considered to have failed. Then the connection between test component and SUT is deleted.

Finally, the control part simply tells us to execute that single test case.

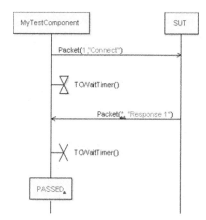

Identifier	MSC_TC_Valid
Reference to requirement	Requirement #1
Initial Condition	Initially in Idle State
Checks to be performed	Test component should now address a port of SUT.
Verdict criteria	Message has been received successfully

Fig. 4. Sample MSC and Objectives Chart

4   Case Study Overview

This paper presents a case study of testing a basic network element developed using UML 2.0 for a high-availability target platform [3]. It also outlines the benefits of TTCN-3 as compared with conventional testing practices using languages such as C, Perl, or Tcl.

In this project, we developed a new mobility management layer for a CDMA network, with high availability and scalability to meet next generation demands. The project involved development of the call processing stack, as well as mobility management, resource management, and link management components of the core network.

The call processing layer was architected using configurable working threads to share the call load (see fig. 5). This layer was developed from UML and implemented on a High Availability platform. A main concern of this implementation was the ability to handle are large call load, and be flexible to support further increasing call loads. Calls are routed by the main thread (Router Thread) to call processing threads (labelled Thr1, Thr2, etc., in fig. 5), which then process these calls with the help of supporting threads. The Router Thread performs load-balancing across the call processing threads. The number of call processing threads can be configured dynamically depending on the call load.

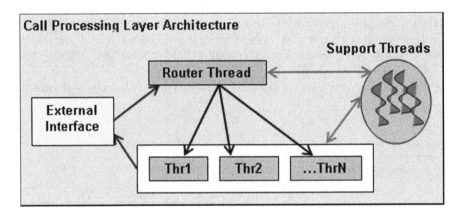

Fig. 5. Architecture of the System Under Test

Test cases were developed for integration testing, system testing, component testing, and load testing. The load system used two components to simulate two interfaces of the system. Along with the test system, user defined library functions had to be integrated to calculate the response times of the SUT. The integration test cases were also used for system testing by systematically integrating each module and interface.

4.1   Architecture

The Abstract Test System may have either one or two components in addition to the encoder/decoder (Adaptation Layer) with ports for message exchange with the SUT (see fig. 6). The Abstract Test System Interface (ATSI) receives two kinds of messages; hence there are two ports, one for each kind of message. The test system ports establish a TCP connection with SUT ports or use UDP data packets to exchange messages with the SUT.

The static test execution setup is shown in fig. 7. It shows the system under test (right-hand side) and the Test System (left-hand side) communicating via a TCP/IP connection. The SUT is comprised of application code (in this case generated from UML 2.0 designs), encoder/decoder, tool-specific run-time library,

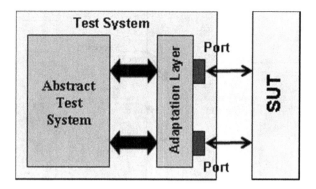

Fig. 6. Test System Architecture

and a communication module, whereas the major components of the test system
are the TTCN-3 generated code, the TTCN-3 run-time library, encoder/decoder
and the communication module. In-coming messages are sent to the application
layer after decoding by the respective decoders. Out-going messages are encoded
by the respective encoders and then sent to the target system. As there are two
types of messages being exchanged, both systems have two threads for receiving
each type of message. The Telelogic Runtime Library simplified the creation of
these threads by providing appropriate hooks, for both SUT and the test system.
The generated application code too executes on separate threads; the underlying
Runtime Library provides mutual exclusion for all these interacting threads.

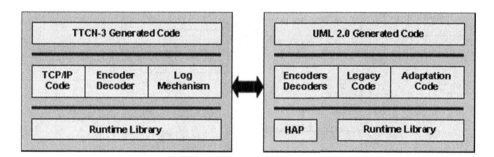

Fig. 7. Static Test Execution Setup

Both single (S-TTCN) and multi component models (C-TTCN) are used for
load testing; the single component model is used for integration and system testing. During load testing, the SUT receives messages from different test systems,
instead of a single test system as in conformance testing and integration testing.
The dynamic execution setup for load testing is shown in fig. 8.

A TTCN-3 implementation has 4 modules: Data types, architecture, behavior, and control modules. The external functions are defined in a separate module. The relationships among the modules are shown in fig. 9.

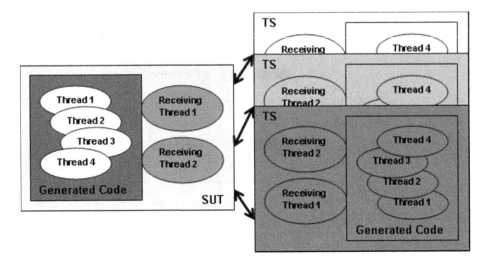

Fig. 8. Load testing execution setup

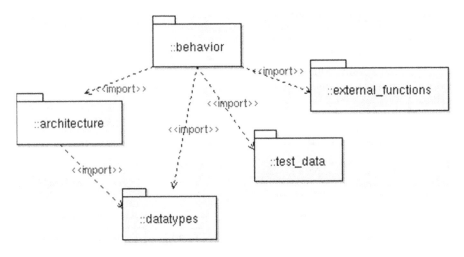

Fig. 9. Relationships among TTCN-3 modules

4.2   Test Case Development

For integration testing, separate test cases were developed for call setup, call termination, and hand-off. Both success and failure test cases were defined to gain further confidence in the system behavior. Most of the system test cases were obtained by reordering and combining the individual integration test cases. For example, the reference MSC in fig. 10 below shows that the system test case "end-to-end Call Test" results from the integration of the three basic test cases for call setup, handoff, and call termination. Such integration is achieved in end-to-end Call Test   interaction **Interaction 1**

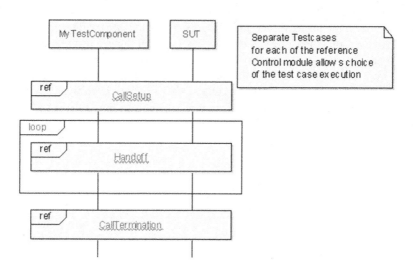

Fig. 10. Reference MSC for Call Setup

the control module; in addition, some templates were changed to obtain invalid behaviors to ensure better coverage of the SUT.

4.3 Load Testing

After ensuring that the system is initialized properly, the test system generates the first call setup message following the single component load test system model. Calls are generated as per the configuration at different rates (from one call per second to 30 calls per second) with other messages interleaved. Timers are used to configure the load on the system. Since the structure of each message was similar, a message type was created, and all messages contained this structure as their parameter. The contents of this structure was changed whenever messages were exchanged by the corresponding systems. On the concurrent component model, the main test component creates the call generator component after every interval, which in turn generates one call and dies after termination of that call. External functions were used to measure the time taken before sending and after receiving messages. These functions measure the performance of the SUT as well as of the test system. Based on performance measurements, the call rate was increased or decreased. The result of each test case was logged to a file.

5   Comparison with Conventional Testing

Languages such as C, Perl, or Tcl are not primarily intended as testing languages, but they do enable us to write test cases. Often engineers think that testing is merely calling a function to send a message and later comparing the result obtained with the expected result; this mentality eventually leads to ad-hoc testing. In such testing, different test environments are often repeatedly developed, and unnecessary logic for comparisons often reduces the time available for implementing test cases and the test system. Conventional languages provide few or no supporting facilities to go beyond ad-hoc testing and to manage testing in a systematic way. Developers have to visualize, plan, and implement everything starting with architecture, the separation of encoding/decoding from behavior, communication, comparison logic, logging, data management, reporting, document generation and so on. However, most of these features are provided directly by TTCN-3, which may immediately impact various business parameters (see Table 2).

Table 2. TTCN-3 impact compared to that of conventional languages

Business Parameters	Conventional Testing	TTCN-3
Productivity	1x	2x (Better)
Impact on Quality	1x	2x (Better)
Impact on CTR	1x	1.5x (Better)
Reuse	1x	2x (Better)
SUT coverage (same effort)	60%	90%

These parameters were estimated before the project and have been verified by other projects. Test coverage was estimated to be at 90% with the same amount of test effort, based on the baselines of the organization (as compared to 60% test coverage with conventional testing).

With respect to features of the TTCN-3 language, the following observations surfaced:

- Templates and timer handling enabled good solutions for integration testing, reliability testing, performance testing, and load testing.
- Control logic, modified templates, and concurrency allowed us to write load generation and processing logic conveniently as part of the test case.
- TTCN-3 code is independent of the platform it is developed on, and it further is very portable. The same TTCN-3 code was used with another tool, with only minor modifications to integration code (adaptation layer).
- Considerable amount of reuse across different types of testing was achieved, in particular resulting from reusing test cases and templates.
- The cost of quality of the test system was substantially less by virtue of concentrating only on test objectives.
- Generated test systems can be used as back ends because of their easy integration with other system components, developed in arbitrary languages.

Table 3 shows the distribution of the total test effort for projects leveraging TTCN-3. From this we can conclude that within a given time one can develop more test cases with better quality using TTCN-3, as compared with the conventional approach (in Table 1). While a new network element was developed during this case study, we feel that the data observed is representative of telecommunication system software in general.

In our experience, the test effort spent on projects following the conventional approach is roughly 1.5 times the effort spent in projects developing test suites using TTCN-3 and leveraging a TTCN-3 execution environment.

Table 3. Effort Distribution using TTCN-3

Test Activity	Conventional	TTCN-3
Test architecture	7%	8%
Test design	10%	7%
Test case identification	8%	15%
Test case development	20%	45%
Cost of Quality of Test System	7%	7%
Communication, encoders and decoders	8%	8%
Test Environment (Logging, Tracing, Defect detection support, Validation, Regression testing, other support activities)	25%	-
Test Management (Test case Organization, description, communication to customer etc.)	7%	5%
Other (Learning, procurement, set-up)	8%	5%
	100%	100%

Table 4 further summarizes the impact of TTCN-3 on testing based on the test projects done in our organization.

6   Conclusions and Recommendations

TTCN-3 enabled the development of a test environment which supported the various types of testing required and the reuse of test artifacts between these test efforts. Further opportunities for automation were identified and implemented, such as the generation of proprietary encoders/decoders and the generation of TTCN-3 data types from UML 2.0 data types.

Based on our experience and observations from this and similar projects, we feel that test automation with TTCN-3 can be beneficially employed for module testing, integration testing, performance testing, conformance testing, and load testing of communicating and event driven systems. Though TTCN-3 is claimed to be general purpose, some enhancements are required to truly make it suitable for testing GUI and data base systems.

We strongly feel that TTCN-3 is well suited for testing in the infrastructure domain. Not only did it help the testing and development teams to generate test cases faster, but also, debugging of test cases became easy. The benefits are significant for medium and long-term projects (but impact is harder to assess for projects with short cycle times). We expect the emergence of TTCN-3 as a prominent testing technology, across a wide variety of domains.

Table 4. TTCN-3 Impact on testing

Feature	Aspects	Our Rating
Test architecture	The framework provides good mechanism with Simple TTCN and Concurrent TTCN	Excellent
Test design	The design is modular and independent from the platform	Excellent
Test case specification	No explicit support but MSC can be used extensively to document the test cases	Very good
Test data	Very good support with templates, parameter-ized templates etc.	Excellent
Test execution	Good support for execution of a test cases from the test control block	Very good. Scope for some improvements
Modifiability of test cases	Templates, modular development	Excellent
Test reporting	Indicates which test have failed and passed, with reasons and byte information	Good.
Reuse	Test case and data level reuse	Excellent
Log management	Supports MSC and text based logging	Excellent
Ease of learning of the language	4 days of learning and practice are needed	Satisfactory
Support for ASN.1	Support for ASN.1 data types	Excellent
Support for Encoder/Decoder generation	Automatic generation of support for encoders/decoders from TTCN-3, ASN.1 and mixed types	Very good for ASN.1
Support for test management	Support dynamic selection of test cases	Good
Support for test case verification and validation	Compilation of the test cases, definitions etc	Very good
Scope for further automation	TTCN-3 encoder/decoder, structures, generation of test cases from requirements, test management integration etc.	Excellent
Legacy and External code Integration in Test System	Library Integration and encoders/decoders for the library parameters have to be written explicitly	Bad

References

1. ETSI ES 201873, The Testing and Test Control Notation TTCN-3, Part 1 (Core Language), Part 2 (Tabular Format), Part 3 (Graphical Format), Part 4 (Operational Semantics), Part 5 (TTCN-3 Runtime Interface), Part 6 (TTCN-3 Control Interfaces) (http://www.etsi.org/)
2. Telelogic Tau Tester: TTCN-3 to C Code Generator, Reference Manuals. Telelogic 2004.
3. Peter Weygant, *Clusters for High Availability: A Primer of HP Solutions*, Second Edition, Hewlett-Packard Company, 2001.

4. Telelogic Tau G2: UML 2.0 to C/C++/Java Code Generator, Reference Manuals. Telelogic 2004.

5. Simon Burton, Andrea Baresel and Ina Schieferdecker, *Automated testing of automotive telematics systems using TTCN-3*, 3rd Workshop on System Testing and Validation - SV04, Paris, December 2004.

6. ITU-T Z.120 (2000): Message Sequence Charts, MSC-2000, Geneva, October 1999.

7. Roger S. Pressman, *Software Engineering A Practitioner's Approach*, Fourth Edition, McGraw-Hill, 1997.

8. Paul Baker, Ekkart Rudolph and Ina Schieferdecker, *Graphical Test Specification - The Graphical Format of TTCN-3*, Tenth International SDL FORUM, Copenhagen, June 2001.

9. ITU-T Recommendation X.680 (1997): "Information Technology - Abstract Syntax Notation One (ASN.1): Specification of basic notation". Geneva, October 2000.

10. OMG: Unified Modeling Language v2.0 (UML). Object Management Group. 2003.

A Compositional Approach to Service Validation

Jacqueline Floch[1] and Rolv Bræk[2]

[1] SINTEF ICT NO-7465 Trondheim, Norway
`jacqueline.floch@sintef.no`
[2] Norwegian University of Science and Technology,
Department of Telematics NO-7491 Trondheim, Norway
`rolv.braek@item.ntnu.no`

Abstract. This paper presents a validation approach that exploits the compositional properties of a system. Our results can be applied on systems modelled by state machines and asynchronous communication by message passing. We consider two axes of composition: horizontal composition across system components, and vertical composition within components. Along the horizontal axis, we reduce the complexity of validation analysis by using a projection technique that allows us to validate interactions between components pairwise. We further simplify by introducing a set of design rules that support the development of well-formed state machines. When these rules are enforced, we are able to apply a simplified compatibility checking algorithm. Along the vertical axis, validation is applied incrementally. Elementary component collaborations are validated first, then their composite.

1   Introduction

A potential benefit of component-based software systems is increased flexibility. Systems built from components may be recomposed - possibly at run-time - to address changing user requirements or variable execution contexts. However, the compositional approaches introduce new complexities both from design and analysis viewpoints. The developers design components that may be used in multiple settings. Some of these settings may not be well understood at design time. Furthermore the developers have to deal with components and component variants that may have been developed by other parties. Our aim is to provide developers with tools that contribute to comprehension of and confidence in component variants and component collaborations. To that end, our work [5] has addressed two issues:

- Modularity and composition. We propose a role-based composition approach that supports incremental system development and contributes to understanding collaborations between components and collaborations among inner parts of components.
- Validation. We propose an incremental validation approach tightly integrated with the composition approach, providing support for checking that components interact consistently.

A. Prinz, R. Reed, and J. Reed (Eds.): SDL 2005, LNCS 3530, pp. 281–297, 2005.
© Springer-Verlag Berlin Heidelberg 2005

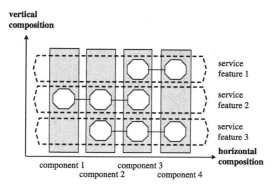

Fig. 1. Composition Axes

This paper presents the validation approach. However, as the composition and validation approaches are tightly integrated, we shortly introduce the composition concepts. More details about composition can be found in [5] and [7].

We distinguish between two axes of composition (see fig. 1): horizontal composition across system components, and vertical composition within components. A Service (or a service feature) is the result of a collaboration between components. Each component provides a partial functionality, called a role, in a collaboration. Horizontal composition deals with linking roles played by different components into a collaboration. Vertical composition deals with the composition of roles within a component. Our validation approach takes the compositional properties of a system into account:

- Along the horizontal or collaboration axis, validation is applied to check the interactions between roles. The interaction behaviour provided (and required) at a component role interface is derived from the component role behaviour by projection [8].
- Along the vertical axis, validation is applied incrementally. Elementary collaborations are first validated, then the collaborations obtained by composing elementary collaborations, etc.

Our work has focused on teleservices: services that aim at coordinating the responsibilities of the participants involved in a telecommunication session. Modelling teleservices in terms of active objects, state machines and asynchronous communication by message passing is widely adopted in telecommunication engineering approaches, and has proven to be of great value. We have favoured the use of the modelling language SDL [13] because its formal semantics enables an unambiguous interpretation of the system specification. However, our results are not bound to SDL. They may be applied to systems specified using other modelling languages that support active objects and state machines, as for example the recently adopted UML 2.0 specification [19].

A major concern in our work has been to provide "developer-friendly" validation techniques: that means techniques that are easy to understand and use.

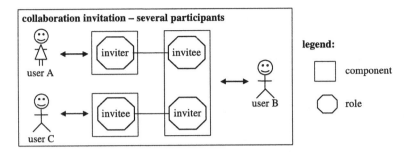

Fig. 2. Service role collaborations

Verification and validation techniques often require high competence and knowledge of formal modelling and reasoning on the part of the system developer, and their use in the software industry is rather moderate. Our approach, although thoroughly justified, remains pragmatic.

1.1   Structure of the Paper

First we shortly introduce the concepts of role, collaboration and composition, and explain how collaboration and composition contribute to increased modularity and flexibility. In section 3, we discuss validation according to the horizontal axis and propose techniques for validating interactions between associated roles. In section 4, we discuss incremental validation along the vertical axis. Finally, we present our experimentation results and plans for further work.

2   Role Collaboration and Composition

As a means to break down the complexity of service design, we have adopted a role-based design approach [20]. A service is modelled as a collaboration between services roles played by components that interact in order to provide services. Service roles enable us to better comprehend the contribution of a component in a service. Beyond increased understandability, experience suggests that role modelling provides better support for system adaptation and reuse than class modelling, because the unit of reuse seldom is a class, but rather a slice of behaviour (or collaboration) [18].

Figure 2 illustrates how an invitation service feature involving three participants may be modelled using roles and role collaborations. Here three components are involved, where one plays two roles in the service.

A particularity of teleservices is that they usually consist of subservices or service features. The features may either occur sequentially (this is the case for a multi-phase service) or concurrently. Figure 3 illustrates the two cases. In (a), the service consists of three phases: invitation, setup and release, that occur sequentially. We propose to model these phases separately. We describe three collaborations and compose the collaborations and associated roles sequentially

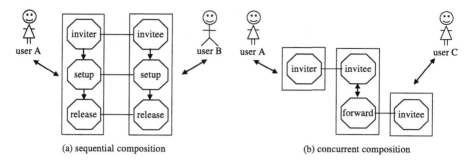

(a) sequential composition   (b) concurrent composition

Fig. 3. Service role composition

to obtain the overall service. In (b), the invitation service feature is enriched with a forwarding service feature. We model this by composing the two elementary roles invitee and forward concurrently.

These simple examples illustrate that composition can be considered along two axes:

- Horizontal composition across systems. This is modelled through role collaboration by the interaction between roles.
- Vertical composition within components. This is modelled through role composition by the sequential or concurrent composition of elementary roles within a component in order to obtain more complex behaviours. There exist various types of dependencies between roles that constrain the form of composition that can be applied. While sequential composition enforces behaviour ordering, concurrent composition supports simultaneous behaviours.

Role collaboration and role composition are modelling techniques that contribute to increased service flexibility and facilitate service adaptation. As shown on fig. 4, services may be modified at different granularity levels:

- A role in a collaboration may be replaced by a new role and/or new roles may be added.
- A role in a collaboration may be partially modified. Composite roles may be modified by replacing or adding elementary roles.

Of course, a main concern when modifying services in these ways is to ensure that the new or modified service role interacts consistently with the other roles. This is the aim of the proposed validation approach

2.1   Role Modelling in SDL

We have used SDL in order to model service roles, role collaboration and composition [5, 7]. The concept of composite state in SDL is especially useful as it allows us to use the same mechanisms for modelling elementary roles and composite roles.In contrast to [21], we do not introduce any new language for modelling

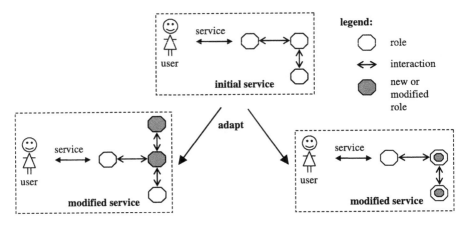

Fig. 4. Service modification

role collaborations. Using SDL modelling concepts uniformly at the elementary and composite levels, we are able to exploit the same techniques for validating collaborations at both the elementary and composite levels.

Note that the proposed validation techniques can be applied to state machines and composite states in general. We use the role concept as it fits well with the notion of a partial component behaviour and it also encourages the designer to produce modular service descriptions thereby increasing understandability of components and services.

3   Role Collaboration and Validation

The first axis of composition we consider is the horizontal composition axis: the collaboration between roles. Recall that we aim to compose services in a flexible way, possibly at run-time. Thus, it should be possible to validate new roles introduced dynamically in a service and ensure that the new service roles interact consistently with their collaborating roles. In that context, we avoid a complex analysis of the whole modified service and seek to develop techniques that restrict the validation analysis to the parts of the service affected by the modification. We propose to check that interactions between collaborating roles are logically consistent. The validation analysis consists of three main steps:

- We derive by projection the behaviour provided by a role on an association, called an association role or a-role [8].
- We ensure that a-roles do not exhibit any anomalous behaviours. If needed, we redesign service roles so that the roles and their projected a-roles are well-formed.
- We apply compatibility checking on interacting a-roles. A simplified algorithm can be applied when a-roles are well-formed.

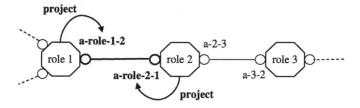

Fig. 5. Association roles

Our work has concentrated on safety properties, so avoiding bad behaviours: unspecified signal reception, deadlock or improper termination. Solutions to extend the approach with progress and goal expressions to enable liveness properties to be checked has been proposed in [22] and [23].

3.1   Association Roles and Projection

Validation is applied on associations between service roles. When a role is associated with several other roles, validation is performed for each association. In order to validate an association between two roles, we need to describe the behaviour of the roles on that association. We introduce the concept of association role (a-role) as the visible behaviour of a role on an association. An a-role hides the internal behaviour of a role, and the interactions on other associations. In fig. 5, the role "role 2" is involved in two associations and provides the two a-roles. The a-role "a-role-2-1" should provide the same behaviour as "role 2" on the association between "role 1" and "role 2".

We have earlier described a projection transformation that can be used to derive a-roles from service roles [8] and we have shown that this projection maintains the observable behaviour on associations between service roles provided that the following design rules are enforced [5]:

– Roles must be save consistent: the saving of a signal is either re-iterated or specified as input in the successor state(s).
– The modelling of alternative signal orderings using save must not overlap with the modelling of concurrent behaviours. Concretely, a signal saved in a state that can consume signals from the same association, should not be retrieved in a state that can consume signals from other associations.

Our approach assumes that these two conditions are enforced. The first rule contributes to collaboration compatibility (unspecified signal reception may occur if this rule is not applied). One may argue that the second rule reduces the power of expression of SDL. Noting that save introduces complexity, we contend that the rule contributes to simplify descriptions. Note that save is still allowed; the rule only relates to special cases.

The a-roles obtained by projection are described as SDL state machines. As a-roles are restricted to interaction behaviour, full SDL is not needed. Some syntactical extensions to the SDL notation are introduced in order to abstract non-observable behaviours. However, the semantics of SDL remains unchanged.

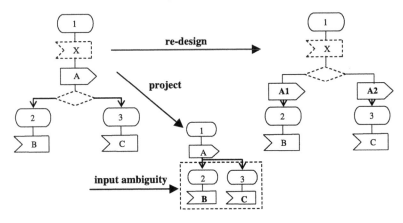

Fig. 6. Removing input ambiguity

3.2   Removing Anomalous Behaviours

A-role graphs are simpler than service role graphs and thus easier to comprehend. As explained in [8], the review of a-role graphs enables the designer to detect anomalous behaviours:

- *Ambiguous behaviours* take place when an external observer is not able to determine which environment behaviour is expected by an a-role. For example, the observer cannot determine whether or not a role expects an input, or which input is accepted.
- *Conflicting behaviours* occur when the behaviours of an a-role and its complementary a-role (the a-role on the other end of the association) diverge.

Ambiguous and conflicting behaviours are usually symptoms of errors. We propose a set of design rules [5] that, when followed, enable the designer to develop well-formed state machines, where anomalous behaviours do not exist.

Input ambiguity and re-design are illustrated in fig. 6. The initial service role is shown on the left hand side; the behaviours not visible on the association to be validated are represented by dashed symbols. The initial a-role exhibits input ambiguity: an external observer cannot determine which input behaviour is expected after the sending of signal "A" and hence unspecified reception is possible. The initial role should be re-designed. For example, distinct signals may be sent before entering state "2" and "3" as shown on fig. 6.

The resolution of conflicting behaviour is illustrated in fig. 7. As a-roles communicate asynchronously, they perceive the occurrence of communication at different points of time. Reception is perceived some time after sending. In fig. 7, both roles may take the initiative to send, leading to conflicting behaviours. The roles should be able to detect and resolve such conflicts. An example of conflict resolution is shown in fig. 7. Other conflict resolution patterns are proposed in [5].

The proposed design rules promote quality in terms of design errors being removed. One may argue that these rules reduce the expressive power of SDL.

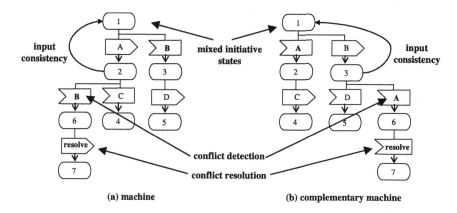

Fig. 7. Resolving a conflicting behaviour

We contend that they do not restrict this power of expression, provided one wishes to design correct services. The design rules aim at eliminating logical interaction errors. They make it difficult to develop incorrect services, and thus they are beneficial for all designers. As we aim at developing flexible and re-configurable services, service roles should not contain behaviours that cannot be explored in a safe way, and developers should design roles that other developers have confidence in.

3.3   Compatibility Checking

Compatibility checking applies to complementary a-roles on an association. As a-roles are modelled using SDL, the reachability analysis techniques developed for state machines can be applied to a-roles [11]. However, we are able to apply a simplified algorithm provided that the design rules defined to remove anomalous behaviours have been followed.

Our compatibility checking algorithm is a simplification compared to reach-ability analysis in the following ways:

- As conflicting behaviours are removed, each branch in a graph following a mixed initiative state (a state where both input and output are possible) can be checked against a single branch in the complementary graph.
- The merging of graph branches following equivoque transitions (similar tran-sitions that lead to distinct behaviours), is performed before compatibility checking. We have shown the merging transformation maintains the observ-able association behaviour provided that equivoque transitions leading to ambiguous behaviours have been removed [5]. Subsequent to merging, a branch in the graph that would be checked against several branches in the complementary graph before merging, can be checked against a single branch after merging.
- Following the two previous points, no message queue is needed to perform the analysis. The algorithm only requires a save signal queue.

The approach also leads to a reduction of the global state space:

- The analysis is performed on projection of roles, not on roles. The a-roles have less states that roles. The reduction achieved here is a factor of 10.
- The algorithm does not make use of a message queue. The number of signals in the save queue normally remains low as the analysis is restricted to one association. The reduction achieved here is significant: a factor of 10^6.

3.4   Discussion

Simplification is achieved by emphasizing the details significant to the purpose of validation of the interfaces, and hiding other details. Simplification, however, causes some shortcomings that are explained in this section.

Over-Specification. Internal role decisions and signals on non-visible associations are hidden by projection. In some cases, however, decisions and signals on non-visible associations are observable from complementary service roles:

- There may exist dependencies between decisions across roles.
- There may exist dependencies between interactions on distinct associations.

By ignoring these dependencies, projection may lead to a non-deterministic a-role behaviour and ambiguity. Our approach encourages the developer to re-design service roles in those cases. When doing so, the new role is over-specified: behaviour is added that is not absolutely necessary.

An example is given in fig. 8. The sequence diagram shows that interactions between the roles ("R1", "R2") and ("R1", "R3") are dependent. Alternative behaviours may be taken after a decision by "R1". The state diagram illustrates that the dependency is hidden by the projection of "R2" on the association between "R2" and "R3". This leads to input ambiguity. Our design rules requires "R2" to be re-designed so that ambiguity is removed. After receiving "A", "R2" should be prepared to receive both "B" and "C" from "R3": the states "3" and "4" may be merged. Furthermore, backward save consistency should be enforced, and the state "2" should be able to save "B" and "C". After such re-design, the role "R2" is overspecified.

Over-specification leads to more complex role state graphs. However, over-specification is harmless with respect to compatibility. It enforces the designer to produce robust specifications towards modifications of collaborating roles that influence dependencies between associations.

Second Order Errors. The projection of roles lead to graphs that may contain spontaneous transitions (t-transitions) that cannot be removed from the a-role transition chart by refinement (by minimization or gathering as presented in [8]). These t-transitions are symptoms of errors. Without the knowledge of the behaviour occurring on other associations, we are not able to decide whether or not those represent errors. The t-transitions may be symptoms of second order errors.

An example is given in fig. 9. A "request-answer" pattern is applied between three roles. We assume that the requesting machine cannot proceed before the

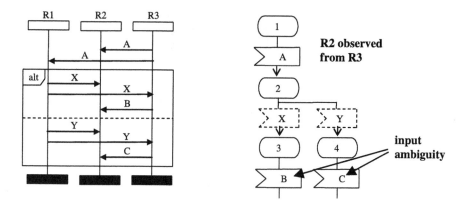

Fig. 8. Dependencies between associations

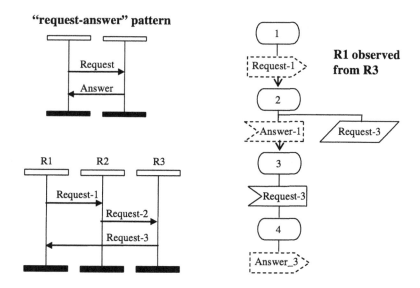

Fig. 9. Second order errors

request has been answered. The sequence diagram shows that the interactions between "R1", "R2" and "R3" lead to deadlock. The state diagram of the a-role "R1 observed from R3" depicts a symptom of error: a t-transition derived from the projection of the non-visible signal "Answer-1" between state "2" and "3". We cannot decide whether there is an error or not by only analyzing the a-role. Neither can we determine the cause of error, if any. Our analysis helps to identify potential problems, but in this case it cannot solve them. A closer analysis of the service roles is required in such cases.

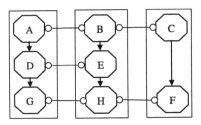

Fig. 10. Sequential collaboration composition

4   Role Composition and Validation

The second axis of composition deals with the composition of collaborations in order to obtain more complex collaborations. This requires a coordinated vertical composition of the roles. The aim of validation along the vertical composition axis is to ensure that roles are consistently composed across components leading to consistent interactions between composite roles. We assume that the elementary roles being composed interact consistently; this can be checked by applying the techniques presented in section 3.

As role composition is modelled using identical mechanisms to the modelling of elementary component roles, the validation techniques proposed for elementary collaborations can be exploited in the validation of composite collaborations. Especially, the techniques apply unchanged to the sequential composition of roles as this form of composition is modelled using composite states in the same way as the modelling of elementary roles [7]. Concurrent composition introduces new associations that are validated separately, also using the techniques for the validation of elementary collaborations.

4.1   Sequential Collaboration Composition

We first consider roles that are composed sequentially. This is illustrated in fig. 10. In that example, the composite collaboration consists of three collaborations that involve three components. One of the components is not involved in the second phase of the composite collaboration. The composite role "A" followed by "D" followed by "G" is modelled using composite states in a similar way as the elementary roles "A", "D" and "G". So are the other composite roles.

We have assumed that the elementary collaborations are consistent, thus we know that the elementary roles execute consistently until they terminate, provided that they start executing in a coordinated way. Note that the detection of improper termination is of special interest with respect to sequential role composition: a collaboration should terminate properly before a successor collaboration starts. Inconsistency may then be introduced by composition if some transition from a role to its successor leads to an uncoordinated start of execution of the successor roles. Two kinds of non-coordinated start may happen:

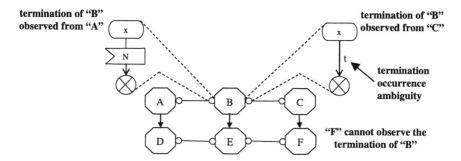

Fig. 11. Termination occurrence ambiguity

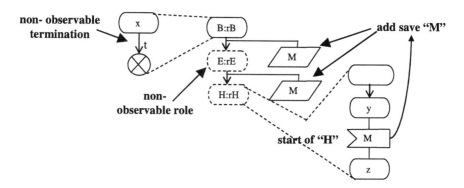

Fig. 12. Backward save consistency

- Interacting roles do not start executing in a synchronized way. In that case, a signal may be sent to a complementary role that has not yet started, leading to unspecified signal reception.
- Interacting roles are entered through inconsistent entry conditions.

Unsynchronized Start. As roles are composed sequentially, roles start execution when their predecessors terminate. Thus non-simultaneous execution start occurs when the predecessor roles, if any, do not terminate in a synchronized way. A simple approach is to constrain roles not to start before all predecessors have terminated. However termination is not always observable, as illustrated in fig. 11.

In order to avoid unspecified signal reception in the transition between composed roles, we introduce a design rule that forces roles to be "backward save consistent": signals specified as input or save in the initial state of a role should be saved in the predecessor role(s). Figure 12 illustrates that rule. We have shown that when this design rule is applied, unspecified signal reception due to non-simultaneous execution start does not occur [5].

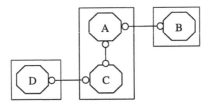

Fig. 13. Concurrent collaboration composition

Inconsistent Entry Conditions. Inconsistency may be introduced when interacting roles are entered through inconsistent entry conditions. Successor roles may either be triggered:

- spontaneously – as part of a logical sequence of actions of the composite role. In that case we simply verify that the entry conditions of elementary roles are consistent. As elementary roles have been validated, consistent entries between interacting a-roles have been identified; or
- implicitly – by signal triggering. The techniques developed for validating elementary collaborations apply.

Extended Forms of Sequential Composition. Guarded sequential composition, choice and disabling are extended forms of sequential composition. As these composition forms are modelled using identical mechanisms as the modelling of elementary roles, the techniques developed for the validation of elementary role collaborations apply. This means that we use the projection technique on the composite role obtained from the elementary role state machines without considering the details described by the elementary role state machines.

4.2   Concurrent Collaboration Composition

In this section, we consider that elementary roles are composed concurrently. This is illustrated in fig. 13. In that example, the composite collaboration consists of two collaborations that involve three components. The concurrent roles may execute more or less dependently. Here the roles "A" and "C" are dependent.

Concurrent collaboration composition introduces new associations that are validated separately. In that way, no new mechanism is needed in the validation analysis.

Dynamic Role Composition. Dynamic role composition can be modelled by the creation of process agents at run-time. Following the dynamic composition of roles, new associations are added at run-time.

The projection transformation was initially defined so that creation is considered to be an internal action and thus hidden by projection. In other words, the start of interaction between a creator role and a created role was not described in the a-roles derived from the creator and created roles; thus the dependency between the creator and created roles was hidden by projection. As explained in section 3.4, hiding dependencies may lead to over-specification. In order to avoid over-specification of the creator and created roles, the projection has been re-defined so that the create operation is maintained in the projection on the association the create relates to.

That redefinition does not however remove any over-specification following dynamic creation. When a third role that is neither creator nor created somehow depends on the creation, for example a role bound to a role created dynamically, that third role may be over-specified when following the design rules proposed by our approach.

5   Experimentation

The proposed validation approach has been manually applied on simple service examples. It has not yet been applied on a large prototype or industrial case. However, our experience from system design and tool design has been used as input and references to ensure relevance and feasibility of the results [6, 10].

A major barrier for starting a larger experiment study is that no tools yet are available that support SDL-2000, and thus SDL composite states and agents. It seems that the SDL tool providers focus on the simplification of SDL rather than on the development of SDL-2000 tools.

As UML was recently extended with concepts that support the modelling of active objects, we now concentrate on UML. UML profiles for SDL are under development. The a-role projection and refinement transformations, and the validation algorithms have been implemented [2, 12]. The integration of the validation tools with UML 2.0 modelling tools that support UML active objects is also challenging as no UML 2.0 tool support both active objects and XMI yet.

6   Related Work

The analysis of finite state distributed systems is usually based on the construction of a global state graph. A main problem in this approach is that the complexity of the global state graph grows exponentially with the number of states of the constituting state machines, and the graph becomes often too large for exhaustive analysis. This is known as the state space explosion problem. Several techniques have been proposed in order to reduce the complexity of the analysis either based on abstraction of the system to be analysed [3, 15], or on reduction of the global state graph [11]. Other techniques exploit the compositional properties of distributed systems, and decompose the analysis of a system into the analysis of the system components [4, 9]. We exploit both the techniques of system abstraction and system decomposition. The approaches described in the literature usually use mathematical formalisms that require specialist competence that normally is not available in an industrial context. We believe that our approach, although thoroughly justified, remains easy to understand and use. As pointed out [3], little work is dedicated to abstracting state machines or SDL. Abstraction techniques are provided for FSMs but not for the more complex structure of SDL.

Various architecture description languages (ADLs) have been proposed to model architectural components and overall system interconnection structure [17]. Of interest for our work are ADLs defined by formal syntax and semantics that allow the analysis of systems. Describing component interfaces and their external behaviour [16] and the semantics of architectural connections [1] are major issues. Surprisingly, these do not discuss how component interfaces are derived from components. Similarly, [14] proposes a component-based analysis where interfaces are described using interface automata, but fails to explain the relation between interfaces and components. Our work defines a projection transformation that ensures that component interfaces exhibit the same behaviour as the components they are derived from.

7   Conclusion

This paper has presented a compositional approach to service validation. The validation techniques apply to systems specified using state machines and asynchronous communication, and aim at checking the compatibility of interactions between service roles played by components. We exploit the compositional properties of systems and propose two simplification schemes:

- Rather than analyzing a whole system, we analyze service interactions between pairs of components. Interaction behaviours are derived from component behaviours by projection. We define a projection transformation that only retains the aspects significant for the purpose of validation of interactions.
- Validation is be applied incrementally. Elementary collaborations between components are first validated, and then the composite collaborations composed from elementary collaborations, etc.

These simplification schemes make it possible to analyze larger systems. Analysis does not require as large global state spaces as traditional reachability analysis techniques.

Our approach provides support, helping to detect and remove ambiguous and conflicting behaviours, and thus develop well-formed state machines. We define design rules that promote quality: many design errors can be removed at an early stage, even prior to compatibility checking.

Finally, we have tried to develop techniques that the developers can easily understand and apply constructively during design. We use the same language for describing association behaviours as the developers use for modelling the component behaviours (SDL). All reasoning is performed using the concepts of the modelling language.

Acknowledgments. This work has been done as part of the Plug-and-Play project supported by the Norwegian Foundation for Research (NFR).

References

1. Allen, R., and Garlan, D., "A Formal Basis for Architectural Connection", ACM Transactions on Software Engineering and Methodology, vol. 6, no. 3, pp. 213-249, 1997.
2. Alsnes, R., Role Validation Tool, M.Sc. thesis NTNU, Spring 2004.
3. Boroday, S., Groz, R., Petrenko, A., and Quemener, Y.-M., "Techniques for Abstracting SDL Specifications." SAM 2002.
4. Charpentier, M., and Chandy, K.M., "Towards a Compositional Approach to the Design and Verification of Distributed Systems", Proc. of World Congress on Formal Methods in the Development of Computing Systems (FM 99), pp. 570-589, Springer, 1999.
5. Floch, J., Towards Plug-and-Play Services: Design and Validation using Roles, Doctoral thesis, Norwegian University of Science and Technology, ISBN 82-471-5598-2, 2003.
6. Floch, J., "Supporting evolution and maintenance by using a flexible automatic code generator", Proc. of the 17th International Conference on Software Engineering (ICSE 95), pp. 211-219, 1995.
7. Floch, J., and Bræk, R., "Using SDL for Modeling Behavior Composition", Proc. of the 11th International SDL Forum, LNCS 2708, pp. 36-54, 2003.
8. Floch, J., and Bræk, R., "Using Projections for the Detection of Anomalous Behaviors", Proc. of the 11th International SDL Forum, LNCS 2708, pp. 251-268, 2003.
9. Graf, S., Steffen, B., and Lüttgen, G., "Compositional minimization of finite state machines using interface specifications.", Formal Aspects of Computing, 8(5), pp. 607-616, 1996.
10. Haugen, Ø., Bræk, R., and Melby, G., The SISU project. Proc. of the sixth SDL Forum (SDL 93), pp. 479-489, 1993.
11. Holzmann, G.J. Design and Validation of Computer Protocols. Prentice Hall. ISBN 0-13-539834-7, 1991.
12. Korda D., Role Negotiation, M.Sc. thesis NTNU, Spring 2004.
13. ITU-T. Specification and Description Language (SDL). "SDL-2000", ITU-T Recommendation Z.100 (11/99), 1999.
14. Jin, Y., Lakos, C., Esser, R., "Component-based Design and Analysis: A Case Study", Proc. of the First International Conference on Software Engineering and Formal Methods (SEFM 03), 2003.
15. Loiseaux, C., Graf, S., Sifakis, J., Bouajjani, A., and Bensalem, S., "Property Preserving Abstractions for the Verification of Concurrent Systems", Formal Methods in System Design, Vol. 6, pp. 11-44, Kluwer Academic Publishers, 1995.
16. Luckham, D.C., Kenney, J.J., Augustin, L.M. Vera, J., Bryan, D., and Mann, W., "Specification and Analysis of System Architecture Using Rapide", IEEE Transactions on Software Engineering, vol. 21, no. 4, pp. 717-734, 1995.
17. Medvidovic, N., and Taylor, R.N., "A Classification and Comparison Framework for Software Architecture Descriptions Languages", IEEE Transactions on Software Engineering, 2000, vol. 26, no. 1, pp. 70-93.
18. Mezini, M., and Lieberherr, K., "Adaptive Plug-and-Play Components for Evolutionary Software Development", Proc. of OOPSLA 98, ACM SIGPLAN Notices, vol. 33, no. 10, pp. 97-116, 1998.
19. OMG. UML 2.0 specifications, 2003. Information available at http://www.omg.org/uml (accessed March 2004).

20. Reenskaug, T., Andersen, E.P., Berre, A.J., Hurlen, A.J., Landmark, A., Lehne, O.A., Nordhagen, E., Ness-Ulseth, E. Oftedal, G., Skar, A.L., and Stenslet, P. "OORASS: Seamless support for the creation and maintenance of object oriented systems", Journal of object-oriented programming, vol.5, no. 6, pp. 27-41, 1992.
21. Rößler, B., Geppert, B., and Gotzheim, R., "Collaboration-based Design of SDL Systems", Proc. of the 2001 SDL Forum., LNCS 2078, pp. 72-89, 2001.
22. Sanders, R., and Bræk, R., "Modeling Peer-to-peer Service Goals in UML", Proc. of the Sixth International Conference on Software Engineering and Formal Methods (SEFM 04), 2004.
23. Sanders, R., and Bræk, R., v. Bochmann, G. and Amyot, D., "Service Discovery and Selection using Semantic Interfaces", Proc. of the 12th International SDL Forum (this conference), 2005.

Consistency Checking of Concurrent Models for Scenario-Based Specifications*

Xuandong Li, Jun Hu, Lei Bu, Jianhua Zhao,
and Guoliang Zheng

State Key Laboratory of Novel Software Technology,
Department of Computer Science and Technology,
Nanjing University, Nanjing, Jiangsu, P.R.China 210093
lxd@nju.edu.cn

Abstract. Scenario-based specifications such as message sequence charts (MSCs) offer an intuitive and visual way of describing design requirements. As one powerful formalism, Petri nets can model concurrency constraints in a natural way, and are often used in modelling system specifications and designs. Since there are gaps between MSC models and Petri net models, keeping consistency between these two kinds of models is important for the success of software development. In this paper, we use Petri nets to model concurrent systems, and consider the problem of checking Petri nets for scenario-based specifications expressed by message sequence charts. We develop the algorithms to solve the following two verification problems: the existential consistency checking problem, which means that a scenario described by a given MSC must happen during a Petri net runs, or any forbidden scenario described by a given MSC never happens during a Petri net run; and the mandatory consistency checking problem, which means that if a reference scenario described by the given MSCs occurs during a Petri net run, it must adhere to a scenario described by the other given MSC.

1 Introduction

Scenarios are widely used as a requirements technique since they describe concrete interactions and are therefore easy for customers and domain experts to use. Scenario-based specifications such as message sequence charts offer an intuitive and visual way of describing design requirements. They are playing an increasingly important role in specification and design of systems. Such specifications focus on message exchanges among communicating entities in real-time and distributed systems.

* Supported by the National Natural Science Foundation of China (No.60425204, No.60233020, and No.60273036), the National Grand Fundamental Research 973 Program of China (No.2002CB312001), and by Jiangsu Province Research Foundation (No.BK2004080, No.BK2003408).

A. Prinz, R. Reed, and J. Reed (Eds.): SDL 2005, LNCS 3530, pp. 298–312, 2005.

Message sequence charts (MSCs) [1] is a graphical and textual language for the description and specification of the interactions between system components. The main area of application for MSCs is as overview specifications of the communication behavior of real-time systems, in particular telecommunication switching systems.

Petri Nets [2] is a formal and graphically appealing language, which is appropriate for modelling systems with concurrency and resource sharing. There are plenty of applications of Petri Nets in modelling system specifications and designs.

We often use MSCs and Petri nets together in a software project [3-5]. Usually, MSCs and Petri nets are used in different software development steps. Even when used in the same step, such as requirements analysis, MSCs are usually used to describe the requirements provided directly by the customers, while Petri nets are used to model the workflow synthesized by the domain and technical experts. Since there are gaps between MSC models and Petri net models, keeping consistency between these two kinds of models is important for the success of software development.

In this paper, we consider the problem of checking concurrent system designs modelled by Petri nets for scenario-based specification expressed by MSCs. We develop the algorithms to solve the following two verification problems: the existential consistency checking problem, which means that a scenario described by a given MSC must happen during a Petri net run, or any forbidden scenario described by a given MSC never happens during a Petri net run; and the mandatory consistency checking problem, which means that if a reference scenario described by the given MSCs occurs during a Petri net run, it must adhere to a scenario described by the other given MSC.

The paper is organized as follows. In the next section, we introduce MSCs, and use them to represent scenario-based specifications. In section 3, we review the definition and some basic properties of Petri nets. The solutions are given in Section 4 and 5 respectively to the existential and mandatory consistency checking of Petri nets for scenario-based specifications expressed by MSCs, and the detailed proofs of the theorems are omitted in these two sections because of space consideration. The related works and some conclusions are given in the last section.

2   Message Sequence Charts and Scenario-Based Specifications

MSCs represent typical execution scenarios, providing examples of either normal or exceptional executions of the proposed system. The MSC standard as defined by ITU-T in Recommendation Z.120 [1] introduces two basic concepts: *basic MSCs* (bMSCs) and *High-Level MSCs* (hMSCs). A bMSC consists of a set of instances that run in parallel and exchange messages in a one-to-one, asynchronous fashion. Instances usually represent process instances, and so are called processes in this paper. An hMSC graphically combines references to bM-

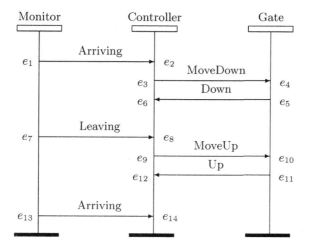

Fig. 1. An MSC describing the railroad crossing system

SCs to describe parallel, sequence, iterating, and non-deterministic execution of the bMSCs. In this paper we just consider bMSCs which are used to represent scenario-based specifications. For example, an MSC is depicted in fig. 1, which describes a scenario about the well-known example of the railroad crossing system in [6]. This system operates a gate at a railroad crossing, in which there are a railroad crossing monitor and a gate controller for controlling the gate. When the monitor detects that a train is arriving, it sends a message to the controller to move down the gate. After the train leaves the crossing, the monitor sends a message to controller to open the gate.

The semantics of an MSC essentially consists of sequences (of traces) of messages that are sent and received among the concurrent processes in the MSC. The order of communication events (message sent or received) in a trace is deduced from the visual partial order determined by the flow from top to bottom within each process in the MSC along with a causal dependency between the events of sending and receiving a message [1, 7, 8, 9]. In accordance with [7], without losing generality, we assume that each MSC corresponds to a visual order for a pair of events e_1 and e_2 such that e_1 precedes e_2 in the following cases:

- **Causality:** A send event e_1 and its corresponding receive event e_2.
- **Controlability:** The event e_1 appears above the event e_2 on the same process line, and e_2 is a send event. This order reflects the fact that a send event can wait for other events to occur. On the other hand, we sometimes have less control on the order in which receive events occur.
- **Fifo order:** The receive event e_1 appears above the receive event e_2 on the same process line, and the corresponding send events e_1' and e_2' appear on a mutual process line where e_1' is above e_2'.

For checking scenario-based specifications expressed by MSCs, we formalize MSCs as follows.

Definition 1. An MSC is a five-tuple $D = (P, E, M, L, V)$ where

- P is a finite set of processes.
- E is a finite set of events corresponding to sending a message and receiving a message.
- M is a finite set of messages. For any message $g \in M$, let $g!$ and $g?$ represent the send and the receive for g respectively. For any $e \in E$, it is corresponding to a send or receive for a message g, denoted by $\phi(e) = g!$ or $\phi(e) = g?$.
- $L : E \to P$ is labelling function which maps each event $e \in E$ to a process $L(e) \in P$.
- V is a finite set whose elements are of the form (e, e') where e and e' are in E and $e' \neq e$, which represents a visual order displayed in D.

$\square$

We use *event sequences* to represent the *traces* of MSCs which are corresponding to the behavior of MSCs. Any event sequence is of the form $e_0 \hat{\ } e_1 \hat{\ } \ldots \hat{\ } e_m$, which represents that e_{i+1} takes place after e_i for any i $(0 \leq i \leq m - 1)$.

Definition 2. Let $D = (P, E, M, L, V)$ be an MSC. An event sequence of the form $e_0 \hat{\ } e_1 \hat{\ } \ldots \hat{\ } e_m$ is a *trace* of D if and only if the following conditions hold:

- all events in E occur in the sequence, and each event occurs only once $\{e_0, e_1, \ldots, e_m\} = E$ and $e_i \neq e_j$ for any i, j $(0 \leq i < j \leq m)$; and
- $e_1, e_2, \ldots, e_m$ satisfy the visual order defined by V for any e_i and e_j, if $(e_i, e_j) \in V$, then $0 \leq i < j \leq m$.

$\square$

Corresponding to the sends or receives for messages, we can transform the traces of an MSC into the *message trails* of the MSC.

Definition 3. Let $D = (P, E, M, L, V)$ be an MSC. For any trace of D of the form $e_0 \hat{\ } e_1 \hat{\ } \ldots \hat{\ } e_m$, replacing each e_i with $\phi(e_i)$ $(0 \leq i \leq m)$, we get a sequence $\phi(e_0) \hat{\ } \phi(e_1) \hat{\ } \ldots \hat{\ } \phi(e_m)$ of the sends or receives for a message in M, which is a *message trail* of D.

$\square$

Notice that for an MSC D, all events in a trace of D are distinct, but there may be the same events in a message trail of D which are corresponding to the message sends or receives. For example, the events e_1 and e_{13} are distinct in the MSC depicted in fig. 1, but $\phi(e_1) = \phi(e_{13}) = Arriving!$.

3   Petri Nets

The Petri nets we consider in this paper are classical 1-safe systems.

Definition 4. A Petri net is a four-tuple, $N = (P, T, F, \mu_0)$, where

- $P = \{p_1, p_2, \ldots, p_m\}$ is a finite set of *places*;
- $T = \{t_1, t_2, \ldots, t_n\}$ is a finite set of *transitions* $(P \cap T = \emptyset)$;
- $F \subset (P \times T) \cup (T \times P)$ is the *flow relation*;
- $\mu_0 \subset P$ is the *initial marking* of the net.

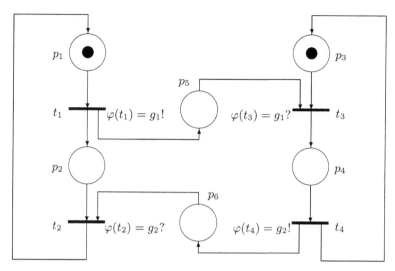

Fig. 2. A Petri net

A *marking* μ of N is any subset of P. For any transition t, ${}^\bullet t = \{p \in P | (p, t) \in F\}$ and $t^\bullet = \{p \in P | (t, p) \in F\}$ denote the *preset* and *postset* of t, respectively. A transition t is *enabled* in a marking μ if ${}^\bullet t \subseteq \mu$; otherwise, it is *disabled*. Let *enabled*(μ) be the set of transitions enabled in μ.   □

As a tool used for modelling systems, the transitions of Petri nets represent the potential events in the systems. Since in this paper we consider the problem of checking Petri nets for scenario-based specifications expressed by MSCs, for any Petri net we consider in this paper, each transition t is labelled with an event which may be corresponding to a message send or receive in a MSC, which is denoted by $\varphi(t)$. That is, for an MSC $D = (P, E, M, L, V)$, for a transition t of a Petri net, there may be a message $g \in M$ and an event $e \in E$ such that $\varphi(t) = g! = \phi(e)$ or $\varphi(t) = g? = \phi(e)$. For example, a Petri net is depicted in fig. 2.

For the firing of a transition to be possible, two conditions must be satisfied.

Definition 5. A transition t may fire from marking μ if and only if the following two conditions hold: (1) $t \in enabled(\mu)$, and (2) $(\mu - {}^\bullet t) \cap t^\bullet = \emptyset$.   □

The first condition is the normal firing condition for Petri nets. The second condition requires *contact-freeness*. The new state is then calculated as follows.

Definition 6. When transition t fires from marking μ, the new marking μ' is given as follows: $\mu' = (\mu - {}^\bullet t) \cup t^\bullet$.   □

Note that since we assume contact-freeness, a self-loop will not be enabled. The behaviour of a Petri net is described in term of *runs*.

Definition 7. A *run* of a Petri net is a finite or infinite sequence of markings and transitions

$$\sigma = \mu_0 \xrightarrow{t_0} \mu_1 \xrightarrow{t_1} \cdots \xrightarrow{t_{n-1}} \mu_n \xrightarrow{t_n} \cdots$$

such that μ_0 is the initial marking of the net, $t_i \in enabled(\mu_i)$ for any i $(i \geq 0)$, and that $\mu_i = (\mu_{i-1} - {}^\bullet t_{i-1}) \cup t_{i-1}^\bullet$ for any i $(i \geq 1)$.   □

4   Existential Consistency Checking

In this section, we consider the existential consistency checking of Petri nets for scenario-based specifications represented by MSCs. The existential consistency checking problem is to check if a scenario described by a given MSC must happen during a Petri net run, or that any forbidden scenario described by a given MSC never happens during a Petri net run, which is depicted in fig. 3.

Fig. 3. Existential Consistency Checking

Now we define formally the existential consistency checking problem. Let $D = (P, E, M, L, V)$ be an MSC, N be a Petri net, and σ be a run of N of the form $\mu_0 \xrightarrow{t_0} \mu_1 \xrightarrow{t_1} \cdots \xrightarrow{t_{n-1}} \mu_n \xrightarrow{t_n} \mu_{n+1}$. For any subsequence σ_1 in σ of the form $\sigma_1 = \mu_i \xrightarrow{t_i} \mu_{i+1} \xrightarrow{t_{i+1}} \cdots \xrightarrow{t_{j-1}} \mu_j \xrightarrow{t_j} \mu_{j+1}$ $(0 \leq i < j \leq n)$, since each transition t_k is labelled with an event $\varphi(t_k)$ $(i \leq k \leq j)$, we get a sequence τ of events: $\tau = \varphi(t_i) \hat{\ } \varphi(t_{i+1}) \hat{\ } \ldots \hat{\ } \varphi(t_j)$. By removing any $\varphi(t_k)$ $(i \leq k \leq j)$ from τ which is not corresponding to the send or receive for a message in M, we get an event sequence $\tau_1 = e_0 \hat{\ } e_1 \hat{\ } \ldots \hat{\ } e_m$ $(m \leq j - i + 1)$. If τ_1 is a message trail of D, then we say that a scenario described by D *occurs* in the run σ, and that σ_1 is an *image* of D in σ. If τ_1 is a message trail of D, $\varphi(t_i) = e_0$, and $\varphi(t_j) = e_m$, then we say that σ_1 is an *exact image* of D. For a Petri net N, for an MSC D, the existential consistency checking problem is to check if there is a run of N where a scenario described by D occurs.

We know that for a Petri net N, there could be infinite runs, and the number of the runs could be infinite. In the following we show how to solve the problem based on the investigation of a finite set of finite runs.

For any Petri net N, for any MSC $D = (P, E, M, L, V)$, let $\Delta(N, D)$ be the set of the runs of N which are of the form

$$\sigma = \mu_0 \xrightarrow{t_0} \mu_1 \xrightarrow{t_1} \cdots \xrightarrow{t_{m-1}} \mu_m \xrightarrow{t_m} \cdots \xrightarrow{t_{n-1}} \mu_n \xrightarrow{t_n} \mu_{n+1},$$

where

- all μ_i $(0 \leq i \leq m)$ are distinct;
- $\mu_m \xrightarrow{t_m} \mu_{m+1} \xrightarrow{t_{m+1}} \cdots \xrightarrow{t_{n-1}} \mu_n \xrightarrow{t_n} \mu_{n+1}$ is an exact image of D; and
- for any μ_i and μ_j $(m < i < j < n)$, if there is not any $t_k (i \leq k \leq j)$ such that $\varphi(t_k) = \phi(e)$ $(e \in E)$ then $\mu_i \neq \mu_j$.

It is clear that the number of the runs in $\Delta(N, D)$ is finite, and that each run in $\Delta(N, D)$ is finite.

Theorem 1. Let N be a Petri net, and D be an MSC. Then there is a run of N where a scenario described by D occurs if and only if $\Delta(N, D) \neq \emptyset$. □

```
currentpath := ⟨μ₀⟩;
repeat
    node := the last node of currentpath;
    if node has no new successive node
    then delete the last node of currentpath
    else begin
            node := a new successive node of node;
            if node is such that the run corresponding to currentpath
                is in Δ(N, D)
            then return true;
            if node is such that the run corresponding to currentpath
                is a prefix for Δ(N, D)
            then append node to currentpath;
        end
until currentpath = ⟨⟩;
return false.
```

Fig. 4. Algorithm for existential consistency checking

For a Petri net N, for an MSC D, a run σ of N is a *prefix* for $\Delta(N, D)$ if it may be extended into a run which is in $\Delta(N, D)$, i.e. there could be a sequence σ_1 of markings and transitions such that $\sigma \char`^ \sigma_1$ is in $\Delta(N, D)$. Based on the above theorem, we can develop an algorithm to check the existential consistency of a Petri net $N = (P, T, F, \mu_0)$ for an MSC D (see fig. 4). The algorithm traverses the state space of N in a depth first manner starting from the initial node μ_0. The path in the state space that we have so far traversed is stored in the list variable *currentpath*. For each new marking that we discover, we first check whether it is such that the run corresponding to *currentpath* is in $\Delta(N, D)$. If yes, then it means that a scenario described by D must happen during N runs, and we are done. Then we check if the new marking that we discover is such that the run corresponding to *currentpath* is a prefix for $\Delta(N, D)$. If yes, then we add the new marking to the current path and start the search from it, otherwise we backtrack. If no run is discovered during the search which is in $\Delta(N, D)$, then it means that any forbidden scenario described by D never happens during N runs. The complexity of the algorithm is proportional to the number of the prefixes for $\Delta(N, D)$ and to the size of the longest prefix for $\Delta(N, D)$.

5   Mandatory Consistency Checking

In this section, we consider the mandatory consistency checking of Petri nets for scenario-based specifications represented by MSCs. The mandatory consistency requires that if a reference scenario described by the given MSCs occurs during a Petri net run, it must adhere to a scenario described by the other given MSC. We consider the following three kinds of the mandatory consistency which are depicted in fig. 5:

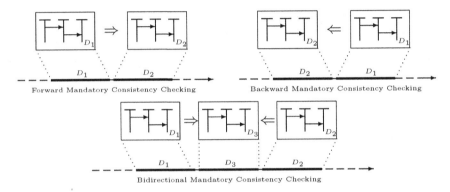

Fig. 5. Mandatory Consistency Checking

- **forward mandatory consistency:** if a reference scenario described by a given MSC D_1 occurs during a Petri net run, then a scenario described by the other given MSC D_2 must follow immediately;
- **backward mandatory consistency:** if a reference scenario described by a given MSC D_1 occurs during a Petri net run, then it must follow immediately from a scenario described by the other given MSC D_2; and
- **bidirectional mandatory consistency:** if a reference scenario described by a given MSC D_1 occurs during a Petri net run and a reference scenario described by another given MSC D_2 follows, then in between these two scenarios, a scenario described by the third given MSC D_3 must occur exactly.

5.1   Forward Mandatory Consistency Checking

For the forward mandatory consistency checking, a scenario-based specification, denoted by $\mathcal{S}_F(D_1, D_2)$, consists of two given MSCs D_1 and D_2, which requires that if a scenario described by D_1 occurs in a run of a Petri net, then a scenario described by D_2 follows immediately (see fig. 5).

The satisfaction problem of a Petri net N for a scenario-based specification $\mathcal{S}_F(D_1, D_2)$ is defined formally as follows. Let $D_2 = (P_2, E_2, M_2, L_2, V_2)$. N satisfies $\mathcal{S}_F(D_1, D_2)$ if any run σ of N of the form

$$\sigma = \mu_0 \xrightarrow{t_0} \mu_1 \xrightarrow{t_1} \cdots \xrightarrow{t_{n-1}} \mu_n \xrightarrow{t_n} \mu_{n+1}$$

satisfies the following condition:

- if there is a subsequence σ_1 in σ of the form

$$\sigma_1 = \mu_i \xrightarrow{t_i} \mu_{i+1} \xrightarrow{t_{i+1}} \cdots \xrightarrow{t_{j-1}} \mu_j \xrightarrow{t_j} \mu_{j+1} \ (0 \leq i < j \leq n)$$

which is an exact image of D_1, then for any subsequence σ_2 in σ of the form

$$\sigma_2 = \mu_{j+1} \xrightarrow{t_{j+1}} \mu_{j+2} \xrightarrow{t_{j+2}} \cdots \xrightarrow{t_{k-1}} \mu_k \xrightarrow{t_k} \mu_{k+1} \ (j < k \leq n)$$

where the number of μ_l $(j < l \leq k)$ satisfying $\varphi(t_l) = \phi(e)$ $(e \in E_2)$ is $|E_2|$, it is an image of D_2.

Now we try to solve the verification problem based on the investigation of a finite set of finite runs. For any Petri net N, for any scenario-based specification $\mathcal{S}_F(D_1, D_2)$ where $D_1 = (P_1, E_1, M_1, L_1, V_1)$ and $D_2 = (P_2, E_2, M_2, L_2, V_2)$, let $\Delta(N, \mathcal{S}_F(D_1, D_2))$ be the set of the runs of N which are of the form

$$\mu_0 \xrightarrow{t_0} \mu_1 \xrightarrow{t_1} \cdots \xrightarrow{t_{k-1}} \mu_k \xrightarrow{t_k} \cdots \xrightarrow{t_{m-1}} \mu_m \xrightarrow{t_m} \mu_{m+1} \xrightarrow{t_{m+1}} \cdots \xrightarrow{t_{n-1}} \mu_n \xrightarrow{t_n} \mu_{n+1} \,,$$

where

- all μ_i $(0 \leq i \leq k)$ are distinct;
- $\mu_k \xrightarrow{t_k} \mu_{k+1} \xrightarrow{t_{k+1}} \cdots \xrightarrow{t_{m-1}} \mu_m \xrightarrow{t_m} \mu_{m+1}$ is an exact image of D_1;
- for any μ_i and μ_j $(k < i < j < m)$, if there is not any $t_l (i \leq l \leq j)$ such that $\varphi(t_l) = \phi(e)$ $(e \in E_1)$ then $\mu_i \neq \mu_j$;
- the number of μ_i $(m < i \leq n)$ satisfying $\varphi(t_i) = \phi(e)$ $(e \in E_2)$ is $|E_2|$;
- there are $e \in E_2$ such that $\varphi(t_n) = \phi(e)$; and
- for any μ_i and μ_j $(m < i < j < n)$, if there is not any $t_l (i \leq l \leq j)$ such that $\varphi(t_l) = \phi(e)$ $(e \in E_2)$ then $\mu_i \neq \mu_j$.

For any $\sigma \in \Delta(N, \mathcal{S}_F(D_1, D_2))$ of the above form, we call the subsequence $\mu_{m+1} \xrightarrow{t_{m+1}} \mu_{m+2} \xrightarrow{t_{m+2}} \cdots \xrightarrow{t_{n-1}} \mu_n \xrightarrow{t_n} \mu_{n+1}$ by the *last segment* of σ.

Theorem 2. A Petri net N satisfies a scenario-based specification $\mathcal{S}_F(D_1, D_2)$ if and only if for any run of N which is in $\Delta(N, \mathcal{S}_F(D_1, D_2))$, its last segment is an image of D_2. □

For a Petri net N, for a scenario-based specification $\mathcal{S}_F(D_1, D_2)$, a run σ of N is a *prefix* for $\Delta(N, \mathcal{S}_F(D_1, D_2))$ if it may be extended into a run which is in

```
currentpath := ⟨μ₀⟩;
repeat
    node := the last node of currentpath;
    if node has no new successive node
    then delete the last node of currentpath
    else begin
            node := a new successive node of node;
            if node is such that the run corresponding to currentpath
                is in Δ(N, 𝒮_F(D₁, D₂))
            then
              begin
                check if the run corresponding to currentpath is such that
                its last segment is an image of D₂;
                if no then return false;
              end;
            if node is such that the run corresponding to currentpath
                is a prefix for Δ(N, 𝒮_F(D₁, D₂))
            then append node to currentpath;
         end
until currentpath = ⟨⟩;
return true.
```

Fig. 6. Algorithm for forward mandatory consistency checking

$\Delta(N, \mathcal{S}_F(D_1, D_2))$, i.e. there could be a sequence σ_1 of markings and transitions such that $\sigma \hat{\ } \sigma_1$ is in $\Delta(N, \mathcal{S}_F(D_1, D_2))$. Based on Theorem 2, we can develop an algorithm to check if a Petri net $N = (P, T, F, \mu_0)$ satisfies a scenario-based specification $\mathcal{S}_F(D_1, D_2)$ (see fig. 6). The algorithm traverses the state space of N in a depth first manner starting from the initial node μ_0. The path in the state space that we have so far traversed is stored in the list variable *currentpath*. For each new marking that we discover, we first check whether it is such that the run corresponding to *currentpath* is in $\Delta(N, \mathcal{S}_F(D_1, D_2))$. If so, we check if the run corresponding to *currentpath* is such that its last segment is an image of D_2. If no, then it means that N does not satisfy $\mathcal{S}_F(D_1, D_2)$, and we are done. Then we check if the new marking that we discover is such that the run corresponding to *currentpath* is a prefix for $\Delta(N, \mathcal{S}_F(D_1, D_2))$. If yes, then we add the new marking to the current path and start the search from it, otherwise we backtrack. The complexity of the algorithm is proportional to the number of the prefixes for $\Delta(N, \mathcal{S}_F(D_1, D_2))$ and to the size of the longest prefix for $\Delta(N, \mathcal{S}_F(D_1, D_2))$.

5.2 Backward Mandatory Consistency Checking

For the backward mandatory consistency checking, a scenario-based specification, denoted by $\mathcal{S}_B(D_1, D_2)$, consists of two given MSCs D_1 and D_2, which requires that if a scenario described by D_1 occurs in a run of a Petri net, then it must follow immediately from a scenario described by D_2 (see fig. 5).

The satisfaction problem of a Petri net N for a scenario-based specification $\mathcal{S}_B(D_1, D_2)$ is defined formally as follows. N satisfies $\mathcal{S}_B(D_1, D_2)$ if any run σ of N of the form $\sigma = \mu_0 \xrightarrow{t_0} \mu_1 \xrightarrow{t_1} \cdots \xrightarrow{t_{n-1}} \mu_n \xrightarrow{t_n} \mu_{n+1}$ satisfies the following condition:

- if there is a subsequence σ_1 in σ of the form

$$\sigma_1 = \mu_i \xrightarrow{t_i} \mu_{i+1} \xrightarrow{t_{i+1}} \cdots \xrightarrow{t_{j-1}} \mu_j \xrightarrow{t_j} \mu_{j+1} \ (0 \le i < j \le n)$$

which is an exact image of D_1, then there is a subsequence σ_2 in σ of the form

$$\sigma_2 = \mu_k \xrightarrow{t_k} \mu_{k+1} \xrightarrow{t_{k+1}} \cdots \xrightarrow{t_{i-2}} \mu_{i-1} \xrightarrow{t_{i-1}} \mu_i \ (0 \le k < i)$$

which is an image of D_2.

Now we try to solve the verification problem based on the investigation of a finite set of finite runs. For any Petri net N, for any scenario-based specification $\mathcal{S}_B(D_1, D_2)$ where $D_1 = (P_1, E_1, M_1, L_1, V_1)$ and $D_2 = (P_2, E_2, M_2, L_2, V_2)$, let $\Delta(N, \mathcal{S}_B(D_1, D_2))$ be the set of the runs of N which are of the form

$$\mu_0 \xrightarrow{t_0} \mu_1 \xrightarrow{t_1} \cdots \xrightarrow{t_{k-1}} \mu_k \xrightarrow{t_k} \cdots \xrightarrow{t_{m-1}} \mu_m \xrightarrow{t_m} \cdots \xrightarrow{t_{n-1}} \mu_n \xrightarrow{t_n} \mu_{n+1} ,$$

where

- $\mu_m \xrightarrow{t_m} \mu_{m+1} \xrightarrow{t_{m+1}} \cdots \xrightarrow{t_{n-1}} \mu_n \xrightarrow{t_n} \mu_{n+1}$ is an exact image of D_1;
- for any μ_i and μ_j ($m < i < j < n$), if there is not any $t_l (i \le l \le j)$ such that $\varphi(t_l) = \phi(e) \ (e \in E_1)$ then $\mu_i \ne \mu_j$;
- for any μ_i and μ_j ($0 \le i < j < m$), if there is not any $t_l (i \le l \le j)$ such that $\varphi(t_l) = \phi(e) \ (e \in E_2)$ then $\mu_i \ne \mu_j$; and
- if there is k ($0 \le k < m$) such that the number of μ_l ($k \le l < m$) satisfying $\varphi(t_l) = \phi(e) \ (e \in E_2)$ is $|E_2|$, then all μ_i ($0 \le i \le k$) are distinct.

For any $\sigma \in \Delta(N, \mathcal{S}_B(D_1, D_2))$ of the above form, we call the subsequences of the form $\mu_i \xrightarrow{t_i} \mu_{i+1} \xrightarrow{t_{i+1}} \cdots \xrightarrow{t_{m-1}} \mu_m$ ($0 \le i < m$) by the *front segments* of σ.

Theorem 3. A Petri net N satisfies a scenario-based specification $\mathcal{S}_B(D_1, D_2)$ if and only if for any run σ of N which is in $\Delta(N, \mathcal{S}_B(D_1, D_2))$, there is a front segment of σ which is an image of D_2. □

For a Petri net N, for a scenario-based specification $\mathcal{S}_B(D_1, D_2)$, a run σ of N is a *prefix* for $\Delta(N, \mathcal{S}_B(D_1, D_2))$ if it may be extended into a run which is in $\Delta(N, \mathcal{S}_B(D_1, D_2))$, i.e. there could be a sequence σ_1 of markings and transitions such that $\sigma \hat{} \sigma_1$ is in $\Delta(N, \mathcal{S}_B(D_1, D_2))$. Based on Theorem 3, we can develop an algorithm to check if a Petri net $N = (P, T, F, \mu_0)$ satisfies a scenario-based specification $\mathcal{S}_B(D_1, D_2)$ (see fig. 7). The structure of the algorithm is the same as the one of the algorithm depicted in fig. 6. The complexity of the algorithm is proportional to the number of the prefixes for $\Delta(N, \mathcal{S}_B(D_1, D_2))$ and to the size of the longest prefix for $\Delta(N, \mathcal{S}_B(D_1, D_2))$.

```
currentpath := ⟨μ₀⟩;
repeat
     node := the last node of currentpath;
     if node has no new successive node
     then delete the last node of currentpath
     else begin
              node := a new successive node of node;
              if node is such that the run corresponding to currentpath
                   is in Δ(N, 𝒮_B(D₁, D₂))
              then
                begin
                   check if the run corresponding to currentpath is such that
                   a front segment is an image of D₂;
                   if no then return false;
                end;
              if node is such that the run corresponding to currentpath
                   is a prefix for Δ(N, 𝒮_B(D₁, D₂))
              then append node to currentpath;
         end
until currentpath = ⟨⟩;
return true.
```

Fig. 7. Algorithm for backward mandatory consistency checking

5.3 Bidirectional Mandatory Consistency Checking

For the bidirectional mandatory consistency checking, a scenario-based specification, denoted by $\mathcal{S}_D(D_1, D_2, D_3)$, consists of three given MSCs D_1, D_2, and D_3, which requires that if a scenario described by D_1 occurs in a run of a Petri net and a scenario described by D_2 follows, then the run segment between these two scenarios must be exactly corresponding to a scenario described by D_3 (see fig. 5).

The satisfaction problem of a Petri net N for a scenario-based specification $\mathcal{S}_D(D_1, D_2, D_3)$ is defined formally as follows. N satisfies $\mathcal{S}_D(D_1, D_2, D_3)$ if for any run σ of N of the form

$$\mu_0 \xrightarrow{t_0} \mu_1 \xrightarrow{t_1} \cdots \xrightarrow{t_{k-1}} \mu_k \xrightarrow{t_k} \cdots \xrightarrow{t_{l-1}} \mu_l \xrightarrow{t_l} \cdots \xrightarrow{t_{m-1}} \mu_m \xrightarrow{t_m} \cdots \xrightarrow{t_{n-1}} \mu_n$$

where all μ_i $(l \leq i \leq m)$ are distinct, $\mu_k \xrightarrow{t_k} \mu_{k+1} \xrightarrow{t_{k+1}} \cdots \xrightarrow{t_{l-1}} \mu_l$ is an exact image of D_1, and $\mu_m \xrightarrow{t_m} \mu_{m+1} \xrightarrow{t_{m+1}} \cdots \xrightarrow{t_{n-1}} \mu_n$ is an exact image of D_2, the following condition holds:

– if there is no subsequence $\mu_i \xrightarrow{t_i} \mu_{i+1} \xrightarrow{t_{i+1}} \cdots \xrightarrow{t_{j-1}} \mu_j$ $(l \leq i < j \leq m)$ which is an image of D_1 or D_2, then $\mu_l \xrightarrow{t_l} \mu_{l+1} \xrightarrow{t_{l+1}} \cdots \xrightarrow{t_{m-1}} \mu_m$ is an image of D_3.

Now we try to solve the verification problem based on the investigation of a finite set of finite runs. For a Petri net N, for a scenario-based specification

```
currentpath := ⟨μ₀⟩;
repeat
    node := the last node of currentpath;
    if node has no new successive node
    then delete the last node of currentpath
    else begin
            node := a new successive node of node;
            if node is such that the run corresponding to currentpath
                is in Δ(N, S_D(D₁, D₂, D₃))
            then
              begin
                check if the run corresponding to currentpath is such that
                its middle segment is an image of D₃;
                if no then return false;
              end;
            if node is such that the run corresponding to currentpath
                is a prefix for Δ(N, S_D(D₁, D₂, D₃))
            then append node to currentpath;
        end
until currentpath = ⟨⟩;
return true.
```

Fig. 8. Algorithm for bidirectional mandatory consistency checking

$S_D(D_1, D_2, D_3)$ where $D_1 = (P_1, E_1, M_1, L_1, V_1)$ and $D_2 = (P_2, E_2, M_2, L_2, V_2)$, let $\Delta(N, S_D(D_1, D_2, D_3))$ be the set of the runs of N which are of the form

$$\mu_0 \xrightarrow{t_0} \mu_1 \xrightarrow{t_1} \cdots \xrightarrow{t_{k-1}} \mu_k \xrightarrow{t_k} \cdots \xrightarrow{t_{l-1}} \mu_l \xrightarrow{t_l} \cdots \xrightarrow{t_{m-1}} \mu_m \xrightarrow{t_m} \cdots \xrightarrow{t_{n-1}} \mu_n$$

where

- all μ_i $(0 \leq i \leq k)$ are distinct;
- all μ_i $(l \leq i \leq m)$ are distinct;
- $\mu_k \xrightarrow{t_k} \mu_{k+1} \xrightarrow{t_{k+1}} \cdots \xrightarrow{t_{l-1}} \mu_l$ is an exact image of D_1;
- for any μ_i and μ_j $(k < i < j < l)$, if there is not any $t_a(i \leq a \leq j)$ such that $\varphi(t_a) = \phi(e)$ $(e \in E_1)$ then $\mu_i \neq \mu_j$;
- $\mu_m \xrightarrow{t_m} \mu_{m+1} \xrightarrow{t_{m+1}} \cdots \xrightarrow{t_{n-1}} \mu_n$ is an exact image of D_2;
- for any μ_i and μ_j $(m < i < j < n)$, if there is not any $t_a(i \leq a \leq j)$ such that $\varphi(t_a) = \phi(e)$ $(e \in E_2)$ then $\mu_i \neq \mu_j$; and
- there is no subsequence $\mu_i \xrightarrow{t_i} \mu_{i+1} \xrightarrow{t_{i+1}} \cdots \xrightarrow{t_{j-1}} \mu_j$ $(l \leq i < j \leq m)$ which is an image of D_1 or D_2.

For any $\sigma \in \Delta(N, S_D(D_1, D_2, D_3))$ of the above form, we call the subsequence of the form $\mu_l \xrightarrow{t_l} \mu_{l+1} \xrightarrow{t_{l+1}} \cdots \xrightarrow{t_{m-2}} \mu_{m-1} \xrightarrow{t_{m-1}} \mu_m$ by the *middle segment* of σ.

Theorem 4. Let N be a Petri net. N satisfies a scenario-based specification $S_D(D_1, D_2, D_3)$ if and only if for any run of N which is in $\Delta(N, S_D(D_1, D_2, D_3))$, its middle segment is an image of D_3.   □

For a Petri net N, for a scenario-based specification $\mathcal{S}_D(D_1, D_2, D_3)$, a run σ of N is a *prefix* for $\Delta(N, \mathcal{S}_D(D_1, D_2, D_3))$ if it may be extended into a run which is in $\Delta(N, \mathcal{S}_D(D_1, D_2, D_3))$, i.e. there could be a sequence σ_1 of markings and transitions such that $\sigma^\wedge\sigma_1$ is in $\Delta(N, \mathcal{S}_D(D_1, D_2, D_3))$). Based on Theorem 4, we can develop an algorithm to check if a Petri net $N = (P, T, F, \mu_0)$ satisfies a scenario-based specification $\mathcal{S}_D(D_1, D_2, D_3)$ (see fig. 8). The structure of the algorithm is the same as the one of the algorithm depicted in fig. 6. The complexity of the algorithm is proportional to the number of the prefixes for $\Delta(N, \mathcal{S}_D(D_1, D_2, D_3))$ and to the size of the longest run in $\Delta(N, \mathcal{S}_D(D_1, D_2, D_3))$.

6   Related Work and Conclusion

In this paper, we solve the consistency checking problems of concurrent system designs modelled by Petri nets for scenario-based specifications expressed by MSCs. The algorithms we present can be used to check if a scenario described by a given MSC must happen during a Petri net run, that any forbidden scenario described by a given MSC never happens during a Petri net run, and if a Petri net satisfies a mandatory consistency specification expressed by MSCs which requires that if a reference scenario described by the given MSCs occurs during the Petri net run, it must adhere to a scenario described by the other given MSC.

To our knowledge, there has been a lack of publication on consistency checking of Petri nets for scenario-based specifications expressed by MSCs. There has been work on checking the state-transition graphs for the properties expressed by temporal logics (CTL, LTL)[10]. It is well known that the state-transition graphs and the Petri nets considered in this paper can be interchangeable, and even there exists an automatic translation of UML statecharts and sequence diagrams [11] into Generalized Stochastic Petri Nets [12], which means that theoretically the problems considered in this paper can be solved by converting to the corresponding formalisms. However, on the one hand, converting from one formalism to the other often leads to a significant enlargement of the state space. On the other hand, the specifications expressed by MSCs are much more acceptable for the industry than the ones expressed by temporal logic. Work close to our own is described in [13] where a tool, HUGO, is designed to check if the interactions expressed by an UML collaboration diagram can indeed be realized by a set of UML state machines in which state machines are compiled into SPIN [14] input model and collaboration diagrams are translated into sets of *Büchi* automata, and SPIN is called for the verification. Compared to that work, the specifications expressed by MSCs considered in this paper are more expressive, and our approach leads to direct and efficient implementation. Live sequence charts [15, 16] is a more expressive formalism to describe the mandatory consistency specifications considered in this paper, but it is less popular in the industry.

The algorithms presented in this paper have been implemented in a tool prototype. The tool is implemented in Java, and its graphical interface allows the users to construct, edit, and analyze MSCs and Petri nets interactively. The tool interface can also read .mdl files of UML sequence diagrams in Rational Rose.

Based on the work in this paper, we are solving the timing consistency checking problem of time Petri nets [17] for scenario-based specifications expressed by MSCs with timing constraints, which requires that if a scenario described by a given MSC occurs during a time Petri net run, the timing constraints enforced to the MSC must be satisfied.

References

1. ITU-T. Recommendation Z.120. ITU - Telecommunication Standardization Sector, Geneva, Switzerland, May 1996.
2. J.L. Peterson. *Petri Nets Theory and the Modeling of Systems.* Prentice-Hall, N.J., 1981.
3. Olaf Kluge. Modelling a Railway Crossing with Message Sequence Charts and Petri Nets. In H.Ehrig et al.(Eds.): *Petri Technology for Communication-Based Systems - Advance in Petri Nets*, LNCS 2472, Springer, 2003, pp.197-218.
4. van der Aalst, W.M.P. Interorganizational Workflows: An Approach based on Message Sequence Charts and Petri Nets. In *Systems Analysis - Modelling - Simulation*, Vol.34, No.3, pages 335-367. 1999.
5. Uwe Rueppel, Udo F. Meissner, and Steffen Greb. A Petri Net based Method for Distributed Process Modelling in Structural Engineering. In *Proc. International Conference on Computing in Civil and Building Engineering*, 2004.
6. Constance L. Heitmeyer, Ralph D. Jeffords, and Bruce G. Labaw. Comparing Different Approaches for Specifying and Verifying Real-Time Systems. In *Proc. 10_{th} IEEE Workshop on Real-Time Operating Systems and Software*. New York, 1993. pp.122-129.
7. Doron A. Peled. *Software Reliability Methods.* Springer, 2001.
8. Rajeev Alur, Gerard J. Holzmann, Doron Peled. An Analyzer for Message Sequence Charts. In *Software-Concepts and Tools* (1996) 17: 70-77.
9. P.B. Ladkin and S. Leue. Interpreting Message Flow Graphs. In *Formal Aspects of Computing*, 7(5):473-509, 1995.
10. Edmund M. Clarke, Jr. Orna Grumberg, and Doron A. Peled. *Model Checking.* The MIT Press, 2000.
11. J. Rumbaugh and I. Jacobson and G. Booch. *The Unified Modeling Language Reference Manual*, Addison-Wesley, 1999.
12. Simona Bernardi, Susanna Donatelli, and José Merseguer. From UML sequence diagrams and statecharts to analysable petri net models. In *Proceedings of the third international workshop on Software and performance*, ACM Press, 2002, pp.35-45.
13. Timm Schafer, Alexander Knapp, and Stephan Merz. Model Checking UML State Machines and Collaborations. In *Electronic Notes in Theoretical Computer Science* 55, No.3, 2001.
14. G.J. Holzmann. *The SPIN Model Checker, Primer and Reference Manual*, Addison-Wesley, 2003.
15. Werner Damm and David Harel. LSCs: Breathing life into message sequence charts. In *Formal Methods in System Design*, 19(1):45-80, 2001.
16. Yves Bontemps and Patrick Heymans. Turning High-Level Live Sequence Charts into Automata. In *Proceedings of Workshop: Scenarios and State-Machines*, 2002.
17. B. Berthomieu and M. Diaz. Modelling and verification of time dependent systems using time Petri nets. In *IEEE Transactions on Software Engineering*, 17(3):259–273, March 1991.

SDL Code Generation for Open Systems

Joachim Fischer[1], Toby Neumann[1], and Anders Olsen[2]

[1] Humboldt-Universität zu Berlin,
Institut für Informatik,
Unter den Linden 6,
10099 Berlin, Germany
{fischer, tneumann}@informatik.hu-berlin.de
[2] Cinderella ApS,
Moselodden 5,
2750 Ballerup, Denmark
anders@cinderella.dk

Abstract. SDL claims to be a language for the description of open systems, allowing the integration of other components into an SDL system and that of an SDL system as a mere component into a greater unit. Indeed, SDL provides the possibility for the interaction of a system with its environment. Signals can be exchanged with the environment and in addition the developer may hide arbitrary actions inside external procedures.

Code generators are widely in use to produce runnable code from an SDL system description, decreasing faults and increasing flexibility. But changes in or changes of the communication protocol to the environment still force a code generator to be adapted, costing precious resources.

This paper presents an automated code generation from SDL to C++, which enables the flexible connection of various communication protocols without changing the code generator or adding code manually. A runtime library contains all necessary means for communication to the environment, an approach which has been tested using CORBA and Web Services, but could be adapted easily to arbitrary protocols.

Problems with the choice of appropriate encodings seem to be solved with the recommendation Z.104, which enables the specification of encodings already in the SDL-2000 system. All results presented in this paper are based on the experience gained in practice during several projects using Cinderella SITE.

1 Introduction

SDL is well suited to design complex autonomous systems. A design progression is supported over several levels of refinement and a concluding automated code generation yielding executables is available at least for older versions of the language. But in the domain of information technologies, how autonomous can a system nowadays possibly be? Such a system consists of physically distributed components, often mobile ones, which only used together to deliver a particular

A. Prinz, R. Reed, and J. Reed (Eds.): SDL 2005, LNCS 3530, pp. 313–322, 2005.
© Springer-Verlag Berlin Heidelberg 2005

service. This requires heavy communication between the separated parts or with central control units.

If the description of a system stems from one source, that is, if it has been developed in one piece by one company, it may be regarded as autonomous enough and leaves only the problem of a later distribution. But far more commonly the necessity is implied to reuse components already there, possibly originating from another manufacturer. In the worst case these parts have been described with a technique different from SDL or even without using any formal technique at all. In addition, the system which is intended to be created may be in itself just a component of a larger unit. Such a sub-system not only has to use particular services from the environment, it also has to offer its own services to the outside (the encompassing system).

SDL provides several language features which enable a system to interchange information with the environment. Data can be delivered to the system as well as originating from it, and external code can be invoked directly. These means for describing interaction with the environment are of particular interest when it comes to automated code generation. Then the question arises whether the system description contains all the information necessary to generate an executable which neatly fits into the desired environment without the need to manually edit the code, to annotate the specification or to fall back to other tricks.

For many years already, automated code generation is one of the main fields at the chair of systems analysis at Humboldt-Universität zu Berlin. This resulted in the SDL compiler tools called SITE which have been successfully employed in the development of various protocol stacks for IN switches at Siemens AG. In this context the integration of SITE with the graphical tool Cinderella SDL (called Cinderella SITE) proved to be prosperous. The aspiration is for new levels of automation to make the process of software development controllable for more complex and dynamic arrangements.

The ongoing standardization of formal languages gives us more powerful and accurate means to express the desired interrelations. For instance, in the context of embedding a system into its environment, the recently published recommendation Z.104 (an extension to SDL) now enables the signal encoding requirements to be described explicitly in SDL [1].

This document is organized as follows. Section 2 reports on the state of the SDL code generation at Humboldt-Universität in general and it sketches structure and strategy of the code generator SITE. Section 3 deals with the problem encountered when executables should be produced from SDL descriptions to fit into interactive environments, and lists and evaluates several approaches. Then follows section 4, which presents the new approach chosen with SITE [2] to provide flexible inter-system communication. Admittedly, that is shown to not being the general solution. Section 5 attempts to summarize the requirements on a method that could provide all the necessary means to enable fully automatic code generation with respect to distribution and integration. A conclusion finalizes the paper.

2   The SDL Code Generator SITE

The code generator SITE is the result of many years of development in the area of automated code generation from SDL. The tool processes SDL-96 [3] and ASN.1-88 [4] in combined use [5] in textual notation. It consists of three components, one of which analyzes the syntax, one analyzes the static semantics and one generates C++ code. Accepting textual input allows the tool to be used both on the command line and in combination with other applications. Previously SITE has been integrated into Cinderella SDL [6]. That combination, called Cinderella SITE, is able to generate executables from graphical SDL specifications.

The code generated from an SDL specification describes a rather abstract level which shows strong similarities to SDL entities. It is based on classes and macros defined in a runtime library, which provides the particular mechanisms inherent to various SDL concepts. There we find base classes for the structural elements (such as package, system, block, process, process set and procedure); for signals; and for the data types of the package Predefined. Other classes will just be instantiated in the code to represent more simple entities, such as channel, signal route and gate. Figure 1 shows the mapping of some SDL entities to C++ classes and objects of the runtime library by example.

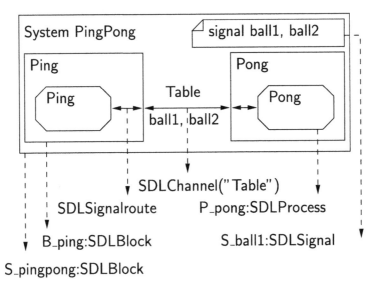

Fig. 1. SITE mapping of SDL entities to C++ classes and objects

The separation into generated code and underlying library is a common approach. There are several reasons for not generating complete code.

keep generated code small. The less code has to be compiled, the faster becomes the compilation; binding libraries is much faster. In addition, the code generator is easier to maintain since it contains fewer lines of output and operates on a higher level of code. The library is quite easy to maintain as well since the code is thus better organized than it possibly could be as mere text in a generator.

introduce an interface. Depending on the intended target environment, the generated code can be combined with an adapted or completely different runtime library. The code resulting from an SDL description always is the same. So the code generator never has to be touched and changes can be applied to the logical organized library.

The latest developments of SITE enable the same code resulting from one SDL specification to be linked with various communication libraries (variants of Selex, see section 4) to yield different executables. Each executable communicates with the environment using the technique determined by the respective library.

Recently, Cinderella SITE has provided another possibility to accomplish similar flexibility (see section 3.1). That approach defines an API which describes the interface to the environment. Arbitrary implementations of that interface in the form of dynamic libraries can be bound to the generated code, completely independent of the communication techniques supported by SITE, overriding them.

3   Interfaces of SDL Systems

Taking the final design step from a completed specification to its implementation, in particular by code generation, requires several parameters to be fixed which have no place on an abstract level. Some of them concern the detailed internal behaviour of the resulting system such as concurrency, internal signalling, timing, and process scheduling. Others can be regarded as independent from the internals. They determine how the system communicates with its environment, which communication protocol is used and which data encoding. These latter parameters are subject to the following inspection.

If an open SDL system, either as part of a decomposition or naturally open, is to be embedded into a concrete environment this usually means that the resulting target code must be combinable with implementations already there. SDL is a language for design and description on an abstract level and therefore it has no concepts to express implementation details. That raises the question whether SDL is well suited to address the communication issue. How could a neat integration of the generated code be obtained? Which possibilities are available and what are the disadvantages?

3.1   Ways for Connecting a System

The problem of integrating the code generated from an SDL system description is solved in every single case, somehow. Some ways are propagated and others could be imagined. In the following, several of them are briefly described and commented on.

Postprocessing the Generated Code. Automated code generation produces source code from an SDL description. It contains some empty classes or functions which the implementor completes manually. These functions form the interface between the generated code and the code which is specific to a platform or application. They could be used for instance to drive hardware gadgets, to manage the communication to remote hosts, or to integrate particular libraries.

This approach is sufficiently customizable and does not need support through SDL. But unfortunately, the implementor gets loaded with the burden of producing a highly complex part of the code himself. That is time consuming and error prone. In addition, similar work has to be done every time the SDL specification changes sufficiently.

Enriching the SDL Specification. An SDL description is augmented with special comments which yield control information for a particular code generator tool. Such comments could actually control the flow of code generation or simply are source code includes which are directly copied to the target code. Most of the tools provide such magic to ease the embedding, for instance the SDL to Java Translator [7] (SITE for other purposes, too). Thus a specification contains all the necessary information but is bound to a particular tool: the one which can interpret the bonus information correctly. In the worst case such enrichment of SDL makes the specification unreadable to other utilities (and maybe their users).

External Procedures. It is possible in SDL to leave functionality unspecified, to leave well defined holes in the specification. This is done by defining external procedures. They can be called like other procedures, but have no body attached. A C++ code generator would just generate the function declaration without the associated definition. The implementor gets the chance to insert arbitrary code in that place. Thus an algorithm (which might be intricate to describe in SDL) could be concisely expressed in some other source code – a recommended use [8].

But everything is left open to to the programmer. In particular, remote hosts could be accessed through some communication technique. But that is completely hidden from the SDL designer and conceals the danger of such a call. In the case of failure the entire system could be brought to a standstill in the middle of two states. It is hard to take into account such hidden communication. To limit the communication of agents to explicit signal exchange is a completely reasonable proposal [9].

Signals to the Environment. An SDL system may send signals to an unspecified environment and receive signals from there, too. In this way data may leave and enter the system at specified entry points, the gates. A code generator could treat all such occurrences of environment signals alike and transform them according to the the communication technique which has been chosen automatically or during configuration.

Such transmission of all signals to the outside is limited to one protocol, but requires neither changes in the SDL nor additional information. If different gates should use different transmission techniques the problem of binding additional information to SDL is there again. Anyway, explicitly exchanging signals with the environment extends the well-defined inner system communication and can therefore be considered to be a neat solution.

Remote Procedures. The name remote procedure may tempt us to consider this feature as a suitable means to define interfaces to remote systems. In fact a remote procedure can be exported and thus made public. But the semantic model explains such a definition to be just a shortcut for an additional signal exchange between importing and exporting agent which at each request is ready to execute the procedure and to deliver the result [10].

A code generator could absolutely create an function for every exported declaration, ignoring visibility rules and make it accessible from the outside. But still the meaning of the parameter data types would be undefined, and in addition it seems not to work the other way, accessing environment functionality.

The TAU tool seems to treat remote procedure like external procedures as described above and encourages the user to use the code generation that way.

Transforming the System. This approach uses both signals to the environment and external procedures in order to gain a flexible mechanism for communication. An SDL specification which uses signals to the environment is rewritten before the code generation. Thus the changes are completely hidden from the designer. An additional process is introduced which becomes the new endpoint of outgoing signals and the new source of signals from the environment. It uses some external procedures as an API to access a communication protocol. It depends on the implementation of the procedures which one that is.

Since the signature of the external procedures is always the same, these can be implemented beforehand and are compiled into a dynamic library, one for each communication protocol to support. One of these communication libraries can be bound to the code generated for the specification. The resulting executable will use the chosen technique for communication with the environment.

This choice can be done dynamically and also permits other implementations of the API. Admittedly, this solution is also limited to a particular tool (Cinderella SDL), and does not allow different protocols to be used for one system at a time.

4   A Runtime Library for Flexible Communication

In the final phase of system design it has to be decided how to distribute the system components physically. To make automated code generation possible the system can be decomposed into several correct SDL systems which communicate with each other via the environment. For such open systems the runtime library Selex, which is currently underlying the code generated by SITE, offers a transmission technique. Differing from the tool APIgen [11], which deals with similar problems using protocols as TCP for signal transport, Selex employs rather higher transmission mechanisms. That difference does not seem to have conceptual reasons, but stems from the field of application. Actually only

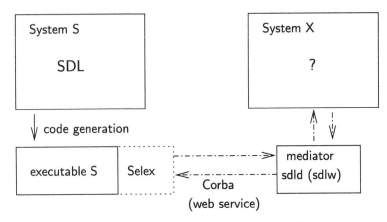

Fig. 2. Inter-system communication using Selex

two kinds of these higher level communication techniques have been tested: web services and Corba [12]. A web service is defined using WSDL [13] and actual messages transmitted as SOAP [14] (at least in the implementation used). Corba services are described using IDL [15].

Selex is the latest innovation to SITE. It defines a general interface using a standardized notation (depending on the communication technique desired) which describes the format of signals and how to send them. Selex implements that interface for the SDL system while the other side could be any peer using that interface. Multiple communication partners require a mediator to distribute the signals. Figure 2 gives a general idea of the signal flow when using Selex.

At the system boundary, SDL signals are mapped to the signal structures use by the outside communication and vice versa. During the mapping the SDL signal parameters, which are constrained to ASN.1 types, are encoded/decoded using one of the ASN.1 encoding rule sets.

This is an extract from the description of the general communication interface for systems. Variable **data** contains the parameters of SDL signals encoded by BER/PER [16, 17]. Every program which is able to call the operation **transfer_signal** can thus send a signal **name** to the generated SDL system which implements the IDL interface **CorbaSDLShellInterface**.

```
struct CorbaSDLSignalStruct {
  CorbaSDLSignalName                    name;
  CorbaSDLSignalData                    data;
};
interface CorbaSDLShellInterface {
  oneway void transfer_signal(in CorbaSDLSignalStruct signal);
}
```

A global variable decides about the encoding to use when exchanging signals with the environment. Either BER or PER can be chosen at program start. When using BER the parameters are simply encoded and sent. The tag/length/value encoding allows identification of the parameters even if some are left out. To find out which parameters have been sent when using PER, a bit field is prepended containing one bit for each parameter; if it is set the parameter is present.

There are some shortcomings in the Selex approach.

double encoding. Strictly, it should not be necessary to encode the signal parameters since the communication techniques use their own encoding. So the parameters are encoded twice. But otherwise the interface could not be general and would depend on the actual signal definitions. In that case somehow the two peers, the SDL system and its unknown partner, must have exchanged their interface definitions. The SDL signal parameters then need a mapping to the types of the interface description language (WSDL, IDL).

fixed encoding. A system can only use one of the encodings. In addition, the chosen encoding of the enclosing signal is proprietary. To improve usability implementing Z.104 seems to be a good choice.

single technique. Only one technique at a time can be used. It is not possible to have the system exchange signals via two different gates bound to different protocols. To enable such flexibility we come back to the need for a means by which additional information on communication can be specified in SDL.

5   Requirements for Smooth Integration

When it comes to the implementation of an SDL system it becomes obvious that additional information is needed to automate this final step of software development. We have to specify how the different components comprising the system are to be distributed onto physical nodes. These components require instructions how to communicate with each other and with other peers outside the scope of the specification. An open system without further need for distribution at least has to be connected to its intended communication partners and as such only is a special case of the scenario mentioned above. In general an SDL system is missing information at least about:

– which parts of a system belong together and make up a functional component,
– how to find the communication partners,
– which data description to use and which encoding. In fig. 3 some example protocols and encodings are shown.

The latter two often are not distinguished from another in a protocol description and therefore are mentioned together. When employing Z.104 for a system description ASN.1 could be specified to be used for the signal exchange along with one of its available encodings.

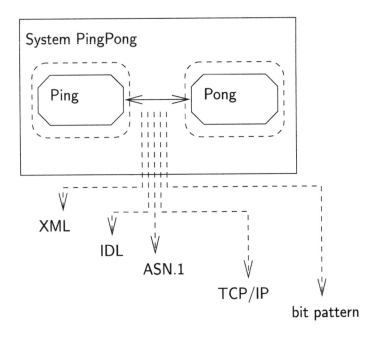

Fig. 3. Break system into components and choose protocol

6   Conclusion

Code generators like SITE and APIgen try to connect some of the missing information to the system but succeed only partially. Is that just more evidence that SDL is missing a vital power of expression? Should SDL be extended to provide the description of implementation aspects to support code generation and embedding? Possibly SDL should remain what is is – a language which is describing behaviour on an abstract level by interacting state machines.

In this paper we reported our experiences in automated code generation deriving C++ code from SDL-96 and ASN.1-88 specifications. The flexible approach of the generator SITE bases the code on a runtime library, the communication binding of which we showed to be more detailed. The conclusion is to confirm the suspicion that it was not possible to host all information in an SDL specification necessary for automated code generation. Recommendation Z.104 has pursued the way introducing additional concepts concerning the encoding of signals. One could be tempted to add in a similar approach other implementation details, too. But after some reasoning that seems not to be the way to go for an abstract description language. Rather, every language should be used for the purpose it is suited best. Tools for code generation surely could manage to gather missing information, but could do so in a more uniform way.

References

1. ITU-T Z.104: Encoding of SDL data. International Telecommunication Union (2004)
2. Schröder, R., Böhme, H., von Löwis, M.: SDL Integrated Tool Environment. Web site, Humboldt-Universität zu Berlin (1997-2003) http://www.informatik.hu-berlin.de/SITE/.
3. ITU-T Z.100: Specification and Description Language (SDL). International Telecommunication Union (1996)
4. ITU-T X.208: Specification of Abstract Syntax Notation One (ASN.1). International Telecommunication Union (1988)
5. ITU-T Z.105: SDL combined with ASN.1 modules. International Telecommunication Union (2003)
6. Cinderella I/S: Cinderella SDL. product (1995-2004) http://www.cinderella.dk.
7. Kavadias, C., Perrin, B., Kollias, V., Loupis, M.: Enhanced SDL Subset for the Design and Implementation of Java-Enabled Embedded Signalling Systems. In: SDL2003: System Design. LNCS 2708 (2003)
8. Weil, F., Weigert, T.: Guidelines for Using SDL in Product Development. In: SAM2004 System Analysis and Modeling LNCS 3319 (2005)
9. Kollias, V.D., Li, Q., Prinz, A., Skelton, W., Yiannakoulias, A., Moss, K.: Back To the Basics. In: System Analysis and Modeling: 4th International SDL and MSC Workshop. http://www.site.uottawa.ca/sam04/pres/Prinz.pdf
10. ITU-T Z.100: Specification and Description Language (SDL). International Telecommunication Union (2002)
11. Schaible, P., Gotzhein, R.: Development of Distributed Systems with SDL by Means of Formalized APIs. In: SDL2003: System Design LNCS 2708 (2003)
12. CORBA: Common Object Request Broker Architecture (CORBA/IIOP), Version 3.0.2. Object Management Group (2002) formal/2002-12-02.
13. W3C: Web Services Definition Language (WSDL). specification (2004) http://www.w3.org/TR/wsdl.
14. W3C: SOAP Version 1.2 Part 1: Messaging Framework. specification (2003) http://www.w3.org/TR/soap12-part1.
15. IDL: Interface Definition Language, Part of CORBA. Object Management Group (2002) formal/2002-06-07.
16. ITU-T X.690: ASN.1 Encoding Rules: Specification of Basic Encoding Rules (BER). International Telecommunication Union (1992)
17. ITU-T X.690: ASN.1 Encoding Rules: Specification of Packed Encoding Rules (PER). International Telecommunication Union (1992)

SDL Versus C Equivalence Checking

Malek Haroud[1] and Armin Biere[2]

[1] STMicroelectronics NV,
Advanced System Technology Group,
Champ-des-filles 39, 1228 Geneva, Switzerland
[2] Johannes Kepler University,
Institute for Formal Models and Verification,
Altenbergerstr. 69, 4040 Linz, Austria

Abstract. We present a tool that automatically checks the existence of a bisimulation relation between an SDL specification and the corresponding auto-generated C code. The tool has been used to verify part of the C implementation of a WiFi Medium Access Controller (IEEE 802.11) that has been derived from its original SDL specification using the Telelogic CAdvanced Code Generator.

1 Introduction

In embedded SW design, especially in the telecommunication field, the developer usually starts with a functional model written in SDL [1, 2, 3] or in any other similar high-level executable language. This model is extensively simulated, revised and sometimes model checked [4] until it becomes the golden reference model. In a second phase, this model is translated into an optimized implementation model, usually written in C [3, 5]. The translation is usually automatic using for instance compilers from SDL to C. Many companies still rely on manual translation for efficiency reasons with respect to speed, power or other technical issues.

Currently, the implementation model is simulated again and compared to the reference model to look for discrepancies. Unfortunately, simulation requires a great deal of time to set-up test benches. Additionally, simulation inputs are necessarily redundant at times and incomplete at others especially when concurrency features of the system are at stake.

The inefficiencies of simulation can mean dramatically higher costs, longer run times and persistent doubts [6]. As a direct consequence, verification becomes a very expensive process and is today swallowing up almost all resources and manpower. Our goal is to have a more efficient validation procedure than testing to assert the correctness of the implementation refinement. Moreover, verifying a code generator formally is very expensive since all the proofs have to be conducted all over again when the code generator changes whereas the validation we propose here occurs at each run of the compiler with a specific SDL program at hand. We present a tool called SCEC (SDL C Equivalence Checker)

A. Prinz, R. Reed, and J. Reed (Eds.): SDL 2005, LNCS 3530, pp. 323–338, 2005.

that provides a fast and accurate validation of the C implementation derived from SDL models. Currently our tool handles SDL-96 language constructs with few exceptions and targets mainly the Telelogic CAdvanced Tau 3.5 code generator. We argue that our approach is not limited to this version of SDL and to this particular tool, but can be applied to a broad class of asynchronous languages and compilers targeting imperative languages.

2   Related Work

Originally applied to synchronous languages, the concept of *translation valida-tion* was introduced by Pnueli, Siegel, and Strichman [7, 8]. Necula [9] generalizes the work by applying it to the verification of optimizing compilers. In the field of behavioral circuit description [10], C is verified against Verilog and uses Bounded Model Checking to verify the consistency [11, 12] between the two descriptions.

In the SDL context, [13] proposes a method to check refinements between SDL models by translating them into a process algebra formalism called CCS [14]. The main problem is that all the data part is abstracted away and the translation leads to overly simplistic CCS models. Our approach is more general in the sense that it addresses the implementation language and handles both the control and data flows [15, 16]. Moreover, we propose a practical equivalence model for asynchronous languages in general.

3   SCEC Tool

SCEC is a tool that has been developed in ANSI C (18 000 lines) together with Flex and Bison generators to produce the scanners and the parsers for C and SDL. A WxWidgets based graphical user interface has been developed in order to browse the intermediate representation of the programs. Starting from the syntax tree, SCEC can record all the transformations that are applied on the trees up to the final normal form. This feature was valuable to debug the tool itself.

4   Flow

SCEC (see fig. 1) generates the Abstract Syntax Tree for both SDL and C programs and performs standard semantic analysis. For the C part, AST comprises data type definitions, global data declarations, and complete function bodies, whereas for the SDL part, SCEC stores type definitions, signals and process bodies. The ASTs are gradually transformed using rewrite rules. Some of them are generic while others are specific to the CAdvanced code generator. At the end of the rewrite process, we obtain on the one hand, a number of state transition graphs representing the SDL processes and on the other hand, the corresponding

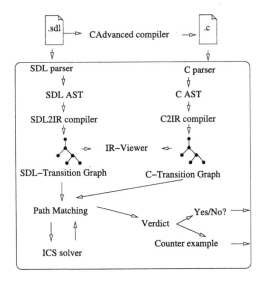

Fig. 1. SCEC Flow

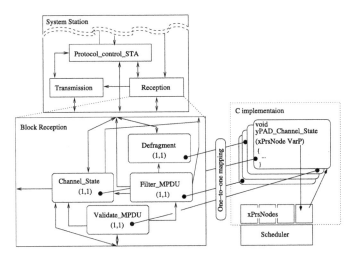

Fig. 2. Process yPAD correspondence

C functions (that is yPADs) that implement them. All SCEC has to do, is to compare the SDL processes and the yPADs pairwise.

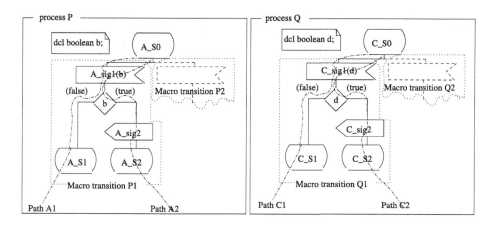

Fig. 3. Path matching

5   Process and yPAD Correspondence

A yPAD (see fig. 2) is a C function that defines all the transitions of the related
SDL process. The yPAD is called by the Telelogic CAdvanced scheduler that controls the pseudo parallel execution of the communicating state machines. When
the head of the signal queue contains a signal instance that can be consumed
in the current state of the associated state machine, the scheduler fires the associated yPAD that will run one selected transition completely. The execution
control returns back to the scheduler after changing the state of the last fired
yPAD function.

6   Path Matching Concept

To grasp the concept of path matching, let us consider the two SDL processes
P and Q that are depicted in fig. 3. Starting from state A_S0, P can either execute the path A1: $state(A\_S0), input(A\_sig1(b)), guard(\neg b), state(A\_S1)$ or the
path A2: $state(A\_S0), input(A\_sig1(b)), guard(b), output(A\_sig2), state(A\_S2)$.
A path represents one transition from one state to its successor. We refer in the
following to a *path* with the term *micro transition*. Moreover, a group of micro
transitions under the same signal input are structured further to form a *macro
transition*. Now, P and Q are considered to be equivalent if the paths A1 and
A2 can be matched with the paths C1 and C2 respectively. Basically, if P and Q
have an identical internal state and they both consume the same signal instance,
then, at the end of the matching paths, they will have modified their internal
state in the same way and they will have output the same signal instances. In
our case, we need to compare an SDL process to a yPAD function, which is why
SCEC has to align the SDL and C internal representations by regenerating the

original SDL process from the yPAD function. To cope with the combinatorial explosion of paths, *cut points* are introduced at four levels (see fig. 4). These cut points are used in our approach to establish a formal correspondence between two descriptions.

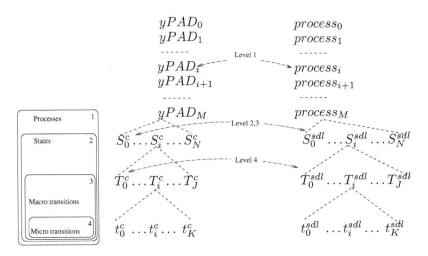

Fig. 4. Modular verification using cut points

By restricting the type, abstraction level and number of cut points considered, we help the tool to establish the correspondence, since fewer pairs of cut points have to be checked. On the other hand this implies less verifiable but equivalent programs. However, no automatic tool can be expected to be able to check all equivalent programs completely, since in general translation validation and software equivalence checking are undecidable problems. One of our main contributions is to list those potential cut points that allow verification of equivalence in practice.

7   Cut Points

We assume that the compiler or the developer respects some naming convention that will allow SCEC to establish correspondence between cut points in order to prove equivalence of the two descriptions. There are four levels of cut points:

1. process name versus yPAD function names.
2. state and connection names.
3. label names defining termination points of control edges.
4. Macro transition names.

A macro transition starts with one of the following:

- an input signal.
- an enabling condition.
- a continuous signal.

A free action identified by the SDL keyword *connection* allows a split of the graphical representation of an SDL process so that it can span over more than one page. We use the label present in the *in* and *out* connectors as a cut point. In addition, we exploit the fact that any control edge that the user defines when drawing the SDL process will appear in the form of a *join* statement to a label defining the termination point of that control edge. This means that all the loops are cut allowing SCEC to reduce loop equivalence problems to path equivalence problems.

8   Code Generator Assumptions

A yPAD does not contain enough information needed for SCEC to regenerate the finite state machine. In fact, we still need to understand the interface between the yPAD and the scheduler. The scheduler needs to store the execution context information (an xPrsNode) and may shift some information that lies originally in the SDL process definition, out of the yPAD in order to avoid firing idle processes. Therefore, SCEC needs to analyze the xPrsNode structure as well. The xPrsNode contains:

- A list of input signals denoted xInputSignals.
- A list of states occurring in the SDL process denoted xStateIdStruct.

Each xStateIdStruct element contains the following:

- A macro transition type table yStaH.
- A transition table called yStaI.
- A reference to enabling conditions denoted yEnab (optional).
- A reference to continuous signals denoted yCont (optional).

This concludes the list of information that has to be extracted by SCEC to regenerate the original SDL process. In the next section we precisely define the kind of equivalence we are referring to.

9   Equivalence Relation

We assume that both the SDL model and its C implementation can be compiled into a normal form that we call a *process network*. Process networks can be compared using an *equivalence* relation.

Proposition 1. *Any process (i.e.; extended finite state machine) can be transformed into a* state transition graph *such that each micro transition is represented by:*

  – *a sequence of terms built over the local data.*
  – *a path predicate defining under which control condition that path is followed.*

Proposition 2. *Each micro transition in the state transition graph is closed with either a nextstate statement or with a join statement referring to a connection name.*

9.1   Equivalence Between Two State Transition Graphs

Definition 1. *Let f and g two terms be in a micro transition (a path). We say that f is equivalent to g written $f \equiv g$ iff f is structurally identical to g.*

Definition 2. *Let t_i and t_j be two micro transitions. We say that t_i is equivalent to t_j written $t_i \approx t_j$ iff:*

  – *t_i and t_j contain equivalent sequence of terms.*
  – *the guards in t_i and t_j are logically equivalent.*
  – *the data and control dependencies between terms and guards are preserved.*

Definition 3. *Let $G_{sdl} = \langle S^{sdl}, s_0^{sdl}, \longrightarrow \rangle$ and $G_c = \langle S^c, s_0^c, \longrightarrow \rangle$ be two state transition graphs.*
G_c simulates G_{sdl} if it exists a binary relation $\sim \subseteq S^{sdl} \times S^c$ such that:

  – *$\forall s_{sdl} \in S^{sdl}, \exists s_c \in S^c : s_{sdl} \sim s_c$*
  – *$s_{sdl} \sim s_c \wedge s_{sdl} \xrightarrow[t_{sdl}]{} s'_{sdl} \Rightarrow \exists s'_c \in S_c : s_c \xrightarrow[t_c]{} s'_c \wedge s'_{sdl} \sim s'_c \wedge t_{sdl} \approx t_c$*

if G_{sdl} simulates G_c via $\sim^{-1}$ then $\sim$ is a bisimulation.

Proposition 3. *If two state transition graphs can be reduced to the same state transition graph S_3 then S_1 bisimulates S_2*

In fact, each rewrite rule performed by SCEC is a reduction. Therefore, if after composing a number of reductions on the C state transition graph and on the SDL state transition graph we can reach the same transition graph then we can conclude using proposition 2 that there is a bisimulation between the C and the SDL.

9.2   Process Network Equivalence

Definition 4. *A process network is a set of processes that communicate with each other and with the environment asynchronously using signals and queues.*

Assume we have two isomorphic process networks PN_{SDL} and PN_C such that related components are equivalent in the sense of definition 3. If we compose components of PN_{SDL} and PN_C with the same deterministic scheduler and with the same environment then we can conclude that PN_{SDL} and PN_C are also equivalent. We are definitely in the case of bottom up compositionality principle of *components-based design* defined in [17].

9.3   C to IR Translation

Translating SDL into the intermediate form was straightforward, since by construction IR was built in such a way, that it subsumes a low level representation of SDL models. For the C part it was less obvious. As a general principle, we have chosen to unify concepts of both languages instead of reducing them to atomic statements that would have made the correspondence almost infeasible [18].

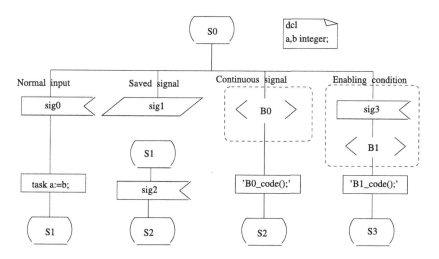

Fig. 5. SDL program fragment

In the following, we present some elements describing how the SDL process represented in fig. 5 is regenerated from the components depicted in figs. 6 and 7.

- **Local data retrieval**: SCEC dereferences a pointer to an xPrsNode (see fig. 6) passed as a parameter to the yPAD and then extracts the integer fields a and b representing local data definitions.
- **Transition number resolution**: This is done by looking up the yStaI tables to determine to which state and macro transition it corresponds. For example, the transition number 4 (see fig. 6) occurs in the yStaI list that belongs to the state S1. Moreover, the position of the transition number 4 in yStaI list corresponds to the position of sig2 in the xInputSignals list. At last, to determine the macro transition type related to sig2, SCEC looks up yStaH (see Table 1) at the position of sig2 in xInputSignals list and infers that it is a normal signal input. The complete transition matrix of the process depicted in fig. 5 is given in Table 2.
- **Next state name regeneration** The name corresponds to the element of xStateIdStruct list that is indexed by the second parameter passed to the SDL_next_state function. For instance, SDL_next_state(yVarP,1) corresponds to nextstate(S1).

xInputSignals =<sig0,sig1,sig2,sig3>
xStateIdStruct
xPrsNode
(*yPAD)
TransitionNumber
State
a
b
S0
S1
S2
S3
yStaH=<1,2,0,3>
yStaI= <1,0,0,3>
(*yEnab)=yEnab_S0
(*yCont)=yCont_S0
yStaH=<0,0,1,0>
yStaI= <0,0,4,0>
(*yEnab)=NULL
(*yCont)=NULL

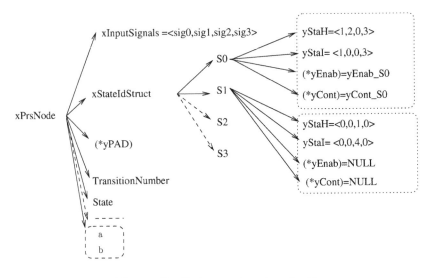

Fig. 6. xPrsNode structure (see fig. 5)

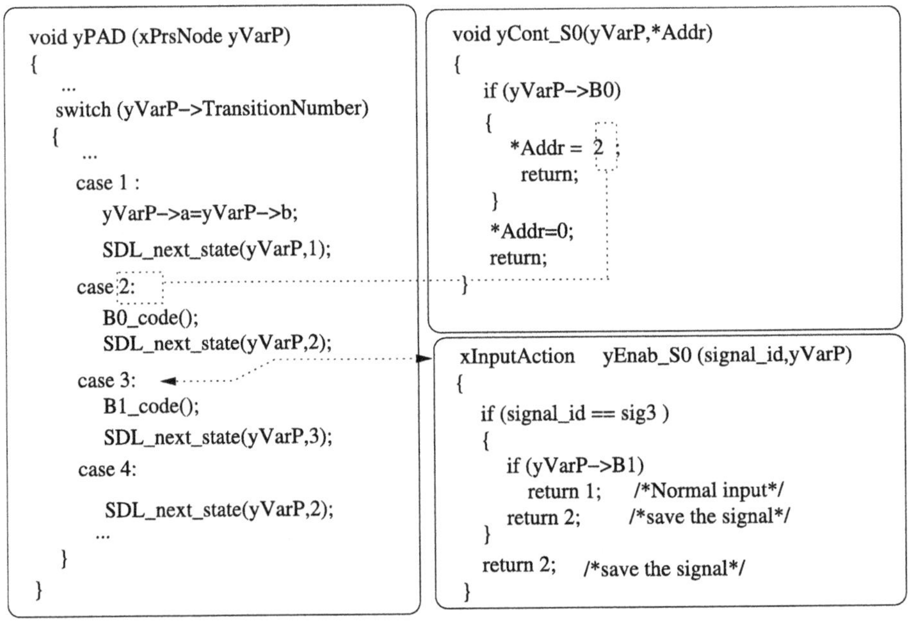

void yPAD (xPrsNode yVarP)
{
...
switch (yVarP->TransitionNumber)
{
...
case 1 :
yVarP->a=yVarP->b;
SDL_next_state(yVarP,1);
case 2:
B0_code();
SDL_next_state(yVarP,2);
case 3:
B1_code();
SDL_next_state(yVarP,3);
case 4:
SDL_next_state(yVarP,2);
...
}
}
void yCont_S0(yVarP,*Addr)
{
if (yVarP->B0)
{
*Addr = 2 ;
return;
}
*Addr=0;
return;
}
xInputAction yEnab_S0 (signal_id,yVarP)
{
if (signal_id == sig3)
{
if (yVarP->B1)
return 1; /*Normal input*/
return 2; /*save the signal*/
}
return 2; /*save the signal*/
}

Fig. 7. yPAD, yEnab and yCont correspondence

– **Input reconstruction:** Figure 8 illustrates how an SDL input statement is translated to C. In fact, the scheduler passes to the yPAD a pointer to the received signal (ySVarP) before firing the transition. This pointer is

Table 1. yStaH interpretation

yStaH value	Interpretation
0	unexpected signal
1	normal input
2	saved input
3	enabling condition

Table 2. Transition matrix

state	event	transition
S0	sig0	1
S0	B0	2
S0	sig3	3
S1	sig2	4

SDL

input sig1 (a,b,c) ; $\Longrightarrow$

C

yVarP –>a=((yPDef_sig1*)ySVarP)–>Param1;
yVarP –>b=((yPDef_sig1*)ySVarP)–>Param2;
yVarP –>c=((yPDef_sig1*)ySVarP)–>Param3;

Fig. 8. SDL input statement translation

converted to the type of the signal corresponding to the selected transition. Signal parameters are then stored to the local data of the SDL process.

- **Output reconstruction** The sending process allocates the necessary storage to hold the signal instance at the receiver input queue using the get_signal function. The returned pointer yOutputSignal is used then to build the actual parameters of the signal from the local data fields (see fig. 9).

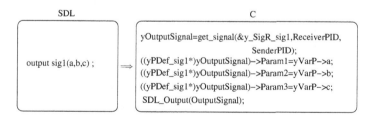

SDL

output sig1(a,b,c) ; $\Longrightarrow$

C

yOutputSignal=get_signal(&y_SigR_sig1,ReceiverPID,
                         SenderPID);
((yPDef_sig1*)yOutputSignal)–>Param1=yVarP–>a;
((yPDef_sig1*)yOutputSignal)–>Param2=yVarP–>b;
((yPDef_sig1*)yOutputSignal)–>Param3=yVarP–>c;
SDL_Output(OutputSignal);

Fig. 9. SDL output statement translation

- **Saved signal set reconstruction**: Basically all the signals that have the value 2 in the yStaH list are saved in the context state in which they appear. For example, sig1 which is located at the second position in the xInputSignals list is saved in state S0 (see fig. 6).

- **Enabling condition regeneration**: By parsing the yEnab function referenced in xPrsNode, SCEC extracts the guard associated to the signal. For instance, sig3 is guarded by the expression B1 at state S0. When the guard evaluates to false, the signal is saved.
- **Continuous signal regeneration**: The yCont function body referenced in xPrsNode contains the boolean condition B0 and the transition number to be fired in case the condition is fulfilled.

10 A Concrete Example

In the following subsections, we show how a concrete SDL example is translated into C in order to figure out the kind of transformations that are applied by SCEC to align the two internal representations.

10.1 SDL Transition Definition

The SDL process is represented in the yPAD function by a switch case statement over the transition number. For instance, the state From_LLC together with the signal input MaUnitdata.request (lines 1 and 2) is mapped onto transition number 1(line 102). The case statement is immediately followed by the process local data update statements. In fact, all the parameters conveyed in the input signal pointer are copied into the corresponding local data using the reference yVarP that points to the xPrsNode structure (see fig. 8).

```
1   state From_LLC;
2   input MaUnitdata.request(sa, da, rt, LLCdata, cf, srv);
```

```
100    switch(yVarP->TransitionNumber)
101    {
102      case 1:
103        yAss_z0A_octetstring (&(yVarP->z0017_sa),
104                             ((yPDef_z02_MaUnitdatarequest *)
105                             ySVarP)->Param1,0);
106        yAss_z0A_octetstring  (&(yVarP->z0018_da),
107          ((yPDef_z02_MaUnitdatarequest*)ySVarP)->Param2,0);
108        yVarP->z0016_rt = ((yPDef_z02_MaUnitdatarequest *)ySVarP)->Param3;
109        yAss_z0A_octetstring (&(yVarP->z0015_LLCdata),
110          ((yPDef_z02_MaUnitdatarequest*)ySVarP)->Param4,0);
111        yVarP->z0014_cf = ((yPDef_z02_MaUnitdatarequest*)ySVarP)->Param5;
112        yVarP->z001A_srv = ((yPDef_z02_MaUnitdatarequest*)ySVarP)->Param6;
```

10.2 SDL Conditional Assignment

A transition contains typically a sequence of actions to be performed when it is fired. The transition presented in subsection 8.1 is followed by a conditional SDL assignment (lines 3 to 9).

```
3        task stat :=
4            if rt /= null_rt then
5                nonNullSourceRouting
6            else if (length(LLCdata) > sMsduMaxLng)
7                    or (length(LLCdata) < 0) then
8                excessiveDataLength
9            else successful fi fi;
```

The CAdvanced code generator preserves the structure of the assignment (lines 113 to 116) which allows SCEC to do a simple structural term comparison instead of adding another factor in the number of paths to be matched. Note in passing that the SDL synonyms resolution rewrite is necessary before unifying the two assignment terms.

```
113   yVarP->z001B_stat = ((yVarP->z0016_rt) != (0) ? 5 :
114     (((((z0M1M_length (yVarP->z0015_LLCdata)) > (5678)))
115     ||
116     ((((z0M1M_length (yVarP->z0015_LLCdata))<(0)))))?4:0));
```

10.3   SDL Decision

The SDL decision (lines 10 to 29) comprises four micro transitions closed with a *join* statement.

```
10        decision stat = successful;
11        (true) :
12          decision srv;
13          (strictlyOrdered) :
14            decision
15              import(dot11PowerManagementMode);
16            (sta_active) :
17            else :
18              task stat := unavailableServiceClass;
19              join grst29;
20            enddecision;
21          (reorderable) :
22              join grst28;
23          else :
24              task stat := unsupportedServiceClass;
25              join grst29;
26          enddecision;
27        (false) :
28            join grst29;
29        enddecision;
```

In the generated C code, the translation reflects the same branching structure as in the SDL code and simply converts *join* statements into *goto* statements. In a manual translation, we would more likely find a function call when the label is referring to a free action or the introduction of an equivalent C iteration statement in case of looping. In both cases, the cut points could still be derived automatically.

```
117     if ((yVarP->z001B_stat) == (0))
118       {
119         yVarP->yDcn_z08_ServiceClass = yVarP->z001A_srv;
120         if ((yVarP->yDcn_z08_ServiceClass) == (1))
121           {
122         if (((*(z00_PwrSave*)
123                   xGetExportAddr(
124                     &yReVR_z001H_dot11PowerManagementMode,
125               xSysD.SDL_NULL_Var, (int) 0,
126                   VarP))) == (0))
127             {
128         }
129         else
130           {
131             yVarP->z001B_stat = 9;
132         goto L_grst29;
133           }
134         }
135         else if ((yVarP->yDcn_z08_ServiceClass) == (0))
136             goto L_grst28;
137         else
138         {
139           yVarP->z001B_stat = 8;
140           goto L_grst29;
141         }
142     }
143       else
144       goto L_grst29;
```

11   Path Matching

To establish the correspondence between SDL and C paths, SCEC needs to match terms structurally. For example, the SDL terms defined between line 10 and 12 can be matched with their corresponding C terms defined between line 23 and 25. A path also contains guards representing the chosen alternatives when conditional statements are met along the macro transition. To cope with guards and auxiliary variables, SCEC relies on an external solver to verify that the conjunction of guards on both sides are indeed equivalent.

```
1   SDL_path_ns_RXC_Idle(
2     guard(or(ftype(pdu)=reasoc_rsp,ftype(pdu)=asoc_rsp,
3               ftype(pdu)=reasoc_req,ftype(pdu)=asoc_req,
4               ftype(pdu)=disasoc,ftype(pdu)=null_frame)),
5     guard(or(sau=1,sau=2)),
6     guard(or(ftype(pdu)=reasoc_rsp,ftype(pdu)=asoc_rsp,
```

```
7                    ftype(pdu)=reasoc_req,ftype(pdu)=asoc_req,
8                    ftype(pdu)=disasoc,ftype(pdu)=null_frame)),
9     guard(not(ftype(pdu)=null_frame)),
10    output(MmIndicate(pdu,endRx,strTs,0)),
11    label(grst50),
12    nextstate(RXC_Idle))

13    C_path_ns_RXC_Idle(
14    assign(z13_TypeSubtype,ftype(pdu)),
15    guard(or(or(or(or(or(z13_TypeSubtype=null_frame
16                         ,z13_TypeSubtype=disasoc)
17                         ,z13_TypeSubtype=asoc_req)
18                         ,z13_TypeSubtype=reasoc_req)
19                         ,z13_TypeSubtype=asoc_rsp)
20                         ,z13_TypeSubtype=reasoc_rsp)),
21    guard(or(sau=1,sau=2)),
22    guard(not(ftype(pdu)=null_frame)),
23    output(MmIndicate(pdu,endRx,strTs,0)),
24    label(grst50),
25    nextstate(RXC_Idle))
```

12   Solver Invocation

The ICS [19] solver is particularly useful to cope with auxiliary variables added in the generated C code (as in an SDL decision) and also to remove the redundant clauses that are added by the path extractor algorithm. Basically, if $\neg(Path_{sdl} \iff Path_C)$ is unsatisfiable then $Path_{sdl} \iff Path_C$ is valid. The following ICS code represents an SCEC satisfiability query.

```
1     def z13_TypeSubtype := ftype(pdu).
2     prop c_path :=     [[[[[z13_TypeSubtype=null_frame
3                            |z13_TypeSubtype=disasoc]
4                            |[z13_TypeSubtype=asoc_req]]
5                            |[z13_TypeSubtype=reasoc_req]]
6                            |[z13_TypeSubtype=asoc_rsp]]
7                            |[z13_TypeSubtype=reasoc_rsp]]
8                         & ~[z13_TypeSubtype=null_frame]
9                      & [sau=1 | sau=2].
10    prop sdl_path :=   [ftype(pdu)=reasoc_rsp|ftype(pdu)=asoc_rsp
11                         |ftype(pdu)=reasoc_req |ftype(pdu)=asoc_req
12                         |ftype(pdu)=disasoc|ftype(pdu)=null_frame]
13                        &~[ftype(pdu)=null_frame]
14                        & [sau=1 | sau=2]
15                        & [ftype(pdu)=reasoc_rsp |ftype(pdu)=asoc_rsp
16                            |ftype(pdu)=reasoc_req |ftype(pdu)=asoc_req
17                            |ftype(pdu)=disasoc |ftype(pdu)=null_frame]
18                        & ~[ftype(pdu)=null_frame].
19    prop path_eq:=[~c_path|sdl_path]&[~sdl_path|c_path].
20    sat ~path_eq.
```

13   Results

The 802.11 MAC layer is IEEE standardized. The original SDL diagrams (4 000 lines) came from the specification [20] and were automatically translated to C (17 000 lines) using the CAdvanced 3.5 compiler. Using SCEC and ICS, the whole verification process takes less than one minute on an Intel Centrino 1.5 GHz, since most of the verification conditions turn out to be trivial after extracting the proper cut points. Figures 10 shows statistics extracted from the intermediate representation. We can see clearly that the number of micro transitions does not exceed one hundred paths for the biggest process (TX coordination). This is due to the fact that free action cut points allowed factoring out all the paths that precede the *join* statements and therefore reduce drastically the number of paths to be matched. To check the soundness of SCEC, we injected random defects into the correctly generated C code. Our tool found these inconsistency instantly.

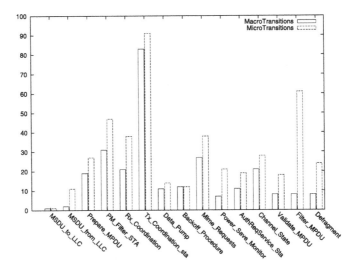

Fig. 10. Macro and micro transition statistics

14   Conclusion

We have described a practical method to check the equivalence between real world SDL programs and their corresponding auto-generated C code. One key feature is the full automation of the process. The SDL and C programs are translated into a common intermediate representation for which we presented a bisimulation equivalence argument. The translation into the intermediate form is done by applying specific rewrite rules that capture the FSM encoding method and the optimizations done by the compiler. Our method was successful in validating the translation of a commercial compiler and should be certainly very useful for checking manually translated code. Our plans for the future include the integration of the Telelogic CMicro compiler which targets embedded applications and also to provide the user with a better diagnosis capability for failed proof attempts.

References

1. Olsen and Pedersen and Reed and smith: Systems Engineering Using SDL-92. Elsevier Science 1994.
2. Juha Sipilä and Vesa Luukkala: An SDL Implementation Framework for Third Generation Mobile Communications System. Nokia Research Center, Mobile Networks Laboratory 2001.
3. Hannikainen and Takko and Knuutila and Hamalainen and Sarrinene: SDL-to-C Conversion for implementing Embedded Wireless LAN Protocols. IEEE Journal 2000.
4. N.Sidorova and M.Steffen: Verifying Large SDL Specifications Using Model Checking. 10th International SDL-Forum 2001.
5. Haroud and Blažević and Biere: HW accelerated Ultra Wide Band MAC protocol using SDL and SystemC. Radio And Wireless Conference 2004.
6. James A.Whittaker: What Is Software Testing? And Why Is It so Hard? IEEE Software 2000.
7. A. Pnueli and M. Siegel and E. Singerman: Translation Validation TACAS 1998
8. A. Pnueli and M. Siegel and and O. Strichman: Translation validation: From SIGNAL to C. Correct System Design 1999.
9. George C. Necula: Translation validation for an optimizing compiler. ACM sigplan notices 2000.
10. Kroening Daniel and Clarke Edmund and Yorav Karen: Behavioral Consistency of C and Verilog Programs Using Bounded Model Checking DAC 2003.
11. Biere and Cimatti and Clarke and Strichman and Zhu: Bounded Model Checking Advances in Computers Academic press 2003.
12. Clarke and Biere and Raimi, and Zhu: Bounded Model Checking Using Satisfiability Solving. Formal Methods in System Design Kluwer Academic Publishers 2001.
13. Marsha Chechik Hai: Bisimulation Analysis of SDL-Expressed Protocols: A Case Study. CASCON Conference 2000.
14. Robin Milner: A Calculus of Communicating Systems. Springer-Verlag New York, Inc., Secaucus 1982
15. Susan Horwitz and Jan Prins and Thomas Reps: On the Adequacy of Program Dependence Graphs for Representing Programs Conference Record of the Fifteenth Annual ACM Symposium on Principles of Programming Languages 1988.
16. Ravi Namballa and N. Ranganathan: Control and Data Flow Graph Extraction for High-Level Synthesis Symposium on VLSI Emerging Trends in VLSI Systems Design ISVLSI 2004.
17. L. de Alfaro and T. Henzinger. Interface theories for component-based design. In EMSOFT 01: Embedded Software, Lecture Notes in Computer Science 2211. Springer, 2001.
18. Peeter Ellervee et al.: IRSYD: An internal representation for heterogeneous embedded systems. In Proceedings of the 16th NORCHIP Conference, 1998.
19. Jean-Christophe Filliâtre and Sam Owre and Harald Rueß and N. Shankar: ICS: Integrated Canonizer and Solver. Computer Aided Verification 2001.
20. Wireless LAN Medium Access Control (MAC) and Physical Layer (PHY) specifications High-speed Physical Layer in the 5 GHz band grouper.ieee.org

Synthesizing State-Machine Behaviour from UML Collaborations and Use Case Maps

Humberto Nicolás Castejón Martínez

Norwegian University of Science and Technology,
Department of Telematics, N-7491 Trondheim, Norway
humberto.castejon@item.ntnu.no

Abstract. Telecommunication services are provided as the joint effort of components, which collaborate in order to achieve the goal(s) of the service. UML 2.0 collaborations can be used to model services. Furthermore, they allow services to be described modularly and incrementally, since collaborations can be composed of subordinate collaborations. For such an approach to work, it is necessary to capture the exact dependencies between the subordinate collaborations. This paper presents the results of an experiment on using Use Case Maps (UCMs) for describing those dependencies, and for synthesizing the state-machine behaviour of service components from the joint information provided by the UML collaborations and the UCM diagrams.

1   Introduction

Telecommunication services are provided as the joint effort of active objects, which collaborate in order to achieve a goal for their environment. Initiatives may originate from any side, be simultaneous and possibly conflicting. This is what makes tele-services interesting, but at the same time particularly challenging to design.

Traditional service engineering approaches have been object-oriented. They have focused on modeling the total behaviour of objects, normally in terms of state-machines. The disadvantage of focusing on the complete behaviour of objects is that we only get a partial view of the services we want to design, which makes it difficult to understand and analyze them. Since telecommunication services are the result of collaborations among objects pursuing a goal, a collaboration-oriented approach to service engineering seems more suitable [1, 2]. A collaboration view helps to see the service as a whole, to define what roles are played by which objects, and to express what service goal combinations must be met for the successful provision of the service.

UML 2.0 collaborations [3, 4] are intended to describe partial functionalities involving interactions among participating roles played by objects. Therefore, they fit well with our understanding of service. An interesting characteristic of UML collaborations is that they can be bound to a specific context, becoming collaboration uses, which in turn can be used in the definition of larger collaborations. This feature enables a compositional and incremental design of services,

A. Prinz, R. Reed, and J. Reed (Eds.): SDL 2005, LNCS 3530, pp. 339–359, 2005.

which is desirable, but which will only succeed if the dependencies between the collaborations that are composed are explicitly captured [5].

This paper presents our approach to incremental service modeling using UML 2.0 collaborations and motivates the need for explicitly expressing collaboration dependencies in this approach (see section 2). It continues with the results of an experiment on using Use Case Maps (UCMs) [6, 7] for describing such dependencies (see section 3) and synthesizing the state-machine behaviour of service components from the joint information provided by the UML collaborations and the UCM diagrams (see section 4). The paper finishes with a comparison between our synthesis approach and other existing work (see section 5), and with a summary of the presented work (see section 6).

2   Goal-Oriented Service Collaborations

In our service engineering approach we model services by means of UML 2.0 collaborations. They describe a structure of roles that collaborate to collectively accomplish some task, that is – to achieve some goal. The collaboration roles specify the properties that object instances must have in order to participate in the collaboration. The UML standard allows the association of behaviour with collaborations in several forms, such as sequence diagrams involving the collaborating roles, or as state-machines for the roles. Since our approach is collaboration-oriented, we prefer to describe the behaviour of collaborations as sequence diagrams that show the interactions between roles, rather than using state-machines for the roles.

Figure 1 shows a UML collaboration diagram describing a UserLogon service. From the diagram we can see that there are five roles involved in the collaboration (represented by boxes). We can also see the relationships that are needed between these roles to achieve the goal of the collaboration. For example, Terminal is associated with TerminalClientSession, which in turn is a part of TerminalAgent and it is associated with UserTerminalSession. The diagram also shows one interesting aspect of UML collaborations: they can contain other sub-collaborations in their definition, expressed as collaboration uses. When this happens, the roles of the collaboration uses are bound to the roles of the container collaboration (for example rr1's requested role is bound to TerminalAgent). Collaboration uses enable a modular design with small collaborations as units of reuse. Modularity is a well-proven approach to break down the complexity of systems; here we use it to structure services. It also promotes separation of concerns and reuse. These aspects are reflected in the UserLogon collaboration, which contains four sub-collaborations, namely rr1, rr2, lo and ua. The two first, rr1 and rr2, are instances of a RoleRequest collaboration, while lo and ua are instances of a Logon and a UserAuthenticate collaboration, respectively. We can see that the RoleRequest collaboration has been reused. We also appreciate how separation of concerns has been achieved by separately defining the interactions between Terminal and TerminalClientSession, and between TerminalClientSession and UserTerminalSession. Indeed, although logon and authentication protocols are related, they are not exactly the same. For example, it may be perfectly possible for two different logon protocols to make use of the same authentication protocol.

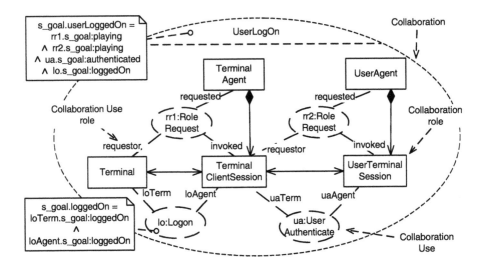

Fig. 1. UML 2.0 Collaboration for `UserLogon` Service

We have just seen the benefits of defining collaborations in terms of other smaller collaborations. However, when looking at fig. 1 we can guess how `UserLogon` works, but we do not exactly know how it does it. Even if we know how each of the four small sub-collaborations works in isolation, we do not know how they work together. Does *rr1* happen before *lo* or afterwards? Does *lo* finish before *ua* starts or do they overlap? Can *lo* succeed with independence of what happens to *ua* or does it depend on its result? These are questions that we have to answer if we really aim at composing collaborations, and we can do it by explicitly describing the dependencies between collaborations, that is, their inter-relationships.

Sanders [8] has proposed associating goals with services considered as collaborations as a means to express liveness properties. *Event goals* (e_goals) are desired events, while *state goals* (s_goals) are properties of collaboration global states that we wish to reach and entail combinations of role goals. Sanders found that service goals may also be used to express the dependencies that exist between collaborations. These goals become then synchronization points between collaborations. For example, we may say that when *rr1*'s goal is achieved, *lo* is enabled, that is, it can happen. Following this approach the problem of showing the dependencies between collaborations turns into the problem of showing the dependencies between their goals, but we still miss a good solution to show such dependencies. Sanders, for example, defined the goal of `UserLogon` (*s_goal:userLoggedOn*) as a logical AND-operation over the goals of its subordinate collaborations, as depicted in fig. 1. However, while such an expression reveals that UserLogon only succeeds if all its subordinate collaborations also succeed, it still does not tell us the order in which the collaboration goals are achieved. To overcome that limitation Sanders also experimented with several UML concepts to describe goal dependencies, such as activity diagrams and interaction overview diagrams. These diagrams are good at expressing sequential and parallel relationships, but they do not meet all our needs, since they fail to express finer relationships between intermediate goals, as those existing when two collaborations overlap. For example, in UML activity diagrams activities can be nested, so if we represent collaborations as activities, it would be possible to show (to some extent) that, for example, *lo* only succeeds if *ua* also succeeds, by nesting *ua* inside *lo*. However it does not seem possible to show, for example, that a collaboration starts, after certain time enables a second collaboration, and from then on both run in parallel (see fig. 3c).

Since UML diagrams do not meet all our needs, we have analysed Use Case Maps to see if they offer better support for expressing goal dependencies, since they are well known for their ability to explicitly capture inter-scenario relationships. The result has been promising, since we have been able to successfully describe several types of dependencies. Moreover, we have experimented with the synthesis of state-machines for collaboration roles using the UCM information to guide the process, and the results are again promising. We take a closer look at these two aspects in the next sections.

3   UCMs for Describing the Goal-Based Progress of Collaborations and Their Inter-relationships

Use Case Maps (UCMs) [6, 7] are a scenario-based graphical notation used to describe causal relationships between responsibilities (tasks, actions, etc), which may be bound to abstract components. Basically, UCMs order responsibilities along a path and link causes (preconditions or triggering events) to effects (postconditions). With UCMs several scenarios can be easily integrated in a single diagram. This is quite useful for showing interactions between the scenarios and understanding their combined behaviour.

In section 2 we argued that the dependencies between collaborations can be expressed in terms of their goals. That is, by relating the event and state goals of different collaborations we can effectively capture their inter-relationships. Our aim is to use UCMs to:

1. describe the goal-based progress of each collaboration (i.e. the causal relationships between its event and state goals) in isolation;
2. integrate the individual UCMs into more elaborated diagrams that show the dependencies between the individual collaborations.

An example is given in fig. 2, where separated UCMs for the RoleRequest, UserAuthenticate and Logon collaborations are shown in the upper box, and

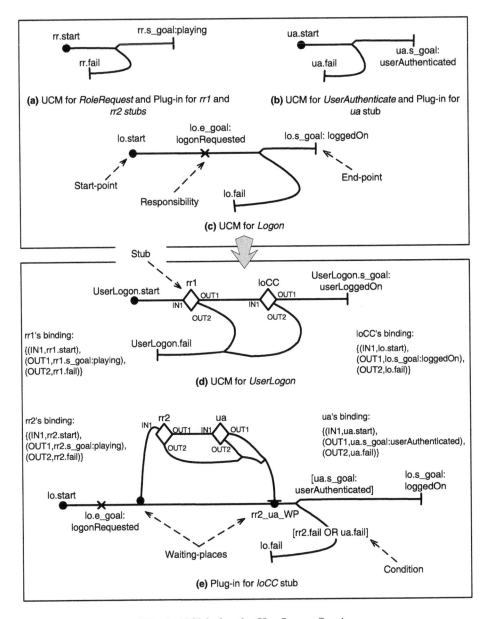

Fig. 2. UCMs for the UserLogon Service

their integration into more complex UCMs for the UserLogon collaboration is shown in lower box. We will explain the dependencies expressed by these UCMs in section 3.2, but before that we will briefly explain the basic UCM elements and how we use them.

3.1   Basic UCM Notation

It is not the scope of this paper to explain how UCMs work, so we will just briefly explain the UCM notational elements needed to understand the figures and concepts presented here. Those notational elements are highlighted in fig. 2. For a more detailed explanation of them, and of UCMS in general, please refer to [6, 7].

In the UCM notation *paths* (depicted as lines) represent scenario flows, so we have used them to represent the lifeline of collaborations. They connect *start-points* with *responsibilities* and *end-points*. A start-point (labeled with '*collaboration_name*.start') is a pre-condition or triggering cause that symbolizes the beginning of a collaboration, while an end-point is a post-condition representing one of its possible outcomes in terms of achievement (or not) of its goal(s). End-points representing achievement of state goals are labeled with '*collaboration_name*.s_goal:*goal_name*', while those representing failure are labeled with '*collaboration_name*.fail'. fig. 2a exemplifies the use of these notational elements. The figure shows a simple collaboration that, after starting, it can reach any of two final states:

one representing the achievement of its goal (labeled *rr.s_goal:playing*);

the other representing failure on achieving its goal (labeled *rr.fail*).

Responsibilities are intended to represent generic tasks or actions. We use them, however, to represent event goals, that is, to show that collaboration achieves some progress (see fig. 2c). Therefore, we interpret responsibilities as "tasks to achieve some progress". We understand that this use of responsibilities is not completely rigorous, but we think it is acceptable[1].

Static stubs can be used to better structure a large diagram. They are containers for sub-maps (called plug-ins) and, in our approach, represent collaboration uses. This is an elegant way of representing the composition of a collaboration from other subordinate collaborations. An example of the use of stubs can be seen in fig. 2d, where the UserLogon collaboration is composed of two other collaborations, namely *rr1* and *loCC*. The plug-ins for these collaborations are shown in figs. 2a and 2e respectively. fig. 2d (at the sides) also shows how the bindings between the inputs and outputs of a stub and the start- and end-points of its plug-in are defined.

Waiting places are points where the path waits for an event to happen (such as an arrival along a tangentially connected path or a connected end-point). They constitute points where interactions with the environment or other paths can happen, so they can be used to couple collaborations and so express causal dependencies between them. As guard conditions for waiting places, we use logical expressions in terms of event and/or state goals of the triggering collaboration. The use of waiting places is illustrated in fig. 2e, where two waiting places are shown. The first one (to the left) is activated when there is an arrival on the *lo*'s path, that is, after *lo* achieves *logonRequested* progress. When this happens,

---

[1] If this interpretation is not acceptable we may use *open waiting places* (see [6]) instead of responsibilities.

the collaboration represented by the *rr2* stub is enabled. The second waiting place (to the right) is used to make the *lo* collaboration wait for the outcome of *ua* and/or *rr2*.

AND-/OR- forks and *joins* can be used to, respectively, split and merge paths.

3.2 Dependency Patterns

A side-effect of decomposing the interactions between components into small collaborations is (as we have already pointed out) that the dependencies between the resulting collaborations must be explicitly captured. The majority of these dependencies can be classified as: sequential dependencies, if they impose a temporal ordering between collaborations; or as goal dependencies, if the goal of a collaboration depends on the goal(s) of other collaboration(s).

We can express collaboration dependencies using UCMs. To do it, we have to couple the UCMs that represent each individual collaboration according to the patterns that we present below.

Sequential Dependencies. Sequential dependencies impose a temporal ordering between collaborations. If a collaboration *c2* depends sequentially on another collaboration *c1*, we say that *c1* enables *c2*. Two UCM patterns can be used to express sequential dependencies between collaborations. The selection of the appropriate pattern is made according to the nature of the condition that enables the dependent collaboration.

If the collaboration *c2* is enabled when *c1* achieves (or not) its goal, the appropriate end-point of *c1* is connected with the start-point of *c2* (see fig. 3a). In situations where stubs are used to represent collaborations, the appropriate output of the "enabling" stub is interconnected with the input of the "enabled" stub (see figs. 3b and 2d).

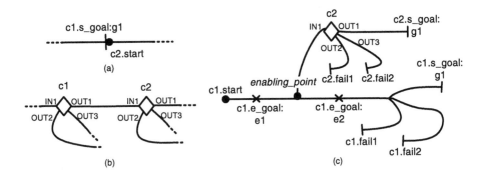

Fig. 3. Sequential Dependencies

If the collaboration *c2* is enabled when *c1* achieves some progress (reaches an event goal), the start-point of *c2* is tangentially connected to the path of *c1*, just after the responsibility representing the event goal that enables $c2$. Note that if a stub is used to represent $c2$, its start-point is not directly connected to the path of $c1$. However, this connection happens indirectly through an auxiliary path with its start-point connected tangentially to $c1$'s path, and its end-point merged with the input of the stub. This is shown in fig. 3c, where $c2$, represented by a stub, is enabled when $c1$ achieves event goal $e1$ (setting its value to *true*). Note also that in order for the interconnection to be effective, the *enabling_point* waiting place[2] must have its guard condition set to *c1.e_goal:e1 == true*. After $c2$ is enabled, both collaborations, $c1$ and $c2$, run concurrently.

Goal Dependencies. A goal dependency exists when a collaboration depends on the success of other collaboration(s) in order to achieve its own goal(s). This dependency can be either *total* or *partial*. When a collaboration C has no own behaviour, but its behaviour has been completely specified by reusing other collaborations, we talk about total goal dependency. In this case, C's goal is completely specified in terms of the other collaborations' goals (for example *C.goal = c1.goal ∧ c2.goal*). However, if the achievement of C's goal not only depends on the achievement of other collaborations' goals, but also on the progress achieved by C itself, we talk about partial goal dependency.

We can show a total goal dependency using a UCM for the main collaboration that does not include any responsibility, and in which the subordinate collaborations are stubs. This is illustrated in fig. 2d, where the UserLogon collaboration is composed of two other collaborations, namely *rr1* (see fig. 2a) and *loCC* (see fig. 2e). The interpretation of UserLogon's UCM is as follows. When UserLogon starts, *rr1* is automatically enabled and runs to completion. If it fails to achieve its goal, so does UserLogon. But if *rr1* succeeds, *loCC* is enabled, which also runs to completion. In the same way as before, if *loCC* fails, so does UserLogon, but if it succeeds, UserLogon achieves its goal. Therefore, this UCM tells us both the execution order of the collaborations and the goal dependency that UserLogon maintains with *rr1* and *loCC*.

According to fig. 2d, *UserLogon.fail = rr1.fail ∨ lo.fail*. We could have given a different meaning to *UserLogon.fail* (or even have defined several types of failure) just by connecting the outputs of the stubs in a different manner, with help of OR-joins and AND-joins.

Note also that UserLogon is a composition of *rr1* and *loCC*, where *loCC* is in turn a composition of *rr2* and *ua*. This shows how collaborations can be nested in several levels.

A *partial goal dependency* can be illustrated applying the patterns depicted in fig. 4 or fig. 5. The key aspect behind both patterns is the interconnection of the collaboration UCMs by means of waiting places.

Figure 4 shows a case in which a subordinate collaboration $c2$ is enabled when the main collaboration $c1$ achieves certain progress. Then $c1$ waits for $c2$ to run to completion and, depending on $c2$'s goal outcome, $c1$ either succeeds

---

[2] *enabling_point* is actually a start-point, but start-points are special waiting places for a stimulus to start a path.

itself or not. This is the same type of dependency expressed in fig. 2e, where the *lo* collaboration is partially goal dependent on *rr2* and *ua* collaborations.

There are four aspects that deserve explanation in this pattern:

1. There is no interaction between *c1* and *c2* other than the one at the beginning and at the end of *c2*. That is, the subordinate collaboration, once enabled, runs without interruption. Therefore we use a stub to represent it.
2. The subordinate collaboration is actually sequentially dependent on the main collaboration. To express that its start-point is tangentially connected to the path of the main collaboration, just after the responsibility that represents the enabling event goal.
3. A waiting place is added to the main collaboration's path at the point where the end-point of the subordinate collaboration must be connected. The main collaboration waits there for the subordinate one to finish.
4. Conditions expressed in terms of the subordinate collaboration success or failure are added to the OR-joins of the main collaboration. By doing this we join pre-conditions (related to the subordinate collaboration) with post-conditions (related to the main collaboration).

The collaboration composition presented in fig. 5 is slightly more complicated. Here the collaborations do not only interact at the beginning and at the end of the subordinate collaboration, but also at intermediate points of the latter collaboration's lifetime. The only difference compared with the previous case is that we have to interconnect the two collaborations at those intermediate points. This is done by using the connectors illustrated in fig. 5. They are paths with one or more start-points, one end-point, and one waiting place connected to the end-point. The start-points are connected to the enabling collaboration and the waiting-place is inserted into the path of the enabled collaboration. Note that both the main and the subordinate collaborations can adopt, at different times, the roles of enabling and enabled collaborations, depending on the concrete interactions that take place between them.

4   Towards Automatic Synthesis of State-Machines

The proposed service engineering process ends up with the translation from the collaboration-oriented view (where a service is described as a collaboration) into the object-oriented view (where the total behaviour of the service objects participating in the service provision is described as state-machines). This translation process basically consists of building the state-machines of the collaboration roles and binding them to instances of objects. This could be a trivial step if a collaboration was not decomposed into smaller sub-collaborations. However, when decomposition is used, as it is the case for the UserLogon collaboration presented in fig. 1, the process is not so trivial. In the figure we see that an object playing

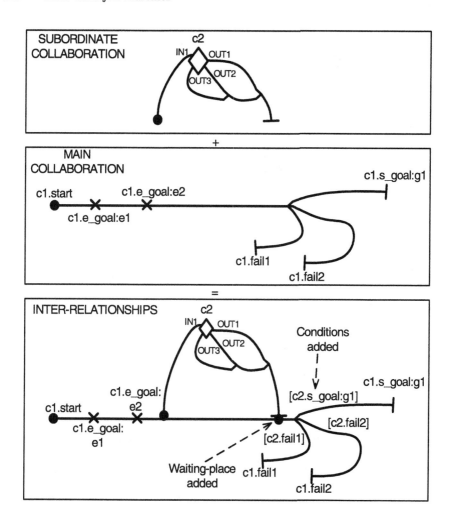

Fig. 4. Partial Goal Dependency (I)

the `TerminalClientSession` role will indeed play four sub-roles[3]: *rr1*, *lo*, *rr2*
and *ua*; each one in a different sub-collaboration. Therefore, we have to compose
the state-machines of those four sub-roles in order to synthesize the behaviour of
`TerminalClientSession`. We need to know then the order in which the roles are
played, and if their executions overlap or not. This information can be extracted
from the UCM describing the UserLogon collaboration (see fig. 2d).

The synthesis process we present here allows mechanical generation of the
aforementioned state-machines. In section 2 we mentioned that, in our approach,

---

[3] The UML standard does not use the word *sub-role* when talking about collaboration
use roles that are bound to collaboration roles. However the informal interpretation
is that of roles of a role, or just sub-roles as we like to call them.

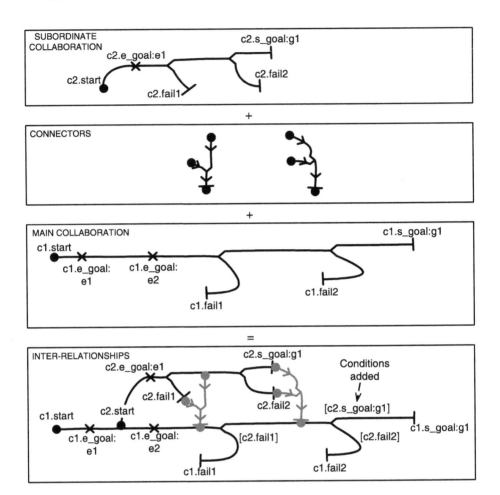

Fig. 5. Partial Goal Dependency (II)

the behaviour of each collaboration is described with sequence diagrams. These diagrams are taken as input for the synthesis process, as well as the UCM representing the service collaboration, which shows the dependencies between its sub-collaborations. In the following we will refer to this UCM as "the composite UCM".

For each collaboration role, the process for synthesizing the state-machine of an object playing that role consists of four steps. These are explained below, and illustrated by the synthesis of a fraction of the state-machine of an object playing the TerminalClientSession role:

1. Determine the sub-collaborations[4] the object participates in. This is necessary because the composite UCM may contain information about other
collaborations not relevant for this object, which should be ignored.
Store the collaboration names, together with the name of the role the object
plays in each collaboration, in a table, which we will refer to as the *Role
Table*. Table 1 is the Role Table for TerminalClientSession.

Table 1. Role Table for the TerminalClientSession

Collaboration	Collaboration Role
rr1	*invoked*
lo	*loAgent*
rr2	*requestor*
ua	*uaTerm*

2. For each collaboration and role in Table 1, project its associated sequence
diagram into the lifeline of the role. This is done to obtain, for each role,
an automaton (still with goal information) describing its behaviour in the
collaboration. Note that this automaton may be stored in the collaboration,
to be reused in the future. This process is shown in fig. 6 for some of the
sub-roles of TerminalClientSession.

3. Use the composite UCM (see fig. 2) to guide the composition of the automata generated in step 3 into a state-machine. The UCM is traversed and
the automata (as a whole or in parts) are added to the final state-machine
attending to the events we find in the UCM's paths. This is done according
to the algorithm described in the Appendix.

4. As a final step, suppress any state existing between consecutive input and
output transitions.

It should be noted that the synthesized state-machine is not complete, because
it does not include internal actions, which have to be added at a later stage by
the designer. We plan to look at how this can be done in future work.

4.1   An Example

In this section we illustrate how the state-machine of an object playing the
TerminalClientSession role can be intuitively synthesized from the joint information provided by the composite UCM for UserLogon and the automata for
the *invoked, requestor, uaTerm* and *loAgent* roles.

---

[4] For the sake of simplicity, the prefix *sub* will be omitted in the following, but the
reader should be aware that when we say "collaboration" we really mean "sub-
collaboration".

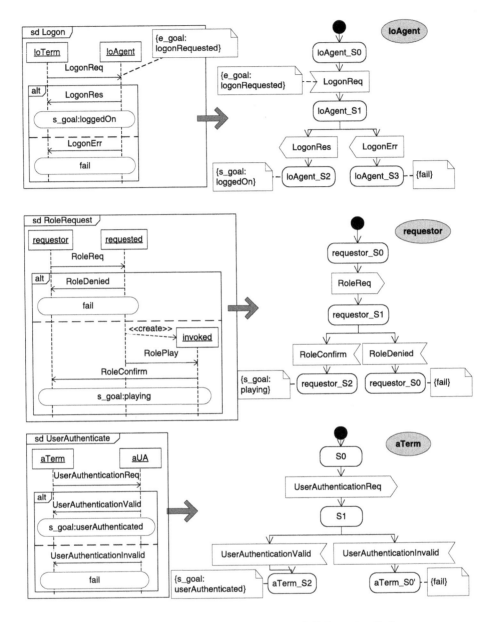

Fig. 6. Projection of Interactions into Collaboration Roles

Looking at fig. 2d, we see that just after UserLogon starts, the *rr1* stub is found. Its plug-in (see fig. 2a) indicates that the *rr1* collaboration starts. Since TCS participates in *rr1*, playing the *invoked* role, we study the details of the plug-in. It indicates that *rr1* starts and runs to completion without interruptions, so we add the whole automaton for the *invoked* role to the TCS state-machine (see fig. 7, step 1). After the *rr1* stub, we find the *loCC* stub. When we look at its plug-in (see fig. 2e) we see that *lo* starts. TCS also participates in this collaboration, where it plays the *loAgent* role. We therefore look at the details of the plug-in and see that a responsibility corresponding to *logonRequested* event goal is reached. As a result, we take, from the *loAgent* automaton, the transitions and states placed between the start symbol and the transition marked with *e_goal:logonRequested* (inclusive) and add them to the TCS state-machine (see fig. 7, step 2). Following the UCM we see that a new path containing two stubs, namely *rr2* and *ua*, is triggered, while *lo* waits at the *rr2_uaWP* waiting place. These two stubs represent two collaborations which TCS participates in, playing the *requestor* and *uaTerm* roles in them, respectively. Therefore, we add the whole automaton for both the *requestor* and the *uaTerm* roles to the TCS state-machine. Note, that the *requestor*'s automaton is added after the transition marked with *e_goal:logonRequested* (see fig. 7, step 3), since the UCM's interpretation is that *e_goal:logonRequested* enables *rr2* and thus the *requestor* role. The *uaTerm*'s automaton is added, in turn, after the state marked with *s_goal:playing* (see fig. 7, step 4), since the UCM tells us that *rr2.s_goal:playing* enables *ua*. Following the UCM we arrive at the *rr2_uaWP* waiting place where *lo* was waiting. That means that *lo* is enabled again. The UCM indicates that if *ua.s_goal:userAuthenticated* was achieved, *lo* achieves its own goal. Thus we take, from the *loAgent* automaton, the transitions and states placed between the transition marked with *e_goal:logonRequested* (the point where we stopped last time) and the state marked with *s_goal:loggedOn* (inclusive) and add them to the TCS state-machine. The addition is performed at the state marked with *ua.s_goal:userAuthenticated* in the TCS state-machine (see fig. 7, step 5). In much the same way, we take, from the *loAgent* automaton, the transitions and states placed between the transition marked with *e_goal:logonRequested* and the state marked with *fail* (inclusive) and add them to the TCS state-machine, at the states marked with *rr2.fail or ua.fail* (see fig. 7, step 6).

The synthesis of the state-machine for TCS is now finished. However, the resulting state-machine is not totally correct. As a final step we need to suppress any state existing between consecutive input and output transitions. This is also shown in fig. 7.

5   Related Work and Discussion

The idea of synthesizing state-machines/state-charts from scenario models is not new, as demonstrated by the number of existing publications in this area. Quite a few papers have been published proposing automatic synthesis approaches that make use of extra information to guide the synthesis process, for example [9, 10, 11, 12, 13]. Our approach is however not currently automated, but there is nothing that prevents its automation.

Leue et al. [9] use HMSCs to explicitly compose a set of MSCs from which ROOM statecharts are synthesized. Mansurov and Zhukov[10] also use HMSCs in their synthesis of SDL state-machines. HMSCs abstract away the details of MSCs

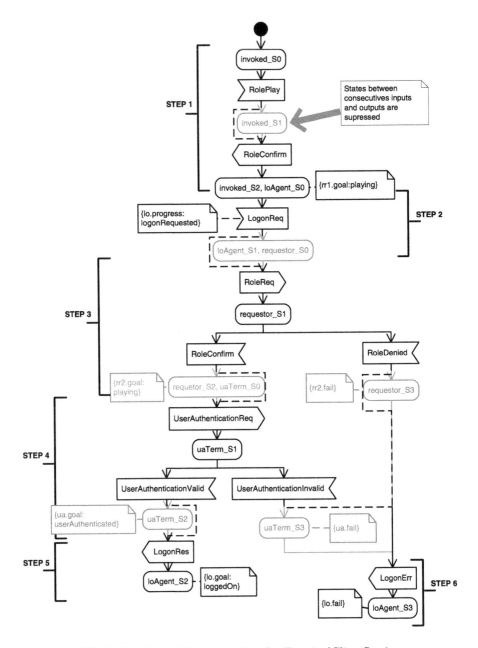

Fig. 7. Synthesized State-machine for TerminalClientSession

and give a high-level view of the relation between scenarios. The disadvantage, however, of using HMSCs (and their UML counterparts Interaction Overview Diagrams) is their lack of support for describing composition of overlapping scenarios, such as those described by the Logon (*lo*) and UserAuthenticate (*ua*) collaborations (see figs. 1 and 6). To express the composition of these two collaborations with an HMSC we should split the sequence diagram associated with the Logon collaboration in two diagrams. By using UCMs to describe the goal-oriented progress of collaborations we also abstract away the details of sequence diagrams, while we are able to describe the composition of overlapping collaborations.

Krüger et al. [12] adopt a different approach for the synthesis of statecharts from a set of MSCs. Instead of explicitly describing the composition of MSCs, state information is included in them, so different MSCs are related on the basis of similar states. This can be compared to our use of state and event goals, which we include in the sequence diagrams associated with the collaborations (see fig. 6) to help during the synthesis process. However, in our approach, the state and event goals are not shared between sequence diagrams belonging to different collaborations, as would be required in order to apply the Krüger et al.'s approach. In contrast, we relate the goals of different collaborations by means of UCMs. Our approach promotes, thus, reuse and separation of concerns between scenarios, at the time that makes explicit their inter-relationships.

The approach by Whittle and Schumann [11] also advocates including extra information in the scenarios in order to relate them. Pre- and post-conditions, expressed in OCL, are used to give semantics to the messages of UML sequence diagrams, from which UML state-charts are generated. The proposed synthesis algorithm does not, however, support overlapping scenarios. This is the main drawback of this approach. Another disadvantage is its low-level of abstraction, since constraints are specified on a per-message basis. Its scalability could also be questioned, since its application to large systems with many scenarios and interactions will probably be a tedious task. On the contrary, with UCMs it is easier to inter-relate the scenarios (that is the collaborations) of large systems in a structured way.

Uchitel et al. [13] present an MSC language with semantics based on scenario composition, state identification and label transition systems (LTS). They further present an approach for synthesizing label transition systems (LTS) from a set of scenarios described in their MSC language. This approach, as ours, tries to combine the benefits of approaches using scenario composition, such as [9] and [10], with the benefits of approaches using state identification, such as [12, 11]. Moreover, the authors show how their approach can be used to support other synthesis approaches and make their assumptions explicit. The drawback of Whittle and Schumann's approach is, however, its lack of support for overlapping scenarios.

A semi-automatic approach for the synthesis of UML state-charts from a set of UML sequence diagrams is given by Mäkinen and Systä in [14]. In their approach no extra information is used to guide the synthesis process. UML sequence diagrams are considered to represent example cases that can be treated in any order. If an ambiguity is found during the synthesis, the user is consulted. This approach recognizes the difficulty of precisely defining the dependencies between scenarios, which by nature are incomplete and many times overlapping.

Specially interesting in this approach is the ability to discover ambiguities in a set of scenarios. Its drawback, however, is the total absence of extra information to guide the synthesis process, which makes it too dependent on the user. It would be interesting to study how the approach we present here may benefit from the ambiguity discovery ability of Mäkinen and Systä's approach.

The work presented here is not the first one that uses UCMs for the synthesis of state-machines from scenarios. In [15, 16, 17] UCMs are also used for that purpose. The differences with our approach lies, however, on the concrete use of UCMs that is done. We use UCMs to describe the dependencies between collaborations at a high level of abstraction. In contrast, Sales [16] uses UCMs to describe SDL state-machines, while both Bordeleau [15] and He et al. [17] use UCMS, at an initial stage, to capture the requirements of services. Then UCMs are translated into MSCs, which are finally used to synthesize SDL state-machines. The approach by He et al. [17] is fully automated, thanks partially to the use of the UCMNav tool [18, 19], which permits graphical construction of UCMs and translation into MSCs, as well as export the UCMs as XML files. These files could be used in the automation of our approach.

6   Conclusions

We have presented a service modeling approach that uses UML 2.0 collaborations, sequence diagrams and UCMs in a complementary way. UML collaborations are used to describe services as a structure of roles collaborating to perform a task or achieve a goal. They help to get a high-level view of services. The low-level details of the collaborations are then given in the form of associated sequence diagrams annotated with goal information. A strong feature of UML collaborations is the possibility to compose them from other smaller sub-collaborations (by using collaboration uses). This allows for a modular approach that promotes reuse and separation of concerns. However, we argue that for such an approach to work, collaboration dependencies must explicitly be described. We use UCMs for this purpose. They are used to describe causal relationships between the event and state goals of isolated collaborations and to effectively relate goals of different collaborations.

Several patterns for the illustration of goal and sequential dependencies between collaborations using UCMs have been proposed. They are not intended to cover all possible cases of dependencies, but just as a starting point in this way.

An experiment has been performed to synthesize the state-machine of a collaboration role from other smaller roles. As input for this process we have used the information provided by the UML collaborations, in the form of sequence diagrams, and the dependency information provided by a UCM. The results have been satisfactory for small services, as the one presented here. However, we need to experiment with other more complex services to really understand the potential of our synthesis approach.

The work presented here is, however, at an early stage of maturity. Further research has to be done in several directions. We are currently working with the improvement and implementation of the synthesis algorithm. We are also investigating rules for choosing appropriate event and state goals, as well as studying the formalization of goals expressions in terms of temporal logic. We would like to study further the classification of dependencies and their illustration with UCMs, so as to make their scope larger. Finally, we would like to extend our approach to the generation of Hierarchical State Machines, as we believe they provide better support for evolving systems.

Acknowledgements

The author would specially like to thank Rolv Bræk, Frank Kræmer and Richard Sanders for their useful comments on this work.

References

1. Rößler, F., Geppert, B., Gotzhein, R.: Collaboration-based design of SDL systems. In Reed, R., Reed, J., eds.: SDL '01: Proceedings of the 10th International SDL Forum Copenhagen on Meeting UML. Volume 2078 of Lecture Notes in Computer Science., Springer-Verlag (2001) 72–89
2. Fisler, K., Krishnamurthi, S.: Modular verification of collaboration-based software designs. In: ESEC/FSE-9: Proceedings of the 8th European software engineering conference held jointly with 9th ACM SIGSOFT international symposium on Foundations of software engineering, ACM Press (2001) 152–163
3. Object Management Group: UML 2.0 Superstructure Specification. (2004)
4. Rumbaugh, J., Jacobson, I., Booch, G.: The Unified Modeling Language Reference Manual. 2nd edn. Addison-Wesley (2004)
5. Bordeleau, F., Corriveau, J.P.: On the importance of inter-scenario relationships in hierarchical state machine design. In Hußmann, H., ed.: FASE '01: Proceedings of the 4th International Conference on Fundamental Approaches to Software Engineering. Volume 2029 of Lecture Notes in Computer Science., Springer-Verlag (2001) 156–170
6. Buhr, R.J.A., Casselman, R.S.: Use case maps for object-oriented systems. Prentice-Hall, Inc. (1996)
7. Buhr, R.J.A.: Use case maps as architectural entities for complex systems. IEEE Transactions of Software Engineering **24** (1998) 1131–1155
8. Sanders, R.T., Bræk, R.: Modeling peer-to-peer service goals in uml. In: SEFM '04: Proceedings of the Software Engineering and Formal Methods, Second International Conference on (SEFM'04), IEEE Computer Society (2004) 144–153
9. Leue, S., Mehrmann, L., Rezai, M.: Synthesizing ROOM models from message sequence chart specifications. Technical report, Dept. of Electrical and Computer Engineering (1998)
10. Mansurov, N., Zhukov, D.: Automatic synthesis of SDL models in use case methodology. In Dssouli, R., von Bochmann, G., Lahav, Y., eds.: SDL Forum, Elsevier (1999) 225–240
11. Whittle, J., Schumann, J.: Generating statechart designs from scenarios. In: ICSE '00: Proceedings of the 22nd international conference on Software engineering, ACM Press (2000) 314–323

12. Krüger, I., Grosu, R., Scholz, P., Broy, M.: From mscs to statecharts. In: DIPES '98: Proceedings of the IFIP WG10.3/WG10.5 international workshop on Distributed and parallel embedded systems, Kluwer Academic Publishers (1999) 61–71
13. Uchitel, S., Kramer, J., Magee, J.: Synthesis of behavioral models from scenarios. IEEE Trans. Softw. Eng. **29** (2003) 99–115
14. Mäkinen, E., Systä, T.: MAS - an interactive synthesizer to support behavioral modelling in UML. In: ICSE '01: Proceedings of the 23rd International Conference on Software Engineering, IEEE Computer Society (2001) 15–24
15. Bordeleau, F.: A Systematic and Traceable Progression from Scenario Models to Communicating Hierarchical State Machines. PhD thesis, Department of Systems and Computer Engineering, Faculty of Engineering ,Carleton University, Ottawa (1999)
16. Sales, I.: A bridging methodology for internet protocols standards development. Master's thesis, School of Information Technology and Engineering (S.I.T.E.), Faculty of Engineering, University of Ottawa, Ontario (2001)
17. He, Y., Amyot, D., Williams, A.W.: Synthesizing SDL from use case maps: An experiment. In: SDL Forum. (2003) 117–136
18. Miga, A.: Application of use case maps to system design with tool support. Master's thesis, Dept. of Systems and Computer Engineering, Carleton University,Ottawa (1998)
19. Use Case Maps Web Page and UCM User Group. http://www.usecasemaps.org.

Appendix: Synthesis Algorithm

The algorithm presented here has not been tested thoroughly yet, so it may contain some inconsistencies. The algorithm steps should therefore be taken as guidelines, rather than as strict steps.

We present guidelines for a recursive algorithm. First, state-machines for the inner-most stubs are synthesized. These are stubs whose plug-ins do not contain other stubs. The state-machines are synthesized following steps 1 - 9 (see below). Once the state-machines for the inner-most stubs are synthesized, the state-machines for their container UCMs, up to the composite UCM, can be synthesized following steps again steps 1 - 9 (see below). Note that state-machines are only synthesized for those UCMs whose start-point refers to one of the collaborations in the Role Table.

The algorithm uses the following variables:

- *currentRole*: stores the name of the collaboration role we are dealing with.
- *currentUCM*: stores the name of the currently active collaboration
- *currentRoleState[currentRole]*: array that for each collaboration role stores the name of the last automatons state added to the object's state-machine. Initialized to "start".
- *currentSMState[currentUCM]*: array that for each collaboration/UCM stores the name of the state where other states and transitions can be added. Initialized to "start".
- *ucmsCurrentPoint[currentUCM]*: array that for each UCM stores the last processed element. Initialized to "start-point".

And it consists of the following 9 steps:

1. Set *currentRole* to the collaboration role that the object plays in the collaboration that the UCM/stub represents and *currentUCM* to that UCM/stub. Go to step 2.

2. Traverse *currentUCM*'s path, starting at *ucmsCurrentPoint[currentUCM]*, until a responsibility, a waiting place (either belonging to the path or tangentially connected to it), an OR-fork, an end-point or a stub is found. If a responsibility is found go to step 3. If a waiting place is found go to step 4. If an OR-fork is found go to step 6. If an end-point is found go to step 8. And if a stub is found go to step 9.

3. For the *currentRole*'s automaton, take the states and transitions between (but not including) *currentRoleState[currentRole]* and the transition marked with the responsibility's event goal. Add these states and transitions, together with the event goal transition and its succeeding state, to the *currentUCM*'s state-machine at *currentSMState[currentUCM]*. Update *currentRoleState[currentRole]* and *currentSMState[currentUCM]*, and set *ucmsCurrentPoint[currentUCM]* pointing to the just handled responsibility. Go to step 2.

4. If the waiting place is tangentially connected to the path (i.e. other collaboration is enabled), a search for a second waiting place, this time inserted in the current path, is performed. If it is found, a partial goal dependency pattern has been encountered. Go to step 5. If it is not found, or a new tangentially connected waiting place is found, a sequential dependency pattern has been encountered. The enabling collaboration and the enabled one run then concurrently. A composite state with concurrent sub-states (or two orthogonal regions in UML) should preferably be used to represent this behaviour. This treatment is left as further work.

5. If the path between the first and the second waiting place is not empty (i.e. any responsibility, stub or other element is found) both the enabling and the enabled collaborations run concurrently for a while. At the time of writing this paper we have not yet decided the best way of dealing with this situation. This is left as further work.

   Otherwise, if the path between the first and the second waiting place is empty, set *ucmsCurrentPoint[currentUCM]* pointing to the second waiting place and synthesize an automaton for the just enabled collaboration, according to steps 1 - 9 (the automaton is not necessarily synthesized for the whole collaboration, but maybe just for a part of the collaboration, which is represented by a fragment of its UCM enclosed between two waiting places). Add the synthesized automaton to the *currentUCM*'s state-machine. To do it, eliminate the start symbol of the automaton and merge each of its succeeding states with a state of *currentUCM*'s state-machine in the following way: if the automaton state is labeled, merge it with a state of *currentUCM*'s state-machine with the same label; if the automaton state is not labeled, merge it with the state pointed by *currentSMState[currentUCM]*. Update *currentSMState[currentUCM]*, so it points to the last added state which is not labeled with any state goal or fail, and go to 2.

6. Set *ucmsCurrentPoint[currentUCM]* pointing to the OR-fork. Check if *currentRoleState[currentRole]* precedes a choice. If so, go to 7. If not, traverse the *currentRole*'s automaton, starting at *currentRoleState[currentRole]*, searching for a choice. If a choice is found, take the *currentRole*'s automaton states and transitions between *currentRoleState[currentRole]* and the state preceding the choice and add them (except the first state) to the *currentUCM*'s state-machine at *currentSMState[currentUCM]*. Update *currentSMState[currentUCM]* and go to 7. If a choice is not found, it means that the OR-fork describes aspects of other collaboration roles. Take then all the *currentRole*'s automaton states and transitions from *currentRoleState[currentRole]* and add them to the *currentUCM*'s state-machine at *currentSMState[currentUCM]*. The state-machine for *currentUCM* is finished.

7. For each of the fork's outgoing paths, synthesize an automaton according to steps 1 - 9. Eliminate the start symbol and label the first state with the guard condition of the path. If there is no guard condition, the state is not labeled. Return to previous active step.

8. For the *currentRole*'s automaton, take all the states and transitions from (and including) *currentRoleState[currentRole]* to the state marked with the end-point's goal/fail. Add these states and transitions to the *currentUCM*'s state-machine at *currentSMState[currentUCM]*. If there are no more paths in the UCM, the state-machine for *currentUCM* is finished, otherwise return to previous active step.

9. If the stub does not represent a collaboration in Role Table, bypass it and go to step 2. Otherwise, add the stub's state-machine (without the start state) to the *currentUCM*'s state-machine. If the stub is enabled by an event goal (i.e a responsibility), the addition is done at the state succeeding the transition marked with the event goal. If the stub is enabled by a state goal (i.e. and end-point), the addition is done at the state marked with the state goal. If the stub is enabled by a start-point labeled with a start label, the addition is done at the *currentUCM*'s state-machine start state. Go to step 2.

Author Index